To Dan –

    With deep appreciation
for your friendship and help
in those memorable years.

                    Spring 2004

Re-understanding Japan

ASIAN INTERACTIONS AND COMPARISONS

Re-understanding Japan

Chinese Perspectives, 1895–1945

Lu Yan

ASSOCIATION FOR ASIAN STUDIES

and

UNIVERSITY OF HAWAI'I PRESS

Honolulu

Asian Interactions and Comparisons, published jointly by the
University of Hawai'i Press and the Association for Asian Studies,
seeks to encourage research across regions and cultures within
Asia. The Series focuses on works (monographs, edited volumes,
and translations) that concern the interaction between or among
Asian societies, cultures, or countries, or that deal with a comparative analysis of such. Series volumes concentrate on any time
period and come from any academic discipline.

Library of Congress Cataloging-in-Publication Data

Lu, Yan.
  Re-understanding Japan : Chinese perspectives, 1895–1945 /
Lu Yan.
    p.   cm.—(Asian interactions and comparisons)
  Includes bibliographical references and index.
  ISBN 0-8248-2730-9 (hard : alk. paper)
    1. China—Relations—Japan. 2. Japan—Relations—China.
3. China—History—20th century. I. Title. II. Series.
DS740.5.J3L83   2004
303.48′251052′09′041—dc22   2003026810

University of Hawai'i Press books are printed on acid-free paper
and meet the guidelines for permanence and durability of the
Council on Library Resources.

Designed by University of Hawai'i Press production staff

Printed by The Maple-Vail Book Manufacturing Group

For Aunt Yan Bo
Friend, teacher, and artist
and
To the memory of my parents
Lu Yixin and Yan Biya

CONTENTS

SERIES EDITOR'S PREFACE

When I first began teaching courses on modern Sino-Japanese relations about twenty years ago, it was all but impossible to put together a credible reading list of materials in English. Slowly, that lacuna is now being filled with marvelous new studies. Lu Yan's book marks an important step in this process, a step that might have been difficult to take twenty years ago. By focusing on the first decades of the twentieth century but abjuring both a global and a biographical approach, she has been able to build on the significant research available and take us to ground that might not have been fertile before. That is, by adopting the prosopopraphic approach, Lu looks at the lives of four Chinese who were central to introducing aspects of Japan and its culture to China during the difficult decades under study, and she can immediately go beyond the introductory lessons about Sino-Japanese ties in these years without having to do all the groundwork herself.

Jiang Baili, Zhou Zuoren, Dai Jitao, and Guo Moruo had little in common aside from a shared interest in Japan. Dai and Guo developed into political enemies and remained so for many years; Jiang was a military man, Zhou a man of culture. Nonetheless, all contributed to fashioning a variety of images of Japan in China. Getting a handle on the voluminous primary writings of these four men was a major undertaking, and in addition each has spawned a massive memoir literature as well as other genres of writings necessary to this study.

Reading through all of this material, though, requires a certain process of forgetting—or, perhaps, more acute remembering. We risk the temptation of historical hindsight unless we creatively jump back over the highly troubling years of the mid-twentieth century to understand what these four men thought about Japan before that time. This is especially true in the case of Zhou Zuoren, Lu Xun's younger brother, who has been the subject of much speculation and condemnation for his accommodation to the Japanese occupation from the late 1930s. Before Japan's war of aggression against China and her neighbors, Sino-Japanese relations were multivalent, full of promise, and open to genuine bilateral exchange. There were certainly insidious sorts who would become more prominent in the 1930s and 1940s, but it would be largely ahistorical to read Japanese belligerence too far back in time. That things turned out as they did is thus all the more tragic. In this sense, Lu's book is a fascinating discussion of what might have been. Had the Japanese military not risen to ascendent power on the mainland and pushed Japanese foreign policy in the catastrophic direction it took, the possibilities of ever greater interaction between China and Japan might have continued to grow.

This was not to be, however, and even now, when China and Japan have reached unprecedented levels of contact, they are still hampered by memories—"memories" often passed from one generation to the next. Suffice it to say that Lu's valuable contribution to the literature on Sino-Japanese relations through this study of four seminal figures from four different discursive arenas recaptures a world of interaction and exchange that we have tried to make the hallmark of the series in which this volume now appears.

Joshua A. Fogel, Series Editor

ACKNOWLEDGMENTS

The completion of this book would have been impossible without the encouragement and assistance of many. I was most fortunate to have had several great teachers at Cornell University whose guidance and encouragement continued as I worked on transforming my dissertation into this book. Sherman Cochran has been the most nurturing mentor and has generously given his insight, patience, and sensibility to help me prepare, launch, and complete this project. Robert J. Smith not only guided me into the field of Japanese society, he was also the first person who encouraged me to use literary sources for historical studies and, later on, with his numerous red marks throughout the dissertation, taught me how to shape my ideas. Walter LaFeber sets a standard of excellent scholarship that I admire and must strive for. Warren I. Cohen, formerly of Michigan State University, has also been a source of unfailing encouragement. I might have abandoned the snow country in North America long ago if not for his guidance and support at the critical phase of my graduate work here in the United States.

My research in Asia has been fortuitously facilitated by teachers and friends. I owe a great debt to Professor Hamashita Takeshi of Tokyo University (now at Kyoto University), who supported my research with a hosting office, research funds, and the arrangement of several research trips and interviews in and outside Tokyo. Professor Fujii Shōzō of Tokyo University kindly provided information about current Japanese research on Chinese literature and connected me with Dr. Izumi Hyōnosuke of Fukui Prefectural University. An accomplished researcher on Japanese medical personnel in China, Dr. Izumi investigated all conceivable sources and even traveled to Tokyo and Niigata Prefecture to find needed information for me, whom he knew only through correspondence. I am also grateful to Professor Kobayashi Tomoaki for sharing his research materials on the Army Officers' Academy and to Liao Bizhen for locating information on medical education in Tokyo University.

I owe special thanks to Y. M. Bau, a Chinese born in Japan and a long-term correspondent with Zhou Zuoren in his later years, for always responding promptly and generously to many of my questions and requests for source materials. Lo Fu, a veteran journalist, granted me an interview concerning his experiences in wartime China and provided me with materials on Zhou Zuoren. Thanks are also due to Cao Jingxing, who helped me make indispensable research connections. In Shanghai, Ding Jingtang opened doors to archives that would have been otherwise inaccessible to outsiders. My former colleagues at the Economic Research Institute of the Shanghai Academy of Social Sciences, especially Shen Zuwei and Zhang Zhongmin, provided indispensable help in my research at archives and libraries in China; and so did Prof. Ku Weiying of Taiwan University in my research at Taibei. Surviving relatives of the four Chinese discussed in this book have kindly shared their information and insights with me; to Iguchi Hirokazu, Jiang Ying, Jiang Zukang, Qian Yonggang, Satō Kihachirō and his family, Tao Naihuang, Tao Titu, Tao Fangzi, Tao Yiwang, and Zhou Jin, I am grateful for their assistance.

On this side of the Pacific Ocean, Joshua A. Fogel, the editor of this series, has provided unfailing support to this project and to my other endeavors in the research on Sino-Japanese relations. Allen Linden, Paula Harrell, Edward Gunn, Robert Culp, Fu Nianzu, Beth Murphy, Thomas McGrath, and Adam Schneider read all or part of the earlier version of this work and provided constructive comments. Yoko Miyakawa Mathews, with her ever-present cheerful smile and laughter, saved me from many mistakes in the translation of Japanese materials. My sincere gratitude to them all.

I am fortunate to have the most supportive and congenial colleagues in the history department of the University of New Hampshire (UNH). Special thanks are due to Jeffry Diefendorf and J. William Harris, my former and current chairs, who read the entire manuscript and provided stylistic suggestions as well useful questions. Thanks, too, to Cinthia Gannett of the English department at UNH for helping with stylistic improvements on one of the earlier versions of the introduction. I especially appreciate the support of Dean Marilyn Hoskin, who provided funds for a research trip to Taiwan and granted me an academic leave during 1999–2000 for revising the manuscript.

The many librarians I encountered throughout my research have provided the kindest support; my special thanks to Teresa Mei and Amy Blumenthal of the Kroch Collection at Cornell University and Abe Nobuhiko and Ma Xiaohe of the Harvard-Yenching Library. I also wish to thank Patricia Crosby and Ann Ludeman of the University of Hawai'i Press for their support during the publication process, and Susan Biggs Corrado for her excellent work in copyediting.

The research and completion of this project has been funded by the Lam Travel Grant for South China Research and the Japan Travel Grant from the East Asia Program of Cornell University in 1993–1994 and 1995, a Mellon Fellowship from the history department of Cornell University in 1994–1995, a Summer Faculty Fellowship from the graduate school at UNH in 1997, an ACLS/SSRC International Postdoctoral Fellowship in 1999–2000, and a travel grant from the College of Liberal Arts at UNH in 2000.

While credit goes to the help and suggestions of others, I am responsible for any remaining mistakes.

NOTES ON NAMES AND TERMS

Names are given in the Chinese or Japanese order, surname first.

Occasional double references to Chinese and Japanese pronunciations of Chinese-character words use the following notation to distinguish the two: (C: *shendao,* J: *shintō*).

INTRODUCTION

In the long history of Sino-Japanese relations, the decades following the Sino-Japanese War of 1894–1895 were marked by the rise of a new Chinese consciousness about Japan. Although a few Chinese had already proposed a Japanese model for China's modern reform in the 1880s,[1] such a view began to grip the Chinese mind only after 1895, when their country suffered a humiliating defeat in its war with Japan. In official and popular statements, the Chinese demonstrated an eagerness to learn from a country they had historically looked down upon as a mere "little island country *[zuier daoguo]*." The attraction of Japan soared even higher during the first decade of the twentieth century, after Japan's victory over Russia. New enthusiasm swept through China from its littoral provinces to the remotest corners, attracting tens of thousands of Chinese into a movement to study in Japan.[2] The Chinese government, which took the lead in sending students to Japan, also brought in Japanese advisers and made use of Japanese expertise in China's institutional reforms in its educational, police, and prison systems.[3] During the first half of the twentieth century Japan educated the largest group of foreign-trained Chinese, far more than America and Europe combined. As a result, the influence and leadership of Japan-educated professionals became especially pronounced in the military, in politics, and in literature.[4]

As much as the expanding firsthand experiences in and intimate observation of Japan heightened Chinese consciousness about their neighboring country, Japanese presence on Chinese territory further contributed to the complexity of this growing consciousness. Although the Japanese had been in direct contact with the Chinese since the third century, their interactions with the Chinese after 1895 developed into a vastly different scale and nature as a result of the changed power relationship between the two. Not only did the number of Japanese who went to China in the five decades after 1895 surpass the combined number who traveled there over the preceding one and a half millennia, but the purposes of their travel underwent significant change as well.[5] Many went to China as mere travelers, some lived there as expatriates disillusioned with their own government at home, and some worked there as progressive journalists with great sympathy to China's modern predicament and struggle.[6] Still more arrived and remained as agricultural settlers in the fertile Manchuria as colonial functionaries, profit seekers, or adventurers in the semicolonial treaty ports, or as soldiers stationed in the Japanese garrisons in north China or in the Kwantung Army in Manchuria. They became "men on the spot" responsible for defending and expanding Japan's newly established empire. It was through the work of these "subimperialists" in the four decades after 1895 that China was transformed into Japan's "informal empire."[7] Their accumulated efforts climaxed in 1937, when Japan plunged into yet another war against China for eight years, bringing more than one million Japanese soldiers to China and claiming the lives of more than twenty million Chinese.[8] In a somber comparison, political scientist Allen S. Whiting views the war as "surpass[ing] any foreign aggression in modern Chinese history."[9]

How might a Chinese, living through these turbulent decades, comprehend a Japan that appeared in such dramatically antithetical images? How might a Chinese reconcile the hopes that Japan's model inspired with the anger and despair that Japan's destruction generated? For those Chinese living through the drastic swings of Sino-Japanese relations, easy answers to these questions were not available. They ended up responding with varied approaches because, in part, of the vexing nature of these questions and, moreover, the fact that many of the time-honored values in their world had been profoundly shaken by what Marius Jansen called the "deep currents" of change.[10]

None of the countries in East Asia was able to stay above the pull of the deep currents of revolution and reconstruction. Yet China during the past one and a half centuries was more thoroughly submerged than Japan by the tumultuous torrents of revolutionary change. The fifty years between the two Sino-Japanese wars, especially, were times of violent political and social upheaval. In the span of roughly a generation, it was not only the central government in China that changed hands from the imperial court to a dictator in 1912, to various warlords after 1917, and finally to the national government under the Guomindang in 1928. All of China was rocked by the rise of anti-imperialist nationalism, numerous mass protests involving an increasingly larger segment of the population, a cultural revolution and renaissance, and the rise of the Communist movement. China in those five decades, in other words, was undergoing constant destruction of the old order and unending reconstruction of the new. But the revolutionary change was not clear-cut. What had been reconstructed, as a number of studies remind us, was not always a total departure from the past.[11]

In these decades of upheaval, Japan was the cardinal outside force that contributed to and complicated China's passage to social, political, and cultural reconstruction. In addition to the Japanese experts eagerly sought and used by the Chinese government in its modernization drive, the Japanese government as well as its marginal social elements were deeply involved in the rebellious activities of Sun Yat-sen and his fellow revolutionaries. From the mid-1910s on, Japan's imperialist demands repeatedly aroused wave after wave of Chinese mass protests. In the 1930s and 1940s, the "kill all, burn all, destroy all" policy of the invading Japanese army became instrumental in transforming the otherwise apathetic Chinese peasants into passionate nationalists, who in turn formed the popular basis for the rise of the Communist power.[12] Whether through well-intentioned assistance, crafty manipulation, or ruthless destruction, Japan became inextricably entangled in China's revolution and reconstruction.

Yet without Chinese initiation and participation, Japanese assistance could not easily be brought in. Without Chinese internal weakness, the Japanese army could hardly set foot inside Chinese borders. Indeed, the awareness of China's weakness and the desire to transform it into a strong nation was at the heart of the many Chinese who otherwise had pursued widely diverse approaches to Japan. It was through their mediation that Japan was able to influence China's revolution and reconstruction. It was through their articulation that Japan made a lasting impression on Chinese minds, even long after its immediate impact ebbed.

This book is my attempt to follow these two related themes in Sino-Japanese interaction—how the Chinese engaged Japan in their national revolution and reconstruction and how they articulated their understanding of Japan—during these pivotal fifty years. In order to move the vicissitudes of Chinese engagements with Japan in their multidimensional reconstruction to the foreground, I have chosen to focus on the intersection of purposeful experiments and articulated thoughts, of individual experiences and collective consciousness. Hence the study takes a shift in perspective away from that of Japan's role in China's state building. Taking the view that the fifty years between the two Sino-Japanese wars was a seminal period in modern Chinese rediscovery and Chinese re-understanding of Japan, this book thus works its discussion on Sino-Japanese interactions through the prism of Chinese thoughts and actions. It asks the questions of what motivated certain Chinese to seek, distribute, and use various resources of Japanese origin, how their deeds and words bridged or widened the gap between the two peoples and two cultures, and how the various ties with Japan affected the lives of those Chinese who made the connections. Ultimately, it seeks to explain how new experiences in Sino-Japanese interaction helped to reshape Chinese understanding of Japan in the first half of the twentieth century.

The book, however, makes no claim on comprehensiveness. I am fully aware that there was an overwhelming and unprecedented number of Chinese who came to experience Japan's influence and that not all Chinese were equally active in engaging Japan or took the same views about it. Therefore, I have made use of some selected cases in order to go beyond political narrative and to explicate the diversity and complexity in these two entwined themes of engagement and understanding in some depth. At the center of this study are four Chinese who grew up in a time of revolutionary change in China's education and political institutions and became prominent leaders in China's military, political, and literary circles. Born during the last two decades of the nineteenth century, just before the reversal of Chinese attitude toward Japan took place, they were raised in the tradition of the Confucian classics and prepared for the Civil Service Examinations. Yet before they were able to take the first step onto the "ladder of success in imperial China," educational reforms diverted them to modern schools and threw open the doors to study in foreign lands. In the span of a decade these men sailed to Japan one after another and studied military science, literature and language, law, or medical science.

In the course of each of these men's careers and personal developments, the Japan connection constituted a critical and lasting element. From their youth and into their mature years, these individuals established personal and professional ties with the Japanese, and their Japanese connections in turn stimulated their experiments with and engagements in China's political and cultural changes. Three of them married Japanese women; one had a Japanese mistress. For all of them, the engagement with Japan was at once intellectual, physical, and emotional. Their multidimensional links and enduring preoccupation with Japan in thought and action distinguish them from many other Chinese men or women who by their occasional involvement with Japan might have attained momentary importance in Sino-Japanese relations, but none, to my knowledge, matched the seriousness and lengthy span of these four individuals' engagements.[13]

Sociologically, politically, or ideologically, however, these four Chinese do not make a cohesive group. Only occasionally did their lives intersect with one another. In twentieth-century China's newly emerged social landscape, each acquired a distinctive and distinguished position. Jiang Baili (1882–1938) was a famous strategist whose advice was sought by warlords as well as by the nationalist leader Jiang Jieshi (Chiang Kai-shek); Zhou Zuoren (1886–1967) was a leader in the New Culture Movement, an innovative essayist, and a leading social and cultural critic; Dai Jitao (1891–1949) made a national name for himself first in journalism and then as a leading politician intimately associated with Sun Yat-sen and Jiang Jieshi; Guo Moruo (1892–1979), a romantic poet of great popularity among young Chinese readers during the May Fourth era, made significant scholarly contributions to Chinese philology and later became a propagandist during the eight-year war with Japan in 1937–1945. During the rapid shifts and quick succession of political regimes of this period, they all started as supporters of the anti-Qing revolutionary cause, but soon parted ways to take sides as China's political situation fragmented and polarized.

How each made his way into these dissimilar and often conflicting positions is a story in part of the unique combination of circumstances and influences, yet in no instance can their individual developments be separated from the large-scale processes that affected millions of others. Central to these individuals' social activism and to their efforts in getting Japan involved in China's revolution and reconstruction was their association with a variety of social and political institutions. Jiang Baili found in radical student groups and the military establishment his venue of nationalist activities and modernization experiments. Dai Jitao built his political career within the Guomindang and became its leading advocate for building special relations with Japan. A teaching career in China's most prestigious Beijing University placed Zhou Zuoren in the center of the New Culture Movement, which, in turn, stimulated his efforts to bring Japanese inspiration into China's cultural reconstruction. The radical practice of marriage by free contract and pursuit of romanticism in literary creation defined Guo Moruo's place in China's new culture, and his social rebellion took on political significance when he embraced the cause of Communism. All of these institutions in their time emerged as revolutionary forces with the goal of dismantling China's existing political and cultural order; all became instrumental in these men's efforts to implement, with success or failure, their ideas about reconstructing China and its relations with Japan.

Just as indispensable as their language skills, social contacts, and intimate knowledge in making transnational and transcultural connections, mass media was a critical tool for reaching a national readership beyond professional circles. Having been imbued at a very young age with Confucian classical training and a sense of the power of the written word, they quickly grasped the significance of the print mass media as soon as it appeared on the horizon. Three of them—Jiang Baili, Dai Jitao, and Guo Moruo—actually made their first successful debuts in journals printed in Japan. Zhou Zuoren, on the other hand, was already a published translator and a budding writer before he went to Japan in 1906. This early success with print media, as we will see in the following pages, soon led each man to a long career as a publicist. Writing, and in some cases translation, became an inseparable part of their lives. Through writing they analyzed their experiences in Japan; through the print media they transmitted the influences they had received from Japan, interpreted Japan for the Chinese audience, and engaged in national discourse about China's relations with Japan.

While taking the leadership in refashioning Chinese understanding of Japan, these individuals did not always endorse the mainstream opinion or the overwhelming Chinese sentiment. On large questions of national concern in relation to Japan, their interpretations were often at odds with the mainstream argument. It is therefore important to remember that their views should not be taken as archetypes of "the Chinese understanding" of Japan, but rather as particular and prominent instances in the long continuum that produced many variations upon a unified but not uniform theme of modern Chinese consciousness of Japan. It was an unfolding process that had, to borrow a term used by psychologist Jerome Bruner in describing the development of self, a "longitudinal version"[14] of continuous development and a latitudinal version of simultaneous existence of differences. Once placed together in comparison, these men's experiences and thoughts offer to illuminate a wide spectrum of perspectives that emerged and evolved through these turbulent and tragic decades.

Sources and the Narrative Structure

As well-known leaders in modern Chinese history, Jiang Baili, Zhou Zuoren, Dai Jitao, and Guo Moruo have already made their appearance in monographs or articles published in English. As the reader can ascertain from browsing the bibliography, these studies treat the four individuals separately and chiefly in terms of their professional achievements—as political leader (Dai Jitao), military strategist (Jiang Baili), or leading writers (Zhou Zuoren and Guo Moruo). Unlike the approaches taken in earlier studies, this book attempts, for the first time in any language, to explore collectively and comparatively the Japanese connection that distinguished and divided them. While works in English are referenced wherever relevant, the essential sources I rely on are the voluminous writings by these individuals. Each of them has left a collection of works ranging from six to seventeen volumes, plus many articles scattered in newspapers and journals such as the *Tides of Zhejiang (Zhejiang chao)*, *Threads of Talk (Yusi)*, and the Literary Supplement of *Capital Daily (Jing bao)*, which are not included in these individuals' work collections. My focus is, of course, on their writings about Japan, but rather than single these specific writings out as isolated evidence, I place these writings on Japan within the life histories of these individuals and within the context of their evolving ideas as found in their other writings.

In reconstructing the life histories of these four men, I have found several kinds of source materials to be of particular importance: explicit autobiographical materials such as memoirs, autobiographical fiction, occasional essays, and personal correspondence reveal the processes of personal growth as well as social and intellectual connections. Archival documents are particularly important in the cases of Jiang Baili and Dai Jitao, who either took refuge in Japan or were assigned to official missions to Japan by the Chinese government. The available documents found in the Archive of the Japanese Foreign Ministry, in China's Second Archive in Nanjing, and in several government and party archives in Taiwan, though sporadic and sparse, provide telling information about the delicate relationships these men had in international and domestic affairs. Recollections by relatives, friends, and colleagues, as well as critiques or comments by their contemporaries, are often indispensable for understanding their social positions and networks. Interviews with more than a dozen descendants, relatives, or friends of these subjects during my research trips to Beijing, Nanjing, Haining, Tokyo, Kyoto, Niigata, and Hong Kong further helped me to verify the written records and revealed occasionally the concealed dimensions of historical connections.

Due to the changing political circumstances and ideological atmosphere, the scholarly treatment in China and Taiwan of these four prominent individuals was uneven during the second half of the twentieth century. In the three decades after the founding of the People's Republic of China (PRC) in 1949, only three of them—Guo Moruo, who was the cultural minister of PRC and president of the official China Academy of Social Sciences; Dai Jitao, who before his death in 1949 was president of the Examination Yuan of the National Government; and Jiang Baili, who had a troubled relationship with the National Government but reconciled with Jiang Jieshi when Japan's threat to China became all too grave—had their works published in multivolume collections. Even in these collections, presumed to be comprehensive, there are deliberate emphases and omissions. For instance, the seven-volume collected works of Dai Jitao, published in Taiwan in 1959, excludes many of his pre-1919 writings, a period when his anti-imperialism and his sympathy with socialism were most evident. In Guo Moruo's 1957 collection there were omissions, too, of some of the works deemed too petit-bourgeois. Interest in Zhou Zuoren, while kept alive in Hong Kong, was generally absent both on the mainland and in Taiwan until the late 1970s, a telling indication of the fate of a defiant thinker. Having served for complex reasons in the collaboration regime under Japanese occupation during the war, Zhou was sentenced to a ten-year term of imprisonment by the Guomindang's National Government and, after being released before completing his term, continued to be treated as a "traitor literati" *(hanjian wenren)* in the People's Republic and could publish on the mainland only under pseudonyms.

Thanks to the new intellectual openness and the booming book market that have come along with recent economic reforms in China, some previously unknown or concealed materials have been brought to light since the late 1970s. Notable additions to the source materials on Dai Jitao are the several volumes of his pre-1919 writings, published in China and Hong Kong, which provide rich details about the intellectual growth of a man before he became, as several works in English portray him, a stiff and zealous right-wing ideologue in the Guomindang.[15] A two-volume collection of Guo Moruo's personal correspondence and several compiled volumes of recollections by his friends, relatives, and colleagues, published in the 1990s, present valuable information about the various social connections of a writer and the many dramatic turns in his life, such as his connections with the Chinese Communist Party and his several marriages, which have not yet been adequately explained in scholarly works so far.

The most striking change in the scholarly record on the mainland is the rediscovery of Zhou Zuoren, a liberal who took an iconoclastic approach to politics and culture and alienated himself from all the ruling regimes of his time. In the late 1970s, some contemporary witnesses and participants gave interviews and published their memoirs concerning Zhou Zuoren's wartime activities, which triggered a debate among Chinese scholars on the question of Chinese collaboration with foreign invaders that remains alive today.[16] Since the mid-1980s, the popularity of Zhou Zuoren's works among the reading public became so remarkable that it has been named the "Zhou Zuoren Phenomenon." Zhou's works have been recompiled into many different editions, and hundreds of articles and more than a dozen monographs have been written on his life, his thoughts, and his literary contributions. My understanding of this erudite and perceptive thinker would have been far less adequate without the benefit of this recent publication of previously unavailable materials. These include some of his early articles, now part of the ten-volume compilation titled *A Collection of the Works by Zhou Zuoren According to Categories (Zhou Zuoren wen leibian)* (1998), his diaries, and a complete compilation of his correspondence with a friend in Hong Kong, Bau Yiu-ming, during his final years. In analyzing his life and thoughts, nevertheless, I have preferred to read and cite his words from the original edition of the essay collections he compiled, because it was through the way he arranged and compiled his essays that he revealed the logic of his thoughts and his intended arguments.

With its focus on Chinese connections with Japan, my comparative biography must be selective in presenting the details of the four subjects' life histories. The reader may see slight overlaps in time between some chapters but will also find a general chronological order in four parts, each of which is comprised of two or three chapters intended for comparison and contrast. Part I (together with some segments of Part II) traces the emergence of an array of motivations and approaches as these four young men set out for Japan during the early decades of the century. Part II focuses on the possibilities and limits of making political or familial ties with Japan and the Japanese during the 1910s, with Dai Jitao and Guo Moruo as two contrasting cases in public and private relationships. Part III further explores the successes and failures in seeking cultural inspiration from Japan and making an international alliance with its government, as exemplified by the efforts of Zhou Zuoren and Dai Jitao. Part IV moves to the 1930s and 1940s, when war loomed and eventually became reality. It examines the inner struggles and outward approaches these four men adopted when facing the challenge of violent and total conflict, with the actions and thoughts of Guo Moruo, Jiang Baili, and Zhou Zuoren discussed extensively in individual chapters and those of Dai Jitao's sketched in that part's epilogue. In the concluding chapter, I summarize the scope and depth of modern Sino-Japanese relations by explicating a spectrum of possibilities and limitations as seen in the four life histories, discuss the novel departures in practice and perspective of these four modern Chinese in comparison to those who came before them, and suggest the implications of this study for understanding the Japan connections in modern China's development.

Zhou Zuoren, an ever-controversial figure in Chinese history, once wrote with poignancy in occupied Beijing in 1943: "It now really makes one feel rather surprised and strange when one recalls how much the Chinese then [at the turn of the century] admired and praised Japan's Meiji Restoration, and how much they wished Japan's victory in the Russo-Japanese War. To be honest, these feelings were several degrees more earnest and passionate than that of last year when the Greater East Asian War broke out. If there had not been so many unexpected turns in the past thirty years, such feelings might have been sustained to the present, and any difficult problems would have been solved a long while ago."[17] Zhou's criticism of Japan's aggression, though masked by the allusion and analogy that had been the hallmark of his style since 1928, can hardly escape an attentive reader. Yet beneath the anger there also lay a profound sense of loss. What had been those hopes so dear to Chinese hearts? What were the "many unexpected turns"? What were the "difficult problems" as those who lived through the trying decades experienced them, and how well had they fared when they confronted these turns and problems? We can find answers only from those people who lived through these eventful decades between the two wars. But before we turn to their stories, a few words about the pre-1895 Chinese understanding of Japan will be needed to put their lives and thoughts in perspective.

Chinese Writings about Japan before 1895

China's long history of writing about Japan can be traced back to late third century.[18] Over the next seventeen hundred years, the major genre of Chinese writings about Japan was the biography (*zhuan*) in the official histories of imperial dynasties. Among the twenty-four such official histories (with the exception of the incomplete *Draft History of Qing [Qing shi gao]*), sixteen of these included a "Biography of Japan" of various lengths. The first of these, the "Biography of the Japanese" ("Woren zhuan") in the *Treatise of Wei (Wei zhi)*, written by Chen Shou (233–297), was a two-thousand-word description of Japan's geographical location, social customs, and administrative structure. Scholars in China and Japan generally agree that this was the first reliable and substantial record of Japan ever written, though the writing style as well as the "between-line small notes" *(xiao-zhu)* indicate that this first record extant drew heavily from an even earlier work, *An Outline of Wei (Wei lue)*, and appears to be a compilation from more than one source.[19] The "Biography of the Japanese" in the *Treatise of Wei* not only established a tradition of official writing about Japan, but also became the source material for several later dynastic histories. Some copied Chen Shou's work without alteration, despite the passage of long periods of time, while others amended the text by adding fantastic and imaginary details.[20]

Yet Chinese writings about Japan were not merely reiterations or fanciful creations. New varieties of genre and shifting focuses can be found, as historian Wang Xiangrong's intertextual comparison demonstrates, over the following four phases. In the first phase, during the pre-Tang times, Chinese writings about Japan can be found only in the officially sponsored dynastic histories. The information in these histories was drawn from visiting Japanese missions, and the writings focused on the description of Japan's internal affairs rather than on Sino-Japanese interactions. In the second phase, during the Tang-Song period, while new details and new awareness of some of the peculiarities of Japanese government entered official records, socially active literati such as poets Li Bai and Ouyang Xiu also recorded their relationships with Japanese friends or their praise of Japanese art works. The focus of writings after the Song dynasty shifted to the relations between the two countries. In the third phase, during the Ming dynasty, monographs on Japan written in response to the coastal conflict with the so-called Wo-pirates, or "Dwarf-pirates," flourished within and beyond the fold of official history. In quantity and in quality, Chinese writings about Japan during the Ming period surpassed those in previous times. The achievement of the Ming writings on Japan was rivaled only by the works written in the last two decades before the Sino-Japanese War of 1894–1895, the last of the four phases, when China and Japan established modern diplomatic relations and some Chinese official-scholars authored new monographs based on firsthand experiences and observation.[21] The Chinese wrote about Japan in travelogues or travel diaries, poetry, and geographical treatises, all well-established genres in China's long, evolving literary tradition.[22] In the long run, however, it is evident that the form and content of the Chinese representation of Japan had expanded to parallel the enlarging scope of actual contact.

If increased variety is one way to characterize the changing forms of Chinese representation of Japan, persistent bias is another. The phenomenon is not unusual in any intercultural relationships, even in modern times, despite the fact that expanded means of transportation and communication have enabled more intimate contact and close observation. But the limitation and peculiarity of Chinese understanding of Japan before 1895 was inextricably linked to imperial China's self-consciousness of being the embodiment of Civilization on the one hand and the tributary-suzerain relationship it established with its neighbors in premodern times on the other. Japan, or "Wo" as it was called before the mid-seventh century, "readily fitted into this tributary relationship with China," as Edwin Reischauer has observed.[23] Since their first appearance in Chinese records, the Japanese had been categorized as one of the "Eastern Outsiders" *(Dongyi)* who were considered beyond the pale of Chinese Civilization, but, like all other outsiders, would be allowed to participate in this Civilization and hence become "Chinese" in the all-embracing Chinese world order.[24] Japan, indeed, had actively sought to borrow Chinese culture in the interest of its own and was thus viewed as an aspirant going up the ladder of Chinese Civilization during the Tang period. But later conflict with the so-called Wo-pirates in the Ming period, though not simply a Sino-Japanese conflict since it was complicated by the participation of Chinese merchants and fishermen along the coast, added negative color to the Chinese image of Japan. If the word "Wo" used in the *Treatise of Wei* was simply a proper name for Japan,[25] by the fourteenth century, when the imperial government of the Ming dynasty came into protracted conflict with the coastal pirates, "Wo" had definitely become a pejorative term for the Japanese "Dwarf" and "Eastern Barbarians."

In this sketch of the history of Chinese writings and Chinese perception of Japan, a trajectory with an ascending curve of increased contact, however intermittent, is quite obvious. Yet it is also tempting to argue that the increased intimacy in contact seemed to have only hardened certain stereotypes in Chinese writing about Japan and Chinese understanding of Japan. If by the late imperial period the restrictive policy toward overseas trade, epitomized by the problem of the "Wo-pirates," was one of the major reasons for the chain reaction leading toward the downturn in Chinese views of Japan, did the change of international relations in the late nineteenth century undermine this basic Sino-centrism?

The answer, as both Noriko Kamachi and D. R. Howland argue, is no. Huang Zunxian, one of the first Chinese diplomats to Japan who made many friends among the Japanese in the 1870s and early 1880s and wrote influential works on Japan, praised Japan's adoption of Western technology but criticized its abandonment of the Confucian ethic.[26] While firsthand experience allowed Chinese visitors or sojourners to observe Japan more intimately, their writings—either in the more subjective and lyrical compositions of poetry or travel diaries or in the more objective compositions of treatises on geography—demonstrate much cognitive continuity despite the changed circumstances. There was a habit of viewing Japan as "a cultural variant" of China on the one hand and, on the other, an epistemological strategy that was intended to contain the disturbing reality of westernization in Japan by way of an analogy to the Warring Period in Chinese history.[27] In other words, the Chinese during the decades prior to the fateful Sino-Japanese War of 1894–1895 changed little in terms of their fundamental understanding of the basic pattern of Sino-Japanese relations. The price for this complacency was high. It took a devastating defeat to shock the Chinese out of their illusions and force them to make a determined move to catch up with the changed reality.

PART I
Paths to Japan

How Japan's victory over China in the war of 1894–1895 became
a landmark event is a familiar story for the student of modern
Chinese history. More than destroying the Beiyang Fleet, the
symbol of China's modernizing military power, the war demolished
a mental block deep in the Chinese psyche and opened the Chinese mind to the need for broad-ranging institutional changes in
the country's political and educational systems and social mores.
One such reform was the decision to send students to Japan, a
move that nobody could have imagined before China's defeat in
1895. Starting with just thirteen students, sent by the Qing court
in 1896, this centrally controlled program soon exploded into a
nationwide movement, attracting many local initiatives sponsored
by provincial governors and thousands of self-financed participants. Young boys just entering their teens, men as old as in their
seventies, and women tottering with bound feet all joined the rush
to the east. By the mid-1900s the ever-growing human traffic had
become the "first truly large-scale modernization-oriented migra-
tion of the intellectuals in world history."[1]

What moved so many Chinese, and why did they go to Japan
in the first place? What did they discover in Japan? How did such
discoveries make an impact on their personal lives and on China's
future development?

Looking back on China's increasingly radicalized political
history in the first half of the century, some scholars emphasize
the link between radical student activities in Japan and the revolution in 1911, which brought down the ruling Qing dynasty. Japan
(or rather, Tokyo, where the majority of Chinese students studied
and lived) freed the Chinese from close government surveillance
on the one hand and, on the other, introduced them to radical
ideas imported from the West.[2] But stressing the radical impact,
others have argued, gives us a biased answer; the link between
Japan's influence and China's modern experience lay elsewhere.
What Japan induced was "not merely political overthrow, but,
more profoundly, China's intellectual and institutional transformation."[3] The potential for diverging developments in the future, in

fact, was present in initial Chinese encounters with Japan during the early years of the century.

Part I of this book, limited to some fifteen years after the first Sino-Japanese War of 1894–1895, will leave the question of long-term impact to later chapters. Instead, it looks for answers to the simple but indispensable questions of motivation and discovery in this study of human actions and cross-cultural connections. In two chapters, this part investigates the personal circumstances of, and external influences on, two young Chinese, Jiang Baili and Zhou Zuoren, who hailed from Zhejiang, one of China's most cultured and prosperous provinces and one that produced the highest number of degree holders in the national Civil Service Examinations. During the final years of the nineteenth century, the study of Confucian classics was their education, entry into governmental service their vocational goal. But the war and the institutional reforms in China reoriented their paths. Going to Japan opened new vistas to these curious and ambitious Chinese; their views, their visions, and their future careers would take off from there.

Riding the Crest of Chinese Nationalism

Neither his ancestors nor many of his fellow Chinese would have dreamed of this day in the fall of 1904: twenty-two-year-old Jiang Baili, once a child prodigy of Confucian scholarship in his highly cultured hometown, now stood among the ranks of Chinese and Japanese cadets at the graduation ceremony at the Army Officers' Academy (Rikugun Shikan Gakkō) in Tokyo. For the past eleven months, he and ninety-four other Chinese had been taking lessons and running drills alongside 549 fellow Japanese cadets in this best military school in Asia, known as the "West Point" of Japan. The Army Officers' Academy offered the most stringent training as well as the highest reward for those who were lucky enough to enter and graduate from it. With top-notch credentials, the graduates filled the lower-middle ranks at the beginning of their careers, and they expected to rise eventually to the upper echelons of the Japanese army. The ceremony was held to single out the very best from the cream of the crop and award the outstanding Top Five of the year's graduates an imperial sword from the emperor.[1] At this ceremony in 1904, Jiang Baili, who ranked number one in the infantry department, was one of the winners of the coveted prize.[2]

It was a day of glory for Jiang, though the journey leading to it had not been a smooth one. He had left China four years before, in 1900, against the objections of his clan's elders and only with his widowed mother's blessing. Besides the age-old belief that one should not travel far when parents are alive, there were indeed good reasons for Jiang's clansmen's opposition. Jiang's hometown in eastern Zhejiang Province was known for its many excellent private libraries and its scholarship in the tradition of the "Zhejiang

School," after the great scholar Huang Zongxi (1610–1695).[3] During the Qing dynasty the province had produced hundreds of degree holders in the provincial and national Civil Service Examinations.[4] With such a record of scholarship and achievement, why would one need to go to a foreign country for an education? It would be even more unthinkable for the clansmen that Jiang Baili, a child prodigy in scholarship, should choose to become a soldier, a profession thoroughly despised in the Confucian tradition.

To his proud clansmen, Jiang's choice of a military career might have seemed a rejection of the tradition that had nurtured him since his childhood. Yet in his own mind, Jiang had no doubt that he was following the guidance of that tradition and assuming a mission that any educated Chinese in any time would accept. He understood, however, that the changes that were unfolding in his time had made his task more demanding: he had to seek tools that ancient sages had not created and bridge the best of two worlds in the shortest possible time so that China would not perish but regenerate during his own generation.

Childhood

Jiang Baili was born in 1882 in Xiashi, a small town that lies some forty miles north of Hangzhou, the famous scenic city and capital of the coastal province of Zhejiang. According to their genealogy, the Jiangs came to the area around the turn of the eighteenth century and made a living as pawnbrokers. A century after their emigration, the Jiangs had extended their family fortune through land acquisition, while the clan grew to became the largest and most prominent in town. When Jiang Baili's grandfather, Jiang Shengmu, became head of the clan, the Jiangs were prosperous enough to make acquaintance with the regional gentry. The grandfather collected rare books and set up a "Biexia Library," which became famous in the Jiangnan area; he also wrote scholarly works of textual criticism and made friends with well-known Confucian scholars, including Yu Yue, Guan Zhixiang, and Xu Guangzhi. In 1875, Jiang Shengmu's thirteenth son received a provincial degree in the Civil Service Examinations, gaining the family formal membership in gentry circles and leading the way for the next generation.[5]

While the clan's scholarly success nurtured young Baili's intellectual propensity, the unusual circumstances of his immediate

family helped to shape the boy's emotional complexity and prepared him for life's adversities. Baili's father, Jiang Xuelang (1851–
1894), was the nineteenth child in the family and was born without
a left arm. The disfigured child terrified his otherwise loving father,
who made arrangements to send him to a temple when Xuelang
turned ten. Later, a local doctor named Zhu Xingbo helped Xuelang renounce monkhood and taught him medicine. Having become economically independent, Xuelang married an orphaned
girl and began to lead a normal life. Handicap and abandonment, it
seemed, did not make Baili's father a bitter person, but instead led
him to seek solace in a cultured life. He was said to have played the
flute well and enjoyed writing poetry in his leisure time. He remained a devoted sibling to his brothers and sisters and visited
Xiashi often, yet he never requested readmission into the clan and
maintained a separate household in a neighboring county, Haiyan,
by the Hangzhou Bay, where the residents could hear the tides
from the Qiantang River as it flowed into the sea.[6]

Jiang Baili's mother, Yang Zhenhe (1855–1923), became the
most powerful influence on her only son's initial outlook, even before his father's untimely death in 1894. Herself an orphaned child
from a local gentry family, Mrs. Yang acquired literacy through self-
education and learned at an early age the local craft of making
bamboo shirts to make ends meet. She began teaching Baili to read
and write when he turned four. By the age of seven he had already
read some Tang poetry and all four Confucian classics. She also
fascinated her son with stories from *On the Water Margins (Shuihu
zhuan)*, *Legends of the Three Kingdoms (Sanguo yanyi)*, *Journey to the
West (Xiyou ji)*, and *Tales of the Gods (Fengshen bang)*, all of which
kindled Baili's love for heroic drama. One particular story that
stimulated his aspirations for a righteous and chivalrous career was
"Vegetable Stems and Porridge Chunks" ("Duanji huazhou"), a
story about the upright scholar-official Fan Zhongyan (909–1052)
of the Song dynasty. Growing up in a poor family, Fan in his early
youth sustained himself through a long period of study and preparation by carefully rationing his meager food, vegetable stems and
jellied porridge cut into chunks. Eventually, Fan successfully passed
all levels of the Civil Service Examinations and became a high official. Owing to his devoted and benevolent service to his people, his
name became a synonym for altruism, and his two lines of poetry,
"to worry and suffer before everyone under heaven suffers, to enjoy

after everyone under heaven enjoys" *(xian tianxia zhi you er you, hou tianxia zhi le er le),* became the motto for many scholars who emulated him. In Fan's story the young Baili must have heard echoes of his own life and his mother's great expectations for him. As he recalled some forty years later, the story left "so profound a romantic impression on a seven-year-old that it always restrains the negative and stimulates the positive in my life."[7]

Sino-Japanese War of 1894–1895

Jiang Baili might indeed have pursued a career in scholarship and become a dedicated official like Fan Zhongyan had Japan not engaged in a war with China in 1894–1895. By 1894, the twelve-year-old Baili had been in the traditional family school for five years and was recognized, along with his best friend Zhang Zongxiang, a future scholar of Chinese classical literature and textual criticism, as one of the two child prodigies in town. In the early fall, Haining was in an expectant mood, awaiting the sessions of the triennial provincial examination. One of Baili's cousins, who was preparing for the examinations, asked for young Baili's help in finding information on current events, which would be one subject in the tests. For the first time in his life, Baili borrowed a newspaper from the native bank in town. He was astonished and fascinated as he read the news about the war and the brewing national anger against government officials who pursued a policy of reconciliation with Japan. The newspaper spread in front of him suddenly opened up a new vista on a world he had never encountered in the books by the ancients:

> I remember one article, which attacked Li Hongzhang vehemently.... It was the time of the Sino-Japanese War, which stimulated my desire for new knowledge, and I began to read the newspaper. From then on, I became familiar with the geographical names, such as Pingrang, Yashan, Dadongguo, Jiulian Cheng, Weihaiwei, and Liugong Island [all battle sites in the Sino-Japanese War] and began to mention them often. Getting a map was not easy at that time; only by chance I found one at somebody's home. Because national borders on it were painted with color, my attention was drawn to the area of Vladivostok and Huichun.[8]

To the young Baili, it was a moment of a sudden broadening of his mental horizon, of touching the pulse of a world that was beating in a pace unknown in the peaceful town of Haining. In the following spring, the news of the peace treaty between China and Japan reached Beijing, where the scheduled national examination was in session. More than a thousand examination candidates from eighteen provinces signed a collective memorial to the emperor urging him to reject the humiliating treaty with Japan. Although Baili's small town was to learn about that event a month or two later, how it was stirred by the war and China's subsequent defeat seemed too obvious to escape the eyes of the observant boy. The teacher of the family school, meanwhile, had begun to bring in newly published books about the recent conflicts between China and Japan, among them *An Account on the 1895 Petition by the Examinees to the Capital (Gongche shangshu ji)* and *Records of the Indignation under Heaven (Putian zhongfen lu)*, and conspicuously left them on his desk during class breaks. A local library, Shuangshan Shuyuan, also started to purchase new books on contemporary subjects, such as commentaries on current affairs, mathematics, and physics. With their teacher's acquiescence, Jiang Baili and Zhang Zongxiang left the school one or two hours early every day and went to the Shuangshan Shuyuan to read the recently arrived books. They were eager to lay their hands first on books like *Treatises on Japan (Riben guozhi)* by Huang Zunxian, one of the first Chinese diplomats to Japan, and *Records of the Indignation under Heaven*, a collection of memorials by court officials concerning the 1894 war.[9] Although neither Jiang nor Zhang left any record of their specific reaction to these readings, the image of Japan—as both a neighboring country with its unique culture and an enemy that had brought humiliation to China—had made permanent marks on the boys' minds.

The 1898 Reforms

In the eventful year of 1898, when reformers Kang Youwei and Liang Qichao and the Guangxu emperor joined forces to initiate China's first comprehensive institutional reforms in modern times, Jiang Baili moved further toward the pursuit of new knowledge. His ten-year schooling in Confucian classics had come to an end when he gained a county-level degree with a *"shengyuan"* title after successfully passing the examinations in the spring. He was now qualified for provincial examinations, eligible to pursue the ambition of becoming a scholar-official. Instead, he turned to seek a modern education in one of the many new schools that were opening in response to the emperor's reform program. With ten yuan borrowed from a relative, Jiang Baili went to Shanghai and entered a School of Economics (Jingji Xuetang). Unfortunately, the school was soon shut down when a conservative coup d'etat in Beijing ended the "One-Hundred Day Reforms."[10]

A second chance for Jiang Baili came when he returned home and took a teaching position in a family school. In the spring of 1899, Fang Yuting, a newly arrived county magistrate in neighboring Tongxiang County, distributed a "Climate Testing Questionnaire" ("Guanfeng juan") in the area. Jiang Baili responded to the reform-oriented questionnaire enthusiastically and won a "super grant" with a scholarship of thirty silver dollars. The next spring, he was invited to Fang's official residence, where the magistrate advised him to give up the Civil Service Examinations and pursue "practical knowledge" (shi-xue). With Fang's encouragement and the grant, the eighteen-year-old Jiang Baili entered Qiushi Academy (Qiushi Shuyuan), a new school just opened in Hangzhou, the provincial capital.

Qiushi Academy and the Boxer Uprising

The few months at Qiushi, from spring to fall 1900, formed Jiang's first eventful season of political activism. He was among those students who circulated reformers' books, then censored by the government. With a few others, he also started a student group called the Zhejiang Society (Zhe-hui). When it was quickly banned by the government, the students renamed it the Society of Zhejiang Scholarship (Zhe-xue Hui). Jiang's antagonism toward the government further intensified during the Boxer Movement that year. He saw much shame in the Qing court's opportunistic approach, which first sided with the anti-foreign Boxers and then abandoned the capital to the advancing Western expeditionary forces. In essays and poetry, Jiang voiced his indignation toward the inept ruler and his sympathy toward the reformers.[11] His rebellious activities so irritated conservative administrators in the academy that they threatened to expel him from the school.

Contrary to these conservatives' expectations, the intimidation only moved Jiang further on the road toward radicalism. Chen Zhongshu, a reform-minded administrator and teacher in the school, mediated his case with the help of Fang Yuting and the magistrate of Hangzhou. Together, the three officials worked out an arrangement to send Jiang to Japan as a nominal official student of Zhejiang Province, with a donation of one hundred silver dollars from the generous Magistrate Fang.[12] Upon sending his student away from trouble, the sympathetic teacher felt obliged to caution Jiang against imprudent action if he hoped to achieve any tangible reforms. Taking these words as subtle encouragement, in April 1901 Jiang Baili embarked on a voyage to Japan that none of his ancestors could have imagined and only a few of his contemporaries were willing to attempt.

Reorientation

When Jiang Baili landed in Tokyo, the officially endorsed study-in-Japan (Liu-Ri) Movement was still in its incipient phase. Since the arrival of the first thirteen students in 1896, the number of Chinese students in Japan had remained small until 1899, when it jumped to around a hundred, and by 1901, when Jiang Baili came, the community of Chinese students had expanded to 280.[13]

The sudden increase of Chinese students at the turn of the century was partly a repercussion of the abortive 1898 reforms. Kang Youwei and Liang Qichao, the reform leaders, had settled in Yokohama after they fled from persecution in the wake of the palace coup. The energetic Liang Qichao immediately turned to mass media and created the *Journal of Disinterested Criticism (Qingyi bao)* within weeks of his arrival and the *Journal of the New Citizen (Xinmin congbao)* in 1902. The journals found broad readership and attracted many students to Liang's ideas and his editorial room. Months after his arrival, Jiang made the acquaintance of Liang Qichao and became a part-time editor of the *Journal of the New Citizen.*[14]

In that highly politicized atmosphere and with his intense concern for his country's fate, Jiang reconsidered his personal preference and his career choice. By temperament, Jiang Baili was inclined toward the liberal arts; he had been the winner of many composition competitions during his Qiushi Academy years. But the reality of China's recent defeat was still so vivid before him; witnessing a modernizing Japan must have further reminded him that military power was the key to national survival in the modern world. Such a view was not his alone, but was shared by many of his fellow Chinese in their small community in Tokyo; when they advanced from language studies to professional training, the most competitive ones often elected to attend military schools.[15] It was not a comfortable path, certainly, for the training programs in military schools were the most stringent, and those who could not endure the hardship often dropped out. But Jiang quickly made up his mind once he completed language training at Seika Gakkō (C: Qinghua Xuexiao) in the summer of 1901; he enrolled at Seijō Gakkō, a privately owned middle school with semiofficial status, which provided the preparatory program for the elite Army Officers' Academy.[16]

To Awaken the "National Soul"

If Japan, with its modern schools, provided a better environment for Jiang to acquire "practical knowledge," it surely did not confine him to his study, but instead opened new doors for his political activities. Perhaps the most stimulating experience in Japan for Jiang was meeting like-minded fellow Chinese from faraway provinces whom he might never have encountered had he remained in his small hometown. Once enrolled in Seijō, Jiang quickly discovered that people from almost every corner of China had gathered there: from Zhili, Jiangsu, Zhejiang, Hubei, Guangdong, Anhui, Hunan, and Fujian.[17] Among them he soon found a kindred spirit, Cai E (1882–1916), a native of Hunan in central China and former student of Liang Qichao at the School of Current Affairs (Shiwu Xuetang) in the provincial capital of Changsha. With Cai E, Jiang Baili and a few others at Seijō initiated the first transprovincial Chinese student society in Japan. They vowed over blood wine to overthrow the Qing court. Then in the fall of 1902, more than a hundred students from Zhejiang organized the Association of Zhejiang Provincials (Zhejiang Tongxiang Hui) in Tokyo. Jiang was elected to the executive committee at its first conference and was assigned to edit the association's journal, *Tides of Zhejiang (Zhejiang chao)*.[18]

Like other revolutionary journals published by Chinese students in Tokyo, *Tides of Zhejiang* under Jiang's editorship had "nationalism" *(minzu zhuyi)* written on its banner and immediately became one of the most widely circulated student journals calling for political reform. Although banned by the Qing government, the journal found its way into China through a commercial network of more than seventy sales agents, including bookstores, publishing houses, and even fabric shops. Its readership fanned out from thirty cities where sales stations had been set up—including Shanghai, Hangzhou, Beijing, Changsha, Chengdu, Guangzhou, Yokohama, and Singapore—to county seats and towns. Most of its ten issues went through four reprints, with five thousand copies made each time.[19] The ideas propagated by the journal provided powerful weapons for revolution-minded youth. Wherever the journal circulated, "the waves of revolutionary thoughts instantly rose and shook the whole place," as one report from the Zhounan Girls' School at Changsha in central China put it. And some secret societies, like the Restoration Society (Guangfu Hui) in the coastal Zhejiang area, found the journal's title inspiring and used it as part of their communication codes.[20]

For Jiang Baili, editing the *Tides of Zhejiang* was a personal journey that led to the discovery of a new world through his own writing and presentations. He wrote most of the leading editorials under the column "Journal's Opinion" *("She-shuo")* and authored major articles analyzing current affairs, signing with the pseudonyms "Feisheng" (High Flyer) or "Yu-yi." Often, as happened with many journals of the time, he had to contribute several essays for each issue. Although he passed the editorship to Xu Shoushang (1883–1948), another Zhejiang provincial, after the first five issues, he continued to contribute to the journal until its last issue.[21] National rejuvenation emerged as the central theme in his editorial commentaries and essays, and it was explicated by his use of evolutionary theory, then popular in Japan and China.

If Jiang only vaguely sensed the danger that a threatening world posed to China when he read the newspaper at Haining in 1894, by 1903 his focus had become sharper and his vision broader. "Around the turn of the nineteenth and twentieth centuries," he wrote in the first issue of the *Tides of Zhejiang,* "a monster has made its way all over Europe, America, Australia, and Africa. Unsatisfied, it rides the wind and tides of the oceans to invade Asia." The monster was called "nationalism," Jiang told his readers. "Today is a time of rising nationalism," he continued. "As China faces attacks, it must promote nationalism. If not, China will definitely perish."[22] Nationalism, as Jiang saw it, was at the root of Western intrusion into Asia. It was "the father of imperialism," whereas the expansion of economy was "the mother of imperialism."[23]

Drawing from the experiences in nation-building by the Germans, Hungarians, and Romanians, Jiang reached the conviction that unification was vital for the survival of a nation. He argued that the rise of nationalism was an inevitable historical process, developing—like an organism—from the "embryonic phase," through the "transitional phase" and "maturing phase," to the "phase of expansion," evidenced by the history of Europe and Asia, as presented in his chart below.[24]

To Jiang, and perhaps to his readers as well, the disparity between Asia and Europe must have been astonishing: only after a long chain of events in Europe had the Asians begun to catch up. In this vertical examination of historical development and horizontal comparison with other nations of the world, Jiang found both

Nationalism

Asia	Europe
	Embryonic Phase
	French Revolution
	Napoleon Wars
	Vienna Conference
	Transitional Phase
	Italy's reaction
	Germany's reaction
	Hungary's reaction
	Maturing Phase
	Unification of Italy
	Unification of Germany
	The Irish question
	The Eastern question
Embryonic Phase	Expansion Phase
Japanese Restoration	The scramble for Africa
Boxer Rebellion	Future of Asia
	Future of the Pacific

negative and positive lessons for China. The negative ones were Poland and India; both had glorious cultures in the past, but both had declined in modern times. The positive ones were Italy and Germany; both had revived in modern times after a period of decline and devastation.[25] The difference, indicated Jiang, lay in "self-consciousness" or "national soul." India, for instance, was a strong country in ancient times. It had survived under the Mongols but perished under the British rule. Why? The ultimate cause was internal: "The British used Indians to kill Indians, thus the whole of India had to perish. Using Indians to kill Indians is what can be called losing national self-consciousness."[26]

Although the European experiences of nation-building might suggest the overriding importance of material strength, Jiang argued that the path to China's national survival lay elsewhere. In another serialized editorial, "On National Soul" ("Guohun pian"), Jiang maintained that the weakness of the Chinese nation lay in a spiritual disease (guomin jingshen bing) deriving from a conservatism that upheld customs as sacred. Just as a man losing his soul turned into a puppet, he asserted, the Chinese had stopped improving their morality for two thousand years and become dispirited.

Focusing his view on contemporary China, Jiang found that his country had arrived "at the critical point of transition between the old and new." It was "the threshold between life and death for a nation," he said, and the fate of the Chinese nation was now "hanging on one single thread"—the "national soul." Meanwhile, China's "national soul" had reached the edge of extinction, because there was "a degenerating tendency in politics, military and economic production since 1894." The failure of the Chinese to develop a strong self-consciousness, he believed, derived from two causes: the enormous geographical space that made communication within the country slow and difficult, and the habitual indifference that made the Chinese "dull and apathetic" (mamu buren). Consequently, many who lived in the hinterland were not aware of the cession of Taiwan and the lease of Lüshun (Port Arthur) in northeast China. This ignorance and complacency, in turn, reduced the competitiveness of the Chinese. On the closing page of this long, serialized editorial, Jiang printed in oversized letters, "Losing consciousness of self is the vital shortcoming in [Chinese] virtue!" as if shouting, in hopes that his impassioned calls would wake his countrymen from their long-standing apathy.[27]

Far from being discouraged by his comparison of China and the more energetic parts of the world, Jiang was inspired by those who had advanced first. From the countries that succeeded in making historical progress he found models for China to admire and to emulate. The British empire builder Cecil John Rhodes deeply impressed him; Jiang discovered that "a strong religious belief, a lively spirit, and a grand vision" had been keys to Rhodes' accomplishment.[28] But for the Chinese whose "old virtue had gone while the new one is yet to be cultivated," he reasoned, the most relevant model would be the latecomer Japan. The Japanese had succeeded in retaining the old virtues of *bushidō* while cultivating the new. They had been able to modernize so quickly, wrote Jiang, because their leading thinkers, such as Fukuzawa Yukichi and Niijima Jō, helped to cultivate both the scientific spirit and spiritualism among their fellow citizens.[29]

Yet China's situation appeared more urgent, one that demanded "one or two unusual measures to uplift the spirit of all Chinese under the emergency of the intensified foreign peril," said Jiang as he turned his attention again to the question of power. He wanted to find a shortcut. One such approach, he reasoned, would be jingoism (*junguo zhuyi*), a positive attitude contributing to a nation's modern progress. Historically, noted Jiang, China was a country that despised soldiers, thus the notion of "military citizen" had "never entered the Chinese mind." In modern times, however, "only soldiers can save China," because military training would bring about three major changes. First, "jingoism will stimulate progressive spirit" and revive ambition among the Chinese. Second, it "will strengthen discipline" and therefore cure corrupt social mores. Third, it "will cultivate the notion of the public *[gonggong zhi guannian]*," from which public virtue would be nurtured.[30] Elsewhere, Jiang argued that "weak organization and irrational thinking" were vital weaknesses of the Chinese nation.[31] Jiang did not name Japan in this discussion of jingoism, but his line of argument followed closely his own personal experience of abandoning traditional scholarly pursuits for a career as a professional soldier through education in Japanese institutions. The vision here is also broader than the personal; he was speaking not merely from a soldier's viewpoint, but from the perspective of a political leader: the cultivation of jingoism and the training of true soldiers were to be instruments in China's nation-building.

With his emphasis on an organic view of nationhood, the question of survival, and the cultivation of a combatant spirit, Jiang's writings in the *Tides of Zhejiang* suggest the acculturating effect of his two years' exposure to Meiji Japan's educational institutions and intellectual atmosphere. The winds of Social Darwinism had already been sweeping through both China and Japan before Jiang's journey east, but his intermittent enrollment in China's new schools had been too brief to allow a systematic exposure to modern ideas. During the first two years in Japan, he saw before him a model of successful competition and survival of the fittest. Japan's vivid example must have inspired him to pass his new vision immediately to his Chinese audience.

Yet there were also some noticeable differences between Jiang and the thinkers in Japan whom he enlisted to support his arguments. One such difference was his distinctive bent toward voluntarism. Jiang's concern for "national soul," for instance, appears to resemble Fukuzawa's promotion of the "spirit of civilization" as well as Niijima's concern for establishing a moral foundation for Japan's modernization.[32] But unlike Fukuzawa, whose "spirit" was "scientific" in nature, Jiang's "national soul" was more metaphysical and stressed human will. Jiang also differed from Niijima, who explicitly advocated Western Christianity for Japan's moral advancement. In Jiang's "soul," by contrast, there was an awareness of, and even confidence in, China's potential greatness as a culture.

A more significant difference between Jiang's inclinations and those of the Meiji proponents of Social Darwinism lay in their views regarding overseas expansion. For the Meiji thinkers, especially Fukuzawa, Katō Hiroyuki, and Tokutomi Sohō, who had been a student of Niijima, expansion was seen as a necessary means to achieve Japan's modernization. For Jiang, however, an understanding of the stages of progress simply made him keenly aware of the imperialist threat to China's survival, and his advocacy of militarism took self-defense as its goal. His approach to Social Darwinism, to a great extent, resembled more closely that of Liang Qichao, who had also been influenced strongly by Katō's translation of Herbert Spencer during Liang's exile to Japan. Yet Liang, viewing the world from the perspective of a weak nation threatened by imperialist expansion, diverged sharply from Katō's expansionism and promoted a Chinese nationalism that would derive strength from the civic virtue of a "new citizenry."[33]

The Russo-Japanese War

The one-year publication of the *Tides of Zhejiang* coincided with rising international tension between Japan and Russia. The mutual suspicion and eventual confrontation between the two powers can be traced back to the period before the Sino-Japanese War of 1894–1895, when they competed for influence over Korea. As Japan made inroads into the peninsula, Russia countered by sending troops into Manchuria in 1900 during China's Boxer Uprising. Japan's strategic concerns would hardly allow for another strong power in Manchuria, which had become its "defense line" in the logic of General Yamagata Aritomo's theory, and gaining Manchuria became the next goal of Japan's growing empire. The prospect of a show of force became all the more real in the spring of 1903, when Russia, instead of completing its scheduled withdrawal of troops from Manchuria, made the notorious "Seven Demands" to the Chinese government in order to secure Russia a special privilege in that region.

Although both powers blatantly violated China's territorial integrity in this imperialist competition, Chinese students became intensely anti-Russian and thus sided with Japan by default. The fully charged, jingoistic press in Japan during the spring of 1903 must have powerfully shaped Chinese students' outlook on the conflict, as Paula Harrell insightfully points out.[34] Yet they were far from becoming truly pro-Japanese. Once again, the crisis reminded the Chinese students that *China* was in grave danger. Alarmed by the news of Russian demands, Chinese students in Tokyo immediately gathered for a meeting and organized a Volunteer Corps to Resist Russia (Ju-E Yiyong Dui). Jiang Baili, as an executive committee member of the Chinese Student Association in Japan, became one of the initiators of the volunteer corps.[35] Although the volunteer corps enlisted fewer than 20 percent of the eight hundred Chinese students in Tokyo and was soon disbanded under official pressure, the rising anti-Russian and patriotic sentiments, communicated through telegrams and petitions, made Tokyo and Shanghai the centers of the Chinese nationalist movement.[36]

In those intense months, Jiang Baili's new monthly carried in almost every issue one or more essays on Russia. Most of these essays, following the tone set by Jiang in the first two issues, depicted a shrewdly aggressive Russia under czarist despotism. One of his two essays, "The Nature of the Russians" ("E-ren zhi xingzhi"), was reportedly a translation of the work of a British journalist named Howick. It presented Russia as a country that possessed scenes of natural beauty, with a people who demonstrated characteristics of being "rustic yet upright," "enduring yet gloomy." Regarding their racial origin, the Russians were depicted as a complicated combination of both the "round heads" from Europe and the "broad heads" from Asia. The author also praised Russian literature for its "most touching" expression of human feelings. Yet on Russia's relationship with the rest of the world, Howick viewed Russia, with its abundant natural resources and large population, as potentially more powerful and threatening than the British empire. He ended the essay with the following alarming predictions of possible scenarios in the future:

- China's Manchuria, Mongolia and Tibet will fall into Russian hands;
- Turkey will hardly avoid being swallowed;
- Austria and Hungary will separate and the major portion of the Slavs from the Empire will unite with Russia;
- Sweden and Norway will be incorporated into the Russian map;
- Although Germany's power is equivalent with that of Russia, it will fall behind in the future.

  By that time, the power of Slavic race will be ten times that of the Teutons. If China prospers, then the world will be dominated by a Triple-Alliance of Latin, Teuton and China. If China perishes, then the area north of the Yellow River will be swallowed by the Russians. The two races of Latin and Teuton will dominate the world, whereas the yellow race will find no place under the sun.[37]

Although much of the Russophobia in Howick's words seemed to reflect the reality of the then-intensifying British-Russian competition in Persia, Jiang used it for his own purposes to call attention to the prospect of an expanding Russian empire extending its sphere into China. In a follow-up essay titled "Russia's New East Asia Policy" ["E-luo-si zhi dongya xin zhengce"], Jiang characterized Russian diplomacy as "covert," "enduring," and "deft." Russia, Jiang warned, posed a grave threat to China through its construction of railroads and expansion of steamship enterprises in Siberia and Manchuria. He concluded that Manchuria had already been colonized under Russian economic expansion. "Manchuria, Manchuria!" wrote Jiang with a cry of warning: "Today's Manchuria, the reflection of tomorrow's China!"[38]

The denunciation of Russia in the *Tides of Zhejiang* commingled with attacks on the Chinese government when the war finally broke out between Japan and Russia. In the final issue,[39] an essay written under the pen name "Mingxin" angrily denounced the Qing court in Beijing for officially maintaining neutrality with the warring countries while simultaneously making secret deals with the Russians. "What a shame for our people," lamented the author, "that there is nobody denouncing the government's crime and stepping forward to first overthrow the government and then force Russia to withdraw!" The current Chinese neutrality only "benefits the government and harms the people," said the author. He also attacked Russia for its occupation of Manchuria and for insulting the Chinese nation, seeing Russia's southward move in search of an ice-free port as the first step toward colonizing China. Japan, on the other hand, was pushed to the background by the author, who saw it as burdened by an exploding population, yet far too weak in comparison to its opponent.[40]

To Jiang, the Russo-Japanese War did more than merely provoke anti-Russian sentiment; it renewed his memory about that area of conflict, which first came to his attention a decade ago. The names of Vladivostok, Huichun, Pingrang, Dadongguo, Weihaiwei, and Liugong Island had already come easily to his lips when he was still a twelve-year-old boy in a small town in China. The ongoing Russo-Japanese conflict only intensified Jiang's earlier apprehension of China's vulnerability and focused his attention more firmly on the northeast.[41]

The war increased his sense of urgency, too, as Jiang pondered the ongoing debate on democracy and constitutional government in 1903. He criticized the advocates of constitutional reforms from above as well as the proponents of creating a new citizenry from below, seeing both "not wrong in theory but mismatches with China's reality." But between the two approaches, he was relatively mild in his critique of the theory of "new citizenry" advocated by Liang Qichao, who believed that China's modern transformation must begin with the rise of a new citizenry with civic virtue. Jiang doubted, however, that even in the most successful democracy in Europe, where people's "character" had been changed through reforms over decades or centuries, the practice of "debating among a hundred viewpoints without reaching the heart of the issue" could be effective; such an approach would be even more problematic in China. The reality in China, said Jiang, demanded that "the new citizenry [come] after a new government."[42] Could the constitutionalists' approach of reforming the current government work? Jiang was even more skeptical. "Can today's government indeed make constitutional reforms? Why it is willing to sell our four hundred million people to the alien races? It only wants to protect a few rice bowls!" The Chinese government today was unable to reform, but it would consider true constitutional reforms as "rebellion." A comparison between contemporary China and Japan during the Meiji Restoration provided more reasons for Jiang to reject a constitutionalist approach in China. Japan had "a few men of high purpose [C: *zhishi*, J: *shishi*] who followed one another to accomplish the reforms," he argued, and "Japan in the early Meiji was widely awakened, whereas today's China is still in deep sleep."[43]

Jiang thus preferred change under elite guidance, yet he saw nobody then who had the ability to guide. At the heart of his rejection of both Liang's "new citizenry" and the constitutional reforms was his anxiety over the dire threats to his country's survival at this moment of international struggle. In the following passage he described his restless mood, shared by his fellow students:

> As I was yet finishing this article, my friend ran in, panting and perspiring. "The Russians have occupied Fengtian," he said to me, "and Britain, Germany, Japan, and France are raising the issue of Russia's old policy and making demands that spheres be cut out. You still argue with words! That's enough! That's enough!" As I listened to him, I showed nothing on my face, but my heart was pounding and trembling.... Alas, isn't this the end of our ancient country with its thousand-year-old civilization?!... Alas, the unenlightened common people do not understand the pain of a conquered country; yet those with high purpose remain hesitant, stopping short of coming out

with a decisive measure to seek life through sacrifice. They always wait until crises come and then regret. Alas, that is why China is being lost, that is why China is being lost![44]

Meanwhile, Liang Qichao remained unshaken in his belief in the long-term viability of the "new citizenry," but he made some modifications in his from-society-up approach.[45] Only nine years older than Jiang, he had befriended Jiang soon after the young man arrived in Tokyo and came to help with the editorial work of the *Journal of the New Citizen*.[46] He responded to Jiang's challenge with generous encouragement and insightful caution. In an essay appearing in the *Journal of the New Citizen*, Liang indicated that Jiang, despite his eagerness to find an effective means to change China, failed to see that an evil government would not change without a new, transformed citizenry. The problem in Jiang's argument, said Liang, lay not so much in his disagreement over whether to change government or the people first, but in a "one-vigorous-effort-ism" *(guqi zhuyi)*. Although "one-vigorous-effort-ism" had become popular among the Chinese students in Tokyo, cautioned Liang, it merely led them to an illusion that one effective stroke would complete national transformation.[47]

Liang was not the first to warn Jiang against hasty action. Since his meeting with Fang Yuting in China in the spring of 1899, Jiang had been advised repeatedly to pursue "practical knowledge" *(shixue)* and to seek proper means for desirable ends. Under the lasting influence of this concern over practicality, Jiang in fact stood apart from many of his fellow Chinese students in Japan, who often were long in words but short in deeds. Liang's admonishment was well heeded by Jiang. When he and Liang exchanged views in their journals, he had in fact already made another significant step in his pursuit of practical knowledge: in October 1903, he entered the most competitive Army Officers' Academy as a member of the third training class for Chinese cadets.[48]

The Army Officers' Academy, founded in the first year of the Meiji Restoration for the purpose of training low-ranking army officers, was originally named Heigakkō and was located in Kyoto.[49] Over the years, it served as a springboard for many of the generals who rose to national power in the 1930s. Among the Japanese cadets of the sixteenth training class who entered the academy at the same time (as did the third training class of Chinese cadets), there were later luminaries such as Okamura Yasuji (1884–1966), who would serve as commander-in-general of the Japanese army in China during the latter part of the second Sino-Japanese War, 1937–1945; Doihara Kenji (1883–1948), who later won the nickname "Lawrence of Manchuria" for his vigorous efforts to secure Japanese control of Manchuria in the early 1930s; Itagaki Seishirō (1885–1948), who would mastermind the 1931 Manchurian Incident; and Nagata Tetsuzan (1884–1935), who, like Jiang Baili, left the academy as the number-one graduate of the infantry department in his Japanese class of 1904 and would later reign as the most brilliant officer in the army until he was stabbed to death by a fanatic junior officer in 1935.

Although the Chinese and Japanese cadets were trained together, fierce competition seemed to have left little opportunity to nurture friendly feelings. The Chinese and Japanese remained separate groups. Jiang's winning of the imperial sword, it was said, stirred up immense jealousy among his Japanese peers, who were at once ashamed and angry for letting the coveted prize fall into the hands of a Chinese.[50] During the one-year program, Jiang's intimate circle of friends included Cai E, Jiang Zungui, and Gao Erdeng. All were graduates of the Seijō Gakkō, where they had undergone the same preliminary training together, all retained a strong sense of mission, and all were to become top graduates in the cavalry department.

Jiang had been preparing intellectually as well as physically for the rigors of the academy's program. By the time he entered the academy, Jiang had already grown from a frail, scholarly boy into an athletic young man; he became good at horsemanship and gymnastics, and his agile movements on the parallel bars surprised an old friend who had known him since their student years in China.[51] While making high demands on himself, Jiang also tried to help his fellow Chinese cadets improve their professional knowledge and skills. After his graduation from the Army Officers' Academy at the end of 1904, he opened a weekend course for the incoming fourth class of Chinese cadets so as to help them become familiar with the Japanese military system. His eloquent lectures even attracted a student of education, Qian Junfu, who had known Jiang since their Qiushi Academy years in China and who ever afterward admired Jiang's diligence and knowledge.[52]

In the spring of 1906, Jiang Baili returned to China as the top graduate, with high honors, of an elite school in Japan and with the self-designated mission of building a new army for his country. Given the choice of serving as regimental commander in Hangzhou near his hometown or as military adviser for Governor-General Zhao Erxun in Manchuria, he chose the latter. When summer came, Jiang took the northbound train for the northeast provinces, where the national frontier had been calling him ever since he had seen the map of China twelve years before.

This decision may appear to be a dramatic turn for the once radical Jiang. He left no record as to why he had chosen to work within the establishment that he so vehemently opposed for so long. But his passionate writings on the external threat against China, as well as his training at the Army Officers' Academy, with its emphasis on competition and professionalism, indicate two moving forces behind his search for effective solutions. Persistent in his devotion to the nation and methodic in his action, Jiang seems to have combined Mary Backus Rankin's romantic hero in the nationalist revolution and Douglas R. Reynolds' moderate institutional reformers into one. The two strands, as we will see, would remain for the rest of his life.

2 Beyond Chinese Nationalism

Just as Jiang Baili completed his training in Japan and proceeded to his position on the northeast frontier, study-in-Japan (*liu-Ri*) as a movement was developing from a trickle to an incessant and ever-expanding stream. In 1905 and 1906 the number of Chinese students in Japan reached an unprecedented and unsurpassed peak, ranging from twelve thousand to twenty thousand by different estimates.[1] This onrush to the east was propelled by two major events in East Asia. In 1905, Japan won the war against Russia and, along with it, a soaring admiration from other Asians; in the same year, China abolished the Civil Service Examinations after years of educational reforms and recognized, through a formal examination, the equivalence of foreign degrees and education abroad. The coincidental occurrence added to the appeal of Japan, which beckoned idealists and pragmatists alike to its shores.

As the Chinese student community in Japan multiplied, its appearance was transformed. The aspirants for military schools, who had constituted nearly 90 percent of all Chinese graduates from Japanese schools when Jiang Baili lived there, began to drop sharply starting in 1908.[2] Disciplines like law, political science, physics, chemistry, police work, and engineering became major attractions.[3] Less obvious, but no less real, was the emergence of varied attitudes toward Japan among the Chinese. Some began to look more deeply into Japan, not simply to its military might, but to its unique cultural spirit. Such Chinese were still few in the first decade of the twentieth century, but in the long chain of modern Sino-Japanese relations, they formed crucial links leading toward revolutionary changes.

The Amazing Bare Feet

Among the eight thousand Chinese students who sailed to Japan in 1906 were two brothers from Shaoxing, a city in eastern Zhejiang well known for its mellow, aromatic rice wine and the shrewd, well-versed secretaries who rendered service to many mandarins' offices nationwide. Zhou Shuren, the elder of the two, had already spent four years in Japan as a student of medicine. He was summoned back to Shaoxing by his mother in the summer of 1906 to marry a girl whom he had never met before. The elaborate wedding ceremony only intensified his longing for the distant island on the other side of the sea. There, although in a foreign country, he was free from imposed family ties. He had also made a resolution that instead of becoming a doctor to cure the physical diseases of the Chinese, he would become a writer, using words and ideas to uplift them from spiritual degeneration. When that revolution he had hoped for eventually came into full bloom in the late 1910s, he would be known by his pen name Lu Xun and would write "A Madman's Diary" ("Kuangren riji"), the first modern fiction in China.

Unlike Lu Xun, Zhou Zuoren, his younger brother, was far less clear about what lay ahead for him in Japan. A recent graduate of the Jiangnan Naval School (Jiangnan Shuishi Xuetang), he had just been awarded a government scholarship to study architecture in Japan. Like many of his fellow students, he did have a cherished dream: in a heavy wooden trunk he had placed an eight-volume collection of Victor Hugo's novels in English, which he intended to translate into Chinese as soon as he felt ready for the task.[4] Meanwhile, nothing seemed to have made him happier than being reunited with his elder brother and going with him to a foreign land. It was as if they were returning to their Baicao Yuan (Garden of one hundred herbs), a vegetable and flower garden behind their old house in Shaoxing filled with many happy memories of their childhood. The voyage, as Zhou recalled some fifty years later, was "indeed not lonesome at all."[5]

With his preoccupation with European literature, Zhou would keep all things Japanese in the background for a while. Yet before he recovered from the excitement of the long voyage across the sea, he was struck by an unexpected scene, appearing at the very moment he stepped into a Japanese boardinghouse for the first time:

> It was already evening on the day I arrived in Tokyo for the first time. I stayed in Lu Xun's boardinghouse, Fushimikan at Hongō Yushima Ni-chome.... The first person I saw in Fushimikan was Eiko, the younger sister of the owner who also did housekeeping there. She was fifteen or sixteen. She came to help carry the luggage and bring in tea for the guests. The most unusual thing was that she moved around in the room in bare feet.[6]

Writing of that encounter many years later, when Zhou had already made a long career of teaching and writing about Japan, he was still amazed by the force of that transformative moment:

> That was my first actual contact with Japan and Japanese life, thus giving me my very first impression. The impression was not out of the ordinary at all. Yet it was very deep, for I have been keeping it for fifty years without any change or revision. To put it in a simple sentence, it was about the love of the natural and the appreciation of the simple.

> That was an ordinary encounter indeed, so ordinary that almost every Chinese student who entered a Japanese boardinghouse could hardly avoid it. But no one else of his time seemed ever to have cast such an attentive gaze or bothered to ponder the meaning of such an ordinary thing. Yet Zhou should have been taken by surprise, for it was too striking a contrast with what he had left behind in China, where a tangle of conventions and habits fettered human spirits and stifled hoped-for changes and progress.

"The Garden of One Hundred Herbs"

Like Jiang Baili, Zhou Zuoren was the child of a gentry family. But unlike the Jiangs, the Zhous in Shaoxing had been well-established members of prestigious social circles for nearly two hundred years since the early eighteenth century, when one of Zhou's ancestors earned a provincial degree and became a county magistrate.[7] Seven generations later, in 1885, Zhou Zuoren was born at New Gate, one of the clan's family compounds. By then, the Zhous had already passed the zenith of their fortune. Signs of decay, however, remained distant and obscure as life within New Gate carried on undisturbed during Zhou's first eight years of life. His happiest days were spent in Baicao Yuan behind their old house, about which Lu Xun wrote fondly:

> I need not speak of the green vegetable plots, the slippery stone coping round the well, the tall honey locust tree, or the purple mulberries. I need not speak of the long shrilling voices of the cicadas among the leaves, the fat wasps couched in the flowering rape, or the nimble skylarks who soared suddenly from the grass to the sky. Just the foot of the low mud wall around the garden was a source of unfailing interest. Here field crickets would drone away, while house crickets chirruped merrily. Turning over a broken brick, you might find a centipede. There were Spanish flies as well, and if you pressed a finger on their backs, they emitted puffs of vapor from behind.[8]

For the young Zuoren, the world of trees, melons, and insects in the garden would have been far less colorful without his elder brother, his playmate in Baicao Yuan. Lu Xun was his idol. He could make awesome copies of the marvelous pictures from an illustrated *Story of Wiping out the Rebels (Dang kou zhi)*. He could carry his younger brothers to a fascinating world with endless stories about the huge, transmutable ants named A-hei (Blacky) and A-chi (Reddy), or about fairy mountains and the distant Ten Islands. One thing he did that most impressed his younger brother was leading a "squad" of his classmates to punish a local bully who had abused a young student. Although the bully fled before the squad reached his house, the image of Lu Xun wearing a sword beneath his gown brought the righteous heroes of the novel *Water Margin (Shuihu zhuan)* to Zhou's real world.[9]

The boys were able to have such an uninhibited childhood partly because of their tolerant father. Although he was an opium addict and had repeatedly failed the provincial examinations, he was nonetheless an understanding parent. Once or twice he accidentally discovered Lu Xun's cartoons and picture books, hidden in obscure places such as underneath a futon or behind a stairway. Instead of scolding his son for wasting time on an indecent interest, he simply skimmed the uncovered treasures and returned them quietly to his son, wearing a faint smile on his face as his children nervously awaited something worse. Sometimes he frightened Zhou Zuoren with horror stories about skeletons, skulls, and split bodies. But what his children also remembered about him, long after his untimely death in 1896, was his resolution, confided to his relatives, that he would send one son to the West *(Xiyang)* and the other to the East *(Dongyang)* to discover the secret to national strength. It was a wish he had made after failing the provincial examinations for the last time in 1894, the year Japan defeated the crumbling Chinese empire.[10]

The women within New Gate were almost equally as distant from the children as their father had been, though in quite different ways. Unlike Jiang Baili's mother, who exerted a constant influence on her only son's education and shaped his outlook on the world in terms of endurance and diligence, Zhou Zuoren's mother allowed her sons to enjoy Baicao Yuan as much as they wished. But she was also a woman of character. She had the courage to free her bound feet when the natural foot movement *(tianzu yundong)* reached Shaoxing in the late Qing. When some members in the clan accused her of scandalous behavior, she retorted calmly and with cold wit. The daughter of a provincial-level degree holder, she had never had a formal education but had learned to read in her childhood through self-education. Later, in her sixties, when she took up residence in Beijing, she started reading newspapers every day and loved to discuss with her sons and grandchildren the politics of contemporary warlords.[11]

When Zhou Zuoren looked back on his childhood, other women in and outside New Gate appeared to be almost invariably bound by their miserable fate. He remembered vividly a young girl in the neighborhood whose attempt to escape a forced marriage by climbing out of her bedroom window ended with a fall into the river below. She later died prematurely from tuberculosis. Two of his paternal aunts had passable marriages, but one died in childbirth and the other drowned in an accident.[12] One exception to these suffering women was an aunt whom Lu Xun later named "Mrs. Yan" in his "Random Notes" and who had been an inexhaustible source of poisonous rumors. Once she even suggested to Lu Xun that he take money from his mother's drawer and then spread the word that he was stealing things from his household. Her duplicity is what first opened Lu Xun's eyes to the dark side of society. All of the bigotry and decadence of a small city, it seemed, had gathered on the tip of Mrs. Yan's seemingly sweet yet virulent tongue, which eventually drove Lu Xun out of the suffocating New Gate to search for a more breathable atmosphere in Nanjing in 1898.[13]

By then, the course of the brothers' happy childhood had already been changed by a series of events that began in 1893. That spring, Zhou Fuqing, their grandfather and the clan's last national degree holder, returned home for his mother's funeral. For many years he had been away from home, first serving as a county magistrate in another province and then as an official in the Grand Council in Beijing. "Once he arrived home," wrote Zhou Zuoren years later, "he appeared to me at the same time distant and stern."[14] The fifty-eight-year-old official brought with him a twenty-six-year-old concubine and a twelve-year-old son, born to another (deceased) concubine.[15] Soon their grandfather frightened his clan with his explosive temper, and the young Zuoren had his first taste of it when he was awakened by a pounding sound one morning to find his grandfather banging on his bed to make him get up. It turned out that his grandfather had become suddenly fed up by the decadent habit within New Gate of getting up late, and he vented his rage on everyone, including eight-year-old Zhou Zuoren.[16]

Their grandfather's sudden wrath over a trivial matter was not, in fact, without cause. Opium smoking, an addiction that contaminated not only the Zhou clan, but also many of their relatives, was one reason they got up so late in those days. What Zhou Zuoren remembered about his eldest maternal uncle, for instance, was his habit of lying all day in his netted bed smoking, so that his shoes became virtually useless.[17] Also upsetting to their grandfather was the lack of vitality within the Zhou clan, as no one after him had ever been able to go beyond a county-level degree *(xiucai)* on the examinations. One of the clan member's repeated failures on the Civil Service Examinations drove him to madness. He first set himself on fire and then jumped into a river, crying, "Old cow is drowning!"[18] Lu Xun was so haunted by his memory of this tragicomic incident that he eventually immortalized the maniac in his story "White Light" ("Baiguang").

In a desperate effort to keep itself afloat in the gentry world, the Zhou clan made a fateful move in the fall of 1893. Pressured by relatives and friends to get some youngsters in the clan to pass the examinations, Zhou Fuqing made an attempt to bribe the examiner of the upcoming civil service examinations. The bribery was discovered and became a widely known scandal. He was sentenced to "waiting for execution in prison" *(zhanjianhou)*. Every year from 1893 to 1901, while their grandfather was jailed in Hangzhou, the family at New Gate had to send bribes to officials in hopes of obtaining a lighter sentence. They also had to pay for expensive medicines for Zhou Zuoren's father, who died in 1896 after a long struggle with tuberculosis.[19]

Ironically enough, it was in the midst of this double misfortune that Zhou Zuoren began his more serious education. Still in mourning for his father, Zhou was summoned to Hangzhou to keep his grandfather company. The old man often had ill-tempered outbursts, cursing officials as well as Emperor Guangxu and the Empress Dowager, but he was surprisingly kind to the jailers and to his grandson. Under his guidance, Zhou read more Chinese classics and learned the technique of composition. Encouraged by his grandfather and influenced by Lu Xun, he also read widely in history and literature during his one and a half years in Hangzhou. Years later, he realized that his grandfather's unconventional insistence that he read novels had subtly shaped his approach to written works, because it was then that he began "to read words on paper and understand the meanings they expressed."[20]

In late 1898, while his grandfather was still in jail, Zhou Zuoren and Lu Xun took the entry-level examinations for the civil service. Lu Xun took only the first of the three examinations, then returned to the Jiangnan Naval School in Nanjing. Zhou Zuoren took all three but failed to pass. In 1899 and 1900 he made two more attempts, also without success.[21] It now seemed there were two other options available: finding a secretarial position under a county magistrate or entering the world of merchants, which was how the Zhou clan had started some four hundred years before in Shaoxing. Fourteen-year-old Zhou Zuoren found neither choice appealing. He was in a dejected mood when he wrote at the end of October 1899: "Feel ashamed as no progress made in learning yet I am aging; again disheartened that the elder brother is in Nanjing and the fourth brother has gone forever."[22]

Thanks to his grandfather, Zhou Zuoren was able to escape his predicament through yet another option. Seeing that the civil service had become nearly a dead end for the younger generation, his grandfather was open to other options. He suggested opening a small business, perhaps making tofu, for it required little skill and investment but guaranteed self-sufficiency, since tofu was a local diet staple for both the rich and poor.[23] Entering a new school was his other recommendation. While still in jail in 1899, Zhou Fuqing wrote to his grandson and encouraged him to apply at the newly opened Qiushi Academy, the school that Jiang Baili was attending in Hangzhou. Qiushi was attractive for both scholarly and financial reasons: "It teaches both Chinese and Western knowledge by different teachers," wrote the old man to the boy. "The students are provided with three meals, with good dishes. Those who excelled also receive three or four dollars monthly fellowship."[24]

The hesitant Zhou Zuoren was jolted out of Shaoxing at last, when his grandfather returned home under the amnesty of 1901. Although rational in his attitude toward career choices, his grandfather turned out to be abusive toward women and stubborn about the family's gentry image. In moments of ill temper he would shout curses or subtly insult his own wife and make her cry; by so doing, the old man "really disgraced himself" in his grandson's eyes. The most unbearable thing to Zhou Zuoren was that he had to, as ordered by his grandfather, wear a long gown while doing morning grocery shopping in a muddy and crowded market during the sweltering summer. The boy thought this "was an invisible abuse that cannot be endured." Already restless and thinking about "going to the provincial capital [Hangzhou]" for the past year, Zhou Zuoren made up his mind to leave home only two months after his grandfather's return. In the summer of 1901 he left for the Jiangnan Naval School and joined his brother in Nanjing.[25]

"When Reading New Books Has Come into Vogue"

The Jiangnan Naval School, like the Qiushi Academy in Hangzhou, was one of those new schools opened at the end of the nineteenth century in order to bring new knowledge *(xinxue)* into China. Lu Xun entered the Jiangnan Naval School in 1898 with the dream of "taking a different path, finding refuge in a different place, and seeking out different people."[26] He was disappointed when he found the curriculum unchallenging and outdated and some of the teachers ignorant and arrogant. Within half a year, he withdrew from the school and entered Mining and Railroad School

(Kuangwu Tielu Xuetang), which was affiliated with the Jiangnan Army School (Jiangnan Lushi Xuetang).[27]

Zhou Zuoren, too, confronted the deep shadow of the past as soon as he entered the Jiangnan Naval School. Enrollment in a modern school was not difficult then, for it had yet to gain the same prestige as the traditional education; entering Jiangnan Naval School was made even easier for the Zhous from Shaoxing because a great-uncle was an administrator of the school. He was, however, a typical standpat scholar-official. A provincial degree holder, the great-uncle recited Daoist scripture every morning in his prayer room at this new school. He was concerned about his clan's gentry reputation, too, and the first thing he did when the youngsters from his clan entered the new school was to change their names. It was by his instruction that Lu Xun, who had been called Zhangshou, became Shuren; Zhou Zuoren, who had been Kuishou, became Zuoren.[28]

But the great-uncle was just one example of the social and institutional resistance and inertia that enveloped Jiangnan Naval School. Although the curriculum, which included English, mathematics, physics, chemistry, and steamship engineering, appeared modern, the instruction was "slovenly" (mahu), as Zhou Zuoren put it. He could never forget one teacher who told his students about the existence of two earths, one called the Eastern Hemisphere and the other the Western Hemisphere. The fate of a swimming pool on campus, built for training the future sailors, was yet another rude reminder of the old die-hard beliefs. At the time of Zhou Zuoren's arrival, it had already been filled in because two students had drowned in it. A Guandi temple had been built atop the pool so that the ghosts of the drowned would be unable to reemerge to haunt the living.[29]

However disappointing the naval school was, Zhou Zuoren still felt elated about coming to Nanjing. The two brothers now could see each other almost every day. During the six months between Zhou Zuoren's arrival in Nanjing in September 1901 and Lu Xun's departure for Japan in March 1902, Zhou filled his diary with entries like, "Elder Brother came this afternoon, and left this early evening." "Elder Brother came this afternoon, brought me four books."[30] His joy sparkles beneath these simple lines. One of Elder Brother's visits in early 1902 was such a high point of excitement that Zhou had to record it in more detail:

Walked to the Army School after lunch. Road was slippery and difficult. Talked to elder brother, then he took me to hang out at Gulou.... After supper, elder brother suddenly arrived, bringing with him Huxley's *Tianyan lun [On Evolution]*. Its translation was really good.[31]

In his *Dawn Blossoms Plucked at Dusk*, Lu Xun, too, recalled his exhilarating encounter with Huxley's *On Evolution* as he opened its first page at a time when "reading new books has come into vogue":

Oh! Indeed was there such a Huxley, sitting in his study, who thought in this way, and so refreshingly? [As I] read more in one breath, *"wujing"* [competition among beings] and *"tianze"* [natural selection] appeared, Socrates and Plato came out, and the Stoics also showed up.[32]

It was not the first time that the Zhou brothers mentioned "new books." Just ten days before, Zhou Zuoren wrote in his diary about reading *La Dame aux Camélias*, a French novel rendered into classical Chinese by the prolific translator Lin Shu.[33] However, Huxley's *Evolution and Ethics*, published in England in 1893 and translated into Chinese in 1898 by Yan Fu, who retitled it *On Evolution*,[34] made a deep impression on the two brothers because of its "good writing" and refreshing views. In that memorable year of 1902, a period of "reading new books" made its way into Zhou's schedule, which so far had been occupied by reading Chinese classic novels, travelogues, history, or essay collections. In addition to Huxley, he repeatedly read *The Wealth of Nations* by Adam Smith and *On Benevolence* (Ren xue) by the martyr of the 1898 Reforms, Tan Sitong.[35] His reading list expanded after Lu Xun went to Japan in March and sent back books like Katō Hiroyuki's *Hundred Essays on the Law of Evolution (Tensoku hyaku wa)* and Shibue Tomotsu's *History of Poland's Downfall*. In July, a classmate pressed into Zhou's hands the eleventh issue of the *Journal of the New Citizen*, edited by Liang Qichao in Japan, and he "read until going to bed reluctantly at mid-night."[36] Early the next year, the first issue of *Tides of Zhejiang* also arrived from Japan; Zhou Zuoren "opened and read it under the lamp" and burst out in exclamation, "How wonderful, how wonderful!"[37]

The new readings brought Zhou Zuoren to a new state of mind; he began to speak more explicitly about China's decline in the modern world. In a stopover at Shanghai during the summer of 1903, he went to the Bund and recorded his "Feelings about the Park" in his diary:

> On the way to the Sixteen Piers [Shi-liu-pu] we passed the park, which is very spacious and lush with grass and trees. The white men strolled inside complacently, but the Chinese were not allowed to enter. There is a plate hung on the gate, with seven big, gilded words: *"Quan Yü Hua Ren Bu Zhun Ru"* [Dogs and Chinese are not admitted].

And he was at once indignant and filled with shame:

> How sad that our Chinese were regarded as the same as dogs. There are iron fences around the park, and many [Chinese] stand outside, peeking in curiously. Yet no one seemed to show indignation. How incredible that their blood has turned so cold![38]

In that mournful mood, he and his fellow students continued their journey and paid a visit in the following months to the Ming Palace in the suburbs of Nanjing. The ruins of the once-powerful dynasty's ruling site again made him "deeply sad."[39]

Momentarily, Zhou's nationalist indignation remained more a private thought, shared with only a few close friends, though he had begun an experiment that would affect his career in the long run. "We had happened to be in a good time. It was just as we were getting bored, with no good novels to read, that the circles of translation prospered," recalled Zhou. "Yan Jidao's *On Evolution,* Lin Qinnan's *La Dame aux Camélias [Chahua nü],* and Liang Rengong's *Fifteen Chivalrous Men [Shiwu xiaohaojie]* can be said to be representative of three schools." His time for studying classical Chinese "was all spent on reading that kind of stuff," and among these Lin Shu's (Qinnan's) translations of romantic novels "were my favorite."[40] In 1905, Zhou made his first attempt at translating "new fiction" when he learned that a journal, *Women's World (Nüzi shijie),* was looking for contributors. The story he chose came from an illustrated *Ali*

Baba and the Forty Thieves, printed by the Newnes Company in London—a book that struck him with its imaginative stories and delightful drawings. *Women's World* accepted Zhou's first translation from the fable, now titled *Chivalrous Woman Slave (Xia nünu)* and signed with the pen name "Ms. Pingyun." The serialized translation became so popular that the publisher decided to reprint it twice as a book. Encouraged, Zhou Zuoren proceeded to translate Edgar Allan Poe's *The Gold Bug,* which was published by the same journal in May. He even wrote and published two short stories, both centered on women and with a theme of social injustice and righteousness. A novella, *Story of an Orphan (Guer ji),* for which he borrowed heavily from Victor Hugo's *Claude Gueux,* was also accepted by a publisher in Shanghai and brought him his first royalty of twenty silver dollars.[41] One incidental but long-term gain from the practice of translation was his enhanced ability to read English, a language he had learned at the naval school.[42]

In 1905, Zhou Zuoren turned twenty. After a nine-month pause, he resumed daily entries in his diary in a restless tone. Earlier, in the spring of 1904, he became so dejected after trying unsuccessfully to go to study in Japan and join his elder brother that he began to suspect many of his thoughts were totally wrong. Writing in early 1905, he considered that his mind had undergone a great change: earlier he believed in power and Europeanization; now he began to have more faith in compassion and national essence *(guocui).* A few days later, he was paid twenty silver dollars for his translation of *Chivalrous Woman Slave.* Using part of this income he bought a few books, including a bibliography of Buddhism. Later that day Zhou wrote: "Everything under heaven does not go beyond the word 'feeling' *[qing].*"[43] As he looked back five decades later at the age of seventy-seven, Zhou judged that he then had had no coherent outlook on the world but was under the influence of a great many ideas: "there were romantic ideas, humanism from abroad, revolutionary ideas, traditional nihilism, the old and new writings by Jin Shengtan and Liang Rengong, all lumped together." And some of his writings showed "deep melancholy of a youthful age."[44]

That Zhou should be sentimental is not so surprising for a young adult, but there was one particular reason for his restlessness. In 1904, Zhou entered the last year of studies at the naval school and was facing graduation. Having spent most of his time reading new books and even having had some initial success with his dabbling in literature, he could not be excited by the prospect of becoming a naval engineer. Despite the great attraction of the Western world, the financial situation of his family would not allow him to contemplate further education in Europe or America. The alternative, then, would be Japan. In fact, at the beginning of 1903, Zhou had already mobilized three fellow students to petition the newly arrived school principal when he heard that the new principal was going to take four students with him for a study tour in Japan.[45] Although that effort failed, Zhou soon started learning Japanese by himself, encouraged by Lu Xun's suggestion that he consider coming to Japan as well.[46]

Zhou's opportunity came at the end of 1905, when the Military Training Department of the Qing court held an examination to select military students for further training abroad. This time, the graduating students succeeded in convincing the naval school to send them to Beijing, where all of them passed the test. Unfortunately for Zhou and another student, Wu Yizhai, their nearsightedness caused them to fail the physical examination. After waiting in their empty dormitory at the naval school for months, Zhou, who was usually quiet and timid, jumped at an opportunity when the provincial magistrate came for a visit. He and Wu resisted the magistrate's order of assigning them two official positions. They instead pleaded that they be sent to study abroad. The sympathetic magistrate listened and made a decision: they were to receive fellowships to study architecture in Japan. The world so far had lured Zhou only with vague hopes; now it suddenly opened to him a magic door.[47]

For a New Kind of Revolution

Zhou did not become a student of architecture in Japan. Thanks to the loose administration of the Chinese embassy, government-sponsored students needed to provide only the name of the school they were "attending" in order to receive their monthly stipends. A sizable number of students thus squandered the money on drink or women, which helped to create a generally poor reputation for students returning from Japan. Yet out of the pool of Japan-educated graduates, which was much larger than the pool of those educated in the West, a considerable number of them would go on to make

indispensable contributions to developments in China's modern
military, literature, banking, engineering, and other spheres in the
decades to follow.[48]

Meanwhile, Zhou felt liberated as he began his six-year sojourn in Tokyo, as if guided by the spirit of Eiko's free-moving feet.
After a Japanese-language program, he enrolled in a one-year special preparatory program at Hōsei University (Hōsei Daigaku) in
Tokyo in the summer of 1907. There, he chose to concentrate on
learning the Japanese language and Japanese history while skip-
ping lessons on English and mathematics, in which he had already
been well prepared by the naval school. Because of his irregular attendance, he was late for the final examination. Although he thus
missed one of the tests, he still earned the second highest score
among the graduates. That became the last formal program in
which Zhou enrolled, and he later chose simply to audit courses at
Rikkyō University (Rikkyō Daigaku) in Tokyo.

While enjoying their freedom from institutional restraints,
the Zhou brothers undertook a rather serious endeavor. Inspired
by Liang Qichao and the then-influential translations of Western
works, they contemplated the possibilities of writing new literature
and founding a new journal, titled *New Life (Xinsheng)*. The editorial
board and the major contributors included both Lu Xun and Zhou
Zuoren as well as two other friends, Xu Shoushang, a classmate of
Lu Xun at Kōbun Academy and Jiang Baili's successor for the *Tides
of Zhejiang*, and Yuan Wensou, another fellow student. However,
short of funds as well as readership, *New Life* had to be aborted before they could even assemble the first issue.[49]

Refusing to give up their hopes, the two brothers moved on to
other endeavors. They turned their curious browsing of Western
literature into a productive engagement in translation and, in 1907,
collaborated on a translation of Andrew Lang's *The World's Desire*.
The work was done in a style after Lin Shu's: while Zhou Zuoren
translated the novel out loud, Lu Xun wrote it down in a more pol-
ished classical Chinese. The task was accomplished in just a few
months and was published under a new title, *Anecdotes of the Red Star
(Hongxing yishi)*, by the Commercial Press in Shanghai.[50]

From this first success the two brothers proceeded to a second
project: a translation of Aleksey Tolstoy's *Ivan the Terrible*. To their
disappointment, the Commercial Press rejected the manuscript because it had already received another translation.[51] The misstep

made the brothers more prudent, and they decided to focus on lesser-known writers. In the following years they translated three more novellas: "Story of Chivalrous Men in Hungary" ("Xiongnu qishilu") and "Yellow Rose" ("Huang qiangwei"), both by Hungarian novelist Jókai Mór; and "Charcoal Drawing" ("Tanhua") by the Polish writer Henryk Sienkiewicz. In 1909, with the financial help of a friend, they published a two-volume collection of translated short stories, *Collection of Short Stories from Abroad (Yuwai xiaoshuo ji)*, which included works by Sienkiewicz, Anton Chekhov, Leonid Andrejev, V. Garshin, Oscar Wilde, Edgar Allan Poe, and Guy de Maupassant.[52] By then, the experience of translating works by Eastern European writers, though originally prompted by considerations of publishing acceptance, had inspired an explicit intellectual goal: they wanted to arouse their Chinese audience with the rebellious spirit in works from "the oppressed weak nations."[53]

As most of their introduction to European literature had been through the medium of English translation thus far, the two brothers undertook yet another ambitious effort to expand their language abilities. In his second year in Japan, Zhou Zuoren, together with Lu Xun and few other friends, began to take language lessons with a Russian immigrant. In the autumn of 1908, Zhou Zuoren started auditing Greek classes at Rikkyō University. He regularly attended religious services at the Trinity School of Rikkyō University in order to listen to the sermons in ancient Greek, which interested him because "it had been used by 'those who pulled vendor carts'" during Christ's time.[54] Together with Zhang Taiyan, the famous Chinese philologist and anti-Manchu revolutionary, Zhou Zuoren even tried to learn Sanskrit from a Brahman priest, but they soon abandoned the effort when both found its alphabet and sounds too difficult to handle.[55]

Just as they were inclusive and open-minded in their attitude toward foreign literature and foreign-language studies, the two brothers embraced friends of diverse temperaments. In one part of their circle were political radicals, such as Tao Chengzhang, the well-known revolutionary from the Shaoxing area who was organizing secret societies to undertake anti-Manchu uprisings in order to overthrow the Qing dynasty; Tao Wangchao, a relative of Tao Chengzhang and an equally passionate revolutionary who later went to Nagasaki to produce explosives for the uprisings; and Chen Ziying, a third revolutionary who fled China after the failed collaboration with anti-Manchu martyr Xu Xilin in an assassination attempt. A different group of friends consisted of scholars such as Gong Weisheng, Zhang Taiyan's son-in-law, who was then interested in pursuing nationalist revolution through language studies; Qian Xuantong, another philologist who would become Zhou Zuoren's closest friend at Beijing University; and Zhu Xizu, later a scholar of literature and one of the organizers of the Literature Study Association in the New Culture movement. There were even some mutual friends of Jiang Baili, such as Chen Yi, a student at the Army Officers' Academy who later served in the Chinese National Government until he was sentenced to death by Jiang Jieshi for his Communist sympathies in the late 1940s; and Qian Junfu, who for a brief period was a boarding mate of the Zhou brothers in a house once occupied by Natsume Sōseki. Friends dropped in to visit at their boardinghouse in Higashitake-chō whenever they pleased and often joined the brothers in a simple meal as their discussions lasted from early afternoon to supper time.[56]

While sharing strong nationalist sentiments with these friends, the Zhou brothers were, as Leo Ou-fan Lee characterized Lu Xun at the time, "[d]istressed by the superficial utilitarianism" found in some Chinese nationalists' attitudes in their era,[57] and they disagreed with the means these nationalists chose to pursue change. Tao Chengzhang's courage and ambition to wage a revolution in order to "provide a bowl of rice to everybody under heaven" won their great admiration, and the two brothers sometimes provided help when Tao needed a place to hide his secret documents from the Japanese police. But they, as well as Zhang Taiyan, had a strong aversion to Tao's advocacy of violence, and they suspected that Tao would become a brutal man like Zhu Yuanzhang, the notorious founder of the Ming dynasty who killed his old comrades when necessary. Teasingly they gave Tao two nicknames, "Emperor Huan" (Huan Huangdi) and "Robber Huan" (Huan Qiangdao), after Tao's style, Huanqing.[58]

Rather than resorting to violence and imposing revolution, the Zhou brothers preferred a different kind of power to bring about modern change. They had only gradually come to their choice, and living in Japan, especially, helped to broaden their vision and sharpen their focus. Not only was their view of the "West" expanded by the literature from "the oppressed peoples," which was easily accessible in the cosmopolitan book market of Tokyo, but their understanding of Japan and its relationship with China deepened as well. "I was then a believer of nationalist revolution," said Zhou Zuoren some three decades later, "and was full of nostalgia [about China's past]." There was always the "idea of restoration [*fugu sixiang*] in all nationalism," indicated Zhou. "We opposed the Qing court, and felt everything in the past, or things before the Yuan dynasty, was all good, not to mention something even more ancient." In such a frame of mind, he and his friends were instantly attracted by the pervasive influence of Chinese culture that they encountered in Japan. One such sign of the intimate cultural connection between the two countries was the Chinese writing script. Two friends of Zhou's, Qian Quantong, a future philologist, and Xia Mianzun, a well-known educator, were said to have been so fascinated by the shop signs on Tokyo streets that they often raised their hands in admiration. "What an authentic style of Tang," they reportedly said, "which is found no more in today's China."[59]

Just as his friends admired the lost spirit of Tang culture in the shop signs on Tokyo streets, Zhou Zuoren was moved by "the love of the natural and the appreciation of the simple" in Japanese life, a discovery inspired first by Eiko's free-moving, unbound feet. He was enamored of the easy and simple style of the Japanese house. "I like the Japanese-style house very much. But it is not because I only prefer ancient stuff.... What I like about it is its usefulness that especially suits a simple life." In his view, the standard four-mat, furnitureless room in a boardinghouse was more versatile than a fully fashioned house: the whole room became "a big desk for paper and books" when a short-legged, small table was put in for writing; it could be turned into a spacious living room that allowed six or seven guests to sit wherever they pleased; "there is no need for a sofa, because one can lie down right there when tired"; and it converted to a bedroom when bedding was taken out of the closet and laid out on the floor. Such an arrangement allowed the Japanese to travel light: "I remember seeing Japanese students moving. They put everything—bedding, cloth bundle, short-legged table, and bookcases—all in one rickshaw and followed it with one glass oil lamp in hand." That lightness and simplicity made the Japanese house far superior to Chinese ones: "A Chinese apartment makes one feel confined," said Zhou, "since little space is left after bed, table, chairs, trunks, and shelves are all put in it."[60]

Zhou's appreciation of this unrestrained lifestyle extended to Japanese clothing as well. For him, the ideal outfit for an evening stroll in the hot summer was the kimono, because it made one feel "at ease."[61] He also favored geta, or the wooden clog. In his opinion, it was equal to the "best, most beautiful footwear" in the world, on par with Greek sandals and the straw sandals from south China. All were better than leather shoes because they "do not hide, do not decorate, and they follow the natural." It was "fortunate," said Zhou several decades later, "that I had experienced such a life in Japan, despite that I did not have the luck to see ancient Greece.... Even if I returned with nothing, whenever I went out for a stroll, I saw only the ordinary people who hither and thither passed by, and none of them had bound feet ... which indeed was most delightful."[62]

And one thing in particular made Zhou feel a special intimacy with Japanese life. The Japanese diet, he recalled, was a surprise to many Chinese because of its "rarity of animal meat." For him, however, there was not just a kindred spirit of simplicity as seen in Japan's house and clothing; its diet, too, had a surprising similarity to the ordinary diet in his hometown. "My hometown is quite poor; there people work hard and feel content with three meals a day, and their main dishes are simply pickled vegetables, pickled bean curd, and snail. Therefore, we neither mind the salty and the stinky nor crave grease. Eating any kind of Japanese food is hardly a problem [for me]." Rather than hating the lightness and coldness of Japanese food, he found it "comparable to those in my hometown" and could see the similarities in a long list of pairs: Japanese miso and the bean paste in his hometown, Japanese *takuanzuke* and the pickled yellow radish from Fujian Province, Japanese sashimi and the *yüsheng* from Canton, Japanese sushi and the *yüzha* that appeared in *Qimin Yaoshu,* an ancient text on agriculture and socioeconomic life in the late Northern Wei period (500–534). The likenesses in food, Zhou suggested, "inhabit the history of cultural exchange; they are food not just for mouth, but for thoughts as well."[63]

In 1909, Zhou Zuoren took one step further into Japanese life. He had fallen in love with Habuto Nobuko, a meal provider *(makanai)* to one of the boardinghouses where the brothers lodged in Nishikata-chō.[64] The two lovers were married in late summer. While Lu Xun returned to China to find a job so as to bring income to the family,[65] Zhou and his bride moved into a rented house in Azabu Ward by Akabane Bridge.

Thus Zhou Zuoren began to live among ordinary Japanese for the first time. Their neighborhood was occupied by people of the laboring class.[66] The move from elitist Nishikata-chō in Hongō Ward to the more plebeian neighborhood near Akabane Bridge reminded Zhou of the experience of riding different railroad cars. In Nishikata, he recalled, neighbors "pretend to be gentlemen and never speak to each other, as if riding in a second-class car." But Zhou had had the irritating, repeated experience of discovering a pile of dirt in his yard, swept from the neighbor's side. In Azabu, the residents "are like riders in a third-class car, where nothing divided them. They say hello upon seeing each other, and chat at ease." There were other kinds of intrusion, of course, though Zhou recalled them with amusement rather than annoyance. He remembered hearing his next-door neighbor, a worker in the paper trade, berate and beat his daughter because the girl made friends with some young boys and girls who frequented Shiba Park nearby. The father was afraid that his daughter would become a "bad girl." But the daughter forgot the beating the next day when she heard the boys' whistles and "slipped out of the house instantly, as if her young soul was seized by magic incantations." When the women in the neighborhood tried to reason with her, the young girl responded with a giggle, "You really don't know how much fun it is to play outside!" And Zhou Zuoren agreed: "That really sounds sensible!"[67]

Living intimately with ordinary Japanese enabled Zhou Zuoren to turn his attention to the native forms of Japanese literature. Among various genres, he became particularly interested in the "humorous kind"—*kyōgen* and *rakugo*. He used Haga Yaichi's *Twenty kyōgen (Kyōgen nijū ban)* and Miyazaki Sanmai's *Selections of rakugo (Rakugo sen)* as his language textbooks and found in them "great materials for [understanding] human feelings and social customs of contemporary society." He also came to appreciate haiku and enjoyed its lyric style of "using the ordinary but transcending the vulgar *[yong su er li su]*." Like the girl next door, Zhou Zuoren, too, became spellbound by the outside world. *Yose*, the storyteller's theater, drew the twenty-four-year-old Zhou Zuoren just like Shiba Park had lured young boys and girls, and he became part of its cheerful, laughing crowd.[68]

By 1911, Zhou Zuoren had grown so attached to Japan that he was extremely reluctant to leave when Lu Xun urged him to start a teaching career in China. He wanted to extend his sojourn and learn French, after becoming fluent in Japanese and highly literate in English, Russian, and Greek. Yet their family's meager resources could not support this ambition. He returned to Shaoxing with Nobuko. But even after months at home, his heart still remained on the other shore: "To return to Shaoxing this summer after living in Tokyo for six years, I feel lonesome even though this is my homeland," wrote Zhou toward the end of the year. "Whenever I recall the days there, I become homesick. I have taken that foreign land as my home and made people there members of my family. Can it be anything but human feelings?"[69]

***

Although fascinated by his "second homeland," Zhou Zuoren nevertheless had had a glimpse of another Japan, which took him by surprise a few months before his departure. In late January 1911, as he enjoyed a peaceful afternoon of browsing through secondhand bookstores, he heard the shouts of a newspaper extra edition as he strolled past the Red Gate of Tokyo University. As he glanced at the news, "it stunned me and halted me right there." That was the day when the verdict on the so-called "Great Treason Incident" (Taigyaku Jiken) was delivered.[70] Since the previous May, the government, after the discovery of a plot to assassinate the emperor, had rounded up hundreds of socialists and charged twenty-four of them with treason. Kōtoku Shūsui, a leading socialist thinker who was not involved in the extremists' plot, was among the twelve who were condemned to death in the final verdict. The government's handling of the incident so shocked the Meiji intelligentsia that it reacted in either open defiance or despair. The essayist Tokutomi Roka, in his address to the students at the First Higher School, urged that "we must not be afraid to become rebels ourselves." The novelist Nagai Kafū, on the other hand, "felt intensely ashamed of [him]self as a writer" who "remained silent in this matter of principle"; subsequently he abandoned his active involvement in literary circles and retreated into the study of Edo arts in protest.[71] Zhou Zuoren, who had grown so fond of Japan's way of life for its expression of "human feelings," was also "greatly shocked." He was indignant about the hypocrisy of Japanese officials; the way the officials handled the case, he thought, was "hatefully fiendish yet pitifully clumsy." Although he believed that a country's politics should generally not be of concern to a foreign sojourner, he felt he could not turn his eyes away from this incident because "it had gone beyond politics and become an issue of human fellowship."[72]

Zhou's encounter with and reaction to the Great Treason Incident, or rather, the sinister side of the most powerful state in Asia, might appear to be personal, but its implication was hardly private. How a modern man might deal with state power is a concern implicitly shared by Rankin and Reynolds, despite their different assessments on the Japanese influence on Chinese approaches. It was a troubling issue for any concerned Chinese of Zhou's time, and it would, in the long run, leave him in a predicament as the two nations clashed in a bloody war. During his youth, Zhou might have wished to avoid it altogether; others, like Jiang Baili, first tried to confront it through radical actions and then wanted to use it to gain national strength. By 1910, Jiang had made yet another resolution when he returned to China from his second stint training abroad. During the previous four years, he had been in Germany for further miliary training with "the strongest army in the world." The professionalism of the German army had made a deep impression on him, and he decided upon his return not to involve himself in politics, but instead to concentrate his energy on building China's new army. After a brief period serving in the Palace Guards for the Qing court, he was once again invited by the governor-general of the three northeastern provinces to become chief of staff of the new army there. By now, Jiang had dramatically modified his approach to the government, yet his commitment to building a strong China only deepened as he continued to advance in his military career.

Jiang Baili in Germany, receiving military training after graduating with high honors from the Army Officers' Academy (Rikugun Shikan Gakkō) in Japan, circa 1911. Reprinted from He Suihua et al., eds., *Jiang Baili xiansheng jiniance.*

Zhou Zuoren (center, standing) in Japan, with wife Habuto Nobuko and brother-in-law Habuto Shigehisa, circa 1909. Photo courtesy of Y. M. Bau.

Guo Moruo (center, in dark uniform) with friends at Kyūshū Imperial University, 1919. Reprinted from *Guo Moruo quanji*, vol. 3:15.

Dai Jitao with Sun Yat-sen at a meeting in Kobe with their Japanese supporters, November 25, 1914. Front row from left: Ōkubo Takaaki, Sun Yat-sen, Tōyama Mitsuru; back row from left: Yamada Junzaburō, Dai Jitao, Li Liejun, Fujimoto Hisanori. Reprinted from *Chūgoku* no. 62 (January 1969), 33.

PART II

"Can China and Japan
Be Friends?"

By the 1910s, "same culture, same race" had been a familiar term in Sino-Japanese discourse for nearly a generation. The idea behind the phrase had a distinct Japanese origin and can be dated at least to the last two decades of the nineteenth century, when a small group of Japanese formed the Asian Revival Society (Popularly called Kō-A Kai) in 1880 with the declared purpose of fostering a friendship between China and Japan.[1] In the following decades, the idea developed into an alternative to the approach for "Leaving Asia and joining Europe *(datsu-A nyū-ou)*" advocated by the famous Meiji publicist Fukuzawa Yukichi. By the turn of the century, a Pan-Asian alliance between Japan and China had garnered more emotional and strategic appeal among the Asians, who were alarmed by the widespread discussion in the West about the "Yellow Peril" and the inevitability of a racial struggle. The sense of urgency attracted people of otherwise widely diverging political positions to the cause of Pan-Asianism. High luminaries such as Prince Konoe Atsumaro, ultranationalist Toyama Mitsuru, and discontented and dislocated former samurai such as Miyazaki Tōten, though socially distant, all viewed Western aggression in Asia in racial terms, arguing that both China and Japan shared a common interest in survival. In 1898, the East Asia Common Culture Society (commonly known as Tō-A Dōbunkai), a larger and more ambitious organization than the Kō-A Kai, was founded under the auspices of Prince Konoe and blessed with a secret regular fund from the Japanese Foreign Ministry, with a mission to carry out cultural diplomacy with China.[2]

On the Chinese side, a Pan-Asian alliance with Japan against Western intrusion had its appeal, but it had always been limited. High officials or diplomats occasionally spoke about strengthening China's international position by forging stronger links with Japan, but their verbal endorsements had never been translated, as happened in Japan, into firm policies or sustained activities. The study-in-Japan movement during the first decade of the twentieth century, as Part I demonstrates, did generate an awareness of cultural affinity in the Chinese, and the experience of the Russo-Japanese War, in particular, kindled a sense of racial affinity with

Japan among the Chinese students. Might this hopeful beginning of such positive sentiments develop into something significant and become the basis of a Sino-Japanese friendship?

Part II of this book, in two chapters, explores the question through the emotional and intellectual journeys of two men, Dai Jitao and Guo Moruo, who made determined efforts to cultivate and maintain a relationship with Japan in their public and private lives. Being sons of modestly wealthy land-holding families in China's remote province of Sichuan, they were from less privileged social circles than those of Jiang Baili or Zhou Zuoren. Education in Japan, as it turned out, provided them with inspiration but did not guarantee a sure link to a career. By chance as well as by choice, Dai joined the revolutionary cause in China and emerged as a close associate of Sun Yat-sen; Guo, by contrast, married a Japanese woman, found his personal liberation in a quiet, private life in Japan, and pursued his medical degree and his interest in literature during the decade.

Because of their special connections, these two Chinese would live their lives crossing the boundaries of two countries and two cultures. In the circles of high politics, Dai would discover Pan-Asianism through contact with a Japanese leader and would become a prominent Chinese advocate for this vision; moving between Japan's southern island of Kyūshū and China's semi-colonial city of Shanghai in search of a stable career, Guo found himself repeatedly confronting the stubborn, invisible wall of bias that reminded him and his family of their ambivalent cross-cultural identity. The connections with Japan promoted Dai's career and inspired Guo's literary creations, yet such connections, as each man learned, were entangled with the skewed power relationship between the two nations. As sons of the weaker partner, they could not escape the burden of slights, ridicule, and shame. Although their positions on Pan-Asianism were not identical, their emotions echoed one another, and the experiences of both men foreshadowed the troubled decades to come.

3 A Case of Ambivalence

As the first decade of the twentieth century receded into history, tens of thousands of Chinese students returned home from Japan, bringing with them a sense of cultural affinity with their neighboring country. While for most this sentiment remained dormant, there were some who, with a sharp eye on the reality of imperialist competition and conflict, attempted to use this cultural force for political ends. Sun Yat-sen, the Chinese revolutionary leader who made the overthrow of the Manchu ruler his life's career, was the most important among those who tried to mobilize the sense of affinity to forge a special bond with Japan. Since 1895, when he was forced to flee China after an abortive attempt at an uprising, Sun had not just established in Japan a regular base of activities during his extended exile, but he also recruited Japanese, idealistic or adventurous, into his revolutionary cause. Occasional assistance also came from Japan's government, which saw him as a useful tool in shaping the political situation on the continent. Although its aid began to wane after 1907, Sun continued to hope for a special relationship with Japan, for he had recognized that, among all the powers, only Japan had rendered him both personal and official support.[1] The success of the anti-Manchu revolution in 1911 and the founding of the Chinese Republic had made a partnership between China and Japan all the more logical in Sun's view. Never before had any Chinese been as vocal about Sino-Japanese affinity as Sun when he addressed a party of distinguished guests at a Tō-A Dōbunkai banquet in 1913:

> If there were Europeans here tonight, they would not be able to tell the Chinese from the Japanese.... During the past

twenty years, I have lived in Japan quite often. Therefore, *Japan is my second home, and I regard this as a family reunion.*[2]

Sun was on his first tour of Japan as a state guest, and he was greeted by an enthusiastic public and welcomed eagerly by politicians and businessmen. From the beginning of the month-long tour, the warm feelings on both sides led him to praise the Japanese who "embrace a Greater Asianism" and to promise, on behalf of the newly founded Republic of China, to make further efforts at cultivating friendship.[3]

Sun's optimism, sustained by the recent success of the revolution that replaced the imperial institution with a republic, was not his alone. Among those who came with Sun and attended the Tō-A Dōbunkai banquet was a young man named Dai Jitao, who subsequently wrote candidly about the necessity of a Sino-Japanese alliance:

> The crisis in East Asia has come about because of the expansion of the white race.... Japan and our country now are the only two nations of Asian race that still exist. Yet our country is already in the swirl of the European races' territorial expansion. If Japan does not collaborate with China to work for the cause of preserving the yellow race, it will face extinction soon.... To resist seven European powers with only one Asian power makes survival in this world very difficult. China, however, is a big country with massive population and abundant resources. If China becomes rich and strong, its power will be ten times that of Japan. If China and Japan combine their forces to resist European powers, they will surely force them to change their aggression into cooperation.[4]

The dire sense of urgency about the threat of racial extinction in a power struggle conveyed by Dai's forthright language is typical of his time. But Dai's statement, printed in a widely circulated revolutionary newspaper, was the very first announcement of his belief in the shared interest of the two neighboring countries. The change must have been too abrupt to be missed by his devoted readers, to whom Dai was known by his pen name "Tianchou" and for his many critical commentaries of Japan. But from 1913, Dai was to become one of the foremost Pan-Asianists in China, though his newly acquired confidence in Sino-Japanese racial affinity and hoped-for cooperation would be seriously tested in the uncertain years of the 1910s.

A Youthful Adventure to Japan

Japan in 1913 was already a familiar country to Dai Jitao. Born in 1891 in China's western hinterland province of Sichuan, Dai was fortunate to grow up in an age when his fellow provincials were making energetic efforts to bring in modern education and, in particular, a large number of Japanese teachers. The combined force of familial, local, and national influences encouraged an adventurous spirit in Dai, and moved him to travel to Japan in 1905, when he was a fourteen-year-old boy.

The youngest of four sons in a family of modest wealth, Dai had a pampered childhood. The Dais traced their ancestral roots to Anhui and Zhejiang Provinces. By the time Jitao was born, they had been settled for nearly a century in Guanghan County, a commercial center and bustling town that hosted more than a dozen long-distance trade guilds.[5] The Dais made their living in the porcelain trade, and although their business lacked prestige, they had intense social and artistic aspirations. While all the male children were provided with a formal education, Jitao received special attention. He began learning to read and write at age four, tutored by his grandfather, who also was an amateur artist with a talent for brush painting begonias.[6] Young Jitao was the only child that his grandmother and mother would take along to drama performances whenever troupes came to town. These privileges seemed to have cultivated an aptitude for beauty and excitement in the child. Many years later Dai Jitao would still recall the kaleidoscopic world on stage and in the market with nostalgia.[7]

Eager to find his own place in the world, Dai made his attempt at the Civil Service Examinations when he turned ten. He passed the first two examinations but stumbled on the third, thus failing to obtain a degree. Undiscouraged, he quickly reoriented his pursuit and left his hometown for the schools in Chengdu, the provincial capital. It was a time when new schools were flourishing all over China, and there he received his first modern lessons. One of Dai's teachers, Xu Zixiu, was a passionate anti-Manchu nationalist; he attracted so many students to his lectures on the history of Chinese resistance to the Manchu conquerors that the school had to find a new location to accommodate his large audience. Xu was "not a teacher for children [of my age]," remarked Dai in later years, "but whenever I listened to his lectures, I felt hot blood boiling in my chest." There was also an incident that "profoundly moved the people of Sichuan," when a local rebel called Yu Manzi was sentenced to death for his activities against foreign missionaries; the news brought out thousands of city dwellers to the streets who prostrated themselves outside the city gate, pleading with the magistrate to repeal the order for Yu's execution. Under the influence of the rising revolutionary mood, Dai joined three other students to form an anti-Manchu sworn brotherhood.[8] He became rebellious at school and was expelled for his disrespectful attitude toward a superintendent. Although a change of name got him into another school, the authorities soon discovered his true identity and expelled him again.[9]

Political lessons aside, the schools in Chengdu also opened up new cultural vistas for the young Jitao. At the turn of the century, the inland Sichuan, in its efforts to catch up with the coastal cities, became one of the most active participants in the Sino-Japanese cultural exchange programs. It was one of the provinces in China to experience a large influx of Japanese teachers.[10] The first school that Dai Jitao entered was called Preparatory School for Going to Japan (Dongyou Yubei Xuetang), where Japanese language was an important part of the curriculum. Young and curious, Dai mastered the foreign tongue easily and made fast friends with several Japanese teachers. One of them was Hattori Misao, who came from a family of scholars in Chinese learning and later became the author of several Chinese-Japanese dictionaries.[11] Another was Konishi Sanshichi, who taught physics and chemistry at the middle high school that Dai attended. When Dai was expelled from school for the second time in 1904, Konishi, who had been giving the boy private lessons, offered to hire him as his classroom interpreter with a monthly salary of fourteen silver dollars.

In a place where the average daily wage was eighty copper coins, a fourteen-dollar salary was an astonishing figure, more than a teacher with a provincial degree could charge a student.[12] This surprising good fortune so encouraged the young Jitao that he decided to pursue a degree in Japan. He even cut his queue to pressure his grandmother into acquiescing to his plea. Finally, his eldest brother, who had taken charge of the family business when their father passed away two years before, stepped forward to side with him. The family sold thirty *mu* of land for seven hundred silver dollars and sent the fourteen-year-old Jitao on the journey east in 1905.[13]

Thanks to his friendship with Hattori and Konishi, Dai Jitao took his first steps in Japan with relative ease. Chinese and Japanese alike admired his fluent Japanese.[14] Following the trend then popular among Chinese students, he entered Japan University to study law.[15] But he showed little interest in anti-Manchu revolutionary activities and instead enjoyed his freedom and "did not concern himself too much with serious politics or scholarship," according to one of his close Chinese friends.[16] During his five-year sojourn in Tokyo, Dai's most noticeable public activity was his participation in a negotiation between the Chinese students at Japan University and the Chinese government supervisor. The Chinese official, who had been unsympathetic to students, was impressed by Dai's diplomatic eloquence and agreed to the students' request to form an association. On the day of its inauguration, some two thousand people, including such dignitaries as Japan's Ministry of Education representative, the president of Japan University, and members of the faculty, attended, and the overjoyed students unanimously elected Dai as president. This first public success was apparently too thrilling to bear for Dai: when he returned to his lodging house after the meeting, he had to release his excitement with a loud, protracted wail.[17]

The young Dai, as one close friend recalled, "gets into his feelings deeply; he wails whenever he feels sad or happy."[18] Naturally, this sentimental propensity made Japanese literature in the romantic tradition an instant attraction to him. Works like Tokutomi Roka's *Nature and Life (Shizan to jinsei),* Yoshida Kenkō's *Essays in Idleness (Tsurezuregusa),* and Sei Shōnagon's *The Pillow Book (Makura no sōshi)* were among those that he chose to memorize and recite as a way of enhancing his language ability.[19] He also tried his own hand at writing short stories, signed with the romantic pen name "Sanhong Sheng" [Young man who scatters flowers].[20] He even fell in love with a Korean girl, reportedly from a royal family, and held a ceremony to announce the engagement. But his fiancée suddenly broke off the relationship and disappeared, leaving Dai disheartened and deeply suspicious of possible interference from the Japanese authorities.[21]

By 1909, Dai had used up all of the money he had brought to Japan and had to leave for China before completing the bachelor's program. He left without a degree and without truly deep contacts within Japanese society. While in Japan, his close friends included Xie Jian, Yang Zihong, Jing Ruixin, and a few other Chinese. Most of them were students at Japan University and natives of Sichuan. Upon Dai's departure, it was Xie Jian who pawned his wedding ring and textbooks to throw a farewell party and provide him with ship fare.[22] Beyond this Chinese circle, Dai had made friends with a few patriotic Koreans,[23] a connection that possibly contributed to his frustrated love affair and stimulated his hatred for Japanese imperialism, which would soon influence his first career in journalism.

Revolutionary Journalism and Japanophobia

When Dai landed in Shanghai in 1909, he had only eighty sen of Japanese money in his pocket. He was completely alone in a vast city, one he had barely skirted as he boarded a ship bound for Japan some four years ago. But now, at eighteen, he had inexhaustible energy and boundless ambition, and he had returned to China at the right moment and landed in the right place. In spite of his anti-Manchu sentiments, Dai found government jobs easy to get and soon obtained an advisory position on constitutional reform at the Research Institute of Regional Autonomy Rule in Jiangsu, directed by Ruicheng, the magistrate of Suzhou. Dai's training in law at Japan University turned out to be useful for presenting suggestions and memoranda on provincial constitutions, which impressed the director. But he also made instant enemies in the institute because of his unconventional views and pompous behavior. His colleagues criticized his frequent visits to brothels, and he soon lost his job when Ruicheng left for another position in the spring of 1910.[24] His service in this official institution, though brief and inconsequential, turned out to be crucial in turning Dai away from the fumbling dynasty toward the cause of anti-Manchu revolution, now fermenting all over the country.

In the summer of 1910, Dai's life reached a turning point when he started his first serious career, journalism, by taking an editorial job at the *China and World Daily (Zhongwai ribao)* and later at the *Mandate of Heaven Newspaper (Tianduo bao)*. Soon Dai became well known in Shanghai for his radical editorials, signed with the pen name "Tianchou," a pun indicating Dai's open hatred for the Manchu rulers.[25] In the spring of 1911, he was detained for his anti-Manchu activities and went into a brief exile in Nagasaki. From there he went to Penang in Malaysia, where he joined Sun Yat-sen's Revolutionary Alliance (Tongmeng Hui) and edited its local newspaper, the *Glorious China Newspaper (Guanghua bao)*.[26]

Dai's journalism career began at the moment of Japan's annexation of Korea in 1910 and China's rising fear of Japan's further expansion. The event must have reopened the wounds inflicted by his frustrated engagement with the Korean girl, and his private anger now merged with the grand torrent of anti-imperialism shared by his fellow Chinese. The issue of Korean annexation became the focus of his first commentaries, where he termed it "a matter of life and death for Manchuria." What Jiang Baili had alluded to some seven years earlier now was echoed by Dai in an amplified voice and more explicit terms: "As Manchuria is next to perish after Korea, the Japanese influence on the mainland will greatly increase. Our great land will become a colony of those barbarians from the islands."[27] Soon, the Great Treason Incident drew his attention to Japanese internal politics. Like Zhou Zuoren, Dai was outraged by the unfair trial of Kōtoku Shūsui for his political beliefs and considered it parallel to the Manchu rulers' brutal suppression of the revolutionary Wang Jingwei. "Among Asian countries, China is the biggest and Japan is the most civilized," wrote Dai, "yet their despotic cruelty is identical!"[28] Kōtoku Shūsui's unfortunate death became a symbol in Dai's commentary of the "immoral and cruel country *[wudao guo]*" under Japanese government.[29]

While the annexation of Korea and the persecution of Kōtoku Shūsui were events with geographical distance, life in semicolonial Shanghai presented Dai with a sense of immediacy to what he saw as the "brazen" behavior of the Japanese. In one of his brief reports on Shanghai, he described how a Japanese "in a dusty Western suit, ... forced himself on a second-class seat with a third-class ticket." Only when Dai criticized him in Japanese did he "leave in disappointment." In another report Dai wrote about a Japanese rider on a rickshaw; "when the puller asked for more fare, he growled while showing his fists." That was a hateful "islander's character," commented Dai.[30] In yet another essay he linked Japan's aggressive foreign policy and the Japanese people's behavior as colonists to the "islander's character"; the Japanese "are cunning and changeable, because they are influenced by the constant lash of sea waves," wrote Dai. And he concluded that "even though Japan has become strong, it can never possess the character of a great nation."[31]

Although Dai's political commentaries on Japan were uncompromisingly critical, the few essays he wrote on Japanese literature and Japanese social life reveal ambivalence and even admiration. In a short, telling article titled, "Bits and pieces of a view on Japanese literature," Dai characterized Japanese literature as possessing five distinctive qualities. On the positive side he praised it as a literature of the beautiful, the natural, the sensual, and the sentimental. These four aspects of Japanese aesthetic taste convinced him that the Japanese "are a people who love beauty most." On the negative side he found it too obsessed with details and lacking in comprehensiveness. Comparing it to Chinese literature, Dai believed that Japanese literature bore certain similarities to China's rhythmical prose of the Six Dynasties, characterized by parallelism, ornateness, sentimentalism, and a lack of profound meaning. Overall, he judged Japanese literature as of lower quality, because its focus was narrow and its subject matter insignificant.[32] Following the same line of analysis, Dai found that while he appreciated the progressive spirit (*xianshang de jinshen*) of the Japanese, he disliked their "submissive character."[33]

Envisioning a Greater Asian Alliance

Toward the end of 1911 there came an unexpected turn in Dai's career. In the previous two years since his return from Japan, Dai had established himself within the circles of anti-Manchu journalists and had become a household name in Shanghai. The revolution in October changed China's polity and also catapulted Dai to the center stage of national politics. On Christmas day, Sun Yat-sen, the leader of the Revolutionary Alliance, who "missed an appointment with history"[34] while traveling in America when the revolution broke out, finally arrived in Shanghai. As a reporter for the revolutionary newspaper *People's Rights Newspaper [Minquan bao]* and as a new member of the Revolutionary Alliance, Dai went to greet and interview the revolutionary leader shortly after his arrival on Christmas day. The energetic and handsome young man instantly made a good impression on Sun; shortly after their meeting, Dai was brought up to the higher circles of the revolutionary leadership.

In February 1912, as part of a political agreement between the southern revolutionaries and northern conservatives, Sun Yat-sen turned the presidency of the new Republic over to Yuan Shikai, the powerful leader of the Beiyang army of the late dynasty who had helped to negotiate the Qing court's abdication. The revolutionaries in the south sent an eight-member delegation to Beijing to negotiate with Yuan on the matter of relocating the capital to Nanjing in the south, and Dai was chosen to join this prestigious group, which included such veterans of the Revolutionary Alliance as Cai Yuanpei, Song Jiaoren, and Li Shiceng. Their mission, however, ended in failure when Yuan deftly staged a "mutiny" and used it as an excuse for remaining in Beijing to keep order. While the meaningless negotiations lingered on, Dai discerned Yuan's motivation and quickly sneaked out of Beijing. Back in Shanghai, he launched a barrage of negative editorials, exposing Yuan's manipulative activities and calling him "the criminal to the Republic."[35] Irritated by these relentless attacks, Yuan pressured the authorities in the international settlement to have Dai jailed for a brief period in May 1912.

But the complex relationship between the southern revolutionaries and northern conservatives would soon soften Dai's position and make him a rising star in the new government's diplomacy. In September 1912, Sun Yat-sen, who had just changed his organization's name to the Guomindang (Nationalist Party), accepted an appointment to head the Department of Railroad Development in Yuan's new government and in turn appointed Dai as his personal secretary. In early spring 1913, as we have already seen, Sun embarked on an official visit to Japan to seek financial support for the newly established Republic. It was a hero's return for Sun and perhaps the highest point in his hopes for an alliance between the two East Asian nations. Politicians and businessmen in Japan, who were anxious to strike new deals with the young Republic while other powers were preoccupied with the emerging Great War in Europe, kept Sun on a busy schedule. Dai, fluent in Japanese and experienced with the life of the country, went along as Sun's interpreter.[36]

The trip thus introduced Dai to the highest power circles in both China and Japan and made him a crucial bridge in the communication between the great Chinese leader and his Japanese counterparts. Dai had written about Japanese politicians and businessmen in newspapers, but never had he dreamed of sitting face-to-face and speaking on nearly equal terms with people like Katsura Tarō, the former premier; Katō Kōmei, the current foreign minister; Shibusawa Eiichi, the business tycoon; and Inukai Tsuyoshi, the Pan-Asianist.[37] This elevated and widened political reach also significantly modified his earlier anti-Japanese stance.

One event during this monthlong visit that would exert a decisive influence on Dai's view of Sino-Japanese relations was Sun's meetings with Katsura Tarō, the prime minister who had just been replaced by the Yamamoto cabinet prior to Sun's visit. Still working to return to power, Katsura met Sun twice in late February and early March. According to Dai Jitao, who was the interpreter and the only other person present, the two leaders engaged in discussions that lasted for about fifteen to sixteen hours. The central topic of their conversation was international politics in Asia. The former premier of Japan spoke strongly about the racial divide in the world, arguing especially for Asians' shared interest in resisting the threat from the British and Russian powers. Yet he also pointed out that, after Russia's defeat in the Russo-Japanese War of 1904–1905, the British had become the greatest danger to Asia. China and Japan, then, shared a common mission:

> [O]nly by destroying England's hegemony could the Orient have peace and Japan survive. This question of survival is not simply Japan's. Whether this plan [of preventing a British-Russian alliance] will work also decides the fate of the whole Oriental world from the Tartar Strait to the Pacific. There are three major questions in the current world: Turkey, India, and China. All these countries are under the oppression of British military and economic hegemony. Yet emancipation from British economic oppression will not be a problem if [these three countries] are able to resist its military power....

If China is weak and hence suffers from the oppression of Europe, then Japan is left in grave danger.[38]

From the standpoint of a common cause, Katsura then proposed a division of tasks between their two countries. Japan's best approach to future development, Katsura reportedly said, was to "expand to America and Australia while at the same time protecting the continent [of Asia]," for he believed that "the development of the continent is China's responsibility." He predicted that "a Sino-Japanese alliance will guarantee peace in the Eastern Hemisphere, and an alliance of China, Japan, Turkey, Germany, and Austria will guarantee the peace of the world." Speaking as the former leader of Japan, Katsura offered his support to Sun, the leader of China, so that they might together accomplish the mission of undermining British power and saving Asia and the world.[39]

How Katsura, caught in the deep mire of political trouble at home, could be a viable political ally to China seemed not to concern Dai much. He was excited about being a participant in these highly secret meetings and deeply impressed by Katsura's vision of a Sino-Japanese alliance for Asian revival. He was convinced, too, of the benefits this alliance could bring to China. Upon returning to China after this state visit, he wrote in the *Minquan bao* with a reinforced sense of pride and confidence:

Now the Chinese people have accomplished a great political and intellectual revolution, which has destroyed old things of the past and initiated the construction of a new republic; how deeply the Japanese have come to admire us! That is why they become so anxious to make an alliance with us. . . . Japan is a strong nation in the East, and the strongest nation among the yellow races as well; a collaboration of [our two nations] will help us build our country internally and resist invasion by ambitious countries externally.[40]

Seven months after these conversations, Katsura Tarō died. By then, the Guomindang's political fortunes as well as its relations with Japan had changed drastically. It was this twist of fate that made Dai comment, some fourteen years later, that "if Katsura Tarō were still alive, the situation in the East would be absolutely different from what we have today."[41]

The Changing Face of Japan

In March 1913, while Sun was still in Japan, Song Jiaoren (1882–1913), a leading member of the Guomindang and the most outspoken advocate for parliamentary government in China, was gunned down by agents of Yuan Shikai just as he was boarding the northbound train in Shanghai. Sun cut short his visit and returned to Shanghai to deal with the crisis. Now convinced that the conservatives under Yuan Shikai were determined to eliminate their share in national power, the Guomindang took up arms in July for the Second Revolution. Most Chinese, however, were tired of the social turmoil caused by the revolution of 1911 and showed no interest in joining the conflict. When their ill-planned uprisings were quickly quashed by Yuan's superior military force, Sun, along with thousands of other Guomindang members, once again fled to Japan, where he had been received as a state guest only a few months before.

To their chagrin, the revolutionaries found themselves facing a frosty reception by the Japanese government under the Yamamoto cabinet, which had already decided to endorse Yuan Shikai and to join the international consortium to provide aid to him. Sun and his followers had become an undesirable liability. Only through the strenuous mediation of Sun's old friends Inukai Tsuyoshi and Tōyama Mitsuru were the Chinese allowed to land in Japan after a detour through Taiwan.[42]

During his two-and-half-year exile in Japan, Sun was desperate to regain power from Yuan Shikai and to retain his leadership within the Guomindang. He used all possible means to undermine Yuan's rule, yet none of these efforts—such as assassination attempts with the help of Japanese adventurers or uprisings with the assistance of Chinese peasant rebel Bai Lang and old warlord Zhang Zuolin—produced any tangible results. Sun had less support from overseas Chinese and the Japanese than before; he thus was limited by circumstances to depend on the few faithful Japanese who harbored him. His desperation for backers was shown vividly in two letters, sent to the Japanese Foreign Ministry and the Ōkuma cabinet, and a contract with two South Manchurian Railway officials during 1914 and 1915. To gain their support for his anti-Yuan cause, Sun made sweeping promises to grant the Japanese special rights in the China market, to offer the Japanese a monopoly on armament supplies to the Chinese army, and to guarantee Chinese employment of Japanese advisers—conditions that parallel the Ōkuma cabinet's notorious Twenty-One Demands that outraged the Chinese and agitated the international community in early 1915.[43]

Sun's party was in disarray, endangered by desertion and division. To ensure his followers' loyalty, Sun reorganized the Guomindang and renamed it the Chinese Revolutionary Party (Zhonghua Gemindang). But his demand for absolute obedience, symbolized by his requirement of a fingerprint upon joining the party, alienated many former Guomindang members, who not only refused to join the new party but also began to question his authority. Huang Xing, another leader within the Guomindang, had serious arguments with Sun Yat-sen from the day Sun arrived in Japan. Eventually Huang left for America on his own to organize separate activities.

Dai Jitao, however, remained loyal to Sun Yat-sen and played a key role in Sun's inner circle as his interpreter, spokesman, and liaison with other revolutionaries. He was trusted with several secret missions to Dalian, the port city in Manchuria, to contact the Manchu monarchists for their cooperation in the anti-Yuan movement.[44] He remained an indispensable presence in Sun's many talks with Shibusawa Eiichi, Yamamoto Jōtarō, Inukai Tsuyoshi, and Itagaki Taisuke, and he participated in Sun's many discussions with his *rōnin* sympathizers, including Tōyama Mitsuru, Iino Yoshisaburō, and Kawashima Naniwa, who helped the Chinese plan anti-Yuan assassinations or stage uprisings. When Huang Xing and Sun Yat-sen began their angry disputes and stopped speaking, Dai passed messages between them.[45] When Chinese students in Tokyo held a mass rally on March 1, 1915, to protest the Twenty-One Demands, Dai spoke to them on behalf of Sun Yat-sen. The reports in Chinese newspapers that implicated the revolutionaries in the demands, said Dai, were obviously "the tactic" of Yuan Shikai, who intended to drive the people away from the revolutionaries.[46] Dai also became acquainted with Honjō Shigeru, a junior officer in the army general staff, then teaching military geography at a university. Dai, who was editing a party organ called *The Republic (Minguo)* and writing commentaries on world affairs, found he shared an interest with Honjō in the ongoing Great War in Europe and the situation in the Near and Middle East.[47]

Repeated failures and endless waiting now led Dai to moments of pause and reflection. In contrast with his forthright optimism in 1913, he began to write in a more sober tone about Japan as the earlier enthusiasm about China among Japanese politicians and the Japanese public rapidly dissipated. Writing in Tokyo in 1914, Dai criticized Japan for handling its foreign policy like "scribbling here and there" *(dongtu ximuo)* without a plan or a vision and called it "self-destructive." He continued to promote Sino-Japanese cooperation, however, though with an emphatic note on mutual interest. "Neither Japan, nor China, could resist European countries with a single hand. If China succumbed, Japan cannot survive.... Under the current situation of the world, China and Japan share the same interest; therefore, the view of the necessity of Chinese and Japanese cooperation is not simply based on race or language, nor on religion or history. It is the law of competition and mutual dependence that will not allow Japan to turn away from China."[48] Warning and wooing at once, he maintained a fence-sitting posture necessitated by a political refugee's need for protection in exile.

Dai's disillusionment with Japanese politics was more obvious when he ended his exile and returned to China. He wrote a long essay, "The Recent Political Situation in Japan and Its China Policy," and had it serialized for forty days, from mid-December 1917 to late January 1918, in a Guomindang organ, *Republican Daily (Minguo ribao)*.[49] It began with a harsh appraisal of the Japanese cabinet leaders since 1913. While critical of their collective dependence on the genrō, Dai tried to differentiate the four prime ministers. Katsura Tarō, the late premier who had once inspired Dai, was again praised as a statesman with "political tact" and "insights into world trends." Ōkuma Shigenobu, who came to power between 1914 and 1916, won Dai's compliments for his "democratic propensity." Yet his cabinet, said Dai, would not have lasted long due to the genrō's unfavorable opinion; Ōkuma was saved by his popular move, made possible by World War I, to declare war against Germany and occupy its leased territory in Shandong Province in China. Dai dismissed Yamamoto Gonnohyōe's cabinet, in power when the Chinese revolutionaries fled to Japan in late 1913, as a mere dependent of the regional faction of Satsuma. But he was more critical still of Terauchi Masatake, who was at the time leading the cabinet that endorsed China's warlord regime under Duan Qirui, calling him a "conservative" and "aristocratic, bureaucratic politician."[50] Dai's evaluation of Japanese politicians, certainly, is colored by his unpleasant exile in Japan and his political stand in China. Yet his understanding of the uncertain and opportunistic nature of Japan's foreign policy during this decade, a phenomenon later noted by historian Marius Jansen, was realistic and insightful.[51]

Beyond his likes and dislikes of individual politicians, Dai emphasized the importance of their fundamental similarity in handling foreign affairs. Even as individual leaders pursued different policies toward China, argued Dai, these policies "differ only in method but not in their principle and goal." There were three forces that shaped Japan's policy, in his view: Japan's need of colonies to expand its economic power; the threat of European powers in East Asia, whose expansion into the China market "oppressed China directly and Japan indirectly"; and public opinion in Japan that pressured the government to demand rights similar to those enjoyed by Westerners in China. It was under these shared goals, indicated Dai, that the Japanese debated about where to expand: one opinion, led by the navy, advocated a southward move to colonize Southeast Asia; the other, led by the army, called for a northward move onto the mainland. But now, warned Dai, the Japanese no longer were satisfied with simply either a southward thrust or a northward thrust, but had started to demand a "Greater Asia." It was under such circumstances that the Ōkuma cabinet formed its China policy, with the intention of gaining public support in Japan.

The Twenty-One Demands, the biggest recent event in Sino-Japanese relations, was an issue on which Dai could not avoid commenting. He chose to pass over the ruinous content of the demands, which "must have been known and remembered," and instead guided readers' attention to Japan's domestic politics surrounding the event. Implicitly, Dai showed sympathy for the Ōkuma cabinet, especially for Foreign Minister Katō Kōmei, who in Dai's words "was in the most difficult position among all" because of the genrō opposition to his diplomacy. Besides the complex political conflict at the higher levels of government, Dai also pointed out to his Chinese readers that "[Japanese] society had a very good opinion about the deal." Yet again he put the blame on the politicians: "Ōkuma always claims that 'the conflict between the yellow and white races is the great problem in future world,'... but all his policies harm his own [yellow] race.... The Japanese frequently label their ideal as 'Greater Asianism,' which is not Greater Asianism but Greater Imperialism." Dai also predicted that "definitely Japan is going to demand its rights in Shandong" when World War I ended. Turning to his Japanese audience, he urged them to follow Britain's policy of "glorious isolation" and refrain from continental expansion, because it would only arouse Chinese resentment. And he reminded them of the vision of Itagaki Taisuke, one of the genrō and a prominent leader in the Liberty and People's Rights Movement, who had "farsightedness" in advocating naval expansion and who warned Japanese politicians to change the course of their China policy.[52]

One of the most interesting points in this essay is Dai's caution with respect to Japan's China adventurers, when he warned his Chinese audience against harboring any illusions about Japanese assistance. It was necessary, said Dai, to remain alert to Japan's aggressive activities toward China while at the same time "remember[ing] and prais[ing] those who had helped China." The so-called *shishi* (men of high purpose), for example, had assisted China's revolution. "None of the revolutionaries who went into exile in Japan had failed to receive assistance from them," Dai said. "Yet such reality co-exists with the reality of Japan's intrusion [into China]. Even those so-called *shishi* at the same time want China to reform, and support the expansion of their country's rights [in China]."[53]

Having analyzed Japanese attitudes and behavior, Dai turned to reflect on China's own and struck a rather surprising note. "Is a foreign threat the ultimate cause of China's dangerous situation?" he asked in the end. "Whenever there is a crisis in foreign affairs, our whole country gets extremely excited and indignant; yet as the business lingers on, the country again becomes indifferent and drifts back to a befuddled existence as usual. How is that [indignation] different from nightmarish raves? It is not the attitude of patriots." Japan, then, once again offered "a great lesson" for the Chinese: although the Meiji hero Saigō Takamori was admired by his fellow countrymen for his courage and expansionist ambitions, noted Dai, it was actually the "farsighted policy" of restraint and forbearance advocated by Kido Takayoshi and others, who argued for the priority of internal construction, that led to Japan's development and made it a strong nation. The Chinese, urged Dai, must "gather the courage of Seigō Tagamori and learn from the forbearance of Kido Takayoshi" as they tried to build China's future.[54]

Hopes and Apprehension

And indeed Dai was to turn his attention to internal construction, moved in part by his own determination and in part by new circumstances. By the end of 1917, when Dai was voicing his criticism of Japanese politicians, the exiled Guomindang had already been back in China for more than a year. China now was divided by various warlords who had filled the power vacuum after Yuan Shikai died in disgrace. While the Guomindang tried to rebuild its power base in the south, Dai continued to serve as Sun's liaison with their Japanese contacts and made frequent trips to Japan.[55] But then, in 1919, Dai made an abrupt shift in his activities, as he described in 1920:

> In the past year I have left political activities and again come back to the world of journalism. . . . Moreover, the books I have read, the essays I have written, and the things I have studied, all relate to fast-moving things like machines, engines, electricity, and steam. Naturally, my mind follows the rapid rhythm of the tram, train, steamship, and airplane, and moves in an increasingly fast tempo.[56]

As these words so vividly describe, Dai spent 1919 in great excitement. It was a year of vibrant interactions of new ideas and the rapidly changing physical world. It was a year of nationalist fervor, inflamed by Japan's imperialist demand for Shandong at Versailles, that reached its climax in the May Fourth demonstration, which added force to the long-fermenting restlessness on the continent. These events further transformed Chinese anti-imperialist nationalism into a broader movement for internal reforms, which intensified the "fast tempo" of industrialization that had already been affecting millions of Chinese. In June, when workers all over China stood up in support of the students' demonstration, the Guomindang started two magazines to add fuel to the national movement: *Weekend Review (Xingqi pinglun)* and then, in August, the monthly *Construction (Jianshe zazhi)*. Dai and a few other Guomindang veterans, including Shen Dingyi and Hu Hanmin, assumed the roles of editor and contributor. *Weekend Review* devoted much of its space to publicizing socialist theory and was viewed as a southern counterpart to *Weekly Review (Meizhou pinglun)*, edited by the Communist Li Dazhao in Beijing.[57] The magazine "was very influential among the students and common people," recalled Yang Zhihua, a student activist from Hangzhou who joined the early Communist movement and worked for the weekly from 1919 to 1921. "The students from neighboring provinces coming to Shanghai and looking for the leaders of the *Weekend Review* were mostly received by Dai Jitao and Shen Xuanlu [Dingyi]." Dai's house at number 6 Yuyang Lane served as the headquarters of *Weekend Review* and hosted many of the early Communists.[58] In May 1920, when the Research Association of Marxism was organized in Shanghai, it brought together three groups of people who had been gathering around *Weekend Review:* those from the Guomindang (Dai Jitao, Shao Lizi, and Shen Dingyi), those newly returned from studying in Japan (Li Da and Li Hanjun), and students from Hangzhou Normal School (Chen Wangdao and Shi Chuntong).[59]

Dai's close association with the radicals during the May Fourth era, however, was not merely in line with his party's tactical move to follow the popular trend. When writing for the new year's first issue of *Republic Daily*, Dai admitted that "the passing year for me has been one of the highest satisfaction in ten years" despite "the uninterrupted work day and night," because it created "an infinite hope in my mind."[60] His discussion of the labor question during the May Fourth years marked a revival of an earlier interest, begun in the pre-Republic years when he was a twenty-year-old journalist. In 1910 in Shanghai, then the largest economic center in China, Dai was disturbed by the appalling contrast between rich and poor. He felt deep empathy for the beggars who roamed the side streets of Shanghai, and he wrote often of his encounters with them. "Today's world is a world of inequality," wrote Dai in 1910. "The so-called civilization is merely for the peace and happiness of a handful."[61]

Despite his sympathy, Dai had long been skeptical about the workers' choice of violent means to achieve change. Already in 1910, when Dai was first becoming interested in new theories and solutions for the labor question and reported on labor strikes in France and Germany, he gave his coverage a sensational title, "Great Actions of Socialism"; yet in the same report he also indicated that the workers suffered more from the bankruptcy that strikes caused.[62] Thus he came to prefer a milder approach and praised Leo Tolstoy's humanism. In one of his many commentaries in 1910 Dai called Tolstoy "the number one great man of our time." He admitted that he "deeply admires" Tolstoy's thoughts, which took "peace as the principle, humanity as the goal." Although he occasionally had doubts about the absolute renunciation of force as a workable approach to ending social injustice, Dai considered Tolstoy's advice—to work—as the best solution to what he called the "vices of the city," such as urban crime, the pursuit of extravagance, venereal disease, and moral degeneration caused by competition and wealth disparity, for work was the best way to purify the heart and strengthen the body.[63]

During the uncertain decade of the 1910s as his party struggled to survive and regain power, Dai had been modifying his views on the relationship between state power and social problems, and his moral bent carried him to the more conservative side during those anxious years. With the exception of the ritual of kowtow, wrote Dai during his exile in 1914, all the ancient rituals that the sage promoted, especially the idea of using music and performing rituals to achieve peace and order, could help "to purify the mind and enhance social morality." There was a shift in his view on women's issues, too. Whereas in 1911 he advocated women's independence and gender equality, in 1914 he wondered if placing women at home to perform their "natural duty as good wife and wise mother" would be a more desirable way to guarantee social stability.[64] Then he also steered away from his earlier support and sympathy for anarchism. Whereas Dai in 1911 had felt that anarchism was "following the just way of heaven" to eliminate injustice in human society,[65] in 1914 he saw it as the enemy of the social order he desired, and he claimed that "anarchism is the greatest among all false beliefs."[66]

Thus by 1919, when Dai returned to a life in journalism during the May Fourth movement and wrote once again on the question of labor, his preoccupation had shifted away from social protest, a position taken by radical social critics, toward the need to prevent chaos. He remained deeply sympathetic to the workers—especially women and child laborers—and wrote detailed accounts of their appalling working conditions and their meager wages. Yet once again, he found strikes an ineffective means to change their plight.

He explained his feelings in a conversation with Sun Yat-sen, when the latter asked him why he wrote about the labor question:

> When the boycott developed into a great strike earlier this month,... no intelligent person was not worried. All of us tried to convince those in the labor circle not to go on strike. Why? Because those strikes, without organization, education, training, and preparation, are not only of great danger [to the society] but also of no benefit to the workers themselves.

Dai recognized the power of workers but believed that they needed guidance:

> However, as the situation this time indicates, workers have stepped on the stage to participate in the social political movement. If the educated people do not study the problem and provide them guidance with thoughts and knowledge, [the movement] might go gradually toward the irrational and unfortunate. It will be very dangerous. Thus, moved by the labor strike at this time, I feel that using mild social theory to guide the majority of this society has become an urgency.[67]

It was with this intention to "guide" that Dai Jitao pursued again the question of Japan and, two months after this conversation on the labor question, wrote "My View of Japan."[68] The Chinese, indicated Dai, had been "hating Japan and cursing Japan," yet all remained "a closed-nation in mind" regarding the question of Japan. In comparison with the Japanese accomplishments in the study of China, a subject that "the Japanese have analyzed tens of thousands of times on their dissecting platform," the Chinese refusal to know things Japanese demonstrated a shameful attitude of "intellectual Boxers."

The angle of analysis that Dai chose in 1919 differed from that in his 1917 essay, which had been focused on Japan's politics. His new perspective was broader, with an emphasis on cultural matters, especially on behavior and beliefs. His terminology was newer, too, marked by the distinctive vocabulary of class differentiation as well as a notion of stages of social development, which he and his fellow Chinese absorbed in their discourse through the influence of Marxism. His overall tone of judgment of things Japanese remained negative, but the negativeness now was set in contrast to things Chinese.

One distinctive feature of Dai's discussion is his focused concern on the Japanese belief in Shintō. There is an intriguing contradiction, noted Dai, in the Japanese's easy acceptance of modern science and their strong attachment to a belief in the sacred origin of their nation. He used a law professor at Japan University, Kakei Katsuhiko, with whom he had studied, to illustrate the deep influence of what he called "superstition." Although a scholar of "truly profound and broad knowledge," Kakei had gradually turned to "superstition" and ended up by opening and closing all his lectures with "prayers, with his eyes closed and palms together, to pay respect to the ancestral gods in his imagination." Many such people could be found also in the army and navy, said Dai; "Kakei is just one of those who believed in their national essence."

Shintōism as "Japan's native thought," explained Dai, developed "before written language was created in Japan" but became the "ideological basis" of Japan's nativist school. It had served as the foundation for Japanese understanding of their nation. Dai found such faith very "naive" because it was based on legends, especially on the legend of creation and human reproduction. He found this naïveté all the more apparent when he compared the persistence of Shintō belief in Japan, all the way through modern times, to the development of Chinese thought, for "since the time of Confucius China had already broken off from legendary superstition and belief in divine origin of the monarchy."

Another negative aspect of Japan, which Dai again set in contrast to Chinese history and culture, is the pervasive use of force in its long history of feudal rule, under which "the distinction of classes was very prominent." Because of "the numerous wars since the time when Heishi [1166–1185] and Genji [1185–1199] controlled the central power, the *samurai* became all the more powerful with the endless wars." One of the examples of the "cruel character" of this ruling class was the practice of testing the sword: "when the *samurai* forged a new sword, he could take a *hinin* [outcast] to test the sharpness of the blade. Such cruel social organization and cruel character of the ruling class are absolutely not what the peace-loving Chinese want to accomplish." Only when Chinese learning began to flourish in the Tokugawa period, Dai argued, did Japan build the "foundation of its modern civilization." It was through the promotion of the Confucian idea of benevolence *(ren-ai)* by Japanese scholars such as Nakae Tōju and Fujiwara Seika that the Japanese began to benefit from this "idea of human fellowship *[tongbao guannian]*." Therefore, concluded Dai, "the progress of Japan's modern civilization went up in proportion to the spread of the 'idea of human fellowship.'"

In spite of his criticism of samurai violence and of Japan's long feudal conflict, Dai viewed samurai ethics with both contempt and admiration. On the one hand, he contended that Japanese praise for samurai virtue, especially the two forms of the most celebrated behavior, revenge *(katakiuchi)* and ritual disembowelment *(harakiri)*, as representing "the most beautiful spirit," was mere "self-indulging complacency." And he viewed such behavior as similar to that of "African and Australian aborigines." On the other hand, he recognized that the custom of revenge in reality often led to chivalrous deeds such as *suketachi* (lending a helping hand). *Suketachi* had moved many people, both men and women, to sacrifice themselves out of compassion and loyalty. The more meaningful aspect of *suketachi*, wrote Dai with a nod of approval, was not revenge but "its social spirit [of mutual help]."

With the dimension of history added to his interpretation of Japan, Dai now felt more certain that he had mastered the key to understanding the politics in Japan that had disappointed him. The corrupting power of the profit-seeking merchant class, asserted Dai, played an important role in this new age as Japan "moved from the force of sword to the force of money." Dai listed several cases of embezzlement and bribery to demonstrate that "no big business in Japan fails to collaborate with the army and the navy, none of the genrō fails to collaborate with big business." Under such circumstances, "political parties must make use of bureaucrats as well as merchants." Dai concluded that "parties have become mere brokers among warlords *(gunbatsu)*, bureaucracy *(kanbatsu)*, and big business *(zaibatsu)*."

Given these negative attributes of Japanese society, was the future of Japan and its relationship with China hopeless? Surprisingly, Dai was optimistic. He advised his readers to take a long-term perspective with regard to Japan's aggressive policy toward China instead of blaming a few politicians like Terauchi, Tanaka, and Yamagata. The history of Japan, he said, demonstrated the power of "an inherited situation" (J: *ikigakari*, C: *yinxi*), which was formed by various forces, including the traditional ones. And the key to changing this *ikigakari* lay in "a change of Japan's political system." He stressed the importance of differentiating the small group of Japanese politicians from the masses of workers and peasants. And with the development of industry, Dai believed, Japan was entering a "democratic age," a "socialist age," and "an age of man" rather than "an age of gods." He saw that "the fate of warlords and big business was sealed." In this hopeful mood Dai ended his long 1919 essay with the following words: "Those Japanese who have never taken up the twin swords [of the samurai] or become servile merchants are still China's good friends."

4 A Case of Frustration

Can the Chinese and Japanese be friends? That was the question for debate among the respondents who wrote to *Black Tides (Hei-chao),* a monthly that appeared in Shanghai in August 1919.[1] With its focus on the question of Japan, *Black Tides* was a rare species among the hundreds of magazines on the questions of labor, family, women, and new theories that mushroomed during the May Fourth Movement. The editor echoed Dai Jitao's dismay at the contrast between Chinese and Japanese attitudes toward studying one another and argued for immediately creating "an open forum of Japan Studies." "Whatever happens in East Asia anytime in the future," wrote the editor in his first editorial, "it will always involve the close relations between China and Japan." The Chinese "must find solutions" so that they might avoid becoming "narrow-minded patriots" and hence "slaves to emotion."[2] His call for participation in a new column, "Can China and Japan Be Friends?" instantly attracted some two hundred submissions; some contributors argued for the possibility of Sino-Japanese friendship, others contended that it was impossible, and still others proposed ways to forge the friendship where none had previously existed. The editor summarized these various views, but also selected a few to be published in their original form.

Among those chosen for publication were two essays written by Guo Kaizhen, a Chinese student in Japan. The first essay, titled "On the Same-Culture and Same-Race," dealt with the notion of sameness between the Chinese and the Japanese, a notion that influential politicians on both sides such as Konoe Atsumaro, Sun Yat-sen,

Katsura Tarō, and Dai Jitao were using to justify a Sino-Japanese alliance against the West. Guo marshaled linguistic, genetic, and cultural evidence to prove that the Japanese were closer to the Malays in Southeast Asia than to the Chinese. He also noted that in their recent "romanization movement," the Japanese were making efforts to eradicate the use of Chinese characters in their written script so as to lead their culture farther from China.

But explaining this widening gap between the Chinese and Japanese was not the author's central concern. Rather, Guo intended to clarify the meaning of "same culture, same race" and found it merely a "superficial" claim. Citing history in Asia and elsewhere, he argued that peoples of the same race and same culture could fight bloody wars against one another, as had the British and the Americans in the War of Independence. On the other hand, he indicated that the British and the Japanese in fact had formed an alliance in 1902 despite their racial and cultural differences. Thus Guo concluded that "if the way of benevolence and justice is followed, friendship can be forged even if there is difference in race and culture."[3]

Guo's second essay, "The Inner Story of the Anti-Japanese Boycott," showed similar fair-mindedness. He used the statistics of Japanese trade with China during 1914 to 1918 to show that Chinese boycotts had failed to stop Japanese exports to the mainland and instead allowed them to increase. He suggested two responses: the Chinese people should use more Chinese products as "passive" resistance to Japanese products; they should also promote vocational education in order to improve Chinese industry and transportation so as to achieve "positive" independence from Japanese imports. The ultimate solution to their problems, hence, lay in the Chinese themselves.[4]

It was perhaps coincidence that these two essays became the first publications of Guo, a twenty-seven-year-old medical student with literary aspirations. Before long, he would launch a writing career and gain national fame with his romantic poetry, signed with his pen name "Moruo."[5] Although these first two essays would be eclipsed by his more colorful poetry, fiction, and scholarly works on philology and history in the following decades, they remain as testimony to a hopeful episode in his long but frustrated engagement with Japan.

In Pursuit of Personal Liberation

In 1892, Guo Moruo was born in Shawan, a small town on the Dadu River in Sichuan Province. The Guos had a big family—Moruo was the fifth of eight children who survived into maturity. They were also the richest family in Shawan; thanks to his father's diligence and business acumen, the family owned a winery, oil mill, money exchange, and land, and it was involved in the opium trade as well.[6] Moruo's mother, the surviving orphan of a Qing official, brought to the monied Guos the social prestige of the gentry and an aspiration for scholarship. As Jiang Baili's mother had done for her son, Guo Moruo's mother also began to teach Moruo Tang poetry when he turned four. At age five he was sent to family school to begin his formal education.

Isolated from the provincial city, Shawan lagged behind the pace of change that had already swept through places near the coast and large urban centers in the hinterland. But in 1903, six years into Moruo's studies in the Confucian classics, new courses of arithmetic, geography, geology, and world history entered the family classroom. That same year, Japanese language also crept into the vocabulary of school instruction; when a new physical education teacher from the provincial city arrived, he shouted his commands in Japanese, amusing and enchanting the children in Shawan. What most impressed them, it seemed, was the addition of a map of East Asia on their classroom wall. The map gave them a totally new vision, said Guo years later. "That map of East Asia was made of four big pieces of paper and was colored red, yellow, blue, and green; it suddenly renewed our senses. At that moment we indeed felt enlightened."[7]

The year 1903 was also when the Guos began to connect to a different world, as Moruo's two elder brothers went to attend new schools in Chengdu, the provincial capital some one hundred miles north of Shawan. The "books of new learning," such as *Illustrated Magazine of Enlightenment (Qimeng huabao), Stories of State Administration (Jingguo meitan), New Novels (Xinxiaoshuo)*, and even the Tokyo-based *Tides of Zhejiang*, "were collected in Chengdu by our eldest brother and began to flood our family school." The young Moruo most enjoyed the *Illustrated Magazine of Enlightenment*, where he read stories about Napoleon and Bismarck and saw pictures of them. "I admired them to the extreme at the time," Guo later recalled.

Bismarck's enthusiasm for dogs made a special impression on the boy: "We too had three big dogs in our house; so I took them along whenever I went out, as if I was a Bismarck in the East." That was probably the starting point of Guo's great expectations of the outside world. By 1907, when Guo entered middle school, he was speculating on four possible choices for his future. Europe and America "of course were the most tempting for me, but that seemed quite impossible." His two elder brothers had already gone to Japan, which "was also a very desirable place." If that was out of the question, then he "wanted to go to Beijing or Shanghai." Finally, he would accept Chengdu, the provincial capital, if all other options were closed to him.

Given these dreams, young Moruo's first contact with the Japanese turned out to be somewhat disappointing. In the summer of 1904, Guo Moruo's elder brother invited two Japanese teachers from the School of Eastern Culture to visit their village. One of them happened to be Hattori Misao, who had become friends with Dai Jitao. As befitted a rich family in Shawan Village, the Guos treated the two Japanese visitors with generosity during their visit, but it was soured by a small incident, as Guo later described it:

> What surprised me was that these two Eastern Foreigners [dongyang ren] were very stingy. They had a tin can painted with a picture, which probably had been a biscuit container; I liked it very much. One day we were to go fishing at Hanwang Temple together, and I wanted to take that can to go fishing. Elder Brother taught me a sentence of Japanese, meaning "may I take this can to put fish in?" I brought the can with me and said what I learned from Elder Brother. I was not sure if I did not parrot correctly, or my Elder Brother's Japanese did not reach the level after a half year's study, but that sentence completely failed to win their consent.[8]

Later, Moruo heard that Hattori had advised his elder brother not to teach complicated sentences to a beginner, but to start with simple sentences. Both brothers' pride was hurt, not by the language problem, but by the refusal of a guest who was receiving their family's hospitality. Guo's elder brother now regretted having let him ask for the can. The Guo family was further shocked when their hospitality was reciprocated with, long after the Japanese guests had returned to Chengdu, "four picture albums on the Russo-Japanese War" via mail. "Now my father also began to be overwhelmed by their generosity," wrote Guo sarcastically when he recalled the episode.[9]

It became a fated irony for the young Moruo that, though his family was the richest in Shawan, its resources were not enough to send him to Bismarck's or Napoleon's land, but only to Hattori's island country. In 1912, while Guo Moruo was still attending high school in Chengdu, his family arranged for him to marry Zhang Qionghua (1890–1980).[10] Guo, then aged twenty, did not particularly desire a marriage and, to excuse his immediate desertion of the bride, described how astonished he was when he lifted her veil and saw "a pair of chimpanzee-like nostrils pointing towards the sky!"[11] Only five days after the wedding, Guo left Shawan and returned to his school in Chengdu. In the early summer of 1913, he passed the examination for the Military Medical School at Tianjin and left Sichuan for the north. The medical school once again failed to satisfy him, for "there is not a single foreign teacher in it."[12] Turning to his elder brother, who had graduated from a law school in Japan, Guo Moruo asked for help in going abroad. Japan turned out to be the best choice given the family's available means. Toward the end of 1913, Guo boarded a train in Tianjin, which took him to the northeast and Korea and arrived in Tokyo in January 1914.

"The Pure Light"

Guo began the "most diligent time" in his life as soon as he arrived in Tokyo. Within half a year, he passed the entrance examination for the preliminary program of the prestigious First Higher School in Tokyo—an examination that took most other Chinese students at least a year to prepare for—and was awarded free tuition and a monthly stipend of thirty-three yen.[13] At the First Higher School, he was viewed by others as one of the best students in his class, always prepared to answer the most difficult questions in mathematics.[14] In the summer of 1915, Guo advanced to the Sixth Higher School in Okayama, where he was to spend the next three years preparing for a more specialized university education.

Guo's quick progress in scholarship was achieved only at the price of great loneliness, an experience not uncommon for a foreign student. But it was worse for Guo, for he had a nervous breakdown when transferred from Tokyo to Okayama. Many sleepless nights so troubled him that for a while he even contemplated suicide. In a chance discovery, he was inspired by the works of the neo-Confucian scholar Wang Yangming to practice meditation, which helped to alleviate his insomnia.[15] Guo also began to read and admire European literature while receiving language training in German and English at the Sixth Higher School, and he was particularly drawn to works in the romantic tradition, such as Heinrich Heine's poems and Ivan Sergeevich Turgenev's novels. One of his classmates introduced him to the poetry of Rabindranath Tagore, the Indian Nobel laureate who was then popular in Japan. Guo was immediately captivated and, after purchasing and reading all of Tagore's poetry collections then available, found himself "intoxicated by Tagore's poetry, floating in a sentimental state" whenever he practiced meditation.[16]

Guo's search for solace in literature was reoriented to a new passion by an incident in the summer of 1916, when he traveled to Tokyo to take care of a Chinese friend who had become deathly ill and eventually died from tuberculosis. During his friend's treatment in the hospital, Guo came to know a nurse named Satō Tomiko, whose tall and slender build and outgoing personality, unusual for girls of her time, strongly attracted him.[17] Perhaps as an excuse for further contact, Guo went to request his late friend's X-ray negative. In his autobiographical novel, written four years later, Guo dramatized that encounter and explained how everything else followed (italics in the original):

> The first time I met my Anna [Tomiko], I found an incredible pure light glowing in her eyes.... About a week later,... she sent me my friend's negative, and with it attached a long letter in English to comfort me with some advice about religious *resignation*.... I truly felt *bitterish sweetness* at that time! I thought that God really had mercy to me, for he sent me a beautiful companion when I lost a close friend.[18]

Three years younger than Guo Moruo, Satō Tomiko (1895–1994) was the eldest of eight children in a Japanese missionary's family in the Ohira Village of Kurokawa District, Miyagi Prefecture, some twenty miles from the city of Sendai. In her teens she had begun boarding at Shokei Women's School in Sendai, a school established by Baptist missionaries. Upon graduation, she learned that her mother was arranging a marriage for her and would not let her continue her education. Alone, the twenty-year-old Tomiko went to Tokyo and found a job at St. Lukes Hospital, just a year before she met Guo.[19]

In part because of their similar experiences with undesirable arranged marriages, the two were drawn together, and in each other's empathy they found a great deal of comfort. Soon the two were writing to each other three or four times a week. Knowing that Tomiko intended to pursue a medical career, Guo suggested that she leave her nursing job and come to Okayama to prepare for her entrance examination for medical school. Tomiko, now called "Anna" by Guo, came at the end of 1916 and then left for Tokyo Women's Special Medical School (Tokyo Joshi Isha Senmon Gakkō) the following spring. But her pregnancy with their first child soon forced her to quit school.[20] Over the next twenty years, she lived with Guo as his common-law wife and bore him five children.

Despite their mutual affection, the union of Guo Moruo and Satō Tomiko was adamantly opposed by both families. Tomiko's name was stricken from her family register when she was punished with *hamon* (expulsion); Guo's parents refused to write to him until they heard a grandson was born.[21] Just as their families rejected them, so did some of the Chinese in the student community. When the news about Japan's demand for Germany's former leased territory in China reached Tokyo in 1919, Chinese students responded with characteristic radical actions. They held meetings and demanded that those who had married Japanese women divorce their wives. Those who refused to do so were invariably accused of being traitors *(hanjian)*. Guo became one of them.[22]

Such were Guo's initial experiences with the people of his own race and culture when the question of national conflict and loyalty was debated in the summer of 1919. It was only natural that he rejected the crude logic that "same race and same culture" guaranteed friendship, and he remained hopeful about the power of benevolence and compassion to link all humankind.

Guo had not just gained intellectual insight, but had also found the muse for his literary aspirations, a light of hope that purified his senses and lifted his spirit. It was Anna, he believed, who finally delivered him from the verge of madness. But instead of bringing him tranquility and contentment, her love threw him into waves of restlessness, for "between summer and fall in 1916" Guo "began to truly feel the desire to write poetry." The poems, "Crescent and White Clouds," "The Temptation of Death," "Parting," and "Venus," which were later published in *Goddess (Nüshen)*, his celebrated poetry collection from China's cultural Renaissance in the post–May Fourth era, were all dedicated to Anna.[23] In 1919 Guo had already graduated from the Sixth Higher School and entered Kyūshū Imperial University to pursue a degree in medical science. Toward the end of that year he wrote "Earth, My Mother!" in an intoxicated state, as he later described it:

> That day I went to Fukuoka Library to read. Suddenly I felt the attack of inspiration and left the library. I took off my *geta* and walked barefoot on the quiet, cobblestone-paved path behind the library. For a while I simply lay down on the path, so that I could be closer to the "mother earth" by touching her skin and being caressed by her.... In such a state I was pushed and moved by the poetry and finally perceived her completion. I rushed back home and put her on paper, feeling as if coming back to life like a new person.[24]

Meanwhile, Guo found his literary audience by sheer coincidence through Chinese students' anti-Japanese activities in Fukuoka. In the summer of 1919, he and a few other Chinese at Kyūshū Imperial University responded to the May Fourth Movement by organizing a Xia Society [Xia She] and decided to focus their activities on translating materials about Japan's China policy and public opinion toward China.[25] To stay in touch with China's internal developments, they subscribed to *Current Affairs Newspaper (Shishi xinbao)*, one of the leading newspapers of liberal bent in Shanghai. One day Guo read in it a poem in modern colloquial Chinese, which moved him to send two of his poems, "Bathing in Hakata Bay with My Son in My Arms" ["Bao he-er yu bodowan"] and "Egret" ["Lusi"], to the newspaper.[26] For the first time, he used the pen-name "Moruo" in remembrance of the two rivers, Mo and Ruo, that flowed by his Shawan Village in Sichuan.

Despite Guo's anonymity, Zong Baihua, the young editor in charge of the literary supplement column titled "Xuedeng," welcomed the new poet with open arms and published everything that Guo sent him.[27] He also began to write to Guo frequently and brought Tian Shouchang, then a student at Tokyo's Higher Normal School (Kōtō Shihan Gakkō) and later known as Tian Han the playwright, into their discussions of literature and life.[28] The three young men's correspondence during the spring of 1920 was compiled into a small book and titled *Kleeblatt (Sanye ji)* to symbolize their friendship.[29] With its focus on questions about life and love, the book immediately became a best-seller among young men and women, who were looking to justify their liberation from the family system. Sales during the 1920s were so brisk that the book had to be reprinted at least seven times.

Guo's poetry won a wide readership among middle- and high-school students. Writers who later achieved fame, such as Bing Xin and Cao Yu, recalled the inspiration that Guo's poetry gave them.[30] The pantheism and heroism of his poetry captured well the mood of his time, and its shining images of the sun, lightning, and thunder became symbols of the post–May Fourth Chinese awakening and revival. In 1922, Guo's translation of Goethe's *The Sorrow of Young Werther (Shaonian Weite zhi fannao)* was published, and it, too, became a bible for China's young generation.[31]

To Guo himself, the instant success of his literary creations produced a double effect. While it helped him gain more confidence in his literary creations, it undermined his determination to pursue a career in medical science, which had already been impeded by his impaired hearing, a result of the *typhus abdominalis* he had suffered as a teenager. Frequent ecstatic seizures during composition moved him to ponder the possibility of becoming a professional writer, and he finally made two attempts, in July 1920 and in early 1921, to leave Fukuoka to work on literature in Shanghai or Kyoto. His first try was stopped only by a sudden change in his fellow traveler's plan and the second try by the persuasion of his close friend, Cheng Fangwu (1897–1984), who argued for the need to study science so as to set up a solid base for literary creation.[32]

Guo's irrepressible yearning to write literature also became a source of domestic conflict. Anna, now a mother of two sons, fiercely opposed his intention to become a writer, for she knew that such a vocation could never secure a stable income and would instead bring endless poverty.[33] Unable to reconcile his own desire to write with his family responsibility, Guo fell into an agitated state in the spring of 1921 and stopped going to school for several months.

He spent all his time on the top floor of his house, reading only literature. Seeing him become "a madman" again finally moved Anna to give up her opposition.

On the eve of Guo's departure for Shanghai in 1921, Anna cooked a special dinner to wish her husband success. Some ten years later, Guo still remembered the dishes of that dinner, a red porgy and rice cooked with red beans. He understood that for Anna, red-colored food symbolized good luck. That dinner, said Guo, "was full of genuine expression of Japan's ancient customs, which were very close to Chinese folk practice." As Guo hesitated at the prospect of a long separation, Anna encouraged him and strengthened his determination. Reflecting on that turning point, Guo was full of gratitude:

> Her personality is stronger than mine. As soon as she made the decision, nothing could move her. Whenever I started to hesitate, it was she who encouraged me to pursue the planned course.[34]

Coming Home as Foreigners

Guo's trip to Shanghai in the spring of 1921 yielded encouraging results. He and his friend Cheng Fangwu succeeded in reaching a verbal agreement with the Taidong Publishing House to issue a literary magazine. He returned to Japan that summer and found a number of like-minded students, including Zheng Boqi (1895–1979) and Mu Mutian (1900–1971) at the Third Higher School in Kyoto, and Yu Dafu (1896–1945), Tian Shouchang (1898–1968), Zhang Ziping (1894?–1959), Xu Zuzheng (1894–1978), and He Wei at Tokyo University. Although none of them majored in literature, all were writing stories or poetry and all were enthusiastic about having a forum of their own. Their quarterly, *Creation (Chuangzao)*, finally made its debut the following spring and became an instant success.[35] Encouraged, the group, now named the Creation Society, initiated *Creation Weekly (Chuangzao zhoukan)* a year later. The society also began to contribute regularly to the *Zhonghua xinbao*, a daily newspaper in Shanghai, with a column called "Creation Daily" in its literary supplement.[36] Guo Moruo, Yu Dafu, and Cheng Fangwu now became pivotal figures in the group and had to keep writing so as to sustain the pace of these regular publications.

Just at this moment of literary success, Guo had to choose once again between medicine and writing. In March 1923 he graduated from the Kyūshū Imperial University, thus opening up the possibility of entering the medical profession. He told Qian Chao, a friend and schoolmate in Kyūshū, that he looked forward to going back to China and to opening a hospital in Sichuan.[37] In fact, his eldest brother was then arranging a position for him in a hospital at Chengdu. Meanwhile, Beijing University, at the initiation of Zhou Zuoren, also offered Guo a professorship in Japanese literature. After some hesitation, Guo turned down both options.[38] On April 1, 1923, the "fool's day," as he pointedly noted, he went to Shanghai with Anna and their three sons. The journey was Anna's first to the "unknown foreign land," yet she felt "inexplicable happiness" because Guo had finally graduated and "life in the future seemed to move only towards the better."[39]

Contrary to Anna's beaming optimism, poverty followed the Guos to Shanghai. Once Guo turned down the teaching position at Beijing University, he became more determined to live by his pen. Soon after their arrival, Cheng Fangwu and Yu Dafu came to Shanghai to join them. The three families took up residence at Minhou Nanli in a row house owned by the Taidong Publishing House. Crammed together, they lived rent free and wrote and edited *Creation Quarterly* and *Creation Weekly* for Taidong without any salary or royalties. Their writings and translations brought a sizable profit to the publishing company, yet their relationship with it, whether as guests or as employees, was never made clear. Pressured by their embarrassing existence, Guo had to go to the Taidong office every few days as a representative of the three writers, asking for five or ten dollars for pocket money. The manager of Taidong kept promising Guo and the others shares of Taidong stock in lieu of royalty payments or monthly salary. His words, however, always disappeared into thin air, never amounting to anything.[40]

Near-destitution exacerbated the Guos' isolation. Being the wife of a poor Chinese writer, Anna could not reach out to the large and well-to-do Japanese community in the international settlement of Shanghai. Speaking virtually no Chinese, neither was she able to make friends among the wives of Guo's acquaintances, who were educated either in China or in the West. Her world, therefore, was confined to the kitchen whenever Guo's Chinese guests came. Xu Zhimo, the Cambridge-educated poet and a leader of the Crescent

Society, recorded in his diary one visit that he and the American-educated Hu Shi made to Guo's residence six months after their return from Japan:

> Moruo answered the door himself, holding a baby in his arms; he was bare-footed, wearing an unbuttoned student uniform, and looking haggard,... but in fact with a pleasant personality.... Moruo's living quarters appeared cramped, with all sorts of things scattered everywhere. His children were running around, constantly in need of their father's comfort when they fell down, or his help to wipe away snot and tears. None of them could speak Chinese. From the kitchen came distinctly the clicking sound of wooden slippers, which must be from his Japanese wife.[41]

Xu immediately noticed that Guo was embarrassed and behaved rather strangely that day, and "there seemed to be a barrier of ice between the host and guests."[42] Although Guo later regained his congenial manner when he and these well-to-do colleagues entertained each other in restaurants, he seemed unable to shake off the shame of exposing his hopeless poverty and became even more sensitive to the invisible hierarchy of the Chinese literary world. In his memoir *Ten Years of the Creation Society,* Guo sarcastically mentioned that "the Great Doctor Hu Shi is indeed an outstanding person, who even humbled himself to visit us at Minhou Nanli." As for the first issue of the *Chinese Learning (Guoxue jikan)* quarterly that Hu offered him, he simply "did not even bother to read a word of it."[43]

Trapped by poverty and pressured to rush the writing for three periodicals, Guo's writing changed drastically. He no longer wrote refreshing poems like those in the *Goddess;* instead, he produced a series of autobiographical stories describing the humiliation and frustration that he and his family suffered in their destitution. The quality of these works, remarks the insightful critic Jaroslav Průšek, is that of "the raw material rather than the finished product of literary art, records and notes of personal experiences rather than stories and novels in the accepted sense."[44] Raw and below standard, Guo's literary attempts in the post–May Fourth years nevertheless left an open record leading directly to his intimate experiences and intense emotions.

In the midst of this clash between dreams and reality there came a dramatic turn in Guo's view of his homeland. While in Japan, as he emerged from anonymity to become a celebrated poet with his widely acclaimed "Nirvana of the Phoenixes," Guo's poetry was imbued with an overflowing sense of rebirth. He spoke about his China after the ablution of the May Fourth Movement as a "young and fresh girl, full of promises and future." That feeling of "being born again" carried him through his first journey back home in 1921 and enchanted him so much that he "wanted to jump into the Huangpu River to be in my lover's arms" as the ship approached the mouth of the Yangtze River from the sea.[45]

But Guo was instantly thrust back into reality by the appalling scenes of Shanghai. As the ship moved into the Huangpu River, his image of the city as a bucolic oasis evaporated as soon as the towering cigarette billboards and factory chimneys that dotted both sides of the river came into view. Stepping on shore into the bustling streets, he saw the pale faces of men and women clad in the bizarre fashion of long sleeves, "moving like corpses." And the coolies and beggars roaming about the city reminded him that he, too, belonged to "the same unfortunate race descending from the Yellow Emperor." Guo realized that he "could not continue his dream." When his fellow countrymen groaned "under the foreigners' whip," admitted Guo, he had only "national consciousness but not class consciousness."[46]

His sense of national shame, as he would soon discover, was ambivalent, partly because of the corruption of his fellow Chinese, partly because of his own ambiguous identity. That frustration vividly surged to the forefront in his description of a trip from Shanghai to the neighboring city of Hangzhou. Upon boarding a second-class carriage, Guo found himself in the midst of a colliding world. In one corner were some politician-like Chinese, drinking, talking loudly, gambling, and playing with prostitutes. In another corner were a few Westerners, "reading their documents in silence as if the world did not exist besides themselves." In yet another corner were a few Japanese passengers "talking loudly and frequently casting disdainful glances at the gambling and drinking party of Chinese." And some of them also "gestured with glances" to Guo and his friend Cheng Fangwu, mistaking them for Japanese students because of their uniforms of the Japanese imperial university. Ashamed of his fellow countrymen and annoyed by these glances, Guo was helpless even to hold back his own tears.[47]

That involuntary membership in the ranks that shamed his country inflicted a double humiliation on Guo. "Lunar Eclipse" (Yueshi), a short story about an evening outing in 1923, drives home a sense of his uprooted drift and loss. It was late August when news of an upcoming eclipse prompted Guo to plan a family outing to Wusong Bay so that his three sons, who had been confined to a row house for months, might breathe some fresh air. But an inquiry about the taxi fare forced him to change his mind: a trip to Wusong could cost as much as three months' wages for their maidservant! So he decided instead to go to the nearby Huangpu Park. While their sons became excited and anxiously watched the ticking hands of the clock, Guo and Anna sank once more into despair: what to wear? They knew well that they could not put on the clothes they usually wore because the placard by the park gate forbade both Chinese and dogs from entering. Only after a long while of trying on the clothes they kept did they put on Western suits, ride on the tram, and enter Huangpu Park. Hiding their anger and shame beneath the tight Western clothes, Guo and Anna mingled with the foreigners in their leisurely world. They talked about their dreams while watching the two elder boys dashing back and forth on the lawn. Guo described his bucolic home village by the Dadu River in Sichuan, and Anna recalled her nightmare of the previous night in which she found her husband transformed into a skeleton in a beautiful house. That was when they both realized that the world on the other shore might be a better home:

> When we were in Japan, we lived by the sea, in the embrace of the forest. The pure wind and bright moonlight were indeed priceless. Recalling the happiness of that time increases our frustration with the present.[48]

About six months later, in February 1924, Anna returned to Japan with their three sons. She hoped to learn midwifery there so that she could return to support her family in Shanghai.[49] Six weeks after Anna's departure, Guo, unable to work and live alone any longer, abandoned his work for *Creation Weekly* and left to join her in Japan.

"You Ungrateful Japanese!"

Having struggled to simply survive in Shanghai for about a year only to see all his dreams disappear in poverty and humiliation, Guo finally came to heed Anna's voice. With bitterness he admitted that without securing material sustenance, he "could meet the icy cold Girl of Truth very often." He planned to write a novel, *Pure Light* (*Jieguang*), for Anna and, after that, "to bury myself in scholarly research at the biology laboratory here [in Japan] for the rest of my life." Guo had been inspired by Dr. Ishii, a professor of biology at the Kyūshū Imperial University and had been interested in physiology during his undergraduate years. With hopes of getting a government scholarship to work with Dr. Ishii for an advanced degree, Guo made a trip to Tokyo at the end of April to see the government representative of Sichuan Province. But the official had no sympathy for Guo's aspirations and turned down his application. Once and for all, the Guos had to accept his insecure life as a writer.[50]

Guo did not write *Pure Light*, either. He was able, however, to make the remaining months of 1924 one of the most productive periods of his life, partly out of financial desperation and partly from the peace of mind regained by reunion with his family. Between April and October, he completed translations of Turgenev's *Virgin Soil* from German and Kawakami Hajime's *Social Organization and Social Revolution (Shakai soshiki to shakai kakumei)* from Japanese. The latter translation, in turn, brought Guo the "spiritual food" that he was so hungry for, and he wrote excitedly to his friend Cheng Fangwu about the inspiration that Kawakami's book had given him:

> I am not so satisfied with the content of this book, such as his disagreement with any attempt at an early political revolution, which I thought differs from Marx's original idea. But what I learned from this book is indeed enormous! Before I only had a vague hatred toward individualist capitalism and had confidence in social revolution; now I have gained the perspective of reason and no longer rely on emotions.... I am so thankful to the author, I am so thankful to Marx and Lenin, I am so thankful to those friends who helped me to finish the translation of this book. I have spent two months completing the translation, during that time I was most surprised to find that

Lenin and Trotsky, whom we used to take as ruffians, are true scholars with such meticulous minds![51]

About a year and a half later, Guo's letter was published in the *Chuangzao* monthly. Although the letter read like a declaration of conversion to Marxism, in actuality Guo had not yet, as David Tod Roy has pointed out, made a clean break with his earlier attachment to romanticism.[52] Especially indicative of his attitude toward the newfound social theory is the religious undertone and the following: "the translation of this book ... wakes me from my half-sleepiness, guides me out of my wandering on forked roads, and redeems me from the dark shadow of death."[53]

And the feeling of being redeemed so purified and elated Guo that the prose poetry he wrote during this period conveys a sensitivity and tenderness rarely seen in his previous work. These works focus on small scenes in his immediate world and are mainly concerned with the suffering, joy, and impermanence of life. Only a few days after his letter to Cheng Fangwu, Guo jotted down the first such prose poem in which he "found a bundle of discarded roses by the side of a trail in the woods"; taking the roses home, he put them into a broken wine bottle so that the roses "will not be trampled by the passers-by." In another prose poem, he guided the reader to his backyard, where in the dusk he played with his three children on the lawn, and from there, they heard Anna's cheerful voice "echoing and swimming through the golden rays of sunset." In yet another piece he led the reader into a barbershop, where he had his last haircut "on that spring night three years ago" by a "young, very young girl"; in the mirror this time he saw the same girl gently pull away a piece of his gray hair, and it made him murmur in his heart, "Young girl, ... this wanderer has been drifting for three years since he last left; it is your pitiful heart that brings me back my youth."[54]

The pity of an unknown girl and the joy of returning to a bucolic Fukuoka, though heartwarming to Guo, still could not dispel the chill of poverty that followed them to Japan. Since Guo's graduation the previous year, the meager but regular student stipend from the Chinese government had stopped coming. Fortunately, Guo received three hundred yen of the "allowance for returning to China" when he visited Tokyo in April, which sustained the whole family until the early summer.[55] When the weather warmed up, the Guos were able to pawn their winter clothing and other belongings to pay for food. Starting in June, they began to move from one place to another, often being evicted by landlords who would not wait for their overdue rent.

It was one of those endless moves that brought the Guos to Karatsu, a port in northwest Kyūshū. The city was so named—the two Chinese characters meant Tang Port—because it was the old port where Japan in the ninth century sent students to learn the Chinese language and political system of the great Tang dynasty. The port had become a summer tourist resort in recent years because of its fine beaches. In his autobiographical fiction *Strenuous Passage (Qilu)*, Guo related an incident when "Ai-mu"—a name that stands for "I am" as Guo explained it—went to look for a house in Karatsu. Ai-mu found a chatty and hospitable landlady who was obviously delighted to have a medical student from Fukuoka, as Ai-mu told her he was, rent her rooms. Ai-mu, for his part, was dazzled by the elegance of her tailored casual wear and her extravagantly furnished living quarters and began to doubt if his poor wife and children could share the same yard with this lady. In a flurry, he jotted down his address using a fake Japanese name. Just as he regretted doing this, the landlord returned home, and suddenly everything turned upside down:

> The man glanced at him with eyes more ferocious than a hunting dog's.
> "Hmm, your gracious country? Shanghai? Or Korea?"
> *Ah, the guy has seen through me! How shameful! How shameful! Great!*
> "I am a Chinese student."
> "Ah, is that *shinajin?*" Thunder rolled out of the landlady's mouth.
> *Ah, damn it! Damn it!* Ai-mu thought, but he could not say anything.
> "Do you want to rent a house? You probably cannot find one here. Our empty room is for the Ping-Pong table."

Fleeing the Japanese couple's mockery, Ai-mu ran to the beach, but the laughter of men and women bathing in the sea sounded like jeers to him. Worse still, the beach instantly reminded him that this very place of his humiliation was where Japan sent off its students to Tang China; he wondered "if those Japanese in

China had ever suffered the same abuse as we have to endure now."
The very thought of China's benevolence to those who came for
knowledge and understanding made him even angrier:

> Japanese, Japanese! You ungrateful Japanese! What does our
> China owe to you to make you despise us so? Only saying the
> three words "Shi-na-jin" reveals so thoroughly your utterly evil
> intention. You purposely wrinkle your nose when saying "shi"
> and prolong that nasal sound when saying "na." Ah, do you
> understand the origin of these two words "Shi-na?" When it
> was the time of the "Chin" Dynasty, you were still barbarians!
> You probably were still living on coconuts in the South Sea!
>   Ah, you ungrateful Japanese! Do you understand I took
> your name not because I admire your culture. I took your
> name only to avoid your plot against me! Your imperialism has
> succeeded, but your conscience has died as well. You often say
> that we "misunderstand" you; you often say that others' de-
> fensiveness is "conspiracy." Ah, you arrogant Japanese! How
> thoughtful is your mind, that is worthy of other's "misun-
> derstanding?" The intention of Sima Zhao was an open secret,
> don't take others as idiots! Do repent! Do repent! I do not
> worry that I took your daughter as my wife. If you do not re-
> pent, I will always oppose you, even my wife will always oppose
> you![56]

Through Ai-mu, Guo poured out the bitterness he had stored
for years. He knew that he was a worthier man in knowledge and
ability than this well-to-do Japanese couple; he knew, too, that not
all Japanese were as "ungrateful" as this arrogant couple. But their
conceit and vulgarity still hurt him badly, deeply. And as a sojourner from a powerless country, he was defenseless in a hostile
world.

Having realized that the natural beauty of Japan was irrelevant
as long as they remained penniless, Guo finally convinced Anna to
move back to China. During that rootless summer Guo completed
his translation of Turgenev's *Virgin Soil* into Chinese. By August,
when he wrote to Cheng Fangwu, Guo had endured two months
of wandering around Kyūshū Island, just as Ai-mu had done in
Karatsu. Armed with his newly acquired Marxist terminology, Guo
declared that he had "killed Nejdanovs," the superfluous man in

Virgin Soil, in his heart; he was now ready to join "the ongoing social revolution" in China, where the situation resembled "the Russia of the 1870s after the emancipation of the serfs."[57]

***

Guo had chosen an opportune time to return to his homeland. China in 1924, though appearing as chaotic and divided as in the previous decade, was gathering force for a new revolution. Sun Yat-sen, having been marginalized by powerful opponents for a decade, was now ready to return to center stage. After twice setting up governments in Guangzhou (Canton) and twice being ousted by the local force and a rebellious subordinate, he came upon a decisive encounter with representatives from Soviet Russia when his own revolutionary movement was at a lull. In the fall of 1922, Sun met for the second time the Comintern agent J. F. M. Sneevliet (pseudonym Maring) and, in early 1923, the Soviet representative Adolf Joffe. The meetings reaffirmed Sun's determination to turn to the Soviet Union for assistance and to initiate his new policy of coalition with the Chinese Communists. The new alliance developed in earnest, and by late 1924, the Guomindang had firmly consolidated its hold on Guangzhou. With Soviet financing and expert advice, the party had also created the Huangpu Military Academy and built up its own armed forces; with the assistance of the Chinese Communists, the workers and peasants in the south were mobilized to join the revolutionary movement. With a solid base in Guangdong, Sun now had both the military and political means to pursue his goal of national unification.

The turn to a Russian approach, however, did not lead Sun away from his goals of Chinese and Asian revival. It was, in his view, a move to embrace one more participant in the cause of Pan-Asianism. Speaking to a Japanese reporter in 1922, Sun stated that "Russians are Asiatics" and that he considered them natural allies against "the aggression of the Anglo-Saxons."[58] Nevertheless, the effective and prompt assistance from the Soviet Union must have set too striking a contrast to the reluctance and indecision of Japan, whom Sun had always regarded as a natural ally and in whom he had placed great hopes that too often ended in disillusionment. In 1924, several months after Guo's frustrated encounter at Karatsu, Sun had come again to Japan. He had been on a trip to Beijing for negotiations with the provisional government on matters of national unification; stopping over in Kobe, he once again made appeals to the Japanese on behalf of a Pan-Asian cause, though his emphasis this time was not on extolling the Sino-Japanese friendship, but on the threat to it:

> The culture of Europe is a culture of dominance.... The culture of Asia is a culture of benevolence.... In this new world, what should be the basis of our Pan-Asianism? The basis should be our inherited culture based on morality and on justice....
>
> What is the purpose of talking about Pan-Asianism? It is a question of how the suffering Asian nations can resist the strong nations of Europe. In a word, it is a question of bringing justice to the oppressed. You the Japanese people have acquired the culture of dominance from Europe, but you have also inherited the essence of the benevolent culture of Asia; for the future of world culture, you must carefully consider whether to be the running dogs of the culture of dominance in the West, or to become a champion of the Eastern culture of benevolence. You the Japanese people must make your choice![59]

Were the Japanese listening? Was the culture of benevolence to prevail? By 1924, Guo Moruo could answer the question only with despair. The root of the problem, as he saw it, was the growing disparity of power that fueled the arrogance of the Japanese, who had abandoned the culture of benevolence. Jiang Baili had anticipated the emerging conflict much earlier. With a more realistic assessment of power on both sides, he had been working since he had left Japan on building up China's defense and searching for a grand strategy for what he saw as an inevitable clash (chap. 8). Zhou Zuoren and Dai Jitao, on the other hand, looked at China's relations with Japan with unyielding optimism. It was not that they were unaware of the conflict between the two nations, but they perceived the possibilities of reducing the potential for conflict through reconstructing the Chinese state and society and hence building an alternative relationship with Japan. The two, however, would take sharply divergent routes in pursuit of their goals, and the changing cultural and political conditions in the 1920s would provide them with hopes and means, as we shall see in Part III.

Guo Moruo with the members of the Creation Society, circa 1924. From left: Wang Duqing, Guo Moruo, Yu Dafu (seated), and Cheng Fangwu. Reprinted from *Guo Moruo quanji,* vol. 3:9.

Guo Moruo with wife Anna (Satō Tomiko) and their children, circa 1924. Reprinted from *Guo Moruo quanji*, vol. 3:9.

Jiang Baili (in military uniform) with the Chinese Observers's Delegation to the Paris Peace Conference, 1919. Liang Qichao is third from left, next to Jiang. Reprinted from *Jiang Baili xiansheng jiniance*.

Jiang Baili with wife Satō Yato and their daughters in 1925. Reprinted from *Jiang Baili xiansheng jiniance*.

Dai Jitao with Sun Yat-sen (both center) at a press conference in Shanghai on November 22, 1924, the day they departed Shanghai for Kobe, where Sun was to give his famous speech on Pan-Asianism. Reprinted from *Sun Zhongshan quanji,* vol. 11.

Zhou Zuoren with friends and colleagues on New Year's Day 1929 in his Bitter Rain Study at his home in Beijing. Front row from left: Zhang Fengju, Yu Pingbo, Ma Mengming's son, Ma Mengming, Qian Xuantong; back row from left: Shen Yinmo, Xu Zuzheng, Zhou Zuoren, Shen Shiyuan, Liu Bannong (far back, standing), Ma Youyu, Li Zihe, Shen Jianshi, Zhang Bingda. Photo courtesy of Y. M. Bau.

PART III
Culture and Politics

In 1924, when Sun Yat-sen made his Kobe speech and his last appeal to Japan to give up the "culture of dominance" for the "culture of benevolence," his criticism carried unusual gravity at that moment. China had changed since Sun had taken his humiliating refuge in Japan after the failure of the Second Revolution. It was now poised for another revolution. In some sense, this was a truer "second revolution" that sprang from a widely shared determination to bring China's internal chaos and international weakness to an end. The goals of anti-imperialism and anti-warlordism galvanized the population, and, within less than half a decade, the nationwide support for this new revolution would climax in the Northern Expedition and propel the Guomindang to national power.

The early 1920s was a time that was both politically hopeful and culturally exciting. It was the cultural awakening of the May Fourth era, after all, that turned the political inertia and frustration of the 1910s to the political activism of the 1920s. There was, in Akira Iriye's words, "as much internationalism as nationalism in the May Fourth phenomenon."[1] It was this dynamic interaction of internationalism and nationalism that placed Sino-Japanese relations on a new terrain.

The question of how China's cultural and political relations with Japan encountered new opportunities and limits in the 1920s is explored in Part III. In the realm of culture, the Chinese quest for inspiration from Japan, which had started at the turn of the century, did not end with the rise of nationalism. The need for references and models from outside, in fact, became even more urgent as Chinese cultural leaders turned iconoclastic toward China's cultural heritage. Japan, in this regard, was at once the most pertinent and most disputable example available to the Chinese. The Chinese had long been aware of Japan's energetic assimilation of Western knowledge to their modernization efforts; yet with the memory of Japan's audacious pursuit of its colonial interests on the continent in the recent past, it had become emotionally difficult to accept things of Japanese origin. Adding to this emotional barrier was a historical awareness of China's cultural

influence on Japan, which in a time of rising national consciousness easily transformed itself into a burden of cultural arrogance.
For those who had seen the value of Japanese experience and who
hoped to emulate it in Chinese experiments with modernization,
Chinese hostility to and rejection of things Japanese presented
both a challenge and an opportunity. It was in meeting this twofold
challenge of translating Japanese cultural inspiration into Chinese
practice while differentiating it from Japan's colonialism that Zhou
Zuoren created a new kind of Chinese understanding of Japan
and a connection that effectively linked Japan to China's cultural
transformation.

The story in the realm of international politics, on the other
hand, was one of hope turned to disillusionment. Possibilities for a
better international relationship than that of the previous decade
did emerge in both Japan and China. The Japanese government,
whose foreign affairs during most of the decade were in the hands
of the moderate diplomat Shidehara Kijūrō, was the most observant and well informed among all foreign powers; it also had sought
to reach an understanding with the rising Guomindang. On the
Chinese side, proponents for a pro-Japanese policy within the
Guomindang also gained the upper hand just as the party approached
victory in its campaign to attain national power. Their ascendance,
or rather their reassertion of power within the Guomindang, was
entangled with the intense power struggle, which ended with the
bloody purge of the Communists in the spring of 1927. Dai Jitao,
who had grown increasingly conservative in the wake of a personal
crisis and who had always maintained a fascination with Pan-
Asianism, became a moving force behind the Guomindang's turn
against the Chinese Communists and its strategic shift from a pro-
Russian approach to a pro-Japanese approach. For Dai, the pursuit
of a Pan-Asian alliance with Japan combined personal passion,
political necessity, and national interest. Yet his long-cherished
vision would materialize only as much as Japan was willing to
collaborate.

5 Pro-Japanese or Anti-Japanese?

"Dr. Sun Yat-sen's proposals, I think, are based on sound reasons," wrote Zhou Zuoren in early December 1924, shortly after Sun's Pan-Asianism speech. He must have been commenting on Sun's proposals for national unification, the purpose of Sun's journey north via Kobe, but he had strong reservations about Sun's appeal to Pan-Asianism, for he added quickly:

> Yet I cannot agree with his Asianism, because these are just empty words—if it is diplomatic rhetoric, that's another matter. I am not an activist in the anti-imperialist movement; but my thoughts have just returned to the path of nationalism.[1]

That Zhou, an unreserved admirer of the Japanese way of life who had taken Japan as a second home, should have rejected Sun's Pan-Asianism out of hand is indeed surprising. Almost two decades had passed since Zhou first set foot in Japan in 1906. In 1924, Zhou was nearly forty, the "age of confidence" in the Chinese saying, and a father of three young children. He was also at the height of his career as a leader in China's New Culture movement and a specialist on Japan. Beijing, China's political and cultural center, had been his home since 1917, and several influential newspapers and magazines there, such as the *Chen Bao Supplement (Chen bao fukan)*, the *Jing Bao Supplement (Jing bao fukan)*, *New Youth (Xin qingnian)*, and *Talking Threads (Yusi)*, were regular forums for his opinions. He was no longer a quiet aspirant but had become a leader of China's intellectual revolution. In 1924, when he voiced his objection to Sun's appeal for Pan-Asianism, his admiration for Japanese culture had not waned; on the contrary, it had grown deeper in recent years along with his efforts to bring Japanese culture into cosmopolitan discourse in China's modern Renaissance. His objection to Pan-Asianism, as proposed by politicians, can be understood only in the context of his ongoing activities on the cultural front and his unique perspective on the intricate relationship between the culture and politics of his time.

Beijing, 1917

In the spring of 1917, Zhou Zuoren went to Beijing for the second time in his life. Some twenty years earlier, while still a student at the Jiangnan Naval Academy, he had been in the capital to take a government examination for a study-in-Japan scholarship. By 1917 he had already returned from Japan, spent six years in his hometown of Shaoxing, and taught English in a middle school while chairing the Shaoxing Educational Association. During those years Zhou had developed an interest in children's literature and psychology, which was most likely kindled by the arrival of his children, a boy and two girls, between 1912 and 1915.[2] Life in Shaoxing was comfortable and quiet, and occasionally there were moments of excitement, when packages arrived from the Maruzen or Sagamiya Bookstores in Tokyo. Some of them contained books on haiku and *kyōgen,* his old interest. Other packages had new magazines that enabled him to keep up with current trends in Japanese literary circles. Two new schools of writers and scholars, especially, had caught his attention just before he left Tokyo in 1911: the idealist writers surrounding the magazine *White Birch (Shirakaba),* edited by Mushanokoji Saneatsu (this group would become known as the Shirakaba school), and the folklorist Yanagita Kunio, who published 350 copies of *Tales of Tōno (Tōno monogatari)* in 1910, one of which was purchased by the eager Zhou Zuoren in Tokyo. Once he returned to China, Yanagita's *Local Studies (Kyōdo kenkyū)* and Mushanokoji's *White Birch* were mailed to Shaoxing and became part of Zhou's regular readings.[3]

Although remote from the center of the political storm, the tranquility in Shaoxing was often upset by disturbing news from the outside. Zhou returned from Japan just in time to witness the excitement of the 1911 Revolution, but the factional struggle within the revolutionary camp soon dampened his optimism. Tao Chengzhang, his Robin Hood friend in the Tokyo years and the head of the Restoration Society, was assassinated by a rival faction in the Revolutionary Alliance in 1912. In the same year Zhou's elder brother, Lu Xun, left Shaoxing for Nanjing to work in the Ministry of Education, which soon moved to the capital, Beijing. There, government secret agents kept intellectuals under close surveillance, an activity deemed necessary by Yuan Shikai, the president of the Republic, who had to be vigilant against the rebellious Guomindang and other opposition forces. For fear of inviting suspicion, many returned students, now serving in the government, began to cultivate "personal interests"—going to brothels or taking concubines, or busying themselves with collecting antiques. When Zhou Zuoren arrived in Beijing in April 1917, he found Lu Xun preoccupied with making rubbings of ancient stone tablets.[4] Later Lu Xun wrote that he felt then like he had been "left helpless in a boundless desert," and in order to dispel the loneliness, he "used various means to dull my senses"; copying ancient inscriptions turned out to be an effective one.[5]

The depressing atmosphere had begun to lift slightly in the summer of the previous year, when Yuan Shikai died in disgrace. Toward the end of 1916, the government, under the new president Li Yuanhong, assigned the chancellorship of Beijing University to Cai Yuanpei, a Guomindang veteran and accomplished scholar, who immediately began to reform the university by recruiting intellectuals of diverse views as faculty members. In 1917, Zhou was invited by Cai to Beijing University with an offer of a professorship in Greek literature and English literature. Zhou arrived just as the ancient city had gone restlessly to the edge of yet another momentous change.[6]

In appearance, Beijing in the spring of 1917 seemed to be the old imperial capital as Zhou remembered it; almost everywhere he sensed the obstinate force of a passing age. In a cross-city rickshaw ride two days after his arrival, he came upon the surprising discovery of a wall, about a dozen feet high, erected on the bridge across the lake surrounding the palace. The purpose, obviously, was to block pedestrians' view into the old palace, where the last emperor and his court still lived their privileged life. "Walking underneath that high wall," Zhou later wrote, "was indeed very unpleasant."[7] In the Shaoxing Guild Hostel, where he and Lu Xun lodged, he again confronted the shadow of a repulsive past. There was a locust tree outside their living quarters on which a concubine had once hanged herself. Although the tree had grown so tall that its lush shade covered the whole yard, the guild was still haunted by her presence and forbade women to take up residence at the hostel. But the two brothers were bothered more by the seasonal worship of ancestors in spring and autumn, which always took place on a Sunday. On such occasions, they would rise early and flee to Liu-lichang, a famous bookstore and antique district in Beijing, before their fellow townspeople arrived at the hostel for the ritual.[8]

Zhou was yet to dispel his disappointment with the inertia of the old city when the apparent peace in the capital was upset by the so-called "Zhang Xun Restoration" in July. It was a Sunday morning, recalled Zhou, when the caretaker of the guild hostel rushed in and shouted, "The dragon flag is hung up everywhere in the city!" For months Zhou had been hearing rumors about Zhang Xun's pigtailed soldiers and the possible restoration of the Qing dynasty by force, so the news did not come as a surprise. Nevertheless, during the next two weeks of fighting and chaos, he and Lu Xun had to move out of the guild to avoid being robbed or injured. Finally, Zhang Xun was defeated by the troops of Duan Qirui, a warlord from Anhui Province who came to take over the premiership. The warlord period then began to unfold.[9]

Although the Zhang Xun Restoration passed as quickly as an episode in the Beijing Opera, the brief return of the old dynasty magically summoned nostalgia in certain corners in Beijing. Watching how the Chamber of Commerce in Beijing had "defended" the late dynasty, Zhou came to realize that "China's reform has not succeeded, and there must be an intellectual revolution [sixiang geming]."[10]

That feeling was not his own. A few weeks after the restoration attempt, Zhou Zuoren and Lu Xun met with Qian Xuantong, one of their old friends from the Tokyo years and now their colleague at Beijing University. Qian had been editing the New Youth monthly, which so far had met "no reaction, favorable or otherwise." Yet that night, under the same locust tree where the concubine had ended her life, the three friends talked about the recent incident, and Lu Xun said in despair:

> "Imagine an iron house without windows, absolutely inde-structible, with many people fast asleep inside who will soon die of suffocation. But you know since they will die in their

sleep, they will not feel any of the pain of death. Now if you cry aloud to wake a few of the lighter sleepers, making those unfortunate few suffer the agony of irrevocable death, do you think you are doing them any good?"

And answered the guest:

"But since a few have awakened, you can't say there is no hope of destroying the iron house."[11]

"Human Literature" and "New Village"

As recaptured by Lu Xun in his preface to *Call to Arms,* Qian's words were agitating, but the two brothers hesitated. They still remembered their own failure in the *New Life* a decade earlier, they had seen an even grander revolution in 1911 accomplish little toward eradicating China's apathy, and they suspected "it is still too early" for a call to arms.[12] And yet another voice added force to Qian Xuantong's prodding: that of Mushanokoji Saneatsu, the leader of the humanist Shirakaba school, which had been gaining attention in Japan since 1910, whose idealist writings urged them to overcome their passivity and break free of the suffocating iron house. Lu Xun, in an introduction to his translation of Mushanokoji's play *A Youth's Dream (Aru seinen no yume),* explained, "Mushanokoji said in his 'Random Thoughts on the New Village,' 'Those who have fire in your houses, don't hide it in the dark; take your fire out, put it at the place we can see, tell us—here also are your brothers.' They have lifted a torch in the storm, how could I cover it with darkness so as to please the sleeping men?"[13] The urgent appeal by Mushanokoji to those few "with fire" apparently struck a responsive chord in the two brothers; they were moved to action, albeit with lingering doubts.[14]

A few months after the conversation under the locust tree, Lu Xun wrote *A Madman's Diary,* which soon appeared in *New Youth* in May 1918. In the same issue Zhou Zuoren also contributed an essay, "Reading Mr. Mushanokoji's *A Youth's Dream.*" Both of them took the lack of human compassion as a central issue in China's reform, though they chose to approach the problem differently. Lu Xun launched a frontal attack on the hypocrisy of the Confucian tradition that disguised the reality of "men eating men." Zhou Zuoren, on the other hand, remained rather tentative; he encouraged his fellow Chinese to follow what Mushanokoji proposed in *A Youth's Dream:* "to actively seek peace."[15]

But Zhou soon found his own voice and made a bolder proposal in "Human Literature," the first of several critical essays on what he regarded as the principles of new literature. With a title designed to present unmistakably his agenda, Zhou, in the spirit of anti-Confucianism, criticized Chinese literary production as being dominated by "inhuman literature" *(feiren de wenxue)* that promoted "inhuman morals." Using "European discovery of the truth of 'Man'" through the Renaissance, Reformation, French Revolution, and World War I as a yardstick, Zhou pointed out that "the question of Man has never been solved [in China], not to mention that of women and children." The Chinese must make their efforts "from scratch," and the function of literary creation, declared Zhou, should be "making a start to promote humanism."

This pronounced Western orientation aside, the essay reveals the noticeable influence of the Shirakaba school, which had given him the courage to strike out. Like these Japanese intellectuals who made their journal a window on European arts and literature, Zhou Zuoren in "Human Literature" also advocated cosmopolitanism; he urged his fellow writers to look beyond the Chinese tradition, to seek inspiration in works by Western writers such as Ibsen, Tolstoy, Hardy, and Turgenev, and even to focus more on introducing foreign works "so as to broaden our readers' perspective that includes the whole humanity of the world."[16] Like Mushanokoji, who wrote in 1912 that the self contained various desires—to be an individual, a social animal, a human being, and an animal—which were reconciled through an effort of "realizing the self,"[17] Zhou in 1918 also saw both divine and savage attributes coexisting in human life. Developing further the central notion in Mushanokoji's philosophy that the goal of life is "for the self," Zhou pointed out that what he called "humanism," a theoretical principle for China's new revolution, was not philanthropism but "individualistic humanism." The term *"geren zhuyi de renjian benwei zhuyi"* is a direct adoption from the Japanese and thus sounded fairly awkward in Chinese.[18]

Yet that foreignness was ignored by Zhou's readers, who embraced the idea of "human literature" with open arms when the essay first appeared in *New Youth* in December 1918. The essay spoke so explicitly of the sentiment among the writers of the May

Fourth era that Hu Shi, when assessing the overall development of new literature a decade later, considered it to be "the most important statement of literature reform at the time" and "a great yet most common-sensical statement."[19] Encouraged by the public response, Zhou followed with a series of essays, elaborating on such issues as literature about common people, children's literature, and the question of women, all related to his concern for a revolution of the Chinese spirit and Chinese literature.[20] These writings carried his radical and idealist thoughts to many and established his position as a leading thinker in the "New Culture community," which had *New Youth* as its major forum and some faculty members at Beijing University as its core members, but whose constituency was rapidly expanding during the late 1910s.[21] As Zhou's reputation spread, he was invited to teach regular courses on European literature and modern Chinese literature at the Beijing Women's Normal University and Yenching University. He also became a popular speaker despite his rather quiet, reserved manner in lectures, and in 1920 alone he gave at least ten public speeches to diverse audiences, ranging from middle-school students to social reform groups.[22] The enthusiasm of his audience in those hopeful years made Zhou more confident about China's future, and his passion to promote historical change assumed an almost religious tone: "The writer of this new age is an iconoclast," said Zhou in one of his speeches to the newly organized Young China Society. "But he has his new religion—the ideal of humanism is his belief, and the will of mankind is his god."[23]

Optimistic and excited about his discovery of the "new religion" of humanism, Zhou joined hands with the New Village movement in Japan, initiated in 1918 by Mushanokoji and his friends in the Shirakaba school. The New Villagers conducted a communal life "celebrating cooperation and honoring individuality, promoting shared spirit and encouraging freedom."[24] Anxious to see the work of the New Village, Zhou decided to take a trip to Mushanokoji's village in the spring of 1919. Yet barely had he settled his wife and children in Tokyo when the news of the May Fourth Movement made him rush back to China. He was kept busy with efforts to rescue Chen Duxiu and other jailed students for two months, until July, when he was able once again to board a ship in Tianjin and head directly to the New Village at Hyūga in southern Japan.

The journey from Tianjin to Hyūga on Kyūshū Island, today only a matter of hours by airplane, took Zhou Zuoren five days and involved various means of transportation—ship, train, bus, and horse-drawn carriage. It was an ordeal for Zhou, who seldom made long trips, but the thought of approaching an ideal kingdom kept his spirits high. At the train station in Moji he even enjoyed being in the crowd and was amused by a few fat pineapples rolling between the hurried human legs. When Zhou entered the last phase of his long journey, Mushanokoji and three other New Villagers came down from the hills to welcome him; in drizzle and darkness they climbed the muddy road, their clothes and lanterns drenched with rain. Never had Zhou experienced such a difficult journey, but the calls and torches from the village sustained him to the end. When they finally reached the village, it was near midnight.

The four days in the village brought Zhou to his "greatest joy in life," where the best of the intellectual and physical worlds united into a harmonious whole. Zhou lived in the Mushanokoji household and browsed through albums of Van Gogh, Cézanne, and Goya while recuperating from the trip. In the following days he joined the villagers in planting sweet potatoes. Laboring in the field made him feel "very tired," yet he thought it was his first taste of "the happiness of 'human life'" that had been wanting in his life of over thirty years.[25] He was deeply impressed by a "religious spirit" among the villagers, all of whom "confidently believe in their ideal," though not all of them subscribed to the same religion.[26] The villagers' brotherly embrace made Zhou feel an overflowing compassion that transcended national boundaries. And his feeling was shared by Mushanokoji, when he asked Zhou to write two scrolls to commemorate the visit, quoting the *Analects:*

> Confucius says, isn't *ren* [benevolence] far away? *Ren* arrives as I come to desire *ren*.
> Confucius says, how can it be worrisome and fearful if one finds no regret in self-reflection?[27]

With that same confidence in the power of benevolence, Zhou returned to China and became an impassioned advocate of the New Village movement. He published essays in *New Youth* and *Morning Newspaper (Chen bao)* and gave many public lectures to promote the idea.[28] In hopes of achieving "an ideal of education and vocation in one," Zhou initiated a Work-Study Cooperative (Gong-du Huzhutuan) with his colleague Li Dazhao, the early Communist leader, and many others in 1920.[29] Through Zhou's connection, Li Dazhao also sent interested young students to the New Villages in Japan. Some early Communists, such as Yun Daiying and Cai He-seng, were attracted to the New Village movement before they con-verted to Marxism. Mao Zedong, the future leader of the Commu-nist revolution, even visited Zhou in April 1920 after having drafted a program for a new village.[30] Some reformist or anarchist journals, such as *Work-Study (Gongxue)* in Beijing and *New Human (Xinren)* in Shanghai, responded to Zhou's call with enthusiasm and carried extensive discussions on the New Village in several issues. The New Village, as one of them saw it, "is not a cave for hermits but … a model of a new society … and a general headquarters in a battle against the old society."[31] For a short period a few students in Bei-jing even experimented with agricultural cultivation to meet their own subsistence needs.[32] The movement, so far as it spread, marked a high point in Zhou's activism during the May Fourth era.

That the New Village movement could have attracted so many youth, especially the early Communists, indicates the widely shared appeal of the countryside, aptly termed an "agrarian impulse" by Arif Dirlik. Yet this is also where the New Village movement de-parted from other contemporary efforts to reach village China. Un-like the Rural Reconstruction movement led by James Yen, the New Villagers viewed rural China as an idealized place, a place to purify the individual, rather than a place to be pitied and lifted with a helping hand of the elite.[33] Nor did the New Villagers develop a vi-sion of reconstructing rural China through reinvigorating the tra-ditional collective organization and uplifting rural production by means of electrification and mechanization, as did the "Last Con-fucian" Liang Shuming.[34] The New Villagers looked to rural China for inspiration to improve the individual, but not as a mass base for an impending political movement, as it would be for the Commu-nists. Zhou Zuoren in those years, after all, was highly idealistic and remained so in comparison to the "pragmatists" James Yen and Mao Zedong. The New Village movement in China thus remained largely an intellectual project, with limited immediate social impact.

Responses to Zhou's optimism and his efforts at promoting Sino-Japanese brotherhood and his "agrarian impulse" were varied as well. Cai Yuanpei, the chancellor of Beijing University, expressed optimism after reading Mushanokoji's letter, "To the Unknown Friends in China," which spoke about hopes for China's rebirth and of both Japan's and China's awakening to work for "the cause of humanity." In response, Cai thought that even those Japanese who supported the imperialist aggression into China "will one day come to awareness and sincerely join hands with the Chinese, just like brothers."[35] The sharpest criticism of the New Village movement, interestingly enough, came from those closer to Zhou Zuoren. If "you promise the golden age to those people's future generations," questioned Lu Xun through a protagonist in one of his stories, "what then do you have to offer to them now?"[36] Hu Shi, moreover, thought the New Village movement had a tendency toward escapism and criticized it for its "individualism only for self-perfection";[37] but Zhou thought his friend misunderstood the idea at the time. By 1921, the New Village movement had receded, as Chinese youth began to embrace a more radical approach to social change—the Communist movement after the Leninist model in Soviet Russia.

What It Means to Be a "Japanophile"

Among those who did not share Zhou's and Mushanokoji's optimism was Chen Duxiu, the editor of *New Youth* and Zhou's colleague at Beijing University. Chen doubted if the hope for brotherly love between the Chinese and Japanese would ever become reality, because "the average Japanese in general follows 'statism' blindly.... Even many of those scholars involved passionately in the social movement and labor movement are taking the position of statism. People who hold truly profound thoughts, like Mushanokoji and Yamakawa Hitoshi and his wife, are probably rare."[38] It was a serious question that Zhou had to face. When the image of an aggressive Japan loomed large in Chinese minds, how could he convince his readers that the Chinese had anything to learn from the Japanese?

To that skepticism Zhou made his first response in 1920, when he wrote an essay, "Japanophiles," for the newly founded *Jing Bao Supplement.* It was a terse composition, fewer than six hundred words; his argument, too, was straightforward: "There is not a single person who deserves to be called 'Japanophile' in China."

With this seemingly impulsive statement came the most important notion in Zhou's study of Japan. There was no single Japanophile in China, he argued, "because there is nobody in China who understands Japan's true glory." To him, those who had been called "Japanophiles" were simply "small men who chase after personal gains." To be a true Japanophile, one had to understand its "glory," by which Zhou meant "scholarship, literature and fine arts." While urging his fellow Chinese to shed their arrogance and find Japan's true glory, Zhou also admonished his "Japanese friends" not to take those Chinese who sold their own country for personal gain as friends, for they would only "harm Japan's glory."[39]

In 1920 Zhou raised the issue of Japan's "true glory" not merely out of his personal appreciation of Japanese culture, but with the task of China's intellectual revolution in mind. Like Chen Duxiu, he was aware of the rising Japanophobia among the Chinese in response to Japanese imperialism toward China. Yet he wanted to go a step further and remind his fellow Chinese of the profound difference between politics and culture. Indiscriminate anti-Japanese boycotts, he warned, would only "cultivate hatred between peoples, foster arbitrary thought, and damage [Chinese] people's integrity."[40]

Deeper in Zhou's heart was the apprehension that the Chinese, blinded by their indignation and ignorance, would miss a shortcut in their search for modern transformation. He first voiced that concern in 1918 when giving a lecture to his fellow colleagues and students at Beijing University. Through a survey of modern Japanese fiction, Zhou made a convincing case for the modern innovations of Japanese fiction in both "forms" and "ideas" through diverse experiments, all beginning with Tsubouchi Shōyō's theoretical discussion, *The Essence of Fiction (Shōsetsu Shinzui)*, in 1886. Yet "the Chinese fiction now [in the 1920s]," he reminded his audience, "still keeps old forms, as writers retain old ideas and old forms in their treatment of literature and life." Therefore, "there has been no achievement, even though the Chinese have been talking about new fiction for twenty years." Some seven years later, in 1925, Zhou made yet another assessment, indicating that "China's new literature ... has gone a parallel path to that of Japan's in the past twenty-five years, yet till now it has only gone as far as what Japan had achieved in the thirtieth year of Meiji (1897), though we ourselves believe that the new literature of the Republic of China has arrived at its golden age."[41]

And the major cause of China's slow progress, as Zhou diagnosed it, lay in Chinese arrogance. Arguing that "by its special circumstances China has the necessity and possibility to understand Japan," he urged Chinese to pay attention to two useful lessons. The most valuable would be the Japanese approach to foreign cultures. He rejected those critics who viewed Japanese culture as merely "the daughter of China" and argued for "a special spirit" in Japanese culture despite the Chinese influence. That "special spirit" became all the more salient in modern literature, indicated Zhou, when the Japanese were seemingly overwhelmed by Western influence: "Japan's new literature ... does not merely imitate [foreign] ideas and forms; it takes the spirit of it, instills it into its own heart, and pours it out again. It hence becomes creative emulation [chuangzao de moni]."[42]

At the heart of this "creative emulation," as Zhou saw it, was an orientation toward independent attitudes and individual expression, for the purpose of imitation was to create one's own. In Mori Ōgai, one of the greatest Japanese modern writers, Zhou found the best example of this unique spirit. Zhou regarded Mori as one of the two most important figures—along with Tsubouchi Shōyō—in the development of modern Japanese literature, because Mori had translated many important European works into Japanese. But the uniqueness of Mori lay not in merely bringing in, or blindly "imitating," foreign forms. Unlike those who followed the vogue, said Zhou, Mori took a "transcendent attitude" when naturalism dominated the literary scene. "Although my cup is not big, I prefer to drink from my own," quoted Zhou with admiration from Mori's story collection *Trickling Drops (Kenteki)*. "That is the profile of Mori," who, in Zhou's eyes, achieved a "rational" and "transparent" attitude toward life and literary creation.[43]

This unique lesson of "creative emulation" aside, Zhou also urged Chinese to study Japan "even for pragmatic reasons," for learning whatever was useful from Japanese experiences in either old or new culture. On the one hand, the Chinese could rediscover their lost culture from Japan, because "Japan was the earliest to begin communication with China, and thus keeps much of China's ancient culture, that is, the cultural traits before the Five Dynasties

(907–960)." Information on the phonetics transition of the Chinese language during the Han and Tang periods, for instance, could be found in the Japanese reading of Chinese words, or the forms and styles of stage performance in the pre-Yuan period Chinese drama could be seen in Japanese kabuki, which had long become obsolete in China. In Zhou's view, the many "similar profiles" between Chinese and Japanese stage presentations resembled the cultural transition from Greece to Rome; studying Chinese ancient drama through Japanese performance, then, would be "just like nowadays rediscovering those long lost Greek comedies in Roman works." On the other hand, Japan's new culture "also can provide help to us," because Japan "has started earlier and made progress faster." The Chinese should feel "grateful" to Japan in Zhou's view, for "having retained so much cultural heritage for us yet at the same time showed us ways of experimenting with new cultures."[44]

The Heart of Japanese Culture: Reconsidering Lafcadio Hearn

Arrogance, of course, was only one of the serious problems for which Zhou faulted his fellow Chinese, though it was a particularly perceptive reminder at a moment when the Chinese seemed to have assumed a cosmopolitan posture during the heyday of the May Fourth Movement. To alert the Chinese to their backwardness in comparison to Japan's achievement, however, was only the beginning of Zhou's work. Once he started this process of introducing the true Japan to the Chinese, Zhou realized there was much more to say about Japan's "true glory." As he charted his own route to the heart of Japanese culture, he found himself departing from the established Western authority on Japan.

Already in 1916 and 1917, before the New Culture Movement was in full swing, Zhou had made attempts to bring his personal interest in Japanese literature into public discourse when he wrote a few tentative, brief essays on Japanese haiku, *obon* dance, and *ukiyo-e*.[45] In 1919, following his call for "human literature," he wrote "Japanese Poetry," a long, more comprehensive essay on *uta,* haiku, *senryū,* and the significant difference between Chinese and Japanese poetry; it was published two years later in *Short Stories Monthly (Xiaoshuo yuebao).* An ambitious endeavor, "Japanese Poetry" shared one thing with Zhou's 1916 essay on haiku: both took Lafcadio Hearn, the Greek-born American Japanophile, as the authority on the subject. Citing Hearn's comment on a unique quality of "allusion" in Japanese poetry, Zhou in 1916 considered it "a very insightful observation." Writing three years later, Zhou once more began with Hearn: "Poetry in Japan is universal as air," quoted Zhou from Hearn's *In Ghostly Japan*. Again taking the lead from Hearn, Zhou added the two reasons that contributed to the pervasiveness of poetry in Japan: it was the result of "Japanese people's innate sensitivity to arts that makes them especially responsive to natural beauty," as well as the nature of Japanese language, a polysyllabic one that required simplicity.[46]

But Zhou had more to say than merely praising, à la Hearn, the aesthetic taste and skill of a poetic people. Already in the 1916 essay on haiku, he had noted that Kobayashi Issa (1763–1827), his favorite poet, wrote "marvelous lines on human feelings and universal truth *[renqing wuli]*." That point developed into an overarching line in his 1919 essay, as he presented several *uta* and haiku in translation, demonstrating how modern poets such as Yosano Akiko, Yosano Hiroshi, and Tamura Kōkon wrote lines of *uta* with "crossed effect of functions" between the human voice and the pale blossom of the morning glory, or about "the sorrow of modern men who wanted to escape pain through merrymaking." He also presented Issa's few lines of poetry in translation, to make visible the way the poet "uses a humorous brush to write out true feelings." Zhou made no specific citations of *senryū,* the satiric haiku, though he stressed the worthy quality of the genre for its "description of human feelings in subtlety and sharp sarcasm."[47]

This balanced emphasis on both poetic taste and the expression of human feelings tilted toward the latter after 1921, the year Zhou suffered a long bout with pleurisy, which confined him to the hospital and bed for nine months.[48] How deeply this flirtation with death had sent Zhou to reflections on the incongruity of human hopes and reality, of the infinite task of change and the finiteness of individual life, may be seen in a sudden outburst of poetry writing. "I have too many dreams, / A knock on the door, / wakes me up right from my dreams; / How cruel are you, the sound … / Where is the light of dawn? / My strength is too small" wrote Zhou after a temporary recovery in early March. He felt paralyzed by the impossible task of reconciling the irreconcilable: "Many footprints left on a wild field, / pointing out the roads taken by the foregoers; / Some direct east, some west, and still some go straight south; / ... But I cannot decide which to take, / being left at the crossroads, staring aimlessly ahead."[49] And the allusion to a crossroads was made specific in his letter to a friend in June, while Zhou was recuperating in a temple in the western hills on the suburbs of Beijing:

> The vacillation and chaos in my mind has gone to the extreme recently. I like and respect them all: Tolstoy's altruist love and Nietzsche's superman, Communism and eugenics, the instruction by Jesus, Buddha, Confucius, or Laozi, as well as scientific logic; yet I cannot reconcile and coordinate them so as to pave out a passable thoroughfare. I only put all these thoughts pell-mell in my head, which has indeed become like a grocery in the countryside.[50]

The vibrant contest among various theories and ideals was not merely a state in Zhou's mind, but a national phenomenon in 1920 and 1921. The time provided opportunities and choices and demanded resolution. The various schools of thought Zhou mentioned had been penetrating Chinese minds for decades, some for centuries; yet the conflict between their appeals might have come especially close to home when *New Youth*, the leading journal of the New Culture movement, took a radical turn after Zhou's colleague Chen Duxiu went to Shanghai to avoid government repression and subsequently turned the weekly into a propaganda instrument for the newly organized Communists. It is not clear whether Zhou knew about the founding of the Communist Party in July 1921, but the radicalization of some intellectuals was made evident by their calls for a total solution to China's problems, an approach that Zhou had viewed as illusory for a long time.

Amid the political oppression of the warlord government and the politicization of the radicals, Zhou sensed a revival of "oppression against freedom of thought." In hopes of sustaining the liberal legacy of the New Culture movement, Zhou after his recuperation opened a column in the literature supplement of *Chen bao* at the beginning of 1922 titled "One's Own Garden." "The so-called one's own garden has a broad latitude," wrote Zhou in his first essay announcing the column. "Whether one plants fruits and vegetables, or medicine herbs, or rose and *di-ding,* one's natural duty is fulfilled as long as he, with his own resolve, does his best to cultivate his big or small ground." To this reaffirmation of a commitment to liberalism he added a specific agenda, "tolerance," upon a broad platform of individualism and humanism. "Literature and arts take the self as the subject and make affecting others as their function; it is both for the individual and for human kind," argued Zhou. "If one uses a grand critical theory to force uniformity, the work of literature and art will lose its only reason for existence even if such an impossible thing became reality." And he considered the principle to have broad implications beyond literature and arts. "Movement and change are the essence of life regardless of the variety of trends, but the development of individuality and an emphasis on creation are the shared direction for both life and literature."[51]

Along these lines of thought on individualist spirit and human tolerance, Zhou directed his Chinese readers to such qualities in Japanese literary and social practice. In 1923, he wrote his first essay on *senryū* to demonstrate its "honest and bighearted attitude toward all human affairs, which makes it superior to other philistine literature." *Senryū* had its shortcoming of indecency, admitted Zhou, for it took such human characters as rakes, pundits, fugitives, or runaway debtors as its main subjects. Yet a good *senryū* "pricks the subtle secrets of human feelings without much poisonous intention," explained Zhou. "We nod while smiling, as we discover the various images of the human world, and we may just feel that the world is even more lovable because of this much human weakness."[52]

And *senryū* was just one example of the empathetic spirit that Zhou found in Japan's popular art of the ordinary people. One Japanese writer in particular would remind him that empathy was the driving force in the dramatic action of *shinjū,* the double suicide, practiced by both the high and low societies. In early July 1923, Zhou rushed to the defense of Arishima Takeo when the news arrived in China that this impassioned writer had committed double suicide with his lover Hatano Akiko. Zhou had been a faithful reader of Arishima's works since the publication of the *Shirakaba;* among them he "liked most 'To the children' ['Chiisaki sha e']" and had just translated it into Chinese. Although the two had never met, Zhou regarded Arishima as one of his "fellow travelers in that wild desert of life," and he admired Arishima's "attitude and criterion toward writing," found in the following lines:

> First, I write because I feel lonely....
> Second, I write because I want to love....
> Thirdly, I write because I want to be loved....
> Fourthly, I write because I want to urge myself forward.

These words must have been echoing in Zhou's mind when he, who also read Arishima's last letters, voiced his view that the dramatic action was "not necessarily just for the reason of a love affair," but an intended statement about life. "We wish to know what caused their death, but want not to make judgment," wrote Zhou, because "no matter what the cause, knowing that they have offered their lives to their feelings or thoughts, solemnity muffles our mouths. We certainly should not toy with life, but neither should we trifle with death."[53] The weight of Arishima's death was probably still with him three years later, when he read another report on a double suicide, this time between a Japanese geisha and a Japanese clerk in Beijing. He took the event as an occasion to write "Double Suicide," expressing his sympathy for those "obsessed men and women" who chose death as the only escape from predicament. "Their wish to 'be reborn upon the lotus seat' may be naive and laughable," wrote Zhou, "yet we dare not laugh at them, but instead wish them fulfillment of that great hope, and indeed go to that Buddha land and resume the unfulfilled relation from this world." The continuous appeal of *shinjū* as a "common practice" in some modern Japanese, once again, made Zhou reflect on Chinese attitudes. *Shinjū* "is not to be found among the Chinese" because they "had never known the weight of life,... not to mention an understanding of something as powerful as death."[54]

By 1925, Zhou's unremitting quest for what was true about Japanese culture reached its climax when he wrote "The Beauty of Human Feelings in Japan" to challenge a claim, popularized by well-known Western Japanophiles—Lafcadio Hearn and Paul Louis Couchoud in particular—that took "loyalty to the ruler *[zhongjun]*" as "Japan's national character." "Loyalty to the ruler," argued Zhou with confidence and emphasis, "was originally the Chinese stuff, though it has been coated recently with a layer of German print; after all it is not their permanent national character." Zhou urged his fellow Chinese to discover the true Japan through common sense. Just as "wearing casual clothing is our normal state," the "true face of the Japanese can be seen, not through watching their dignified posture with the double swords, but through observing their manner of drinking tea and arranging flowers." Although using education to instill loyalty to the emperor had led to Japan's success in modern wars, "that is simply the result of outside influence." There were "things in Japanese culture many times superior to that of China's," asserted Zhou, and the "strength of Japanese national character lies in the opposite direction, that is, the abundant human feelings." Such "is the best virtue of Japan, and why we feel intimacy with its culture."[55]

Like his 1920 essay "Japanophile," "The Beauty of Human Feelings in Japan" can be read as another critical point in Zhou's long discourse on Japanese culture. In the long scroll that Zhou continued to unroll for his Chinese readers to view scenes of Japanese culture, one can always find the original colors by going back to these two essays. They constitute links to many of his views on life and art, on the relations between culture and politics, and on the intimate connections between China and Japan. They were the two pillars underpinning his many essays about Japan. And his insights were not missed by others, as Hu Shi tersely put it: "Among the one hundred thousand Chinese [who went to study in Japan], how many are there like Mr. Zhou Zuoren who can truly appreciate Japan's culture?"[56]

"Japan is China's Enemy"

In appearance, Sino-Japanese relations in the years after the May Fourth Movement were perhaps the most hopeful since the fiasco of the Twenty-One Demands. Having finally emerged from the horror of the machine gun and poison gas of the Great War, the world looked forward to peace and prosperity in the 1920s. Power politics, too, was reoriented under American leadership and the Washington System in 1922, which bound its signers to America's principle of the "Open Door" in China. For most of the decade, Japan's foreign policy came under the care of the more cosmopolitan Shidehara Kijūrō, who considered cooperation with the West as the best way to protect Japanese interests in China. The spirit of Shidehara diplomacy was summarized in a new phrase, "co-existence and co-prosperity *[kyōson kyōei]*," which came along with Japan's officially initiated projects at promoting cultural exchanges.

Yet this new diplomacy had no new foundation, but instead remained dependent on the old practice of unequal relations defined by the treaty system, created by gunboats over the previous six decades. While Zhou wrote so fondly about "the beauty of human feelings in Japan" in 1925, he seemed unable to hold back from striking a disturbing note: "In contemporary Japan these two elements [the beauty of human feelings and loyalty to the state] seem to coexist on equal terms, hence we still feel bits and pieces of brilliance and beauty among many unpleasant things."[57]

The "many unpleasant things" had long been irritating him, and he had made his anger heard in his 1920 essay "Japanophile." In the few years that followed Zhou had attempted a constructive course to bridge the two peoples and two cultures by introducing Japanese culture to his fellow Chinese. But obstacles soon appeared in his way, and his first sobering experience was precisely the loudly proclaimed cultural diplomacy of the Japanese government.

In 1923, after a four-year debate, the Japanese Diet finally decided on the remission of the Boxer Indemnity to China for cultural purposes. The decision, made some thirteen years after America's move to remit part of its share of the Boxer Indemnity for educational purposes, was a belated but anxious effort to maintain "cultural and moral parity with the West" in its influence in China, as historian Sophia Lee aptly puts it.[58] The legislation led to the creation of the China Cultural Affairs Bureau (Tai-Shi Bunka Jimukyoku) to supervise various cultural exchange programs in China. In historian See Heng Teow's words, it "marked an unprecedented development in demonstrating Japan's readiness to promote its cultural image abroad on a planned, long-term basis." The bureau would be simply the first cornerstone of the whole official apparatus that Japan would create in the next two decades to carry out its cultural diplomacy on the continent.[59]

Preparations by the Japanese embassy in Beijing had already begun in the spring when it invited Beijing University, one of the recipients of the remitted funds, to join the effort. In mid-March, Zhou was sent by the school, along with his colleague Zhang Fengju, another Japan-educated professor, to meet Japanese consul Yoshida Shigeru to discuss the application of the remitted funds.

One result of their discussion was to form an eighteen-member Sino-Japanese Learned Society (Zhong-Ri Xueshu Xiehui), inaugurated in October 1923. Its Chinese participants included Zhou, Zhang, and a number of professors from Beijing University who had either studied or sojourned in Japan during their youth. Besides a few scholars, its Japanese members also included such figures as Lieutenant General Banzai Riihachirō, the famous "China Hand" who served as a military adviser to the Chinese government, and Major Doihara Kenji, Jiang Baili's fellow cadet at the Army Officers' Academy and now an intelligence officer of the Japanese army who later earned the nickname "Lawrence of Manchuria" for his expansionist activities in China.[60]

While the Sino-Japanese Learned Society remained a nominal body of cultural exchange only, Zhou's initial optimism about the official participation in Sino-Japanese cooperation quickly evaporated. His change of mind is found in his discussion of anti-Japanese boycotts, as his view evolved from opposition to endorsement of the action. "Most of those who join the anti-Japanese boycotts reject all kinds of Japanese indiscriminately, which generates hatred between peoples, and to which I disapprove strongly," explained Zhou in 1920. "I am not a statist, nor a socialist, but I oppose the anti-Japanese boycott.... I believe that the anti-Japanese boycott is a product of statism," Zhou wrote, reaffirming his position again in the summer of 1923.[61] Yet by the end of 1925, he angrily called out: "Those who truly love China naturally should curse China, just as those Chinese who truly love Japan must become absolute Japanophobes." "'Japan is China's Enemy,' please remember this," wrote Zhou a few months later. He even urged Chinese to "broaden" the activity of anti-Japanese boycotts beyond rallies, public speeches, and distributing leaflets. "The methods ... on the one hand, should be educating our Chinese to destroy the illusion about same-race and same-culture, thus plant the idea of 'Japan is China's Enemy' deeply in our hearts; on the other hand, there should be efforts toward a solid movement aimed at undermining Japanese influence." And the Chinese must "actively help the revolutionary movements in Japan and Korea, just as Japanese *shishi* render support to Chinese revolution."[62]

The change in Zhou's attitude toward the popular anti-Japanese boycott was decisively influenced by two pivotal events in 1923 and 1924. The first took place in Japan amid the popular hysteria against Koreans and socialists shortly after the great Kantō earthquake. On September 16, 1923, some two weeks after the disastrous earthquake, fires, and massacre of foreigners, the anarchist Ōsugi Sakae, together with his wife Itō Noe and his six-year-old nephew, was apprehended by a military police captain, Amakasu Masahiko. Then, at the military police headquarters in Tokyo, the gendarme strangled the couple and the child and threw their bodies into a well. Although the authorities tried to cover up the incident, news of the murders broke out, and Amakasu was brought to trial.[63]

In China, Zhou was so astonished by the "open murder" that he called it "the most frightening event after the earthquake."[64] When news of a public petition—along with a demonstration of fifty thousand people—for a reduction of Amakasu's ten-year sentence reached China some twenty days later, Zhou immediately sent another comment to the *Chen Bao,* with words of great apprehension and disappointment: "If the government releases or reduces the sentence of Amakasu, and the people [in Japan] do not protest, that will bring shame on the Japanese nation"; "I always feel suspicious about the death sentence, yet I support without reservation putting Amakasu Masahiko to death, ... for that is demanded by humanity and justice." He predicted that "the anti-Japanese sentiment will rise higher" if such were the result, warning that Japan was about to lose the goodwill of the small number of intellectuals and become "truly isolated among Asian nations."[65] As it turned out, Amakasu was indeed released after three years in prison and sent to Manchuria, where he became an active participant in the 1931 Manchurian Incident.

The Ōsugi Incident had not yet faded in Zhou's mind when another event close to home directed his attention to Japan's official intentions toward China's republic. In early November 1924, the Chinese government under a new caretaker cabinet acted upon popular demand and decided to evict Puyi, the abdicated emperor, from the palace, where he had retained his court and lived a royal life since the 1911 Revolution.[66] Zhou, who witnessed Zhang Xun's abortive restoration in 1917 and always viewed the surviving court as a potential force of reaction, rejoiced at the "completion of the 1911 Revolution." Toward the end of November, he even wrote a long letter to the abdicated emperor, who had now finally renounced his title, and advised him to "take some more lessons and advance into high school, then after graduation go to study abroad." He even had a plan laid out for the eighteen-year-old: "I think it is best for you to study in Britain or Germany, then you should take a trip to Athens; when you accomplish your study and return, we hope to invite you to Beijing University and assume (or rather open) a lectureship on Greek literature."[67]

But Zhou's enthusiasm was instantly dampened. Just a day before Zhou wrote those encouraging words, Puyi had taken refuge in the Japanese embassy.[68] Although eight years would pass before Puyi once again ascended to the throne, becoming emperor of Japan-created Manzhouguo (Manchukuo) in 1932, this move was Puyi's first step toward his service to Japanese expansion in China. Meanwhile, the sudden turn of events made Zhou "very regretful" for the teenager, though he was even more outraged by foreign countries' interference in this Chinese internal matter. Following the eviction, the British, Japanese, and Dutch ministers sent their protests to the Chinese foreign minister, demanding that the Chinese government guarantee Puyi's safety. Of all the foreign pressures, the most active, as Zhou found, was the Japanese propaganda machine in China. *Shuntian Shibao,* the semiofficial organ of the Japanese Foreign Ministry,[69] fabricated sensational reports of how "so-and-so empress dowager sacrifices her life for the Qing dynasty," called the eviction "bullying widows and the orphan," and described the event as part of the movement of the Reds.[70] Another Japanese organ, *Shanhai,* openly attacked the Chinese government's action and called the eviction a signal of "the end of the republic."[71]

Zhou listened to these waves of propaganda and understood them as more than isolated incidents. "I don't know what is the intention of this author," he retorted in a commentary on the *Shanhai* article. "Does this comply to international protocol? Even if the author is a maniac, why does the Japanese consulate general in Shanghai not come out and stop him?"[72] In the foreign protests he saw clearly that the powers wanted to retain the reactionary forces within China. "When there was the restoration [in 1917], why didn't you come out to interfere?" he wrote in another commentary on a report by the *Shuntian Shibao.* "If then you considered it as a Chinese internal affair and did not interfere, what reason do you have for saying such nonsense this time?"[73]

The foreign objection to Puyi's eviction was not the first time that the powers attempted to intervene in China's internal affairs, yet its timing was critical for Zhou's developing approach to his self-assigned mission. Already in 1922 he had voiced apprehension over the "rise of two tendencies" in intellectual circles, one in favor of restoring ancient ways, and the other leaning toward xenophobia.[74] Up to 1923 he had been focusing on fighting the close-minded xenophobics by making constructive efforts at introducing Japanese culture to his fellow Chinese. But the events in 1923 and 1924 made him more vigilant about the combined threat from reactionary forces within and without. Thus he wrote on New Year's Day of 1925, when Puyi was still under the Japanese legation's "protection":

> My thoughts have finally returned to nationalism this year.... In the May Fourth years I gave many pedantic talks and dreamed of cosmopolitanism. Last spring I cut down its scope and modified it to Asianism. When the Qing court renounced the imperial title and moved out of the palace, survivors of the old dynasty, the Japanese *rōnin*, and British imperialists all made a great deal of fuss; their conspiracies are still going on at this moment. That makes me finally aware of my own stupidity; I realize that the foundation of the republic has not yet stabilized. Now one must be realistic, and everything should begin with nationalism.[75]

To counterattack their joint conspiracies, Zhou aimed at three tools of Japanese expansionism: first, the Japanese press in the Chinese language, "one of the most virulent means" of Japanese imperialism, and especially the *Shuntian Shibao,* "the most virulent of them all,"[76] which "opposes anything that is beneficial to China and advocates everything that is harmful to China"; second, the so-called "China Hands" from Japan who with superficial knowledge about the old China helped to perpetrate "rotten customs"; and third, Japanese colonialists, the "unscrupulous, immoral, and perfidious elements that are unwanted in Japanese society."[77] By 1928, his essays attacking these three evil forces had outnumbered those on Japanese culture, and most were published in the popular newspapers and magazines such as the *Jing Bao Supplement, Chen Bao*

Supplement, and *Yusi.* He hoped that his writings would eventually arouse Chinese readers to resist the imperialist organ that "enslaves" Chinese minds. To his disappointment, few in Beijing seemed to take the detrimental propaganda of *Shuntian Shibao* seriously; some, like the Chamber of Commerce, even echoed its views. This apathy, which resembled so much the indifference to *New Life* that he and Lu Xun had attempted two decades ago, was disheartening. Looking back to that four-year battle with *Shuntian Shibao,* Zhou remarked years later that he was then like Don Quixote, "fighting with that monstrous windmill all alone."[78]

Zhou's participation in the Sino-Japanese Learned Society had already ended by the mid-1920s. Disappointed with Japan's meddling in the Puyi incident, he had withdrawn from the society in late 1924, and subsequently the society was dissolved. In 1925, however, he was again drawn into a Sino-Japanese Education Association (Zhong-Ri Jiaoyuhui), sponsored by the Tō-A Dōbunkai and joined by the same members of the disbanded Sino-Japanese Learned Society. Zhou found little appeal in this second joint venture, but he nonetheless accepted its presidency as a mere title without much responsibility. The major project of the association, the Sino-Japanese Academy (Zhong-Ri Xueyuan) in Tianjin, turned out to be a failure in judgment; all he could remember about it was its administrators' indulgence in fishing, drinking, and womanizing.[79] In other words, the Japanese government-sponsored Sino-Japanese cultural projects only reproduced more of the "China Hands" whom he utterly despised. Official Sino-Japanese cultural relations in those years might appear "relatively cordial."[80] But, guided by the goal of promoting Japan's interests in China, Japan's cultural projects from the beginning failed to win Chinese hearts, including those of Japanophiles like Zhou.

By 1925, Zhou's promotion of Chinese understanding of Japan had attained some success within academic circles. Under his influence, Beijing University established a Department of Eastern Literature; Zhou was appointed chair and taught the course on Edo literature.[81] Beyond the classroom, however, his efforts had achieved little; while general ignorance about Japan prevailed, the Chinese public swung between apathy and sudden bursts of Japanophobia. But he was not yet completely discouraged, as he wrote with candor and resolution in late 1925:

To be honest, Japan is one of the countries that I love, just like I love ancient Greece.... I can live happily almost everywhere in Japan, just as I do in China. Yet I am after all a Chinese.... My opinion nevertheless differs greatly from that of many average Japanese, and I cannot help but feel angry and hateful toward some of their opinions and activities. I feel angry because they hurt my self-respect as a Chinese, I feel hateful because they have disturbed my fondness of Japan. I have not yet destroyed my dream because of that; but I am not a transcendent sage without hatred.... Therefore I no longer complain, but continue to do this: love what is lovable, hate what is hateful; being both pro-Japanese and anti-Japanese, for that may just be the only workable approach.[82]

6 The End of a Pan-Asian Vision

In 1925, the Guomindang reached the threshold of generational change of leadership when Sun Yat-sen, the party's founder, lay dying of liver cancer after he reached Beijing in December 1924. He had not been able to proceed to the planned negotiations with the northern powers for national unification, and the task was left to his successors. Knowing that the recent revival of his revolutionary movement owed much to Soviet assistance, Sun made an emphatic wish in a parting letter to the Soviet Union. "Fate is forcing me to give up the mission I have not yet accomplished," he said in this dictated letter. "In order to liberate China from the semicolonial shackle imposed by imperialism, I have instructed the Guomindang to continue the work for the movement of national revolution and to cooperate with you for that purpose. I believe with certainty that your government will continue to give help to our country."[1]

The timing for a national revolution never seemed so good as in 1925. Not only was the Guomindang in much better shape, having reorganized and expanded itself with the assistance of Russian advisers and Chinese Communists and trained a small but disciplined and spirited army. There was a rising mass awakening across the country as well. Since the late 1910s, the labor movement had been developing at an unprecedented scale and speed. There had been twenty-five strikes in 1918, and the number rose to ninety-one in 1922. On May Day 1924, workers marched in Guangzhou, Wuchang, Hanyang, and Shanghai, demanding better wages and an eight-hour work day. A year later, delegates representing 166 unions and 540,000 workers held a congress in Guangdong and formed an All-China General Union. Meanwhile, labor agitation had been going on without pause in Shanghai since early 1925, when strikes erupted in Japanese-owned cotton mills. On May 30, it escalated into a nationwide movement when the British police inspector, without warning, gave the order to fire into the demonstrating crowd, killing ten and wounding more than fifty. Instantly, strikes spread beyond factories to shops and schools throughout Shanghai, followed by many anti-imperialist demonstrations and protests all over the country.[2]

In the next two or three years, the Guomindang would ride this torrent of popular nationalism to national power. But before it unified the country under a more centralized government, it had to deal with an internal schism that had been developing even before Sun passed the leadership to the next generation. The force that gained upper hand would put an end to the pro-Russian policy, and Dai Jitao would be one of the pivotal few, with battle cries to rally an anti-Communist movement and with efforts in turning foreign policy toward a pro-Japan direction, to leave a permanent mark in China's political history and China's relations with Japan.

Turning Rightward: Personal Odyssey to Partisan Ideology

When Sun died on March 25, 1925, Dai was one of nine Guomindang leaders who waited by his side. He was no longer an impulsive young man who wrote indignant commentaries on imperialism and on labor conditions. Long association with Sun as his personal secretary and active involvement in the party's diplomacy and propaganda had firmly established his position within the highest circles of the party leadership. When Sun moved toward an alliance with the Soviet Union, however, Dai for the first time remained distant from Sun's leadership.

By 1925, Dai, who earlier had been closely associated with the Communists, had become a staunch anti-Communist warrior. His about-face took place just when his Communist friends began to organize a formal party, and it appeared all too sudden and confusing to the other participants. Yang Zhihua, the young student who had come to work at *Weekend Review*, recalled hearing Dai cry one autumn day in 1920. She was told that Dai had refused to join the just-formed Communist group because "he was afraid it contradicts Sun's Three Principles of the People." Dai, who had a propensity to wail under stress, cried this time because he "was shaken, for he cannot match words with deeds, while he could not endure others' criticism at the same time." Other people who had joined the early Communist movement in Shanghai, including Shao Lizi and Chen Gongbo, wrote accounts similar to Yang's.[3]

If ideological differences kept Dai from joining the Communist organization, a personal crisis brought him closer to a turning point and colored his outlook on life and politics. In the autumn of 1922, Dai was sent by Sun to Sichuan, his home province, to mediate the civil conflict and to recruit local forces into the revolutionary movement. Midway toward their destination, at Hankou, Dai and his comrades met several Sichuanese who, as members of certain warring factions, were planning new fighting. Dai's efforts to dissuade them from opening fire met with outright rejection. Already depressed and hoping to rejuvenate himself with this trip home, Dai after the encounter suddenly turned "deadly dumb-stricken," as he recalled later. "I could not hear what others said to me, nor could I see the scenic views around me." He felt he "had no will to live." That night, as their ship approached Yichang, a city in the upper reaches of the Yangtze River, Dai stepped out of his cabin and jumped overboard. After drifting downstream for hours, he was finally rescued and revived by a fisherman.[4]

It was extraordinary that Dai should so react to this frustrated mediation, for until then he had never been crushed by any of the weightier failures in his decade-long political career. Although his official biographer attributes Dai's near-fatal act to his frustration over the official mission, Dai himself admitted, four years after the incident, that he was then in a depression, which "had taken root in 1917, was exacerbated in 1920, and by 1922 had gone beyond cure." The cause was "a mistaken love" started "five or six years" before the suicide attempt. And he blamed himself for being unable to reconcile his "romance" and his "conscience," and the conflict was like a struggle "between heaven and man" that finally sent him to "bewilderment."[5]

These words of self-reproach, written with the intention "to provide a lesson to the sons and nephews of my next generation," were candid about the nature of the incident. And it was indeed a complicated affair with no easy solution. Dai had been married in 1911 to Niu Youheng, a girl from a well-to-do family in the famous silk-producing town of Huzhou in the suburbs of Shanghai. Four years Dai's senior, Niu had become a devout Buddhist at a very young age. That Dai had more reverence than affection for his wife is tellingly demonstrated by the way he addressed her as "elder sister" *(jiejie)* throughout their married life.[6] In the mid-1910s, Dai seemed to have found more freedom and new pleasure in his personal life during his exile in Japan. The routine of his night life, as he recalled with contentment, was visiting geisha houses after running the day's errands for Sun Yat-sen.[7] By late 1916, when Dai ended his exile and returned to China, one Japanese woman had borne him a son. Jiang Jieshi (Chiang Kai-shek), who had become a close friend of Dai during the exile and had also been acquainted with the Japanese woman, stepped in to save his friend from embarrassment and family dispute. He adopted the child, who has been known as Jiang Weiguo ever since.[8] It was in the wake of this family confusion and crisis that Dai was involved in yet another affair: he fell in love with Zhao Wenshu, his wife's niece, who came to help manage his household in 1919 when it was in disarray. Unable to extricate himself, he sought death as his salvation.[9]

Although a failure, this first suicide attempt—there would be several more later in his life—moved Dai to reexamine himself and led to a decisive change in outlook. Repenting for his "many sins in romance," he cursed "Shanghai, this cesspit that degraded humanity" for causing his moral corruption. He laid blame not just on himself, however, but more on the influence of new thoughts and ideas popular during the May Fourth era. He regretted his "muddleheadedness" in "importing the theories from the West in such a confusion." He also angrily blamed "the Communists who follow blindly the few slogans of Communism imported from the West and use such slogans to cover up their own pursuit of sexual desire and appetite." The suicide attempt, then, rescued him spiritually, because, while floating on the Yangtze River Dai believed that he saw "Buddha light," a glowing white circle; he regained the desire to live only at that moment and became a devout Buddhist afterward.[10]

While Dai was in Sichuan recuperating from his spiritual disorientation, the reform of Guomindang moved forward by leaps and bounds. When he finally emerged from seclusion and returned to Shanghai at the end of 1923, Dai was informed that in his absence he had been appointed as a member of the reform committee of the party. Yet he found himself in strong disagreement with

the new policy, fearing that the Guomindang was being taken over
by the Communists. To Liao Zhongkai, another left-wing leader of
the Guomindang who came to Shanghai to persuade him to join
the activities in Guangzhou, Dai was unyielding in his refusal to accept any positions in the party, and he made clear his opinions on
the coalition: that the Communists who joined the Guomindang
should have only one party membership, and that the Guomindang
should not accept Soviet funds.[11] Only under Sun's orders did he
reluctantly make three trips to Guangzhou in 1924, where he attended the party's first national congress and assumed his post as
minister of propaganda and member of the standing committee of
the Guomindang's supervisory committee. He returned to Shanghai's suburbs after each trip angry and frustrated over what he saw
as the increasing Communist control of the political situation.[12]

Out of deference, Dai refrained from announcing his opposition while Sun was alive. Within the Guomindang, however, resistance to the alliance with the Communists never let up. In June
1924, Xie Chi, Deng Zeru, and Zhang Ji—all senior party members and members of the Guomindang's supervisory committee—
submitted a motion of impeachment to the central committee, recommending a suspension of the practice of admitting Communists
into the Guomindang.[13] At Guangdong University and Huangpu
Military Academy, anti-Communists formed organizations such as
the Society of People's Rights (Minquan She) and the People's Society (Min She) to resist Communist influence among youth.[14]

All the discontent and opposition toward the policy of alli-
ances with the Soviet Union and the Chinese Communists surfaced when Sun's death left a leadership vacuum in the already
divided Guomindang. Within two months, the first wave of the anti-
Communist movement arrived with an ideological campaign under
Dai's lead. During April and May 1925, he lectured in Guangzhou
and Shanghai on the meanings of Sun's Three Principles of the
People, establishing himself as the interpreter of Sun's thoughts.
Then he set up a "Jitao Office" in Shanghai and wrote two pamphlets: "The Philosophical Foundation of Sun Yat-senism" ("Sun
Wen zhuyi zhexue de jichu") and "Chinese Revolution and the
Chinese Nationalist Party" ("Zhongguo gemin yu Zhongguo Guomindang"), which appeared in print in June and July. The response to Dai's battle cries was dramatic. "Chinese Revolution and
the Chinese Nationalist Party" ran through several printings of

more than one hundred thousand copies, while more than ten thousand copies had been burned by opposition groups.[15] Under the guidance of Dai's theory, right-wing students in the Huangpu Military Academy organized the Association of Sun Yat-senism (Sun Wen Zhuyi Xuehui) to counterattack the Communist-led United Association of Young Chinese Soldiers (Zhongguo Qingnian Junren Lianhehui). As similar organizations appeared in Shanghai, Beijing, Sichuan, Changsha, and Changde, the grass-roots support for the party purge in 1927 began to grow.[16]

None of the other voices within the Guomindang had achieved the same effect as Dai's. Unlike many opponents of Sun's policy of alliance with the Soviet Union and the Communists who were bogged down in partisan matters, Dai elevated the conflict to the height of principle. The most distinctive tendency, and the most instigative in effect in all his lectures and these two pamphlets, was his strategy to "nativize" Sun's Three Principles of the People. Quoting Sun from his first pamphlet, "The Philosophical Foundation of Sun Yat-senism," Dai wrote, "The Three Principles of the People is the principle of national salvation." Sun's thought was a synthesis of the ancient and the modern, added Dai, because "it inherits the authentic ethics from ancient China, . . . and creates a new theory based on an observation of the economic organization, state system, international relations and various other systems in the modern world." What made Sun's thoughts a theory of national salvation, explained Dai, was his appreciation of "the true meaning of China's own ethics," which he summarized into the neo-Confucian virtues of wisdom, benevolence, and bravery, all unified through "sincerity" in behavior. "The rise and fall of a nation depends on self-confidence in national culture," argued Dai. "Only with national confidence can [a nation's] culture be created. Only through continuous efforts at creating culture and developing culture can a nation gain life and have a prosperous life."[17]

And from that nativist perspective Dai further insisted on a critical difference between Sun's philosophy and Marx's Communism. The two ideals differed not in their final goals to improve people's livelihood, noted Dai, but in their ideological sources and approaches. Whereas Sun's people's livelihood "is founded on China's native ethical philosophy and political philosophy," Communism was "very simple, based on Marx's historical materialism." Whereas Communism "takes the approach of direct revolutionary action by the proletarian class and proposes class dictatorship," Sun's national revolution was "a revolution based on unification of all classes." Dai maintained that there were no clear class demarcations in China, only the differences between the leaders and the followers, or the enlightened and unenlightened. China's approach to national revolution, therefore, derived not from the logic of class struggle but from the age-old ethics of benevolence.[18]

Turning to the current reality, Dai viewed "losing national self-confidence" in China's great tradition as the greatest danger to the Chinese revolution. To rescue the revolution, Dai urged Guomindang members to cleanse the spiritual disease within the party —the rightist tendency that focused on personal interest and encouraged favoritism, and the leftist tendency that made the national revolution just empty talk. As he had done in personal correspondence and internal discussions before, he now openly proposed mandatory registration of party membership and a termination of Communist activities within the Guomindang so that the party could enforce discipline and assume the leadership of the national revolution. Since the alliance with the Soviet Union still remained Guomindang's policy and enjoyed popular support, Dai avoided a frontal attack on Russia and instead tried to emphasize the theme of China's independence: "For its national independence and national freedom, China has the need to form an intimate relation with Russia; for the world revolutionary movement, too, it has the need to make shared efforts with Soviet Russia. Yet the Chinese must always recognize clearly their own needs, especially to respect their own independence. They should not throw away their own independence to depend on Soviet Russia, nor should they forget their own needs to follow Soviet Russia."[19]

Dai's intention to prepare an anti-Communist ideological climate was well understood by his opponents. Michael Borodin, the Comintern representative in Guangzhou, now singled Dai out as a great danger and placed him among the five evils in China, along with imperialism, warlords, comprador capitalists, and Guomindang rightists.[20] Chen Duxiu, once a friend of Dai in organizing the study group on Communism, wrote in *Xiangdao Weekly* to criticize Dai's rejection of the class-struggle theory.[21] And the radical youth depicted Dai Jitao in a caricature "carrying Sun Yat-sen's idol into a Confucian temple."[22] But their "empty talk" proved no real match for a nationalist party that claimed the inheritance of its deceased leader's ideology and controlled his painstakingly built new army. Before long, the pro-Russian policy would be discarded, and the Communists, both Russian and Chinese, would be purged from the country and the Guomindang.

The 1927 Mission: Leap to Greater-Asianism

On several occasions during his campaign to nativize the Three Principles of the People, Dai had hinted at an international alternative to the Soviet Union. Speaking to the cadets of the Army Officers' Academy in Guangzhou in late spring of 1925, Dai said, "Japan is [geographically] the closest to us," and it had been pursuing a nationalism based on the belief of the unique origin of the Yamato race. The Japanese "thus become very strong," indicated Dai, though their nationalism was aimed at "controlling the world" and hence was "in conflict with the Principle of People's Rights."[23] Elsewhere, Dai praised Sun's Pan-Asianism speech at Kobe for "expressing most clearly his central ideas," though he quickly added that Sun "was not an ordinary Pan-Asianist." "If you take a look at all his works," argued Dai, "his proposal for the alliance of the oppressed peoples in theory is not limited to only those in Asia, but includes the weak and small nations all over the world." Here was the relevance of Japan to China's future: "China can indeed become the base of universal peace if she revives the nation and reinvigorates national morale. We only need to look at that very small Japan, whose rise to power had so inspired the nationalist movement in the East." Although it was regrettable that Japan had once "abandoned Eastern morality by following European imperialism, and obstructed Eastern nations' solidarity with its annexation of Ryūkyū and Korea," yet how different it could have been, speculated Dai, if a strong Japan had followed the benevolent Asian morality and taken the responsibility to strengthen Asia in the past thirty years![24]

And developments within China, indeed, would give Dai another opportunity to pursue that alluring vision of a Sino-Japanese alliance. In the two years following Sun's death, conflict within the Guomindang-Communist united front intensified as the national revolution moved north with the commencement of the Northern Expedition in the summer of 1926. The whole country was galvanized by this "Great Revolution" as workers, peasants, and students rose to assist and join the revolutionary force while it marched north. The expedition now brought Jiang Jieshi to the forefront of both the military campaign and power struggle. A pragmatic moderate, Jiang had chosen to focus on his duties as president of the Huangpu Military Academy while keeping his distance from the right wing's campaigns against the Communists. Yet in the spring prior to the Northern Expedition, in the so-called "Zhongshan Gunboat Incident" on March 20, 1926, he had succeeded in ousting three Russian advisers and driving the Communist political workers out of the First Corps under his command. His tilt toward the right became more distinguishable in May when the Guomindang, at his initiative, held a plenary meeting of the Central Executive Committee and passed proposals to severely restrict Communist influence within the party. The appointment of Jiang as the head of the National Revolutionary Army for the Northern Expedition was the culmination of these early achievements, and the success of the military campaigns in the middle Yangtze River region further strengthened his position in the political struggle. By the end of 1926, having won decisive battles in the strategic cities of central China, Jiang's military headquarters in Nanchang, Jiangxi Province, emerged as a rival political center to the leftist-controlled Provisional Joint Council in Wuhan.

As the conflict between the two camps intensified in early 1927, Jiang's faction began to look for alternative international support. Their eyes were set on Japan, which appeared to be not only a restrained power, but also friendly in comparison to others. By then, the United States, which was "the most passive" in the words of historian Akira Iriye, had tried to propose a neutralization scheme to protect its interests in Shanghai's international settlement, but it was rejected by the revolutionaries. Britain took a more aggressive approach by sending thirteen thousand marines in January 1927, which greatly antagonized the Chinese. Japan had not merely refused Britain's proposal to jointly send more marines to defend Shanghai; in addition, it made two moves that attracted the attention of Jiang's moderate right wing. In November 1926, Japan's Foreign Minister Shidehara Kijūrō sent Saburi Sadao, chief of the commerce bureau and a delegate to the Special Tariff Conference in China, to travel south and meet top Guomindang officials in Wuhan and Nanchang. The meetings with the southern revolutionaries appeared to go well, as suggested by Saburi's soothing message home on the gap between the Guomindang leaders' anti-imperialist statements and their pragmatic intentions. Then, on January 18, 1927, Shidehara gave a speech to the Diet reiterating his policy of noninterference and emphasizing the need to promote economic cooperation on the basis of "coexistence and co-prosperity." Japan's friendly gestures elicited an instant response. Jiang in a private conversation with Japan's consul at Jiujiang expressed his intention to respect the treaties with foreign countries, honor foreign loans, and protect industrial development.[25]

While Saburi's contacts with the nationalists seemed to have encouraged an optimistic belief in Japan's sympathy with the south,[26] Huang Fu (1880–1936), a politician and diplomat who had served on several cabinets in Beijing, added particular weight to Jiang's decision to pursue the Japan alternative. Once an active member of the Revolutionary Alliance during the 1911 Revolution, Huang had sworn brotherhood with Jiang Jieshi in their youth. Through his diplomatic career, he had also made key connections to the current Japanese foreign policymakers. In 1921, when serving as an adviser in the Chinese delegation to the Washington Conference, Huang had become acquainted with Shidehara Kijūrō, then Japan's minister to the United States, and Saburi Sadao, Shidehara's trusted aide. Huang and Saburi met again in 1925 in Beijing, when each represented his own government at the negotiation table of the Special Tariff Conference. The two men enjoyed their renewed friendship and found themselves sharing a view on the world from the perspective of East Asians.[27]

Shortly after Saburi's trips to the south in late 1926, Huang Fu, who had stayed in touch with important Guomindang leaders in the south while serving the government in the north, received two personally delivered letters from Jiang Jieshi urgently requesting his immediate presence in Jiangxi.[28] Huang arrived at the scenic mountain resort of Lushan in early 1927, where he found Dai Jitao and Zhang Jinjiang, Jiang's two close advisers, as well as other Guomindang leaders, gathered there for the Chinese New Year. Exactly what Huang advised Jiang Jieshi in their many long conversations probably will never be known. Judging by Huang's vigilant warnings against Russian expansion, which he considered "more dangerous than Japan's," and the rapport established during his contacts with Japanese diplomats, it is very likely that Huang offered an optimistic assessment of a goodwill mission to Japan. Dai Jitao, with the broad contacts established during his 1913–1916 exile in Japan, was then chosen to carry out the mission.[29]

Discreetly disguised to avoid the attention of the leftist faction of the Guomindang as he traveled downstream from Jiujiang, Dai arrived in Shanghai to board the Japanese ship *Yamashiro-maru* on February 14, 1927, and reached Moji on Kyūshū three days later.[30] During his six-week visit, Dai gave more than sixty public speeches and held many private talks at various semiofficial banquets and gatherings in his honor in Tokyo, Osaka, and Kobe.[31] He came "by the order of the Guomindang," Dai announced to the Japanese public, to "explain the sincerity of the Chinese people's nationalist revolutionary movement to Japan and gain the understanding of Japanese people, hence to establish the future friendship between the peoples of China and Japan upon the base of international equality, humanity and justice."[32]

Dai's goodwill message struck a responsive chord in business circles. On March 17, he was invited to the Bankers' Club in Tokyo to have luncheon with leading businessmen, where he met Viscount Shibusawa Eiichi, the industrial tycoon and head of the Sino-Japanese Industrial Association. Four days later, on March 21, Shibusawa hosted a small luncheon with nine guests at his mansion in Dai's honor. The Japanese businessmen were anxious to know "the intention of the southern government," whereas Dai spoke of the "sincerity" of the nationalists and reminisced about the good days of Sun Yat-sen's time in Japan.[33] Again on March 26, at a luncheon with members of the Osaka Industrial Club, Dai had another chance to speak to some two hundred businessmen in the China trade. He assured them that the Guomindang was "not under Borodin's leadership," that the Guomindang took "the protection of business as its natural duty." But he also confirmed that the Guomindang would pursue efforts to secure the revision of unequal treaties in the shortest possible period.[34]

The dialogue with Japanese politicians produced mixed results, however. Dai's meeting with elder statesmen and diplomats, including Saionji Kinmochi and Saburi Sadao, reassured him of their sympathy toward the Chinese revolution and their desire for Sino-Japanese cooperation. Moreover, the people from the Foreign Ministry hinted that the policy of continental expansion was not unanimously supported within the Japanese government.[35] But Dai's encounter with the politicians of the Tanaka faction, which was then ferociously attacking the Minseitō cabinet, cast a dark shadow over that optimism; at a banquet attended by Tanaka's supporters, as Dai revealed years later, some politicians blatantly demanded that China open its doors to Japanese colonization.[36]

The encounter with the military was an even worse episode in Dai's goodwill mission. At a banquet hosted by the army and the general staff, one general in his toast to Dai simply challenged the National Government to military competition. Another banquet hosted by the expansionist Black Dragon Society (Kokuryūkai), Dai wrote, was "full of the smell of gunpowder." The hosts and guests, among them many young fellows, "had lost their normal manner."[37]

The Japanese military's reaction to Dai's goodwill mission, indeed, was a telling indication of the rapidly changing political climate in Japan at the moment. Ever since Hara Kei had been struck down by an assassin in November 1921, there had been frequent cabinet changes throughout the decade. Beneath the fluidity of high politics was social unrest, originating from the economic difficulties following the World War I boom. In the period shortly before Dai's mission, this socioeconomic stress began to find its loudest spokesmen in the military, especially in the middle and lower echelons of the army. Discontent was directed toward the politicians, especially Foreign Minister Shidehara's "weak-kneed policy," as his political opponents called it, of cooperation with the West by refraining from carrying out a more aggressive continental expansion. Tanaka Giichi, the general turned politician, was leading a Seiyūkai opposition against the Minseitō cabinet. His repeated promise to change the current "weak-kneed policy" to a "positive policy" on the continent, along with the military's determination to pursue expansion in China, eliminated room for dialogue when Dai arrived with hopes for a Sino-Japanese understanding.

When Dai returned to Shanghai at the end of March, both China and Japan were moving toward momentous political changes. In historic April 1927, Jiang Jieshi staged a full-scale party purge, beginning with the suppression, arrest, and massacre of the Communists in Shanghai. On the east side of the Japan Sea, Tanaka Giichi defeated his political rival and formed a new cabinet. Although he made no radical changes in his predecessor's policy toward China, Tanaka's call for "positive policy" was an encouraging signal to the expansionists.

And Sino-Japanese relations became potentially more confrontational, for a unified China under Jiang's nationalist government posed a more effective resistance to Japan's continental ambitions.

In the following May, the temporarily halted National Revolutionary Army resumed the Northern Expedition and crossed the Yangtze River. Anxious to protect Japan's vested interests in Manchuria, the Tanaka cabinet met on May 24 and, with the recommendation of the minister of war, decided three days later to send two thousand troops from Manchuria to Qingdao in the north China province of Shandong. The Japanese public, as reported by the *Asahi Shinbun,* welcomed the action as a manifestation of the long-promised "positive policy" toward China by the Tanaka cabinet.[38] The expedition, however, was a slap in the face of the newly consolidated Guomindang, which had just made an attempt to seek a Sino-Japanese rapprochement.

Three days after the Japanese marines were dispatched, *Shishi Xinbao* in Shanghai published a four-day series of Dai Jitao's speeches from his Japan tour.[39] From the carefully selected speeches appearing in the newspaper, Dai emerged as a stately diplomat who responded to the challenge of the "Tanaka-kind fellows" with dignity and who defended Chinese sovereignty with anti-imperialist eloquence. It was a calculated gesture to the Chinese public, whose support remained vital to the Guomindang's campaign of national unification. Yet careful observers of Sino-Japanese relations, Dai included, could not ignore the fact that the future development of relations between China and Japan had now slipped away from a few politicians' hands. As his diplomacy was undercut by the surge of military force, Dai realized that he was left with little power, except his pen, to salvage his cherished dream and to save his party from diplomatic disgrace.

On Japan

In the months after his inconsequential mission to Japan, Dai returned once again to his study and wrote, for the third time, a serious treatise on Japan. He titled it *On Japan (Riben lun)* and intended to make it a more "temperate and fair study" than his 1919 essay.[40] Numbering 176 pages and divided into twenty-four chapters of uneven length, this small book is indeed an enlarged and improved version of his 1919 essay "My View of Japan," for roughly the first half of it uses the same materials and deals with similar topics, such as Shintō belief, samurai and *bushidō,* the cultural relations between China and Japan, and contemporary Japanese society. Yet through his re-presentation of materials old and new, *On Japan* becomes a reinterpretation of Dai's view on Japanese culture and society.

The most arresting change of this 1927 representation of Japan is probably not the "more temperate and fair study" as Dai intended, but a reversed evaluation of Japanese culture. Negativity, as we have seen, underlines his 1919 view of Shintōism, the behavior of samurai, and Japan's modern politics on the one hand, and his comparison of Japanese culture with the Chinese on the other. In his 1927 study, however, Dai placed his discussion on Shintō belief and samurai behavior within the new frame of Japan's successful efforts at modern nation-building during the Meiji period. "We cannot but admit that Japan's native thoughts are indeed naive," Dai concluded on Shintō belief in 1919. "Yet this fact should not be viewed as Japan's shame," he added in 1927. "It was exactly from its innocence that its vitality and its progressive spirit developed." In 1919 he was aware that "Shintō belief is the origin of the Japanese idea of their country," but he dismissed it as only "superstition" that revived during the Meiji Restoration. In 1927, he stopped calling Shintō "superstition" but emphasized that it was "not at all unusual that mysterious thoughts should become the origin of the Japanese idea of their country in ancient times." Moreover, his 1919 criticism against the "cruelty" of samurai practice and against militarism was now overshadowed by praise of the samurai's militant spirit. The samurai were no longer the militaristic simpletons with "heads filled with imagined heroes" that he portrayed in 1919; they were "the moving force of the Meiji Restoration." "What is worth our attention," said Dai, "is that the *bushidō* has been developing from an institution into ethics, then into a system of beliefs. Once into the Meiji era, the old ethics and old belief of *bushidō* has been infused with a spirit of restorative revolution and European thoughts; it thus becomes the foundation of the political ethics in the restoration era."[41]

The novel emphasis on Japan's internal vitality further led to a modification of Dai's earlier comparison between Japan and China. While he retained the view that the Chinese idea of "shared humanity" assisted the progress of Japanese civilization, he now stressed the goal of Japanese borrowing from Chinese knowledge, which was intended "to create the central thought for the Japanese nation." Taking the National Learning scholar Yamaga Sokō as an example, Dai indicated that "all his methods and theory come from

Chinese learning . . . yet his spirit is totally different." And that was a more vigorous spirit than China's. "What we find as the greatest difference between the Japanese spirit and the Chinese one is that the Japanese do not have such degenerative illness as the pure talk and irresponsibility from the Jin periods [265–420] or the hedonic weakness from the Six Dynasties [222–589]. Even the most passive 'literature and arts of *ukiyo-e*' is full of militancy."[42]

Turning away from the repeated view in his 1919 essay that "military force is not as effective as civilian rule," Dai now expounded on the importance of jingoism and of using force in Japanese history: "As we look at the ideological basis of Japanese restoration, we understand better that 'military force' and 'war' are the most critical means of its nation-building." When Japan faced "an extremely adverse environment," argued Dai, "its transformation from a feudal polity to a Jingoist modern empire is not at all extraordinary but, under the circumstances, is very proper." And here was what Dai saw as an immediately useful lesson for China: "If a civilized nation forgets to 'strive forward,' or forgets that 'military force is the moving force of culture,' it will lead to 'degeneration of civilization.'" That, as Dai found, had been proved by the history of Toyotomi Hideyoshi's famous continental ambition: "If the Chinese nation did not degenerate, how would Japan grow the ambition to invade China?"[43]

While admitting that internal weakness under Manchu rule was the cause of Japan's continental ambition in modern times, Dai objectified its overseas expansion as an intricate response to the oppressive international circumstances of power struggle and competition.[44] Here he turned to criticize Japan, not because of its use of force, but for the way it applied force. Already in 1917 Dai had called attention to Japan's diverging approaches between the "northward thrust," which aimed at competing with Russia for the continent, and the "southward thrust," which focused on competing for the Anglo-American sphere in the South Pacific. In 1927, Dai singled out three representatives in Japanese politics to illustrate these two approaches of Japan's foreign policy, and by commenting on their thoughts he made clear where he stood.

On the one side, Dai presented Katsura Tarō, the late Japanese prime minister and the visionary of a Sino-Japanese alliance in the racially divided world, and Akiyama Masayuki, an admiral and a hero in the Russo-Japanese War. Katsura was "the most able and

had the longest political experience among Japanese military politicians," said Dai; his plan for a Chinese-Japanese-German alliance
against Britain and Russia was "astonishing" because it revealed a
vision "unmatched by anyone in today's Japanese political world."
According to Dai, Sun Yat-sen and Katsura had the "highest expectations of each other," for both placed their mutual trust and
understanding on "a global strategy for the revival of Eastern nations."[45] Admiral Akiyama, who had fascinated Dai with his prophetic intuition, was a "scholar" as well as "a passionate and sincere
Shintō believer." He was a good friend of Sun and other Chinese
revolutionaries because he, too, "is a passionate advocate for the
southward strategy." Akiyama held views on global strategy similar
to Katsura's, Dai explained, and his anti-British and anti-American
views were "derived from the goal of the revival of the colored
races."[46]

On the other side, Dai presented Tanaka Giichi, the current
prime minister of Japan, and viewed his rise to power as an indication of a growing "reactionary trend in world politics." "General
Tanaka Giichi is the direct heir of Japan's Chōshū military faction,"
wrote Dai in contempt; "he only lives under Japan's traditional
thought, traditional policy, and traditional power, and worked with
his intelligence and wisdom from day to night, without goal, without sure plan, without sure method, without certainty." Despite
Tanaka's mediocrity, indicated Dai, "all the disputes and chaos
within China had a direct or indirect connection with the policies of
General Tanaka." Recounting Tanaka's support of several regional
forces in China since the mid-1910s—Tang Jiyao, Cen Chunxuan,
Duan Qirui, Zhang Xun, and Zhang Zuolin—Dai pointed out that
the "central point" of Tanaka's policies was "to oppose unification
of China, especially to oppose a China unified under the revolution
and under the revolutionary leader Sun Yat-sen." As a member of
the Chōshū faction, noted Dai, Tanaka was a promoter of the
"northward-thrust strategy." And the recent Japanese expedition to
Shandong must be understood in terms of this strategy and its key
tactic, called "scorpion policy," which aimed at controlling the
continent by establishing Japan's advancing scorpion's tail at Taiwan while stretching its two claws to the Liaodong and Shandong
peninsulas. As the prospect of China's unification became a reality
with the continuous success of the Northern Expedition, the
Tanaka cabinet's decision on the Shandong expedition, indicated

Dai, "has profound implications despite the small number of troops sent."[47]

How deeply Dai regretted the irreversible trend of Sino-Japanese relations and yet how intensely he cherished his dream of Asia's revival with a Sino-Japanese alliance is tellingly revealed in the three concluding chapters of this "temperate and fair study." In a surprising turn in subject and tone, the three chapters on Japanese belief, aesthetics, and society appear structurally disjointed from the rest of the book. Yet the way Dai linked his subjects to his underlying argument, in effect, makes these trailing chapters a logical part of the whole. Here, in a forthright manner and with intimate language, Dai wrote to his readers about a Japan that was eternal in his heart.

The Japanese "are a people who always advance upward with vitality," argued Dai, if "we see how passionate and sincere is their spiritual life." They lived a life that "is pure, positive, and without calculation." The best evidence of such sincerity, Dai once again noted, could be found in their practice of suicide. Although "suicide is the most cowardly and most stupid behavior," he wrote, the practice of *seppuku* and love suicide paradoxically demonstrated "positive meanings." Because ritual disembowelment "causes greatest pain," the *seppuku* suicide "must positively maintain the most clear consciousness of being alive, the very determined spirit to strive, and an unwillingness to abandon the obligation to make the effort, ... till the last moment." The commitment to one's belief as shown by this painful action, noted Dai, was matched only by the love suicide. Such suicide pacts "most often take place in the world of prostitution, as well as in love affairs across social strata." It, too, was a paradoxically revealing practice because "these were the two most calculative situations in society." Yet "the passionate love and beautiful sympathy" could move many men and women to "leave behind all the calculation" to go for death. "In these suicides," he concluded, one found "abundant meanings about life."

Besides "the fighting spirit and the force transcending life and death," Dai also found vitality in Japanese artistic aptitude. As a "moving force of life," he considered true appreciation of beauty as nearly important as belief. Here again comes a modification on his previous judgment. The Japanese aesthetic taste, admitted Dai, "has no such aptitude for the rushing boldness of the great river Yangtze." But whether such taste fit a Chinese standard was not important; "what we need to know most is ... what is it." Dai called attention to "the most commonplace" Japanese art forms, such as garden, bonsai, and flower arrangement, and pointed out "the very special imagination and creativity within them." They were "elegant and exquisite," and the "subtle taste" of such arts, he noted, created an effect that "restores life to dead things."[48]

And finally, in an effort to balance his claim about the Japanese militant spirit, Dai turned to "the gentle habit of mutual help which envelops the Japanese society." And he found the best example in their social relations between the sexes and between the superior and the inferior. "The Japanese take rituals most seriously," noted Dai, "yet their ritual is totally different from the principles hanging on Chinese old fogies' mouths." In China, "especially in the families of upper society," he wrote, "there are such things as extreme as men abusing women, on the one hand, and also extreme facts of women abusing men, on the other," but "Japanese society is absolutely different." There, "men returned women's absolute subordination with absolute protection, despite some exceptions." The "human warmth," noted Dai, mediated the relationship between master and servant in a family, and "there is no such cruel thing as abusing female servants in Japan."[49]

On this soft note, Dai ended his third major work on Japan. With a more empathetic perspective on Japanese history and culture, it indeed has become a more "temperate and fair" treatment of Japan than his other two major essays in earlier years. Yet it is not at all a work of detached objectivity, but a representation of Japan shaped by Dai's partisan interests. In his praise of Japanese culture one hears vigorous battle calls to his intended audience, as the refrain "The youth of China, wake up!" is dotted all over the text and highlights his theme of the importance of belief and commitment to the Chinese nation. Dai interlaced his praise of Japanese willingness to act with criticisms of the Chinese for irresponsible and empty talk, a national disease that he saw as not only derived from a declining spirit but also exacerbated by the importation of a foreign ideology from Russia. In Japan's successful nation-building, moreover, Dai found powerful justification for the Guomindang's military campaigns to eliminate competing forces, especially the Communists allied with the Soviet Union. Chinese youth were called upon to summon their faith and will, once again, to follow their own tradition as the true path to rejuvenation.

And Dai also had a subtle message to the Japanese leaders in power:[50] by "speaking without customary courtesy," he hoped to move Tanaka and his subordinates to "serious introspection" when reading his account of the Sun-Katsura meetings and by their shared vision of a Sino-Japanese alliance. "Tokyo in the past thirty years has evidently gained the position of political center in the East, though its power is still under the sway of Europe, especially that of London," Dai remarked. He believed that "the history of the East ... has entered an age of rivalry for hegemony between the two countries [of Japan and Russia]." In the volatile China, where "those without self-confidence were rushing to either Tokyo or Moscow," Dai saw the shadow of the Balkans before World War I; he was afraid that Tanaka, who "immediately followed British policy in Shanghai by sending troops to Shandong," "might become yet another middle-school student in Sarajevo!"[51] Dai's work was immediately translated into Japanese, but his warning fell on deaf ears.[52] Although Tanaka would leave the political stage in 1928, the tide of expanding militarism had already risen, and none of the succeeding administrations in Japan was able to stop its advance.

**

In October 1926, when the National Revolutionary Army marched up to central China and conquered Wuchang, Zhou Zuoren's heart went out to the south and to the revolutionaries. The recent military conflict, he wrote in the *Yusi* weekly, was not a feud between the south and the north but "a war between ideas" and "a war between democratic thought and tribal thought."[53] Watching from a distance the growth of the revolution in the south, and knowing many of his students were attracted to it, he was hopeful that a real revolution might indeed be coming. He reacted strongly to those who opposed the expedition and saw them as his enemies, and once again he singled out *Shuntian Shibao,* which wrote derogatory reports on the revolutionaries in Wuhan.[54]

Little in Zhou's writings seemed to indicate his knowledge of the internal split in the Communist-Guomindang coalition. Living in China's old political center, his attention had been drawn to things close to home, and one of the concerns underlying his many-sided social criticism had been the tendency of "restoration" and social regression. The apprehension of the "return of the dead" had been with him since the Zhang Xun Restoration in 1917 and had grown more acute in the Puyi Incident of 1924. Studies of Chinese history and folklore in those years deepened his apprehension of how enormous was the task of making real change, and how "deeply and stubbornly savage thoughts lurk beneath modern life." Occasionally his utterances sounded close to despair: "Although waves keep rolling on the surface of the sea," he wrote in 1926, "at its bottom the sea remains just as it was a millennium ago."[55]

Even with "an apprehension that a restoration movement might soon come," that the regression would originate within a once-hopeful revolution and alter the course of history with such abruptness and magnitude still gave Zhou a great shock. In early April 1927, the news reports of an "internal split in Guomindang" raised his fear that the tragedy of the Taiping Heavenly Kingdom would return to the stage. And soon he heard from "the cruel methods of 'party purge'" from "a friend in the south," and "'the rumor fabricated by the Reds'" was proved by the "true fact that numerous people were killed." Among those who died were some of his former students, who "were thoughtful and articulate, and had worked very hard for the Guomindang in Jiangsu and Zhejiang ... but now were killed as leftists." And again, in October, he wrote on the ongoing purge: "Many Communists have died, of course, but the innocents who got killed were even more. Those rebellious youth have been either killed or forced to escape, and the evil gentry and local bullies join the party [of Guomindang] in herds." He was angry that the leading intellectuals of the New Culture movement, such as Cai Yuanpei, Wu Zhihui, and Hu Shi, now had either "become maniac killers" or "stand by as if seeing nothing." The once hopeful Northern Expedition, he mourned, "has gone in a wink like a dream in spring." When the old capital finally fell into the hands of the Guomindang in the early summer of 1928 and the Blue-Sky-Red-Sun flags were hung everywhere, he concluded that "Beijing is not being revolutionized" but "revolution has capitulated to Beijing."[56]

Alongside the cruel purge Zhou noted yet another "appalling" tendency. Years of observation of Japan's behavior toward China convinced him that "any change within China, whether to disorder or peace, is almost always related to Japan, yet at the same time almost always proves harmful to China and beneficial to Japan. Japan is indeed a terrifying country, an immense menace to the survival of the Chinese Republic and Chinese nation." Four months after Jiang Jieshi's massacre in Shanghai, Zhou discovered that "the current Guomindang government in Nanjing has decided to make alliance with Japan and ordered a halt to anti-foreign (Japanese) boycotts; thus, talking about anti-Japanese boycotts in the five southeastern provinces has become almost the same as the crimes of a Communist insurgence, inescapable of capital punishment."[57] A month later, in September 1927, he found that even in the north, where the Guomindang's power had not yet been consolidated, "any talk about the Japanese or the Nanjing government is perceived as dangerous, as if dancing on a volcano."[58] By late 1928, he realized that government censorship, which had arrived in the wake of unification, had put liberal debate to an end. His decade-long social criticism had to stop, unless he wished to put his life in jeopardy. And he could "read behind a closed door" only, commenting no more on current affairs.[59]

But it was a claim that, as in a few other instances, Zhou could never fulfill. In the very same essay where he announced his intention to retreat, he would leave a note on a historical transition recently accomplished. The Examination Yuan, the state bureau for selecting future government functionaries that was presided over by Dai Jitao, announced a new policy: future civil examinations would incorporate Confucian classics into the required texts. Responding to the news, Zhou suggested, not without sarcasm, that the most readable among the traditional four collections of classics was the second category, history, for "it teaches us honestly that what has happened in the past is occurring at the present, and will do so in the future." "Reading old books in reference to living humans," remarked Zhou, "makes dead books live."[60]

Dai probably would agree with Zhou, though he was looking in the other direction for historical parallels. Yet however Dai might use the past to justify his party's quest for power, there was no guarantee that its future would arrive as he wished. What happened between China and Japan in the few years of the Guomindang's unification was, in a sense, a recurrence of the past. Just three months after the publication of *On Japan,* the Tanaka cabinet made the decision to dispatch troops on the second Shandong Expedition, which resulted in the deaths of thousands of Chinese civilians in Jinan. In the next three years, Japan's Kwantung Army twice blew up the railway near Mukden, killing the Manchurian warlord Zhang Zuolin in the first attack and achieving its goal of occupying Manchuria in the second. Amid the crisis, the National Government appointed Dai Jitao to chair the Special Diplomatic Committee. During the three months of its existence, from September to December 1931, the most important decision the committee made was to appeal for international condemnation of the Japanese invasion through the League of Nations. With the Western powers struggling in the valley of the Great Depression and the United States paying lip service to China with its "non-recognition" of Manzhouguo (Manchukuo), the hope of stopping Japan's continental expansion was forever doomed.[61]

Dai Jitao in middle age. Courtesy
of Shanghai Municipal Archives.

Jiang Baili in 1932, after being
released from jail. Reprinted from
Jiang Baili xiansheng jiniance.

Guo Moruo addressing an anti-Japanese mass rally in Wuhan, 1938. Reprinted
from *Guo Moruo nianpu*, vol. 2.

Zhou Zuoren with friends in 1936. From left, Zhou Zuoren, Ma Yuzao, Qian Xuantong, Shen Shiyuan, Zhu Tixian, Shen Jianshi, Xu Shoushang. Photo courtesy of Y. M. Bau.

Zhou Zuoren in 1943, the year he wrote several important articles criticizing the Japanese invasion of China. Photo courtesy of Y. M. Bau.

Dai Jitao at work, circa 1940s. Courtesy of Shanghai Municipal Archives.

PART IV

Parting with Japan

During the fifteen years from 1931 to 1945, China's relationship with Japan was overwhelmed by a pressing reality: the war between the two countries. The anticipation, preparation, and execution of the war added new dynamics to politics and culture in China, causing many shifts that might have been impossible or slow to materialize during peacetime. The exigency of international conflict, above all, gave the claim of national unity a priority over any existing partisan or ideological differences. Seen from the outside in, the most striking change within China at this time of international crisis was the dramatic reconciliation of the two warring parties, the Guomindang and the Communists, who formed a united front just months prior to the outbreak of total war with Japan. The call for national unity also demanded that individuals leave their personal interests behind and place the nation above the self. The coming of war was a time for personal sacrifice; the coming of war was also a time of political integration.

In viewing history from the perspective of the nation, this period seemed to have made sharp breaks from the previous decades, as unity overwhelmed division and conformity replaced demands for individual liberty. But however extraordinary an episode in Chinese history, the war against Japan did not eradicate the political and intellectual divisions within China, which had become a basic reality in the nation's political and cultural life. Only temporarily were these divisions submerged in the nation's struggle for survival. And in the day-to-day existence of the individual, the conflict of competing priorities and values was an ever-present reality and was even sharpened momentarily with the arrival of the international conflict.

The following three chapters explore the question of how individuals negotiated different loyalties during this extraordinary time. By 1931, the year of the Manchurian Incident, the four protagonists in this book had all established their careers and found their distinct places in the nation's complex power structure and intellectual spectrum. At the political center, Dai Jitao was a revered statesman within the newly risen National Government, yet sick in body and spirit, he was no longer active in Sino-Japanese affairs. On the radical end of the intellectual spectrum, Guo Moruo, after having endured racism in Japan and poverty in China, had turned to Marxism and Communism. But in the early 1930s, he had detached himself from the political tumult in China, settled into a comfortable life in Japan, and emerged with outstanding accomplishments in the study of Chinese philology and ancient history. Politically and intellectually a nonconformist, Zhou Zuoren, still a professor at Beijing University, puzzled some of his contemporaries with an increasingly "traditional" flair for premodern texts and a preoccupation with remote subjects detached from current affairs. But most indicative of the rupture between the new state, on the one hand, and its suspected or actual dissenting elements, on the other, was the situation of Jiang Baili. In 1931, Jiang was in jail because of his connection with a rebel force that had mutinied against Nanjing. He was facing a secret execution without trial.

The arrival of the war against Japanese invasion would change the fate of most of them, and each would make a choice that had been impossible to imagine before 1931. Guo would abandon his family life and come back to join the war of resistance in China; Jiang would reconcile with Nanjing and assist with its diplomacy and military planning; Zhou, the radical thinker and innovative writer, would remain in the Japanese-occupied Beijing and be recruited into the collaboration government.

Was the exigency of war the cause of these decisions and turns? As the reader will soon find out, however dramatic these choices might appear, there was an internal logic to each man's deeds and words if we look deep into his life and thoughts. Organizational connections, intellectual priorities, and personalities all exerted their influence as each man confronted international conflict. War, as an extraordinary catalyst in human life, did alter drastically the course of many an individual's life, but it did so only by working upon the already existing potentials.

7 For Survival

During high summer of 1928, as the pursuit and purge of the Communists and leftists raged throughout China, life across the Japan Sea at Ichikawa, a suburban town on the eastern edge of the Tokyo metropolis, was as quiet and placid as it had always been. But the tranquility was disturbed on August 1, 1928, when black-clothed detectives arrived at the Guo residence in town. It was early afternoon, as Guo Moruo, having worked all morning finishing a research article on the ancient text *Book on Change (Yi jing)*, was ready to take a nap. Barely had he spread his futon and lay down when he heard the footsteps of six or seven men rushing into his house. The detectives had come to "invite him to have a talk at the Tokyo police bureau." Anna tried to argue with the intruders, but Guo stopped her. Silently, he put on his clothes and followed the detectives to board the train for Tokyo. He was being detained for his subversive activities in China.[1]

The Guos had just fled China about six months before. During the preceding three years or so they had been in various places in China, often separated. They had drifted back to the other shore and landed in Shanghai in late 1924, when that great city of the proletariat was going through restless preparations for the revolutionary upheaval and the country was on the eve of the "Great Revolution." On May Day that year, one hundred thousand workers had marched together through the streets. And the messages about the upcoming great change continued to radiate from workers' night schools and clubs, where a few dozen Communists lectured and worked diligently to bring the light of hope to the hundreds of thousands who lived in the dingy huts in the city's sprawling shantytowns.[2]

Although Guo had announced his conversion to Marxism just before returning to China, he had yet to connect with the party organization. Arriving in Shanghai penniless, he had tried to strike a contract with the Commercial Press for a translation of *Das Kapital,* but failed. Then he obtained a position at a small university, but his temper led him to clash with the school authorities, forcing him to leave and search for another position. He was frustrated with his experiences in small universities because of their mediocre administrators as well as the meager pay, which could go as low as twenty silver dollars per month. He was in just such a dejected mood when the May Thirtieth Incident ignited anti-imperialist patriotism across the nation.[3] On that famous day in 1925, when Chinese demonstrators clashed with the police force under foreign jurisdiction, Guo was only a few blocks away from the site of the incident, locked inside a department store with many other panicked pedestrians. "Several times I wanted to rush out to grab the pistols from those Western constables and shoot them," Guo wrote shortly after the incident. He was instantly drawn to the protest and rallies, and drafted an anti-imperialist statement for the Learned Society of Sojourners from Sichuan in response to the incident.[4] Being a well-known writer, Guo was invited to speak at various mass demonstrations, where he suddenly discovered a talent for inciting the less articulate audience. While working excitedly on anti-imperialist propaganda, he also became acquainted with Qü Qiubai, the Communist leader who had been a close friend of Lu Xun and many other progressive intellectuals. Before long, Qü went to Guangdong to join the nationalist movement under the Communist-Guomindang coalition, and Guo soon followed when he was invited to chair the Department of Literature at Guangdong University on Qü's recommendation. In that "Red Capital" Guo became friends with more Communists, among them Mao Zedong, Zhou Enlai, Deng Yanda, and Lin Boqu—men who would change China's fate in the next few decades. It was through Zhou Enlai's arrangement that Guo was appointed head of the National Revolutionary Army's Department of Propaganda when the Northern Expedition began in June 1926.[5]

Unlike some other intellectuals, such as Lu Xun and Yu Dafu, who soon became disillusioned with the superficiality of the revolution and left the south even before the Northern Expedition began, Guo enjoyed these restless years and savored his newfound self-esteem as he gave lecture after lecture to the tens of thousands of soldiers of the Revolutionary Army. As the troops advanced north, he rose to the rank of deputy director of the political bureau, carrying a military title of lieutenant general and a monthly salary of three hundred yuan. He was also appointed a service soldier for his miscellaneous personal needs and, most important, a secretary named Li Yimang, who would serve as a critical connection with the Communist Party in the years to come.[6]

Guo's glorious career suddenly turned into a nightmare when the Communist purge began in the spring of 1927. Although he had joined the Guomindang by then, Guo chose to remain a leftist.[7] At the incipient stage of the purge he wrote a widely publicized article, "Please Look at the Jiang Jieshi of Today," attacking Jiang's reactionary activities; as a result, his name was added to Jiang's most-wanted list. This made Guo all the more radical, and he joined the Communists during the Red Army's retreat to the south. Finally, after trekking through the hills of Jiangxi, Fujian, and Guangdong and making several dangerous journeys on boat, he sneaked back into Shanghai's International Settlement and found Anna and their children waiting for him there. At that point Zhou Enlai, who was leading the underground Communists in Shanghai, decided that Guo and his family should leave China and go to the Soviet Union.[8]

The latter half of Guo's life might have turned out very differently if he had not been stricken with typhoid fever in mid-December 1927. While he was hovering between life and death, the last ship for the Soviet Union sailed. Zhou Enlai had to make other arrangements for him and his family, and the optimal choice, based on convenience of transportation and lack of requirement for a visa or passport, appeared to be Japan.[9] Using the pseudonym Wu Cheng, Guo passed through the guarded port of Shanghai and reached Kobe without being recognized. But the Tokyo police found him six months after his return. Guo had long prepared for the moment, though he had no idea what lay ahead of him.[10]

"I Am a Chinese"

When Guo stepped onto Kobe soil in early 1928, he was no longer an anonymous Chinese, as he had been when he left four years before. During the Communist purge of 1927 in China, his and his family's pictures had appeared in Japanese newspapers, some of which had reported that he had already been executed.[11] With help from some Japanese friends, the Guos used the surname Satō to settle down in Ichikawa. But the arrival of the Tokyo police changed everything. Although Guo was detained for only three days, the incident rippled to every connection the Guos had so far established. Muramatsu Shōfū, a sympathetic writer, and Ohara Eijirō, a small businessman who transmitted remittances from Shanghai to Tokyo for Guo, both were detained by the police and after their release refused to see Guo anymore. Yokoda Heizaemon, a local strongman in Ichikawa who had helped the Guos settle down, politely told Guo that he was "too small a hen to protect a big ostrich egg." Worse still, neighbors gave Anna and her family "vigilant and contemptuous looks," forcing them to move out of the area to the outskirts of town.

Guo's detention, in fact, was not an isolated affair but part of a growing police effort by the Tanaka administration to combat "dangerous thought." In March and August 1928 there were mass arrests of suspected anarchists and Communists under the Peace Preservation Law of 1925. The suppression also extended to liberal circles; five professors—including Kawakami Hajime, the prominent Marxist economist whose work had been translated by Guo into Chinese—were dismissed from the imperial universities in 1928.[12] Guo, as a well-known Communist, now was under the constant surveillance of the gendarmes and local police. It was merely an irritating nuisance to have a visit every other day from the local policeman, who viewed Guo as a "prominent figure" (kyotō) and addressed him as "Your Excellency." But the insolent gendarmes, who marched through Guo's home every day, provoked a fury in Guo that increased with each day. At one time Guo tried to stop the gendarme just as he was stepping into the yard, but his protests only invited ridicule: "Our law is not written for you, changoro.[13] You go back to your Shina if you dare. I even dare to do whatever I want to on your Shina land!" The riding boots of the gendarmes continued to step in and march from the front door through the backyard, as if to make a determined statement and to stamp the notes of hatred into Guo's heart. Guo took the gendarme's daily patrol as both a personal insult and national humiliation, and his anger instantly welled up whenever he recalled Ichikawa many years later:

I must be thankful to these riding boots, that dead-end lane, and that small house which was built in such a way that anybody could trespass it so easily. Together they created an opportunity to allow the tyranny of Japanese imperialism, though small in scale, to perform vividly in front of me. The impression will be forever distinct. It reminds me: I am a Chinese![14]

Although a Chinese, Guo's contact with China at this point was all but severed. What bound him to China during this early phase of his exile in Japan was a new interest: the study of ancient China. The work was apparently encouraged by Li Yimang, his former secretary and connection with the Communist Party, who assisted Guo's research by sending materials to him from Shanghai.[15] In the summer of 1928 Guo was already well under way on a research article based on *The Book of Songs (Shi jing)* and *The Book of History (Shu jing)*. He made substantial progress when he was able to make use of recently unearthed oracle bone and bronze inscriptions kept in the Oriental Library (Tōyō Bunko) in Tokyo, where he gained access with the help of Fujimori Seikichi, his former German-language teacher, and Yamagami Masayoshi, a progressive journalist who befriended many Chinese writers, especially those of the Creation Society, while he was reporting in Shanghai and Guangzhou during 1925 and 1926.[16]

When the results of Guo's study were published in 1930 in *Researches on Ancient Chinese Society (Zhongguo gudai shehui yanjiu)*, it was an instant success in China, one that exceeded Guo's expectation. Since 1928, about a dozen scholars had been engaged in a heated debate on the structure of Chinese society. By taking different approaches they aligned themselves along three opposing positions: the Guomindang leftists, the Communists, and the Trotskyites. At the time Guo's book was published, the debate had moved from a discussion of contemporary Chinese society to its historical development. Guo's work provided positive evidence of the existence of a slave society in ancient China, which strengthened the Communist position in the debate. Despite its somewhat rigid and mechanical application of Marxian notions of social development, the work reached a broad audience; even a non-Marxist authority on ancient China regarded the book as the first work that "delineated the contours of the true visage of ancient society."[17] The book sold out so quickly that its publisher had to issue three impressions during the first year of publication.[18] By the early 1930s, Guo's achievement in his research on ancient China, especially on oracle bone and bronze inscriptions, had gained the respect of scholars in both China and Japan. His works began to be published in Tokyo, mostly by Bunkyūdō, a bookstore specializing in sinology.

While retaining the study of ancient China as a major intellectual pursuit, Guo also wrote his autobiographical novels and translated two works by Marx, *A Contribution to the Critique of Political Economics* and *The German Ideology*. Most of his works and translations were published in Shanghai with the help of Li Yimang, now an underground Communist under Zhou Enlai's direct command.[19] By diligently wielding his pen Guo enabled his family to live in relative comfort and security after the Creation Society was closed down by the government and hence stopped sending his monthly allowance.

Thus Guo Moruo spent his late thirties and early forties in Japan, exploring an esoteric field of Chinese studies in the solitude of Ichikawa. Sometimes, as he admitted to occasional visitors, he felt at a loss being so out of touch with his homeland.[20] Writing his autobiography, then, became not simply a means of making money, but a way of reliving the excitement of those revolutionary years and retaining an emotional bond with the China he had left behind.

Interludes between Past and Future

Just as Guo settled into a life of quiet scholarship and material comfort in Ichikawa, the already tense Sino-Japanese relations suddenly reached a crisis when, on September 18, 1931, the Kwantung Army blew up the Southern Manchurian Railroad near Mukden in northeast China. Turning a deaf ear to Tokyo's order to localize the incident, the Kwantung Army resolutely pursued its plan to occupy the three provinces of northeastern China. While the crisis prompted many Chinese students in Japan to return to China in protest, Guo had no alternative but to remain in Ichikawa. He was trapped in Japan, of course, by fear of more severe oppression in China, but he was unable to leave for a more personal reason as well: he and Anna were expecting their fifth child in early 1932. In a letter dated late September 1931 to Rong Geng, a scholar of philology and archaeology in Beijing, Guo hinted at his wish to return to China either at the end of the year or the following spring.[21] To his and many others' relief, the crisis stopped short of developing immediately into a major war. Yet the tension between China and Japan remained, and Guo would soon face a new crisis as the two countries moved further down the road to confrontation.

Across the Japan Sea, the political atmosphere within China began to soften under the pressure of international crisis. In all the years since the 1927 party purge, the National Government in Nanjing had kept Guo's name on the most-wanted list and banned his works. Anyone who possessed Guo's *Goddess,* the poetry collection from the May Fourth days, risked arrest for hiding a Communist's book.[22] Some youth were decapitated for possessing his translations of Turgenjev's *Virgin Soil* or of Kawakami Hajime's *Social Organization and Social Revolution.*[23] But the stringent censorship began to lessen toward the mid-1930s with the rise of popular demands for a united front. After December 9, 1935, when students in Beijing staged a large-scale demonstration demanding an end to civil war and initiation of anti-Japanese resistance, various national salvation organizations sprang up in urban areas. Among the first was the Shanghai Cultural Circles Association of National Salvation, organized soon after the December 9 demonstration. In October 1936, twenty-one famed writers of diverse political inclinations signed a "Statement for Resisting Invasion in Unity and for Freedom of Speech by the Colleagues in the Circles of Literature and Arts," with Guo's signature appearing alongside those of Lu Xun, Mao Dun, Ba Jin, and Bing Xin.[24]

Revived Communist circles in urban China had also reached Guo and helped break his isolation. Already in 1930, underground Communists in Shanghai had organized the Chinese Leftist Writers Association (Zhongguo Zuoyi Zuojia Lianmeng, abbreviated Zuolian), which assembled and coordinated progressive writers in the city.[25] Zuolian also founded a Tokyo branch but closed it for two years when most Chinese students returned to China after the Manchurian Incident. As soon as the branch resumed activities in September 1933, it became an umbrella organization for three literary groups of Chinese students in Japan: the Dongliu Society (Dongliu She), Zhiwen Society (Zhiwen She), and New Poetry Society (Xinshige She).[26] Lin Lin, the special liaison sent by the Tokyo branch of Zuolian, brought Guo Moruo into contact with more Chinese students in Tokyo. Through Lin's arrangement Guo often contributed historical stories to *Dongliu,* a student literary journal. Occasionally he was invited to speak at Chinese student gatherings.[27]

At his home in Ichikawa, which was still under surveillance, Guo began to receive visitors from China. Those who knew Guo during the Northern Expedition years were surprised at his thorough Japanization. They were struck, at the gate of his house, by the nameplate that read "Satō." Inside they saw a typical Japanese residence, simply decorated with a calligraphy scroll and without high furniture or chairs. Everybody in the family, including Guo, dressed in kimono and geta. And Guo admitted that often he did not speak Chinese for months.[28]

Amid these periodic visits, Guo's household received an unexpected guest in the middle of 1934. That summer Zhou Zuoren came to Japan with his wife for a vacation. Although both Zhou and Guo were important contributors to the New Literature movement, they had never met throughout the 1920s. They had missed their only chance to meet when Guo declined an offer by Beijing University, prompted by Zhou Zuoren, to teach Japanese literature there.[29] During the party purge of the late 1920s, Zhou in Beijing often expressed his sympathy for the revolutionary youth, and on some occasions he particularly mentioned Guo's name.[30] In August 1934, while the Guos were on a ten-day vacation at Namihana Village by the sea, Zhou sent his regards through Xu Zuzheng (Yaochen), his colleague at Beijing University who was also one of the earliest members of the Creation Society, and inquired about the possibility of a visit.[31]

Zhou's message took Guo by surprise and made him very uneasy. Despite their mutual alienation from the current nationalist regime, the two men had taken divergent paths in their pursuit of literature. Within literary circles throughout the 1920s it was an open secret that the Creation Society had not gotten along well with the Literature Study Association, with which Zhou was affiliated. Only seven months earlier, Guo had written to the editors of *Contemporary (Xiandai)* complaining that his essay had appeared after Zhou's in sequence; annoyed and sarcastic, he remarked that he "has no intention of being set side by side with an idol."[32] Now Zhou came to Japan as a renowned Chinese writer and Japan specialist, welcomed by the Japanese literary community with much attention and respect. Receiving Zhou's message again made Guo grumpy: "The life of Mr. Qiming [Zhou Zuoren] is really enviable. Mr. Qiming is a descendent of the Yellow Emperor, and I am too. Mrs. Qiming belongs to the race of Goddess of Amaterasu, and so does my wife. Yet Mr. Qiming draws attention from a circle of literati, whereas I attract only police and gendarmes."[33] In fact, when Guo wrote these lines in his diary, he and Zhou had already met by chance at Xu Zuzheng's home near the end of July.[34]

Finally, in the middle of August, Zhou came to Ichikawa to visit Guo at his home. As it turned out, the two men found much to talk about, chatting the entire afternoon. A few days later they met again by coincidence at Bunkyūdō, Guo's publisher. When Tao Kangde, an editor of *Cosmic Wind (Yuzhou feng)* in Shanghai, heard about these meetings and wrote Zhou to inquire about his impression, Zhou replied: "[I] found much to talk about with Dingtang [Guo Moruo] when meeting him. In his writing, though, he seems unable to avoid exaggeration. Since it is a personal idiosyncrasy, [we] should not be too picky about that."[35] As far as Zhou was concerned, the ten years of animosity had become history.

Guo's greater surprise and joy came with a visit from Yu Dafu, a fellow writer of the Creation Society, in November 1936. Without warning, Yu appeared at the door of Guo's house, shouting in his delightful voice, just as he used to during the days of their youth. Yu was invited by schools and organizations to speak in Tokyo and was being hosted that day by Kaizō Publishers (Kaizōsha). In the evening, the two friends went to the publisher for a dinner in Yu's honor. When Guo heard that the president and editorial board of Kaizōsha were compiling *The Complete Collection of Lu Xun*, he suggested that they contact Zhou Zuoren in Beijing. Although the Japanese editors did not take his advice, Guo took the opportunity that day to announce publicly his high regard for Zhou Zuoren.[36]

Yu Dafu arrived in Japan just as a few more critical changes were taking place in both China and Japan. On February 26, 1936, a military coup d'etat in Tokyo further strengthened the army's hand and diminished the influence of liberal statesmen in Japan; mass arrests of Marxists and socialist professors followed in the early summer. While the rise of militarism led to the severe repression of leftists and liberals in Japan, the authorities in China finally gave in to popular demands and loosened harsh political controls. At the end of 1936, the so-called Xian Incident forced the National

Government to abandon its anti-Communist campaigns and form a second united front with the Communist Party for national defense. As Japan and China were now poised for a final confrontation, police surveillance of visiting Chinese in Japan was intensified. Although Yu came in a civil capacity, he was constantly followed by the Japanese police, and a scheduled speech on Chinese poetry at Gakushi Kaikan had to be canceled.[37]

As a political suspect living under police surveillance for nearly a decade, Guo was not surprised that Yu had been put under "police protection." Guo's political caution on public occasions seemed exceptionally impressive even to some Japanese. Takeuchi Yoshimi, one of the three founders of the Chinese Literature Study Association (Chūgoku Bungaku Kenkyukai) and a pioneer in the Japanese study of contemporary Chinese literature, recalled one such evening during Yu Dafu's visit, when Takeuchi's association invited Guo and Yu to dinner in the Mita District of Tokyo. As the hosts and guests left the restaurant after dinner, some of the Japanese in the gathering suddenly became so excited by the meeting with China's famous writers that they started to shout, "Long live the Republic of China!" Without missing a beat Guo responded, "Long live the Great Japanese Empire!" This response so surprised and unnerved Takeuchi that he asked Guo to shout no more. Only in retrospect did Takeuchi realize how naive was this group of young scholars and how astute was Guo, the veteran revolutionary, in a world of pressing danger.[38]

In light of the increasing tension between the two countries, Yu's visit, though centered around the reunion with his personal friends, appeared to Japanese authorities to be a covert mission. They may have been right. A few months after Yu's return to China, Guo suddenly received a telegram from Yu asking him to come back to China as soon as possible because "the government needed his service." Only years later did Guo find out that Yu's telegram had resulted from a meeting in Lushan, where a number of Guomindang decision makers persuaded Jiang Jieshi to cancel the order for Guo's arrest and bring him back to serve the country during a national emergency. The message was passed through Chen Yi, the president of the Fujian provincial government, where Yu served as a consultant. Still in Japan, Guo was struck by the abruptness of the invitation and asked for more information, but no further word came from Yu, and he decided for the moment not to venture back.[39]

"I Have Only One Sweetheart"

The long-awaited showdown between China and Japan finally occurred on July 7, 1937, when a small number of Chinese and Japanese troops exchanged fire near the Marco Polo Bridge in a suburb of Beijing. At the time, many in both China and Japan still thought this incident was just another local clash of the sort that had become commonplace since the Manchurian Incident. Yet the indecision of the Konoe cabinet gave leeway to the already impatient military; within weeks three more Japanese divisions were mobilized and sent to China. By the end of July Beijing and Tianjin fell into Japanese hands, and in early August fierce fighting broke out in Shanghai. Only then, as writer Mao Dun observed, did "people truly feel that a great age had finally arrived."[40]

Watching the unfolding events from the other shore of the Japan Sea, Guo realized that the moment for decisive action had come. For more than ten days after the incident he "had been in torment."[41] All kinds of scenarios must have rushed through his mind: staying in Japan, he might well fall into the gendarmes' prison, like many Communists and socialists did in these years, and be forced to do things; yet leaving for China was not an easy choice either. It was not simply the practical problems of how to elude the watchful eyes of the police and gendarmes who came to "protect him" every day, or how to obtain Nanjing's acquiescence were he to return that troubled him. The most agonizing dilemma involved his family: taking them all with him seemed impossible, yet leaving them behind would be unbearable.

Guo was released from his torment only by the force of circumstances. The technicalities of his escape were solved relatively easily with the help of Jin Zutong, a young Chinese who had come to live in Ichikawa in the summer of 1936. Still in his mid-twenties, Jin had already begun to study oracle bones and bronze inscriptions under the influence of his father, who had been a student of the famous paleographer Luo Zhenyu (1866–1940). During 1935, Jin visited Guo regularly for advice in his esoteric field. In turn, he helped Guo gain access to rare pieces of ancient Chinese stone inscriptions held by a well-known Japanese artist and collector of art works, Kawai Senrō (1871–1945), who was an old friend of Jin's father.

Jin never made clear in his memoirs on his contact with Guo and on the rescue operation that took Guo out of Japan whether he had come on government assignment. But as soon as news of the incident at the Marco Polo Bridge reached Japan, Jin immediately came up with a plan of escape. The key link would be Qian Shoutie (1897–1967), a sojourning Chinese seal-cutting artist who at the time was a covert Chinese intelligence agent in Japan working for the semiofficial Japan Research Institute at Nanjing. Through Qian, word came from Nanjing that the order of arrest from 1927 had been canceled, and travel fare was sent from his research institute to the Chinese ambassador in Tokyo.[42]

At dawn on July 25, 1937, Guo walked out of his small house in Ichikawa wearing only a casual kimono and geta. Pretending to take a stroll, he cut through dew-dampened fields and quickly boarded a train to Tokyo, where he met Qian and Jin. Qian provided Guo with a suit for travel and escorted him and Jin to Kobe. From there, Qian bade farewell to Guo, and Jin accompanied Guo aboard the ship bound for Shanghai.[43]

Despite the swift and successful escape, Guo's guilt and sorrow at leaving Anna and their children never abated. From the moment they began to plan the escape, Jin observed, Guo had become sullen and reticent. Occasionally Guo spoke to Jin about his anxiety over how he should talk with Anna about the escape. He never appeared enthusiastic whenever Jin reported on the progress of their plan, and instead appeared "like a piece of wood." On July 24, when tickets for the next day's ship ride were finally obtained, Guo suddenly began a long discussion with Jin; he doubted whether the Chinese government was determined to wage a war of resistance and feared he would be punished by the government upon his return. To Jin it sounded like Guo was trying to find every possible excuse not to leave and instead stay in Japan with his family.[44]

Nonetheless, Guo hinted at dinner the night before his departure that he might be forced to go back to China eventually. Anna had already expected this and was understanding. Her only worry was that Guo "has such an unsteady personality"; if he would deal with his life seriously, she said, she could endure whatever happened to them. On board the ship to Shanghai, as Guo recorded their fateful conversation and heartbreaking farewell in his diary, he thought the escape was beyond their control.

> I am in fact a man who can endure. But besides walking into this blind alley, I have no way to endure anymore. Since the outbreak of the incident, the gendarmes, the plainclothes police and policemen have been coming to watch and talk nonsense to me. This is not unusual anymore and I do not care. But it is already a moment of death for our nation. Who has the leisure to take care of the safety of only one person or one family?... I believe what I have taken is the only road to life.[45]

During the three-day voyage Guo's mind was preoccupied with the family he had left behind; he felt both guilt and gratitude toward Anna, "a suffering Madonna" whose sacrifice again opened his way to the world. It was her courage in shouldering the responsibility for their family, he thought, that helped him to make this drastic decision.[46] In this frame of mind Guo happened to meet an Afghan merchant on board who, while taking a walk with Guo, sang a love song and translated the lyrics into English for him; drifting on the sea, the two middle-aged men then had the following conversation, opened by the merchant's question (originally in English):

> "Have you sweetheart?"
> "Yes, I have."
> "Chinese or Japanese?"
> "Chinese and Japanese."
> "Oh, have you many, many?"
> "No, I have only one, because she is a Japanese girl and become [sic] my wife."[47]

For the melancholy Guo the hurly-burly of wartime life came to the rescue. As soon as he disembarked at Shanghai he was welcomed by two men from Nanjing. One of them, He Lian (1897?–1975), came from the Department of Administration at the Administrative Yuan and invited Guo to go with him, but Guo declined. Before leaving the dock, he was again spotted and cheered by a few acquaintances who had happened to come for other friends. In a hurry to avoid further attention, Guo and Jin went to see Shen Yinmo (1883?–1971), a liberal scholar of Chinese literature and calligraphy known for his insight and cautious approach to politics. Shen's suggestion that he take a "wait and see" approach, however, did not appeal to Guo. While the discussion was going on, Yu Dafu appeared at Shen's door. Having received a telegram from the Chinese embassy in Tokyo, Yu had rushed from Fuzhou to welcome Guo at the dock in Shanghai, missing him by only a few steps. Yu, generous and gregarious as always, invited all at the meeting to dine at a restaurant. He passed on to Guo Chen Yi's invitation to work at Fujian, which Guo declined as well.[48]

The news of Guo's return spread rapidly; all kinds of people— mostly his literary friends and students returned from Japan—came to visit him at his hotel.[49] Among them was Pan Hannian (1906– 1977), an early member of the Creation Society and now one of the most energetic and capable Communists in urban China. In the past few years Pan had been working directly under Zhou Enlai and was involved in secret talks with the Guomindang about forming a united front; he was now a Communist leader in charge of activities in literary circles. Upon hearing the news of Guo's return, Pan rushed to Guo's hotel and arranged for a new residence in the French Concession to help Guo avoid the many visitors, some un- wanted, who had been overflowing his hotel room. He also brought Xia Yan (1900–1994), an underground Communist who had been active in Shanghai since 1927, to assist Guo.

Some fourteen years before, in 1923, while studying at the Meiji Senmon Gakkō in Kyūshū, Xia Yan had visited the Guos at Hakata Bay. He still remembered Guo as an exuberant poet and Anna as a hospitable hostess who treated him and his friends to lunch. Meeting Guo fourteen years later, Xia Yan observed a noticeable change. Despite his characteristic enthusiasm, Guo now carried an air of restraint, or even the pathos of a middle-aged man. Moreover, Xia Yan found him less talkative than he used to be, and melancholy often showed in his eyes.[50]

Within a month of Guo's escape from Japan, a letter from Anna reached Shanghai describing how she and the children were being harassed by the special policemen who came to their house two or three times a day. In late November another letter came. Anna and their eldest son had spent a month in jail and been tor- tured at the police station; their house was searched and all of Guo's manuscripts confiscated. Guo asked the Chinese embassy in

Japan to help Anna and their children get out of Japan, but the request was denied by the Japanese government.[51]

Hopelessly trapped in Japan for the remaining years of the war, Anna had to grab whatever job came within her reach. For a while she worked at a paste workshop, operating and managing the boiling pot. Later she started a small business peddling groceries on the streets. The youngest son, while still in elementary school, sometimes went with his mother. Despite the enormous hardship, Anna made every effort to give her children the best possible education. With some assistance from the owner of Iwanami Bookstore, a great sympathizer of this special family, the four elder children were able to enter Kyoto Imperial University, and all graduated to become specialists in industrial chemistry, architecture, aquaculture, and mathematics. Resisting pressure from the police and gendarmes, Anna refused to allow the children to become Japanese citizens, thus protecting them from conscription and from going to fight against their father in China. Years of excessive manual labor left Anna with permanent back pain.[52]

Now separated by the unbridgeable Japan Sea, Guo was left to compress his grief into these agonizing lines: "How impossible it was to protect family and country at once, /such a grief shall last for ages to come."[53] Soon after receiving Anna's second letter, he and many others had to be evacuated to the south when greater Shanghai fell on November 21. While in Guangzhou, Guo was called to Wuhan by General Chen Cheng, who invited Guo to chair the Third Bureau in the Political Affairs Ministry and be in charge of propaganda, an appointment Guo accepted in 1938.

In the evacuation southward this time, unlike the trip from Shanghai to Guangzhou some ten years before, Guo did not go alone. He was accompanied by Yu Liqun (1916–1979), with whom Guo had been acquainted since his return from Japan.[54] Just in her twenties, Yu Liqun at the time was an actress in Shanghai and had been close to a few underground Communists in the artist circles. Her elder sister, Yu Licheng, who had committed suicide a few months before, had been an intimate companion of Guo during the Northern Expedition. Guo had always harbored a tenderness for Yu Licheng, who had shared difficult times with him in their retreat from Guangdong to Shanghai in 1927. When Guo arrived in

Shanghai in 1937, Lin Lin, the student liaison between the Tokyo branch of Zuolian and Guo Moruo, brought Yu Liqun and others to visit him daily. Yu Liqun had been planning to go to Yanan when the intellectuals in Shanghai began their retreat to the rear area. But it soon became apparent that Guo's fond memories of Yu Licheng had transformed into affection for her living sister. And the Communist Party agreed to let her stay in Wuhan instead of sending her to Yanan.[55] With Guo Moruo she moved from Wuhan to Guilin and finally settled in Chongqing. One year later, in April 1939, Yu Liqun gave birth to a son, the first of their five children.[56] Their marriage ceremony, presided over by Zhou Enlai and attended by about eighty distinguished guests, was held in late spring of the same year.[57]

Although his new family was not what Guo had foreseen that summer morning when he stepped out of his home in Ichikawa, it certainly brought him peace and comfort and provided an anchor in his life. In ten years, Guo's personal life seemed to have come full circle. In 1927 he was trudging from central China along trails in hilly Jiangxi, across the turbulent sea of southeast China. He had arrived in Shanghai to escape the Guomindang and finally been forced to leave for a foreign country. In 1937 he made the trip in reverse and was reunited with the sister of his previous fellow traveler and admirer and, under a changed political climate, joined hands with many who had once been his enemies. No one could tell for sure whether Guo had wondered how fate had so teased him, throwing him into the deepest sorrow at one moment and raising him to the highest joy the next, or if he had ever secretly relished the taste of this enigmatic drama. All that can be said, perhaps, is that the reverse journey had finally concluded his deep engagement with Japan and that his only "sweetheart" would return to him only in his dreams.

Shared Past, Shared Present

As his private life stabilized, Guo's public engagement also took on a new orientation. During the Northern Expedition, Guo had joined both the Guomindang and the Communist parties, but his period of exile in Japan left him a nonpartisan. This ambivalent identity allowed him to retain friendships with many on both sides, and with his outgoing personality and intellectual prestige he thus became a special link in the united front. In the four months since his return to Shanghai, Guo was frequently invited to give public speeches to government troops, and generals like Chen Cheng and Feng Yuxiang sought his opinions about the war of resistance. Toward the end of September Guo went to Nanjing, where he was received by Jiang Jieshi and met with many high government officials who had been his acquaintances during the Northern Expedition.[58] Declining Jiang's invitation to serve in the government, Guo returned to Shanghai and became president of the Communist-initiated *Salvation Daily (Jiuwang ribao)*.[59]

During the stubborn resistance of Chinese troops between 1937 and 1939, Guo concentrated his energy on writing commentaries on Japan. It was the first time since he wrote his two articles on Sino-Japanese relations in 1919 that he had given his writing such a focus. His articles, appearing mostly in newspapers or popular resistance journals, were understandably charged with high-pitched patriotism and served as war propaganda. The name Guo Moruo, famed scholar and romantic writer, was an added appeal to his wartime commentaries and essays. People who went to buy *Salvation Daily*, it was reported, often said simply, "Give me Guo Moruo."[60] To this responsive audience Guo articulated his understanding of Japan and communicated a sense of the higher purpose of sacrifice when many were overwhelmed by the exigencies of survival and tremendous loss during the war.

Emerging first and foremost from Guo's writings on Japan during this period were the notions of culture and civilization, which interplayed with other subthemes as the war developed. In the early stages of fighting, Guo asked his readers to take a broader perspective on the Sino-Japanese conflict and to see China's resistance as "direct combat" in the struggle between "reason" and "savagery."[61] The Chinese, Guo indicated, were not just fighting for their own survival, but "we are also fighting for the defense of civilization in the world and the welfare of mankind."[62] In "A Letter to Our International Friends," written on behalf of the literary circles in China during the battle of Shanghai in August 1937, Guo compared the Japanese invasion of China to that of cholera and the plague, which threatened to destroy world civilization. Guo had captured the mood of his time well, and his analogy was soon echoed on the other side of the Pacific Ocean in President Roosevelt's "Quarantine Speech."[63]

Once an "insider" of Japanese society, Guo found it too crude a generalization to blame all the Japanese indiscriminately for the savagery of war. Now and then he reminded his readers that the Japanese soldiers and people were not bloodthirsty animals; they went to war only because they were forced to do so by a handful of militarists in the army. But, Guo said in September 1937, revered statesmen such as Saionji Kinmochi, as well as "the bourgeoisie and the proletariat," had lost their freedom. "The situation in Japan," he said, "has entered an era of terror [after a series of assassinations of top-level politicians]. All of the political figures are so terrified that they either shut their mouths tight or become mouthpieces of the Japanese Army Headquarters."[64]

At the end of the 1930s, as the war entered a stalemate after the Japanese occupation of the eastern half of China, "culture" in Guo's writing began to carry a connotation of long-term national vitality, in contrast to war's destruction and degeneration. In "Culture and War," an essay he wrote in 1939 for the liberal newspaper *Da gong bao (L'Impartial)*, Guo argued that any aggressive war not only brought harm to the victim, but, more unfortunately, invited destruction on the aggressor itself. The political culture in Japan, he observed, showed exactly such signs of internal degeneration. From the political oppression of Communists and liberals, to the many assassinations, to the popularity of the erotic, grotesque, and nonsensical among Japanese youth, to government censorship of Tolstoy's *War and Peace* and Shakespeare's *Hamlet,* Guo found that Japan's war in the past twenty months had caused "not just crisis in politics and economy but bankruptcy of thought and culture as well." In contrast to the situation in Japan, he pointed out, the defense of the Chinese nation and culture had "uplifted our spiritual power for material and cultural creation" despite enormous material losses. In that "light of early dawn" of China's "national revival," Guo hoped that the Japanese people would wake up and liberate themselves from "the force of darkness."[65]

The discussion of the relationship between war and culture naturally led Guo into a reexamination of the shared past between China and Japan, and in the light of history Guo found in Japan not only an atavistic predator, but an ungrateful villain as well. In "The Past, the Present, and the Future of Japan," an essay written in late 1937, Guo depicted Japan's historical development in three stages. The initial period of Japanese culture, wrote Guo, was a "primitive state" that had "stagnated" for a long time. And then, contact with China from the sixth to tenth centuries brought an "electrifying" effect and enabled Japan "to jump suddenly from a primitive state to the garden of civilization." For the thousand years since then Japan had been "a cultural dependency, and for a while political vassal" to China. The third period came in the last seventy years, during which Japan benefited from China again: it was China that shielded Japan from Western invasion and offered its resources so that Japan was able to "successfully adopt Western civilization."[66] While China offered its generous gift of a four-thousand-year culture based on benevolence and righteousness *(yi renyi wei ben)* and "had helped the Japanese leave the primitive state and reach the same level [of civilization] as ours," Japan in return sent China "airplane [-bombings], gunfire, poison gas and germicidal warfare!"[67]

In 1942, however, Guo's harsh condemnation of Japan's ingratitude softened noticeably in an essay titled "An Overview of the Development of the Japanese Nation," his last major writing on Japan during the war years. Here Guo cited in detail Japanese language, clothing, food, and housing as evidence of their similarities with the culture of southern China. With their characteristic labial sounds, he noted, Japanese pronunciation *(kunyomi)* of many Chinese characters *(kanji)* actually had their parallels in Cantonese, such as *"kami"* and *"shamisen."* Traditional Japanese clothing such as *fundoshi* (loincloth for man) and *koshimaki* (waistcloth for woman), appeared to Guo similar to the costume worn by southern Chinese. Japanese food like sashimi also had its origin in the *yusheng* (raw fish) that was commonplace in Canton, a similarity also noted by Zhou Zuoren. On the basis of his special knowledge in philology and phonetics, Guo speculated that the pronunciation of "sashimi" in Japanese was derived from *"sa'siem,"* a Cantonese dressing used for eating raw fish.[68]

The reaffirmation of the cultural affinity between China and Japan was meant to bring up a contrast. Living in the rear area, Guo had the opportunity to reconsider the shared past of China and Japan and hence realized that, "although the old Japan was a branch of our Chinese culture, I feel that it had preserved many good things from our China." As he looked for an explanation of Japan's ability to retain and absorb the benefit of foreign influence, he found that the fundamental cause was internal rather than external. More explicitly than ever he praised Japan's successful modernization and admitted that "the Japanese themselves indeed have made a great effort, having endured immense hardship but remained wholeheartedly devoted." Turning to China, he recognized that internal obstacles to its modern progress had been "enormous." Above all, the Qing dynasty's 260-year rule had created "a huge impediment to the development of China's fortune." Toward the end of its reign the damage became particularly severe, Guo wrote, for "it became more conservative, and collaborated with foreign forces to suppress reform movements." As a result, "Japan had speedily progressed on the road to restoration whereas we, in order to wipe away obstacles and thorns, have gone through bloody revolutionary struggles for decades."

To many who were familiar with Guo's high-pitched criticism of Japan, his "Overview" must have sounded impressively remote from the negative descriptions so pronounced in his earlier writings. Yet the shift would not be so surprising if read in the context of the changing political climate in China during the early 1940s: since 1939 the united front between the Guomindang and the Communists had virtually reached a dead end, and in 1941 the partisan conflict reached its peak in the New Fourth Army Incident, when the Communist-led New Fourth Army clashed with government troops in Anhui Province. Guo, who since 1938 had been presiding over the Third Bureau of the Political Affairs Ministry for war propaganda in the central government, was never ambiguous about his bias toward the Communists, an attitude that so annoyed the National Government that it disbanded the Third Bureau in 1940.

Although the government, under Communist pressure, soon assigned Guo to head the Cultural Activity Committee,[69] Guo's defiance of the Guomindang only became bolder. He had written his overview of Japan for the Communist organ *Xinhua ribao*,[70] and his emphasis on the positive aspects of Japan was meant to underline a larger truth: the failure of the Guomindang government was the main obstacle to China's victory, progress, and modern success. As he now turned from anti-Japanese war propaganda to anti-Guomindang propaganda, he energetically explored the theme of resistance and rebellion against internal despotic rulers by writing historical dramas, which became his major literary creations for the remaining years of the war. One of his plays, *Qu Yuan*, depicted the famous poet-official in 300 B.C. and became a focal point of ideological war when it was staged in early 1942, with the Communists and progressive intellectuals praising its unmistakable political message of protests while the authorities and progovernment journals criticized it for its "distortion of history."[71] Guo, speaking through those indignant, defiant men and women of the past, had long ceased to be a "superfluous man"; he had become, as one of his admirers called him, "a trumpet for the [Communist] party."[72]

By the end of 1941 Guo had reached the age of fifty, the landmark in human life that Confucius called "the age of knowing one's heavenly mandate." Then, no one could yet see the end of the war against Japan, and no one could yet predict with certainty the process and outcome of the ongoing conflict between the Guomindang and the Communists—hence the risk and possible reward of leaning to one side. But Zhou Enlai, the famously charismatic Communist leader who had been a crucial influence ever since Guo's escape to Japan in 1928, was able to strike a prophetic note that would ring true in the next thirty-some years. On November 16, Zhou not only orchestrated the celebration of Guo's fiftieth birthday through parties and performances attended by social celebrities, but he also contributed an article to lead a two-page special column in the *Xinhua ribao,* "A Special Issue Celebrating Mr. Guo Moruo's Twenty-Five-Year Writing Career." "Just as Lu Xun was the guide to the New Culture Movement, Guo Muoro is the principal general of the New Culture Movement," wrote Zhou in this front-page article. "If Lu Xun was the pioneer who opened the path where there was none, Guo Moruo is the vanguard who leads all of us to make further progress.... We wish always that he will lead us to strive to the end."[73] As the surviving major general and the vanguard of the New Culture Movement, Guo would join and lead the progressive intellectuals' attack on the Guomindang when civil war erupted in the wake of the anti-Japanese war. When the Communists finally won national power in 1949, Guo was appointed president of the Chinese Academy of Science, the highest official research institution of the new People's Republic. In the decades that followed, he would also serve many other official functions in the cultural arena until his death, at age eighty-seven, in 1978.

8 For Rejuvenation

For China's survival, many Chinese had long argued, China must resist Japan's invasion. But how long could China's resistance last? It was a question that indignant anti-Japanese propaganda could not fully answer, and in the summer of 1938 the reality seemed to point to anything but hope. By then, the eastern coast had fallen into Japanese hands, and the National Government had moved to Wuhan in central China after the fall of Nanjing at the end of the preceding year. In late July, Wuhan, too, came under enemy threat when Jiujiang, a strategic city some one hundred miles east down the Yangtze River, fell into Japanese hands. Japanese military authorities now were gathering the largest force since the conflict had begun in 1937; the campaign for Wuhan, argued war hawks in Japan, would decisively end the military phase of what they called the "China Incident" and bring the Chinese government to its knees.[1] There was an equally tense anticipation of a showdown on the Chinese side, and the call for "defending the great Wuhan" was heard all over the city throughout July and August. Amid the military preparation, government personnel and civilian refugees, who had moved in from the coastal areas, were once again taking to the road, retreating farther west.

It was at this moment of anxious anticipation when *Da gong bao*, the most popular liberal newspaper in China, began to serialize an article titled "The Japanese: A Foreigner's Analysis." The immediate attraction of the article caused a sudden increase in readership, and the already widely circulated newspaper had to print ten thousand extra copies per issue during its serialization; some readers, it was said, even waited at the gate of the newspaper's office every morning so as to get the next issue as soon as it came out. Without knowing the author of the article until the final installment, the readers, struck by its "intimate familiarity with Japan" as well as its passionate language, suspected that the author was the romantic poet Guo Moruo. Some believed it was indeed a translation of a foreigner's work, as the subtitle suggested. Only when "Jiang Fangzhen in Hankou"[2] appeared in the last issue did many nod in assent: "Indeed, he deserves his reputation!"[3] Jiang Baili, having tantalized those who did or did not know him, now confided to them "the story about this book":

> In the afternoon of November 11 of last year [1937], I took a walk in the Green Forest in the suburb of Berlin. Having many troubled thoughts in mind and being not used to the new situation, I lost my way in the woods and began to feel anxious after walking without direction for two hours.... At just that moment a dim light appeared in the far distance, drawing me toward it for help. To my surprise, the light was on the other side of a lake; only after a long detour around the lake did I reach it. I knocked on the door in the dark ... and an old man appeared—he looked almost like an immortal from a fairy tale, with pink cheeks like that of an infant and silky hair as white as silver.... He invited me into his living room, where I saw many things from China and Japan; thus we began a conversation about the East. I realized that this silvery haired, pink-cheeked immortal had more knowledge about the East; he knew all that I knew, yet my understanding had never reached his depth.... It was from his notes that I worked out this book.... When he bade farewell to me, he admonished me:
> Whether in victory or defeat, never negotiate with them![4]

To many who read Jiang's articles, one of his contemporaries said, that particular article became their "beacon of optimism" in the uncertain years of the war. Some took Jiang's last sentence as the essential message of his article, which helped to "stabilize a disturbed popular mood." To others, Jiang's injunction to continue fighting became their motto during the war of resistance.[5]

In this allegorical ending, Jiang indeed was offering the doubtful Chinese a reassuring answer: Chinese resistance would be sustained through a long, trying course, but ultimate victory lay in their own hands. The coming of a total war between China and Japan, in his view, was the moment when "dim light" began to turn into the ever-brightening light of dawn. The tale, too, is a subconscious description of his own search for a guiding principle for China's national defense. His discovery of that dim light—the simple truth that the Sino-Japanese conflict would be a protracted war and the final victory was guaranteed to China—had come at the end of a long and circuitous path, with Jiang arriving at enlightenment only after various experiments with frustrating consequences.

Adversity and Adversary: Pathways to Strength

Japan had long remained Jiang's model of nation-building and military-building, even though his apprehension of Japan as China's next threat can be traced to the moment of its victory in the Russo-Japanese War of 1904–1905. Jiang's training in Germany during 1906 and 1910 only reinforced his conviction about the strength of the Japanese model. "When speaking about today's army in the world," he said in a 1912 lecture, "one must mention either Germany or Japan."[6] His observation of the German army also reconfirmed his earlier decision, made when he returned from Japan, that as a professional soldier he should stay away from politics and devote his energy to building the military. It was with this conviction that he accepted the presidency of the nation's first modern army officers' academy, the Baoding Military Academy, in 1912 and declined his friend Cai E's invitation to head the civilian government in Yunnan Province. The brief, six-month tenure at Baoding, however, led to Jiang's first confrontation with the limits of his vision and conviction.

Jiang came to Baoding when the school was in a morass of conflict between the administrators and the rebellious cadets. In October 1912, only a few months into the first training class, the seventeen hundred cadets at Baoding rose to protest the school's decision to dismiss some students for their revolutionary activities. The cadets, many of whom had fought in the uprisings of the 1911 Revolution, demanded reform at the academy and the removal of the current president, who had no modern training yet had gained his position as a disciple of the war minister, Duan Qirui. The conflict developed into a national incident when the students, defying an order from the war minister to disband, marched into Beijing and sent telegrams to appeal for support from the provincial governments. Public pressure forced the president of the republic, Yuan Shikai, to seek a nonpartisan candidate for the presidency of the academy, and the twenty-nine-year-old Jiang Baili, a rising star within the army with his outstanding records of modern training, was selected for the task.[7]

Jiang arrived in Baoding with the hope of training the best officers, who would be qualified to lead an army comparable to that of Japan and Germany—a hope made clear in his first address to the cadets. "I have been in both Germany and Japan, and have observed carefully their armies," said Jiang after giving high marks to both countries' military power. "But they neither have extra limbs, nor esoteric tricks.... I believe in our intelligence and ability; and I don't believe that our country will forever remain weak, nor do I believe our army will always be inferior to that of others." His goal in heading the academy, he assured the cadets, was "to build it into the best military academy, and to make you the best officers, so that you will lead the army in the future and train an army of excellence." Should he fail to fulfill these goals, he declared, he would "accept the responsibility by committing suicide."[8]

Jiang matched his words with his deeds. His work to improve discipline began with such details as uniforms; as the cadets remembered, he would stop a cadet to straighten a misplaced button or tighten a belt. A unified and serious appearance, he believed, symbolized the civility and modernity of a new army, and he himself provided a model. He came in person to command every barrack or field drill, always arriving on horseback with a cloak over his impeccable uniform. Whenever other teachers requested leave from classroom teaching, he stepped in as their substitute. His concern even extended to the cadets' daily diet, and he was often seen dining with the cadets in their canteen. In addition, he reformed the school's administration by replacing incompetent personnel with those trained in Japan's military schools, and he also had the textbooks rewritten by specialists with modern educations.[9]

Jiang's immediate goal was to instill the essence of both traditional and modern military morale in his students' minds. Among the favorite and repeated themes in his lectures, recalled one cadet, were the Chinese ideals of "loyalty, sincerity, wisdom, and courage" [zhong, cheng, zhi, yong], the Japanese bushidō, the European spirit of chivalry, and the sense of justice characteristic of wandering martial-arts errants in China. All that, Jiang hoped, would be internalized by the cadets when they assumed the duty of defending their new republic.[10]

The various changes, and especially his charismatic leadership, met with an enthusiastic response from the cadets. But his superiors in the Army Ministry saw Jiang as an intrusion into their inherited turf. Using their power, they cut his funding and vetoed his decisions on personnel matters. By June 1913, after returning from yet another fruitless trip to Beijing, Jiang concluded that he could not carry his task any further. He spent a sleepless night writing and drinking alone. In the early morning of the next day, June 18, he assembled the cadets and stepped on the podium in his full uniform. In an unusually low and heavy voice he praised the cadets' achievements at fulfilling what he had demanded, yet he admitted that he himself had failed in his promise to improve the academy and hence must assume responsibility. Giving the command "Attention!" he stepped down from the podium and strode toward the back of the hall, took out his pistol, and shot himself in the chest. Taken by surprise, the cadets watched as he turned around, leaned on his sword, stumbled two steps toward them, and fell.[11]

To the relief of all involved, Jiang's bullet missed his heart, thanks to a watchful servant who had rushed forward and pulled hard at Jiang's arm at the critical moment.[12] Instantly, the incident became a national scandal for the central government as the angry cadets, again, sent out many telegrams to provincial governments faulting the War Ministry for the devastating event. Yuan Shikai responded by sending several high-ranking officials to investigate the case. He also obtained medical help from the Japanese embassy in Beijing, which dispatched a Dr. Hiraga and a nurse, Satō Yato, to Baoding.[13] The doctor left after tending to the wound, leaving his patient in Satō's care. When she discovered that Jiang was again contemplating suicide and hoarding sleeping pills, the twenty-three-year-old nurse tried to encourage her patient with her motto, "Great forbearance is the greatest courage."

These words from a seemingly delicate young woman must have stricken a chord in Jiang and stimulated his desire to fight against adversity. Jiang, in fact, had fallen in love with her. But Satō was hesitant and returned to Japan soon after Jiang's recovery; she could not contemplate their union because, as she ostensibly stated, relations between China and Japan were not going to be harmonious. Indeed, "it would have been difficult to tell [the] villagers that she would get married to a Chinese," as one Japanese medical historian contemplates.[14] The unstated obstacles, however, were their own existing marriages. Jiang had been married in 1911 to Zha Pinzhen, a marriage arranged when he was only eight; Satō had married Nomizu Shinji, a man in her neighboring village, before she came to China as a nurse. Neither of them, though, were happy with these arrangements, and both sought escape in their work.[15] Determined to win her over, Jiang traveled to Satō's home in Niigata and eventually gained her and her family's consent. After Satō's divorce in April 1914, the couple married in Tianjin in the fall.[16]

The suicide attempt, which had brought sudden fame and personal happiness to Jiang's life, had other long-term effects on Jiang's personal career. Jiang had tried to take his own life "for duty" (xunzhi) and "for the nation," as he explained in his farewell letter to his mother. And his brave action following the Confucian tradition of "sacrifice for a cause" (xundao) made him a living hero to the cadets at Baoding.[17] He would be revered as the "president" (xiaozhang) by all Baoding graduates, however briefly he had served the academy. The connection, both personal and professional, with this particular group in China's modern army would make Jiang an unusual military leader in the country and, in the next decade, entangle him in and rescue him from political troubles. But in the meantime, Jiang had to face the limits of this "one vigorous strike" and reflect on the efficacy of personal, heroic sacrifice. The suicide attempt had brought public attention to the corruption and inefficiency of the government but failed to attain the "lofty goal" (zhishan zhi mudi) of modernizing the army and affecting the institutional change that he so desired. Not only did politics in the central government remain the same, but the Baoding Military Academy even took steps backward when Jiang left and the presidency was taken over by an obscurantist. Jiang, upon his recovery, was appointed as military adviser in the central government, a sinecure that guaranteed a comfortable income without any power or responsibility.[18] It was perhaps in view of his wife's words on the power of forbearance that Jiang accepted the position, turning his energy to the research and rethinking of military science.

Jiang had long held the ambition of bringing the strategic theories of the West and the East together, a task that was first inspired by a conversation with a German general, Wilhelm von Blume, a veteran staff officer of the Prussian-French War. The old general, already in his seventies when Jiang met him in the early 1910s in Berlin, reportedly said to the young Chinese, "Napoleon once said, a hundred years from now a strategist from the East will rejuvenate the principles of his ancestors' time-honored lessons and become the formidable enemy of the Europeans. Please do your best!" Jiang took the hint and the encouragement and made the task his personal mission ever since.[19]

In 1914, Jiang compiled "A New Interpretation of Sunzi," using the Prussian military theories of Clausewitz, Moltke the Elder, and von Blume to annotate the first chapter of *Art of War,* the most famous study of strategy in the Chinese classics by the legendary Sun Wu of the Spring and Autumn Period (722–481 B.C.).[20] In 1915, Jiang finished a complete annotation of *Art of War* in which he added to each of the thirteen chapters a new title in modern language; modern concepts such as "relationships between military maneuvers and leadership," "finance," "diplomacy," "domestic politics," and "general war" were used to bridge classical and modern concepts of warfare and politics.[21] In order to make his synthesized theory more accessible to the Chinese military, Jiang wrote a book, *Common Knowledge in Military Science (Junshi changshi).* Taking a broad approach to military conflict, Jiang explored extensively the relations of historical circumstances, national geography, material potential, and human will to military maneuvering. He stressed the importance of organization and discipline as critical steps in training an army of high quality. The book immediately became a popular reader in Chinese armies when it was published by the Commercial Press in 1917.[22] As its circulation expanded, Jiang's fame extended from a small group of the elite to thousands of foot soldiers. Some generals, such as Feng Yuxiang of the northwest army, regarded Jiang's opinions so highly that he compiled Jiang's pithy observations on military maneuvering, along with those by Zeng Guofan, Hu Linyi, and Yue Fei—all famous generals in Chinese history—into a handbook for his troops.[23] From this point forward, Jiang's contemporaries began to view him as the founder of modern Chinese military theory.

From *Common Knowledge in Military Science* also emerged a key element in Jiang's vision of a grand strategy for China's national defense in future military conflicts. It was an old question approached from a new angle: how to build military strength. In his reexamination of the past, Jiang was inspired by successful cases in history: the Japanese victories over China in 1894 and Russia in 1905, the Prussian victory over France in 1870, and the rise of the Huai Army in fighting the Taiping Uprising. The key to all these successes, he concluded, was in defining the adversary, for history proved that "defining the enemy first and training the army next makes the army strong, training the army first and defining the enemy next makes the army weak."[24]

History in the making seemed to confirm Jiang's conviction as he wrote these lines. In Germany's two-front war and in Japan's all-out continental expansion during the Great War, Jiang perceived a historical parallel that pointed toward a disastrous ending. Both strategies, in his view, were cases of failure or potential failure. Writing in 1921 he thus alluded to China's potential enemy in future conflicts, which "is taking an aggressive approach, greedy for this piece of rich land and that beautiful island ... without a sense of focus. Its failure, hence, is written in history."[25] He avoided naming Japan as a matter of diplomatic precaution, but the further development of his thinking made it clear that, from 1921, Japan had assumed the role of China's adversary in his strategic vision.

History's Suggestion: From Offense to Defense

It would be a long while before Jiang could proceed to translate his vision of building a strong national defense into reality. Throughout the first decade of the Republic, Chinese soldiers fought constant wars—not against foreign invaders, but among themselves in the service of opposing warlords. Jiang had broken off from Yuan Shikai in 1916, when Yuan attempted to restore the monarchy and place himself on the throne. Leaving the capital, Jiang joined Cai E, his close friend at Japan's Army Officers' Academy, in a Republic Defense Campaign. As soon as the republic was restored, Cai became gravely ill from exhaustion and malnutrition and had to leave the country for medical treatment in Japan. One early November morning in 1916, Cai was able to stand up with assistance; looking out the window, he saw Japanese fighter planes performing air drills. Turning toward Jiang at his side, Cai expressed his despair that he could do no more to modernize the Chinese army, while Japan had already transformed its warfare from two-dimensional to three-dimensional. "Although it was necessary to wage the Republic Defense Campaign," recalled Jiang of Cai's last words, "after all we pointed the gun inward and cannot take that as an achievement. I regret that I cannot die in a war against foreign enemies."[26] Cai E died the next day; to Jiang, Cai's words of regret became a constant call to duty.

In 1918, two years after Cai's death, World War I ended with the Allies' victory. The war had been a remote event for most Chinese, but for those who understood its deep causes and anticipated its profound impact on the world, it had been the main focus of their attention. Liang Qichao, the famous promoter of constitutional government and one of China's foremost interpreters of the West, had been contemplating a trip to Europe since early 1918. He had served as the minister of finance briefly after Yuan Shikai's death and, after his resignation, retained great influence in the central government as the leader of the Research Clique. Later in the year, he was able to obtain one hundred thousand silver dollars, with 60 percent from the government fund and 40 percent from private donations. He had also assembled a small Delegation of Observation to Europe to serve as a semiofficial advisory body to the official Chinese delegation to the Versailles Peace Conference. The group included five other distinguished specialists, all with whom he had close personal relationships: Jiang Baili, who had been a friend of Liang for nearly two decades since their Tokyo years, was the military specialist; Zhang Junmai (1887–1969, known as Carsun Chang in the West), a professor of political science at Beijing University who had become a close assistant to Liang in Tokyo at the beginning of the century and a pivotal member of Liang's Research Clique in the late 1920s, was the specialist on political affairs; Xu Xinliu (1890–1938), a graduate with metallurgy and economics degrees from British and French universities who had served as secretary to Liang in the Finance Ministry, advised on matters of economics; Ding Wenjiang (1887–1936), an Edinburgh-educated geologist who came to know Liang through Xu, provided advice on matters of science;[27] and Liu Chongjie (1881–?), a Japan-trained professional diplomat who had also known Liang for decades, dealt with diplomatic problems.[28]

The Delegation of Observation to Europe left China at the end of 1918 and arrived in Paris on February 18, 1919. During the ten months in Europe, they traveled through England, France, Germany, Belgium, Holland, and Italy, investigating major battle-fields and meeting famous scholars. In his characteristically passionate language, Liang Qichao recorded his amazement at the ancient architecture of the Roman Empire, the Gothic cathedrals in France, the classical atmosphere at Cambridge, and modern libraries, museums, and astronomical observatories. He was, above all, overwhelmed by the resilient power of culture that affected him throughout this sweeping tour in western Europe. Between trips, these distinguished Chinese turned themselves into diligent students, spending every spare minute reading reference materials and practicing the German, French, and English languages.[29]

This grand tour of post–World War I Europe had so impressed Liang and Jiang that, upon returning to China in March 1920, both reoriented their activities. Liang moved his focus from high politics back to popular education. In the next few years, he organized a Common Learning Society (Gongxue She), which, with Jiang Baili and Carsun Chang as major administrators, sponsored lecture tours of internationally renowned intellectuals, such as Bertrand Russell and Rabindranath Tagore, to China. Jiang also took over the editorship of *Liberation and Reconstruction* (*Jiefang yu gaizao*), a bimonthly sponsored by Liang's reformist group New Knowledge Society (Xinxue Hui), which began its publication in late 1919 and had become one of the major forums of discussion on socialism in China. When it was placed under Jiang's editorship in late 1920, the journal title was changed to *Reconstruction (Gaizao)*; its discussion also shifted noticeably from theories to practical issues such as arms control, provincial autonomy, and popular education.[30]

As with Liang, the impact on Jiang of this grand tour to Europe was almost electrifying. It made him reconsider the top-down approach to social change, which was taken for granted in his elitist education in the Confucian tradition and in the training at the Army Officers' Academy in Japan. He was left disheartened by his many years' work for incompetent and corrupt leaders from Yuan Shikai to Duan Qirui, yet his preference for orderly change trapped him in the service, one after another, of self-serving politicians. On the eve of the delegation's departure to Europe, Jiang had declared to his traveling companions a wish "to find the light of dawn." The ten-month tour of various countries did not disappoint him; he had encountered so many new vistas that, at the end of the journey, he was able to exclaim, "Indeed I have found it!"[31]

Jiang summarized his new discoveries in a new work he wrote upon returning from the tour, *A History of European Renaissance (Ouzhou wenyi fuxingshi)*. In this sweeping survey of the European Renaissance and Reformation, Jiang drew from French and Japanese scholars' lectures and works as well as his own personal observations. He recounted his amazement at the geographical contrast between a bright, passionate south and a gloomy, somber north, where the Renaissance and Reformation respectively originated. Citing Japanese writer Kuriyagawa Hakuson, Jiang explained the Renaissance and the Reformation as cultural dichotomies, rooted in the two separate and somewhat contradictory traditions of hedonic Hellenism and ascetic Hebrewism. Along the same lines he saw the modern development of European culture as bifurcated into southern and northern branches, one passionate and this-worldly, the other sober and religious. He was, above all, deeply intrigued by how suddenly the Renaissance liberated the "human spirit," just like "a spring thunder that brings tens of thousands of flowers to bloom." Thus he concluded that the greatest achievement of the Renaissance, along with the Reformation, was the "immediate contact of man with nature" and the "immediate communication between man and God."[32]

The attention to human spirit, to be sure, had been a persistent strand in Jiang's thoughts from the beginning of his education. The discovery of "human spirit" in European history, then, must have been reassuring to his long-held views on men and history. Yet for his strategic thinking, this discovery also generated a noticeable shift in emphasis. It was the tradition of "humanism," Jiang discovered, that gave rise to an antimilitarist tendency in the contemporary world, which was attested to by both political and military developments in Europe. Among the three major types of modern nations—monarchy, such as France under Napoleon; aristocratic rule, such as Britain and Germany before the war; and democracy based on popular support, such as in today's France and America—Jiang found that only the last type had the vitality to survive. The military failure of Germany in the recent Great War, in particular, "symbolized the 'demise of warlordism' and the 'bankruptcy of jingoism.'"[33] As a strategist, he found that the Battle of the Marne especially illuminated the weakness of an aggressive national policy. The defeat of the German army in the battle, argued Jiang, did not simply result from the deep penetration of an isolated army that had encountered immense difficulties in maintaining a long supply line; more important, it was the injustice of the invasion that weakened soldiers' morale. Although the French had made various mistakes in strategic planning, observed Jiang, it was "the determination to defend one's own homeland" that boosted their fighting spirit and ensured their final victory in the Battle of the Marne and, hence, the Allies' victory in the Great War.[34]

Turning to his own country, Jiang was elated to find that China's political, economic, and military traditions "converged" with the current trend in the world—a trend that endorsed self-defense and anti-expansionism. Politically, he wrote, Chinese tradition contained the seeds of democracy, for history proved that any ruler who failed to serve the people always ended up losing the Mandate of Heaven. Economically, "every aspect of the Chinese people's life ... is self-sufficient, making it unnecessary to be aggressive toward others." Militarily, then, China was a nation "most capable of self-defence," for the awareness of and the need for defending one's own homeland would sustain the Chinese people's determination to prevail in times of foreign invasion. And Jiang felt more confident in perceiving two possible assessments of China's history and strength: "The twenty-four histories was nothing but a history of shame and defeat" if judged by the standards of imperialism, "but it becomes a history of glory if viewed from the perspective of democracy and socialism."

That discovery of the anti-militarist trend and the rediscovery of China's "history of glory" further prompted Jiang to reorient his military thinking. In one of his public speeches he pointed out that "[i]n the past twenty years, what we have seen and learned about strategy and tactics was all imported from the jingoistic, aggressive countries, which contaminated us with the deplorable habit of over-sensitivity and emotional tension." Now China "must rid itself of that expansive and discredited foreign stuff."[35] After all, self-defense as a national strategy had been a proven wisdom in Chinese history, which had been overshadowed by imported aggressive military theory only during the last two decades.

Speaking of China's national strategy in more concrete terms, Jiang advocated "the French tradition" as the best alternative. He considered Switzerland's compulsory military service an economical and efficient approach to national mobilization well suited to China's needs.[36] He realized that France's strategy during the Great War, which "concentrates the military force on the second front," might be applied to China's future conflict with its potential adversary, as he wrote in 1921:

> Regarding the current situation, what worries us most is that most aggressive country in our neighborhood.... The only method we can use to prevail upon our enemy is to do the opposite of its actions. That is to say, if the enemy chooses to fight a speedy war, we use protraction to exhaust it; if the enemy places the gravity of force on the first frontline, we move to the second frontline and preserve our energy deep in the hinterland, thus making its force useless momentarily. I predict that this method will certainly drive the enemy to death.[37]

In the understandable desire to avoid a diplomatic dispute, Jiang never named Japan directly as China's enemy when he publicly discussed national strategy. Yet no one could miss his point when he explicitly rejected the "strategy and tactics ... imported from the jingoistic countries."[38] Meanwhile, Jiang chose to actively promote provincial autonomy and reduction of the armed forces, hoping to eliminate warlordism, the Chinese version of that "expansive and discredited foreign stuff." While editing *Reconstruction* and arranging lecture tours for foreign scholars, he traveled frequently between north, east, and central China and gave particular attention to the reforms in Hunan, where, he hoped, the changes would eventually make that province "a Switzerland," a symbol of self-defense, in China.[39]

Detour through Darkness

Despite Jiang's increasing confidence in his new orientation of military thinking and in China's potential to win a defensive war, his emphasis on the strategy of a protracted war sounded defeatist to others, including those who admired and respected him. In the spring of 1923, Jiang returned from his hometown after attending his mother's funeral and spending a period of mourning there. When the train passed Xuzhou, the strategic city that connected two major south-north and east-west railways, he suddenly remarked to Gong Hao, his former student at the Baoding Military Academy who was traveling with him, that once war broke out between China and Japan, the Beijing-Hankou and Tianjin-Pukou Railways would fall into Japanese hands, forcing China to take the three "Yangs"— Luoyang, Xiangyang, and Hengyang—as the line of defense. Gong thought his teacher was too pessimistic in predicting China's failure to hold its defenses along the coast and its retreat so far to the interior. The war's development in mid-1938, however, would affirm Jiang's prescience.[40]

Jiang had to wait another fifteen years before his insights could be fully comprehended and appreciated by his fellow Chinese. Meanwhile, he realized that he had been over-optimistic about the demise of warlord politics. Contrary to his hopeful prediction, warlordism died hard—witness the Hunan-Zhili War in 1921, the First Zhili-Fengtian War in 1922, the Second Zhili-Fengtian War in 1924, and the Zhejiang-Fengtian War in 1925, to mention only the major conflicts. The endless civil wars cast a dark shadow over Jiang's life because of his personal involvement. The two dominant figures in these conflicts—Wu Peifu, the warlord who then controlled central China, and Sun Chuanfang, the warlord whose base was in Zhejiang Province—had on different occasions solicited Jiang's service as adviser. Jiang, on his part, was not without the illusion that either one of these military men might emerge as a true national leader for China. It was also his hope that these conflicts—all fought against the Fengtian warlord Zhang Zuolin, whom Jiang knew collaborated with the Japanese military—would annihilate Japanese influence in Manchuria and north China.[41]

The desire to use a "good" warlord to achieve national unification was not Jiang's alone. Ding Wenjiang, Jiang's fellow traveler on the grand tour to Europe in 1919 who was now director-general of the Port of Greater Shanghai, shared similar hopes and collaborated with Jiang in advising Sun Chuanfang.[42] Yet neither Wu Peifu nor Sun Chuanfang proved to be a viable candidate for China's leadership, and both were defeated by the advancing National Revolutionary Army in 1926. Disappointed with both men's vanity and thirst for personal power, Jiang distanced himself from Wu in the spring of 1926 and from Sun at the end of the same year. He was disheartened by his own fruitless efforts and perhaps by his vain hope as well and became so exhausted that he decided to leave with his wife for Japan and spend part of the summer in Niigata, his wife's hometown.[43]

The rise of the Guomindang was probably not what Jiang Baili could have foreseen in the early 1920s, when the party appeared to be a mere local power like many others. In the mid-1920s, Jiang was apprehensive of the Guomindang, for he, like his friends in Liang Qichao's circles, suspected it to be an extension of Red Russia's influence in China.[44] But various signs by March 1927 had convinced the members in Liang's circles that Jiang Jieshi was not a friend to the Soviet Union and the Communists. Moreover, many former graduates from the Baoding Military Academy, who all revered Jiang Baili as their "president," emerged as an important force within the National Revolutionary Army as they joined the Northern Expedition and rose quickly to middle and higher positions of leadership. Some voices had been calling for Jiang Baili to be brought into the military apparatus of the newly risen regime. The prospect appeared most opportune in March, when the National Revolutionary Army entered Nanjing. Jiang Baili was invited to the soon-to-be capital to provide suggestions for the future government. Jiang Jieshi, who was four years his junior and who graduated later from another, less prestigious Japanese military school, Shinbu Gakkō, addressed Jiang Baili as "master" (xiansheng). Jiang Baili's recommendation that China should avoid immediate conflict with Japan coincided with the Guomindang's policy; he also agreed to go to Tokyo in a private capacity to make informal contact with Japanese politicians.[45] The trip, made in May, like the one taken by Dai Jitao a month earlier, was fruitless; the Tanaka cabinet had already decided to pursue its "positive policy" and dispatched troops for the first Shandong Expedition.

Not only was Jiang Baili's first service of semi-official diplomacy inconsequential, but his relationship with the new regime soon deteriorated as well. At the end of 1928 Tang Shengzhi, a graduate of the Baoding Military Academy and victorious general in the national army, led a rebellion against Jiang Jieshi. As Tang's former teacher, Jiang Baili had kept in touch with Tang via a radio station in Shanghai, which infuriated Nanjing;[46] he was accused of conspiring with the rebels and put into a special prison in Nanjing in 1930. Jiang was treated with lenience, yet the threat of secret execution—as had happened to Deng Yanda, the leader of the

Third Party and Jiang's one-time prison mate—always hung in the air. In solitary confinement, Jiang busied himself with reading Kant's philosophy, telling stories to his two daughters, who came with their mother for daily visits, and practicing calligraphy by copying Buddhist sutras. From Shanghai he also ordered gramophone records, and Beethoven and Wagner—both celebrating grandness and heroism—became his favorites.[47]

At the end of 1931, Jiang Baili ended his nearly two-year-long prison term and returned to Shanghai with his overjoyed wife and cheering daughters. It was his prestige among the Baoding graduates, now an indispensable force within Jiang Jieshi's army, that had prevented the authorities from taking more drastic measures. Especially important were the efforts by Chen Mingshu (1889–1965), a graduate of the Baoding Military Academy and the Commander in General of the Defense Force of the Nanjing-Shanghai area, who energetically defended Jiang Baili and mediated his case.[48] But the most pressing reason for Jiang's release was probably the escalating tension between China and Japan in 1931. Jiang returned to Shanghai just before the Japanese marines opened a second front in the International Settlement after the Manchurian Incident the preceding September. During the month-long fighting, from January to February 1932, Jiang became an extra chief of staff for the Nineteenth Route Army, whose high-ranking officers often came to his residence for advice and suggestions.[49]

The Shanghai Incident of 1932, as the journalist Tao Juyin observed, was "the first time when Chinese soldiers' guns turned outward."[50] In Jiang's career as a strategist, it also became the first time he was allowed to serve immediately the national interests of defense. In 1933, he made another visit to Japan in a civilian capacity, intending to observe Japan's war preparations. Although it is not clear whether Jiang went with any covert official assignment, he did meet Araki Sadao and Mazaki Jinzaburō, both his seniors (*senpai*) from the Army Officers' Academy and now pivotal figures in the so-called Imperial Way faction (*Kōdō-ha*), recently at the pinnacle of its political influence in Japan. Jiang was also invited to dine with Prince Kan'innomiya Kotonohito, the army's chief of staff. Some of these powerful men made unabashed demands for China's northeastern territory; others demanded that China come to the negotiating table immediately. Reading these signals, Jiang realized that the time for his country's defense preparation was running out.[51]

In response to the radically changing situation, Jiang, upon his return, conducted extensive research on China's strategic materials, suggesting that Hunan in central China be prepared as the strategic base for the upcoming war.[52] During the spring of 1935, when the Japanese army pushed farther from Manchuria into north China, Jiang toured the area and sent a number of suggestions to Jiang Jieshi, recommending that the government pay particular attention to "technical problems" in diplomacy and be flexible in dealing with the ever-changing situation. He thought that it was necessary to take "an endure-humiliation-ism" *[renru zhuyi]* stance so as to "induce international sympathy" and to "stimulate national morale."[53] Toward the end of 1935 Jiang was appointed a senior adviser on the Military Committee of the central government. The national crisis finally had brought him back to public duty.

"Japanese: A Foreigner's Analysis"

The protracted war that Jiang had anticipated as early as 1923 finally arrived in the summer of 1937. During the months that followed, China's policymakers still tried to settle the conflict through negotiation, or at least tried to use diplomatic means to ward off the quick advancement of the invading army. By November 1937, the Sino-Japanese conflict had already extended from north China to the Yangtze delta; but German ambassador Oscar Trautemann's offer of a good office to mediate the Sino-Japanese conflict seemed to have kept hopes for peace alive.[54] To reinforce Trautemann's mediation and to dissuade Italy and Germany from giving assistance to Japan, the National Government sent two missions to Europe, and Jiang Baili was chosen to lead one of them as Jiang Jieshi's personal envoy.[55] In late October, Jiang was received by Mussolini; Il Duce was impressed by Jiang's diplomatic eloquence but nevertheless went his own way and joined the Axis Alliance.[56] Jiang also held confidential conversations with the British and American attachés in Rome, who appeared to be "utterly pessimistic" about constraining Japan, though the British appeared to be more concerned with their interests in southern China.[57] On November 1, Jiang proceeded on to Berlin, hoping to pass along personally the

Chinese leader's message to Hitler. During these days of waiting he received a telegram from home informing him that China's defense had rapidly disintegrated as the Japanese succeeded in outflanking Chinese resistance in Shanghai. The national capital of Nanjing was now exposed to the advancing enemy.[58]

Although Jiang Baili was confident that in the long run China would prevail, he knew that the will of the Chinese people was under the most stressful test when they faced the enormous losses. Meanwhile, his mission to Italy and Germany had failed; Hitler never granted him an audience, and instead sent Göring to meet Jiang briefly at the end of November, without promising anything. For the next few months, while Jiang remained in Berlin to observe the war from Europe, what he heard from home was news of China's repeated defeats and forced retreat. Only on his return voyage in late spring 1938 did he learn of the Battle of Taierzhuang. Jiang was, of course, exhilarated by China's first major victory in the war, but he was more heartened by the international response he saw in the ship captain's congratulatory toast to the Chinese passengers. In that civil gesture Jiang found reassurance, and he turned to his youngest daughter, who had been traveling with him: "You see, international courtesy is so fair—we show one inch of strength, they give us one inch of respect!"[59]

That strength, as Jiang had learned through decades of adversity, ultimately lay in the will to overcome and triumph. "Combating closely within a narrow lane, killing is done like cutting grass without noise!" *(Zaixiang duanbing xiangjie chu, sharen rucao bu wensheng!)* was a line from classical Chinese poetry that had inspired Jiang in the 1920s when he searched for paths to a Chinese Renaissance. The deepest source for change, he then realized, lay in everybody's "narrow lane" of the heart. "Alas! Only when we consciously wage a determined war in this narrow lane, might the eternal light shine all over the world!"[60] Now that the enemy had indeed pressed China into a narrow lane, would China win? How could China win?

It was against fear, the greatest threat to one's ability to win in close combat within the narrow lane of the heart, that Jiang wrote "Japanese: A Foreigner's Analysis." The opening of this long article began with a dramatic tone typical of the Jiang Baili who loved dialectics:

Nobody in this world is more sympathetic toward the Japanese than I am! . . .

Ancient tragedies were caused by unknown fate; modern tragedy is the reflection of its players' personalities, hence is subjectively created. Yet the great tragedy we are watching is the combined result of the two.[61]

Following these lines of empathy and sarcasm came a colorful and allegorical description of the Japanese character. Jiang portrayed the Japanese as "a passionate race," shaped by their southern origin and their natural environment. They "lacked the capacity for introspection" because "the charming and radiant landscape constantly stimulates this passionate race's senses, drawing its attention outward." They were "short-tempered" and "pessimistic" as well, due to the influence of the "limpid but short and rapid rivers" and frequent earthquakes and volcanic eruptions. That pessimism had its ultimate reflection in the Japanese image of their national flower, *sakura,* "for its most beautiful moment also signals its immediate decay." And there was pessimism, too, in Japan's national spirit, *bushidō,* for "the most glorious moment of a samurai is the moment of his death on the battlefield."[62] Many Chinese were familiar with these symbols of Japanese culture, yet Jiang's words provided a timely interpretation when they so badly needed assurance of their potential to prevail in this ongoing battle of weapons and human will.

Having thus set the background, Jiang next moved to Japan's past, or "the unknown fate," as he termed it in the opening lines. On two occasions, noted Jiang, Japan had greatly benefited from that "unknown fate." The first was the rule under Emperor Meiji, whose "painstaking efforts changed Japan into a great, strong nation." Much of Meiji Japan's success resulted from the emperor's determination to forbear: he steered his nation through thick fog on the turbulent seas of world politics, avoiding many tempting but unrewarding conflicts, such as the agitation to invade Korea in the 1870s, the Triple Intervention in 1898, and the decision on the Anglo-Japanese Alliance. Through Emperor Meiji's wisdom and resolution, modern Japan was saved from drifting on to the wrong course.[63]

World War I was another period when Japan was deeply influenced by "unknown fate," yet the result was mixed at best. Although "the influx of money from Europe" had helped bring about an economic boom in Japan, it also "brought great frustration to the Japanese," for the society had since become radically polarized between the rich and the poor. More detrimental, remarked Jiang, was "the temptation" of overseas expansion when European powers were forced to retreat either by defeat or exhaustion. Reinforcing one another, internal agitation and the outside lure had turned Japan into "a fishing boat in a hurricane," which was pushed to the sky by its ambition to conquer the world at one moment and sunk to the hell of pessimism at another.[64]

World War I, therefore, brought various internal contradictions into Japanese politics, policy-making processes, and diplomacy. Jiang called it an "innate split" resulting from the lack of wise leadership during the radical socioeconomic changes in those years. The most powerful forces in acting out this "innate split" in Japanese political life, wrote Jiang, were the young officers in the army. Recruited mostly from peasant families, these officers were shocked by the sharp contrast between the impoverished rural Japan that shouldered the burdens of industrialization and a prosperous but snobbish urban Japan. Once in the army, they emerged as a new generation with up-to-date training in the use of novel weapons that the older, powerful generals did not understand. All the experiences of social disparity and incompatibility between ability and power increased the young officers' frustration and indignation; they became disobedient, easily susceptible to the wiles of "instigators." Being born "short-tempered," Jiang reminded his readers, the young officers eagerly imbibed in the "childish" revolutionary theory of the "fake hero" Kita Ikki as their "Holy Bible."[65]

Adopted by the young officers as a means to implement "internal reforms," terror of assassination had now become the hallmark of Japanese politics. Jiang admitted that such drastic action had been "a reality since the beginning of modern Japan," but it had become so rampant only in recent decades: the great politician Itō Hirobumi; Hara Kei, the first "common people's prime minister"; Inukai Tsuyoshi, the champion of constitutional politics; Takahashi Korekiyo, the seventy-eight-year-old business genrō;[66] Minister of Finance Inoue Junnosuke; and the "transcendent admiral" Saitō Makoto had all fallen to assassins. Such was what Jiang called the "mad reality" in Japanese politics that was driving their politicians to "dance on the volcano day after day!"[67]

Jiang then found that the same pattern of internal contradiction was reflected in both Japan's financial policy and its foreign policy. Hardly any other country, indicated Jiang, kept absolute parity in the budget for both the army and the navy, but that was precisely the case in Japan, resulting from these two forces' fierce competition for greater power. Worse still, the rivalry between the two branches of the military led to "two approaches" in diplomacy, one pro-Russian and the other pro-British. In practice, the ascendence of the military caused "dual diplomacy" as well, for the general staff had its own overseas intelligence system that often took action independent of Tokyo's official line.[68]

The Japanese, Jiang now concluded, had already become weak from the inside out. All these structural problems, unfolding through "the unknown fate," had trapped them in a dilemma and in pessimism. The contradiction in the Japanese mentality was seen in their "admiration of foreigners," fostered by a long history of learning from China and the West. But that admiration "has changed into jealousy" so that the Japanese began to boast of their "unique ability." Yet underneath their proclamation of "national crisis" (C: *guonan*, J: *kokunan*) was "an undercurrent of xenophobia," which also cast "a shadow of pessimism" because the champions for "national crisis" knew that it was "merely propaganda."[69]

From a strategist's point of view, Jiang saw the Japanese military's disobedient and independent action producing a fatal weakness: the lack of consistency in national strategy. The current conflict, he maintained, demonstrated exactly this problem; whereas the navy saw Great Britain as its enemy, the army considered Russia as its adversary, thus leaving the war with China unjustified. How could Japanese soldiers maintain morale when they fought without purpose? How could Japan win the war with Britain or Russia, asked Jiang, if it could not even win a war with China?[70]

War and Rejuvenation

In September 1938, the National Government issued an order appointing Jiang Baili acting president of the Army University.[71] In the preceding twenty-five years, Jiang had preferred to appear in the public in a Western suit, but he began to wear the Chinese long gown more often after his release from prison in 1931. His new appointment resulted in an instant transformation of his appearance. He threw away the long gown and changed into the military attire he had worn at the Baoding Military Academy: uniform, belt, and sword. In the eyes of one observer, suddenly he glowed with youth and exuberance.[72]

Returning with his military uniform was the outspoken optimism that Jiang had discovered during his grand tour through Europe in 1919–1920. Since that time he had made another extended trip to Europe in 1936, investigating war preparations in Italy, Austria, Yugoslavia, Czechoslovakia, Hungary, Germany, France, and Great Britain, returning via the United States to China. The trip brought Jiang firsthand knowledge of current military developments; he was especially impressed by Italian strategist Guilio Douhet's theory of using the air force to destroy an enemy's potential to resist. Returning from the trip he recommended that China follow the Italian practice and build an air force.[73] Yet the most lasting impression for him was the renewal and reaffirmation of his earlier conviction about the vitality of culture. In the early summer of 1937, Jiang was invited to lecture at the Lushan Officers' Training Corps (Lushan Junguan Xunliantuan), a regular training program for high-ranking officers in the national army. In an unusual approach for this military program, Jiang ended his lectures on current military theories and practice with three talks on his tour of Italy. His opening remarks conveyed his amazement at the almost magical power of the birthplace of the Renaissance, and his words were imbued with dialectical imagination:

> Indeed we must celebrate our good fortune! Once we step on the land of Europe, we have entered the oldest as well as the newest place in the world, so rich in history, yet so full of modernity. Only because it is old can it be renewed, only because it renews can it retain the old. . . .
>
> Rome is a sea of cultures, . . . Rome is a mountain of cultures. . . . Just as the western proverb says that every road leads to Rome, Rome also reaches every corner of the world. I differ from many others in defining culture; I call attention, especially, to its fermenting function; whatever it touches, it renews and ferments, [just as fermenting] makes sour grapes into luscious wine.[74]

Just as he found Rome a symbol of a forever-renewing history, in China's ongoing war of resistance Jiang perceived a growing hope for his nation's eventual revival. While on yet another trip to Europe as Jiang Jieshi's personal envoy in 1937, he sent *Da gong bao* an article titled "The Premises of [China's] Resistance War" to clarify "two premises in our Chinese thinking that Westerners find hard to comprehend." The first premise, he wrote, was "an optimistic attitude" nurtured by China's long history. The past and the endless social changes it entailed taught Chinese that "the strong will not always stay strong, and the weak will not always remain weak. Despite the repeated foreign conquest of the Han, Tang, Song, and Ming dynasties, the hope of future revival has always been alive in the people's subconsciousness." The second premise was "an intuitive determination." The current Sino-Japanese War was "a manifestation of our national determination" because history proved that "never has it been possible to break a nation's will for survival and freedom." China's agrarian economy and vast hinterland, he reasserted, would provide the material base for long-term resistance; losing Shanghai and Nanjing, he wrote, meant only losing "a dead port" and "a few modern buildings," but the losses could "never reduce China's potentials for resistance."[75]

In late September 1938, as the Chinese troops poised to defend Wuhan, the Chinese government was preparing to retreat farther west to Chongqing. The war had been going on for more than a year, and in repeated defeat and retreat many apparently had lost faith in China's future. Jiang, however, saw the situation in a radically different light. On the eve of this massive withdrawal, he wrote a long article for *Da gong bao* titled "The Causes and Consequences of the One-Year-Old Resistance War." Arguing against both the pessimists, who saw subjugation to the conquerors as the only alternative, and the optimists, who "took the reality of the one-year-old resistance war as ... making a few speeches, a number of pamphlets, and a few maps," he urged his fellow citizens to comprehend the resistance in terms of "its moving force."

What Jiang called the "moving force" was "a particular trend of cultural development," flowing through China's three thousand years of history and evolving over three great periods: from its origin in northern China during the Zhou period (1100 B.C.–771 B.C.) to the unification of China during the Qin dynasty (221 B.C.); from the early Han dynasty (206 B.C.) to the end of the Song dynasty

(A.D. 1279); and from the end of the Song dynasty to the founding of the Republic in 1912. The earliest period was a time when "the Chinese race had established its own culture," with the unique characteristics of "assimilative offense" *(tonghua de gongshi)* and "military defense" *(wuli de shoushi)*. Over time the Grand Canal became the symbol and means of peaceful integration and the Great Wall the symbol and means of military resistance. Nurtured by "a culture of great plains" *(dapingyuan de wenhua)* the Chinese had cultivated "a magnanimity that allowed others to develop [on Chinese land]." And with that magnanimity the Chinese assimilated cultures from the west (India and Turkistan) during the second period. At the same time, the invasion of the Mongols and the Manchus "trained our ability at resistance," which, at the end of the third period, became the moving force for modern change, when the call for "revolution" around 1910 could be so readily "instilled into ears, transmitted into hearts, and motivated into actions."

Taking this long perspective on history, Jiang concluded that the seeds of both "assimilative offense" and "military defense," which "have been planted three thousand years ago," were approaching the stage of "sprouting and blooming" now. The current war, therefore, was just another trial of China's capabilities for military resistance. The young generation, Jiang wrote, should feel "very fortunate" because the war provided them with a real opportunity "to go to the people," which had been merely a slogan, or an ideal, during the May Fourth movement. With students from the north and the south moving into the southwest and the people in the southwest receiving new things, the war experience "cuts a channel between the ideal and reality for society" and "bridges a pure heart and agile sensitivities for individuals"; that grand scale of change, predicted Jiang, would be "the greatest fruit of this resistance war."

The current war would bring a "minor benefit" to China as well: it would help to cleanse the "cancer," the Chinese traitors, from society and hence purify the nation. But nothing, maintained Jiang, would be so significant as the training of the bodies and minds of millions who had plunged into that great classroom of "practical experiences" and "social test," especially when that test was undertaken amid "the emotions of great grief, indignation, and excitement." Looking back at the past year of war, Jiang found himself deeply impressed by the changes among the youth. In their reportage on the war he found that their observations had become "more thoughtful," their feelings "deeper," and their attitude "more earnest." He urged them to move forward "toward greatness" and, as his teachers once encouraged him, "toward the practical."

In this long commentary on China's resistance, Jiang also gave a few lines of advice to his "Japanese military juniors" (C: *houbei*, J: *kohai*). Since 1922, he reminded them, he had pointed out that failure to define war aims would lead to defeat. Given Germany's failure at fighting a two-front war in the past, Japan's vacillation between southward thrust and northward thrust was the major cause of its weakness. To his "military juniors" in Japan who had learned only a few tricks from the West but never comprehended that truth, Jiang asked, "How can you boast of being the master of Asia?"[76]

Like his article on the Japanese that had just been published in the same newspaper, this review of the past year in light of China's innate "moving force" struck a resonant chord among its readers. In these busy months Jiang traveled back and forth between Wuhan, the temporary capital, and Hunan Province, where the Army University was located. His temporary lodgings in Wuhan, the Deming Hotel, was always flooded with visitors whenever he came. Journalists came most often, seeking comments and soliciting more articles; one of them, Tao Juyin, had become a close friend and wrote the first biography of Jiang soon after Jiang's death. Another journalist, Cao Juren, who had been a history professor for more than a decade, also discarded his long gown and put on a military uniform to become a frontline reporter once the war broke out; that dramatic shift in his career, Cao admitted, was greatly influenced by Jiang's thought and example. Jiang was also, as Cao recalled, the first among many leaders he knew who warned that the upcoming conflict would be a war of attrition.[77]

In 1937–1938 Jiang's family, six in all, were mobilized. His wife had first evacuated to Hong Kong with two of their four daughters, and Jiang brought his youngest daughter back to China from Germany. Only their third daughter, who was in a critical stage of vocal-music study, was left in Germany. Jiang wanted his wife and daughters to remain in China so that they could read the great book of war in this "age of great change that is rare even in a hundred years." That, he believed, was the best way to express his love for them.[78]

At the end of October 1938, Wuhan finally fell into Japanese hands. Jiang Baili was already on his way to Zunyi, Guizhou Province, where the Army University was to be relocated. At every stop he was asked by the local government to give public speeches and provide advice on war preparations. When he reached Yishan, a small town in Guizhou Province, he was too exhausted by the intense social activities to proceed farther immediately, so he decided to postpone his trip and take a few days' break. On the night of November 4, just before his planned departure for the Army University, Jiang died of a heart attack in his sleep.

9 With Sorrow

Unlike Jiang Baili, the military strategist who had foreseen a war with Japan as well as its course of development long before the actual event, average Chinese found themselves overwhelmed by the catastrophe and exigencies of war. As Chinese defenses along the coast collapsed within a year, the civilians in the area had only two basic options: either retreat inland with the government in hopes of protection, or remain in the area under Japanese occupation. The choice was mostly their own, free of public interference. That, however, was not the case for Zhou Zuoren. Ever since the relocation of universities in Beijing (then called Beiping) began in the wake of the Marco Polo Bridge Incident in the summer of 1937, personal letters and public appeals from friends had come to him now and then, urging him to come south with other government institutions.

Why Zhou's whereabouts should attract this much public attention can best be explained by his widely recognized prestige. He was regarded as a leading writer in China by liberals and radicals alike, despite their differences in judging his political inclinations. He was viewed not as a "man of letters" only, but as a "thinker" as well and was given the crown of "the king of the essayists" by the French-educated writer and literary critic Su Xuelin, who in 1934 described Zhou's works as "a proud mountain peak, standing amidst the raging tides [of our time] and revealing its increasingly distinctive color." In 1937, Guo Moruo, who had just fled Japan, wrote about Zhou from yet another perspective: "In recent years, there are only a few who can establish a distinctive style and can stand as equals to international friends and gain human dignity for our nation, and our Zhitang [Zhou Zuoren] is one of them." To the rumor that Zhou had spent nine thousand dollars on a chartered airplane to fly south, Guo responded passionately: "Nine thousand dollars is nothing, though it is an extravagant sum at this time of crisis; yet if we lose one Zhitang, the loss is priceless." And Guo valued highly Zhou's symbolic appeal for China's war efforts: "There are many Japanese who admire Zhitang; if he can fly south, and even if he does not make any statement, the action itself, I think, will be a dose of supreme tranquilizer to Japan's brutal General Staff and the Japanese who have lost human freedom while running amok for military mobilization."[1] The intellectual circles' great expectations for Zhou Zuoren also explained why, in 1938, the news of Zhou's attendance at a meeting in Beijing sponsored by the Japanese *Osaka mainichi shinbun* had so disturbed writers in Wuhan; eighteen of them—including Zhou's personal friend Yu Dafu, but with the noticeable absence of Guo Moruo—wrote an open letter to "admonish" him "to leave Beiping immediately," lest he be considered "a great traitor to the nation."[2] Later that year, Hu Shi, too, sent Zhou a poem from London while he was there on a diplomatic mission, urging him to leave occupied Beijing.[3]

Zhou understood his friends' anxiety but did not share their logic. He was not unconcerned with "national integrity" *(minzu qijie)*, but he found political loyalty too simple an answer to all the problems in real life. His several letters to a friend in the south during the uncertain months after the fall of Beijing contained a straightforward explanation for why he did not leave: he was bound by a responsibility to nine family members, including his younger brother Zhou Jianren's estranged wife, his married daughter, and several children. It would be a daunting task to move all these women and children to the hinterland. He knew that remaining in Beijing would not be easy either, and his anticipation of the difficult days ahead was evident in a change of name for his study, in June 1937, from "Bitter Rain" ("Kuyu Zhai") to "Living-in-Bitterness" ("Kuzhu Zhai").[4] By then, Zhou had given much thought to the approaching war and made clear where his loyalties would lie.

Between "A Culture within Heart" and "A Reality before Eyes"

As with many other Chinese, the thought of a war with Japan had been with Zhou for much of the first half of the 1930s, but he had written very little about Japan—five book reviews in six years since

1928. Unlike many others, he remained an outsider to the strident rallying of national salvation, being at once deeply disillusioned with a government that "stores guns and cannons and gunboats for internal use" and upset by the "empty talk" in popular anti-Japanese propaganda.[5] He had never stopped writing on affairs within China, though his language had noticeably changed to combine both the classical and the vernacular, as necessitated by his many and frequent references to works written in the premodern era. And this allusive and allegorical style sometimes made young radicals think he had "fallen behind the times."[6]

That reticence, however, was broken less than a year after a visit to Japan in the summer of 1934, his first since the 1919 visit to the New Village and his last before the war. His arrival in 1934 became a public event and caused a great stir in Japan's literary circles, bringing together old friends and new admirers. He was greeted by the young generation of scholars in Chinese literature, and eminent writers in Japan such as Shimazaki Tōson, Arishima Ikuma, and Togawa Shūkotsu honored him with dinner parties and receptions. Reporters from newspaper and literary journals such as *Asahi shinbun* and *Kaizō* came to interview him, and a number of cultural organizations invited him to give speeches. While the hospitality and enthusiasm deeply moved him, as evidenced in some of his writings, a Japan that was moving toward violence and militarism, which he directly experienced in this visit, seemed to have so disturbed him that, upon returning to China, he reopened the sealed topic of Japan once again.

A distinct and urgent sense of ominous change surfaced in his first essay, which was prompted by the news, in March 1935, of the death of Yosano Hiroshi, a famous writer of the Meiji era. Zhou had hoped to meet Yosano in his visit the year before but had missed him, and the departure of one of the "giants" once again reminded him that the great Meiji era had fallen into the irretrievable past. Once a "significant link in Sino-Japanese studies" through his work on etymology, Zhou observed, Yosano's death resulted in a particular loss to "the mutual research and understanding" between China and Japan.[7]

As if to retain this special bond between the two cultures, Zhou followed this tribute to Yosano with a succession of essays on Japanese writers and their works. But his interest was rekindled by writers who were significantly different from those of the 1920s: he chose authors who expressed criticism of contemporary Japan and, particularly, of Japan's militarist pursuits. Naka Kansuke, a writer who "neither is influenced by those before him nor cares about the current trends," caught Zhou's attention with his rebellious fiction against Japan's nationalist education.[8] Togawa Shūkotsu, the famous essayist Zhou met during the 1934 trip to Japan, was presented to Chinese readers because of his critical writings against militarism. "It is hard to say that Japanese hold no hatred toward military men," observed Zhou, "but writing of this kind is very rare."[9]

The writer most congenial in thought and in style to his own, as evidenced by Zhou's repeated citations, was Nagai Kafū, who was known for his fiction and his study of Edo arts. Zhou had long been an attentive reader of Kafū's novels and other works but valued most highly his lyrical essays. In an enthusiastic introduction to Kafū's *Hiyori geta* (Geta for bad weather), an essay collection first published in 1915, Zhou wrote in 1935 that he appreciated the author's "subtle" expression of an uncompromising attitude; Kafū, in Zhou's words, "had become very pessimistic, almost with an ultimate hatred, toward the politics and culture of his own country when he was only thirty-six." The reason for this was "clearly explained" in the following words by Kafū from yet another essay, "Appreciating Ukiyo-e," which Zhou quoted at length:

The painter's spirit shows itself in the strong, affirmative colors of an oil painting. On the contrary, if the painter's spirit is also displayed in the sleepy color of woodblock prints, it is the reflection of a despondent mind sagging under the burden of an authoritarian age. It is impossible for me to forget these somehow sad and forlorn colors—their expression of the fear, the sorrow, and the weariness of a dark day, is like the low, muffled sound of a courtesan weeping. In my dealings with contemporary society, I am sometimes outraged at the high-handed ways of the powerful, and I turn back to this art, to its forlorn, wavering colors. The darkness of the past comes back in the sad melody hidden there, making me suddenly aware what is the despotism of the Orient, and understand more deeply how futile it is to talk about righteousness. Greek art came from a land that had Apollo for its god, and the ukiyo-e came out of a rented shack in a dark alley, the work of a townsman whose status generally resembled that of a worm. It is said that times have changed; but that is on the surface only. When the cold, rational eye penetrates deeper, it sees that our militarist politics have not changed in the slightest these one hundred years. It cannot be by accident that the sad colors of ukiyo-e can go so deep into our heart, whispering their secret across the gulf of time.[10]

Across the gulf of space and time, Zhou must have been surprised and heartened when reading Kafū's indignation at "the high-handed ways of the powerful," written some twenty years ago in 1913, which echoed his own. Zhou had always deemed it contemptible, as some Japanese had done to China, to criticize another country without reflecting on one's own faults. As Zhou was paralyzed by the shame of his own government's unwillingness to fight foreign invasion and his agony over Japan's escalating aggression against China, Kafū's penetrating criticism gave him a double-edged sword with which to break through the predicament. He was finally able to begin "A Limited View of Japan" ("Riben guankui"), a serialized essay in four installments, which he had promised to *National News Weekly* since the beginning of the year.

The first "Limited View" came out in May 1935, when the controversy over the notorious Minobe Incident was at its height in Japan. Beginning in February, the liberal scholar Minobe Tatsu-kichi, who argued that the emperor should be viewed as the state's highest constitutional organ, was attacked in the Diet, in the courts, and by the right-wing press for his "treasonous idea." By April, this ideological witch-hunt had "swept over Japan like a typhoon," forced the government to ban three of Minobe's books, and silenced all liberals.[11] It is not clear whether Zhou was immediately informed in detail about the ongoing incident, but the way he began his "Limited View" suggests a perceptive understanding of the roaring calls to clarify "national polity" in Japan's media. Taking *"bansei ikkei"* (the continuous imperial line through the ages), a nationalist claim for the unique origin of the Japanese state, as the central issue, Zhou criticized current Japanese politics by commenting on the relationship between the Japanese emperor and the Japanese people. "The fact of 'bansei ikkei,'" Zhou observed, could have "deep and great influence on the Japanese people's psyche" only because of the "unique fact that Japan was never invaded by foreigners." Yet he insisted that one must acknowledge this claim only with qualifications. In the Japanese feeling of their country's superiority, "there is a difference between the coarse and the delicate, that is, the difference between a love for one's own homeland and the desire for a military empire." And the "deep feelings" that the Japanese people had for their emperor might not be the same as time went on. How he had been struck with admiration, recalled Zhou, when he witnessed the courteous exchanges between the prince and average people on the streets in the late Meiji years! But a barb of criticism immediately followed this praise: "I have heard from Japanese friends that it is now different and the police control is severe; why destroy people's trust and love in this way? It may not be out of ordinary in China, but as this happens in Japan it makes even we foreigners feel truly regretful."

The regrettable change also revealed itself in yet another tradition: the *bushidō*. "After the 5/15 Incident," Zhou wrote, referring to the assassination of Prime Minister Inukai Tsuyoshi on May 15, 1932, "*bushidō* seems to have become a problem: is there such a thing in Japan?" Commiting suicide to take responsibility for breaking the law, said Zhou, was the rule of *bushidō;* yet all assassins received lenient treatment, and their families clasped hands in grateful relief while society applauded the verdict. Of course, the trend had already begun in 1923 with the Ōsugi Incident, noted Zhou, when the assassin, Captain Amakasu Masahiko, had been released after a light sentence. "If there are such things as swordsmen," said Zhou, citing Togawa Shūkotsu for his own comment, "those must be the people who support the strong and bully the weak, and this conclusion now can also be applied to so-and-so." The "so-and-so," indicated Zhou, should be read as "the military" in this context.

The military was precisely the target of this seemingly elegiac tribute to Japan's traditions. The destruction of "people's trust and love" by police control and the decline of *bushidō,* indicated Zhou, derived from "a reactionary trend against the Meiji Restoration," which might lead to "a fascist government organized by military men," which, though it appeared similar to the revival of the *bakufu,* was actually a regression into something worse.[12]

Was that Japan—with its love of simple beauty, its politeness, and its "healthy and straightforward attitude"—going to disappear beneath the "reactionary trend?" Zhou was reluctant to submit to

momentary changes. His second "Limited View," titled "The Clothing, Food, and Dwellings in Japan," took a step back and placed
relations between Japan and China in a long view of the past. It was
a nostalgic essay in tone and content, with intimate descriptions of
his life in Japan as a student underscored by lengthy quotations on
the similarity of Chinese and Japanese ways of life, cited from the
works of Huang Zunxian, the nineteenth-century diplomat who
made the first comprehensive study of Japan by a Chinese. In not-
ing Sino-Japanese cultural parallels that had evolved over centuries,
Zhou reiterated his belief in the affinity between China and Japan
and between Rome and Greece. But his purpose, once again, was to
make a point about the present: "To think carefully about Japanese
life in the past and at the present, I still see very clearly that after all
the Chinese and the Japanese are Asians, in spite of Japan's behavior at this 'moment of emergency' [C: *feichangshi*, J: *hijōji*].
Their fortunes can be different temporarily, but their fates are the
same."[13]

Momentarily, the reality of the escalating crisis between the
two countries seemed to refute Zhou's extraordinary insight into
the "same fate" shared by the Chinese and Japanese. Almost simultaneously with the publication of his second "Limited View," the
Chinese government yielded to the pressure of the Japanese army
and signed two agreements, the Ho-Umetsu Agreement on June 10,
1935, and the Chin-Doihara Agreement on June 23. Together the
treaties promised the withdrawal of Chinese troops and guaranteed
Japan's free entrance into the northern provinces of Hebei and
Chahar. For the rest of 1935, the Japanese army–engineered
North China Autonomy Movement went into full swing, and by the
year's end a provisional government headed by General Song
Zheyuan was set up to meet Japan's demand for "special government in north China."

Zhou, now living on Chinese soil where China's sovereignty
was so seriously impaired, responded to the new events in a third
"Limited View" in which he quoted in total his 1920 essay "Japanophile," criticizing those "small men" who sold China's land to
Japan for personal gains and harmed Japan's true glory. He felt
compelled, too, to comment directly on the relationship between
culture and politics. Although China's understanding of Japan had
"a long precedent [*yin*]" that began with the cultural exchange in
the Tang dynasty, "the most glorious event in the history of man-

kind" without any "sordid motivation," wrote Zhou, "the 'chance' [yuan] has not been good," because "political conflicts in recent years have created enormous obstacles to cultural contact."

While recognizing the impact of political force, Zhou remained convinced of the power of culture, though he realized that there was a need to clarify his notion of it. An investigation of culture, he suggested, should not be limited to arts and literature only, but instead be extended to the "lower part that is influential in the society." Therefore he looked into the practice of *bushidō* in Tanizaki Junichirō's historical novel, *Secret History of Bushūkō (Bushūkō hiwa)*, and picked out a scene where women on the victorious side washed the severed heads of the enemy. In their careful and respectful treatment of the enemy Zhou found overflowing empathy, which revealed, as he put it, "the beauty of human feelings that goes beyond animal instinct." To add one more dimension to his differentiation between the high and low cultures, or between articulated expression and behavior, he suggested making a distinction between a "material culture" *(wu de wenhua)* and a "human culture" *(ren de wenhua)*, the former being the extension of man's ability to survive and including various tools as well as weapons, the latter being human will and practices that prevented people from harming one another for selfish gains. What served as a demarcation, again, was behavior, not any declared statement. "If we in Africa see a white man with his complete set of civilized equipment carrying a gun to hunt and to kill life, and another naked black man on the roadside offering his roasted grubs to share with the passersby," wrote Zhou, "we cannot but admit that the civilized and the savage have exchanged their positions here." And in the practice of *bushidō*, too, "that small gesture of human empathy amidst the slaughter of two sides is perhaps the only bright spot on the extremely dark road of life."[14]

Never had Zhou written such penetrating insight combined with a sense of helplessness. Culture, wrote Zhou elsewhere in July 1936, "is useless, for the good side of it cannot save the nation, while the bad side cannot sell the nation." Those words were his critique of "the calls against cultural invasion and cultural traitors" that had come into vogue in China lately.[15] He felt he had been lecturing students about "the high culture that belongs to only a few," which had "little influence on the majority." And he was "troubled by not being able to answer many questions when teaching Japanese literature and its background."[16] The conflict between "a culture within the heart" and "a reality before the eyes" stopped him from immediately writing the fourth "Limited View"; only after a year and a half did he send the final promised essay to *National News Weekly.* War was only three weeks away.

Unlike his previous three essays, the last "Limited View" was far less allusive, and his anger and despair showed in his sarcastic words:

> For years I have kept in mind a big puzzle when seeing the contradictory phenomena of the Japanese nation, and I have not yet found an answer. The Japanese love beauty, . . . yet they seem to be not at all afraid of doing ugly things toward China. The Japanese are very nimble, . . . yet their behavior is so clumsy. The Japanese love to stay clean, . . . yet their behavior is so dirty and mean as to force others to throw up. That is indeed a great wonder, or perhaps a miracle, under heaven.

Zhou's answer to this big puzzle was what he called a "cultural reaction" *(fan wenhua),* an argument he had touched on briefly when he wrote his first "Limited View." Now he placed what he called "reaction to the Meiji Restoration" in a longer perspective, pointing to two trends of cultural reaction: one was an "anti-Chinese culture" trend, "a reaction against the Taika Reform (645–650)" that introduced Chinese culture into Japan; the other was an "anti-Western culture" trend, "a reaction against the Meiji Restoration" that modernized Japan after Western models. In judging the two trends, Zhou tried to be fair, yet he could not but feel contempt for Japan's turning against one's teacher and benefactor. In turning against China, Japan was "not graceful" but "understandable," said Zhou, because China's decline had made its student "subconsciously ashamed" and "want to rebel violently so as to feel free to breathe." Although Japan "borrowed Western culture and succeeded in the Meiji Restoration," the adaptation, too, provoked reaction. As these two reactionary trends developed in tandem, neither had succeeded because of the fact that Japanese culture, "despite its unique position and value, grows from Chinese and Western cultures." Japan's effort to replace Chinese characters with either Westernized *romaji* or its own alphabet system, *kana,* had never succeeded. Japan's rejection of Western culture was even a farce, according to Zhou. Matsuoka Yōsuke's dramatic gesture of walking out of the League of Nations in 1933, he observed, "appeared to be in the style of an American movie." Even the announcement of the "Shōwa Restoration" was sustained by a claim for *"fascio,"* a term from Italy, rather than an appeal for the revival of *bakufu.* "It's ridiculous indeed," Zhou sniffed, "that this voluntary nativism should use a ghost mask from the West."

The argument of "cultural reaction," of course, merely explained Japan's "ugly behavior" to other nations. But that "is the same in its own country," quoted Zhou of a Japanese friend. To add force to this observation, he drew upon correspondence to the Japanese-language newspaper *New Shina (Shin shina)* that enumerated the cruel repressions since the 1923 earthquake and the violent assassinations within Japan since the Manchuria Incident, concluding that "Japan seems, too, a place that does not care for human life."

The question for Zhou was: How could this happen in a country that he had always thought of as possessing "the beauty of human feelings"? His answer now pointed toward the "unique spirit of Shintoism" that the Japanese "always kept to themselves." How that unique belief influenced the culture of the majority, in Zhou's view, was best illustrated in a description of the village festival by Yanagita Kunio, the folklorist whose works had long interested him. The "fusion of gods and men" depicted by Yanagita in the parade of carriers of god's palanquin through the village in a trance, moving hither and thither, attacking this household or that, or holding suddenly in the middle of the road, "is never seen in the parade of the image of gods in China," indicated Zhou. He had once said, in his first "Limited View," that the Chinese and Japanese shared "a this-worldly attitude." But now, as violence seized Japan and the phalanx of Japanese soldiers was poised for the order to charge, he admitted his oversight. "If I could understand those god's palanquin carriers' minds," he wrote, "I might be able to understand the meanings of Japan's actions toward China. Yet I cannot, because I have no religious feeling ... and I cannot but feel hopeless." The final conclusion he could offer was "I do not understand," which was "the most valuable comment in all the four 'Limited Views'" and the "very proper way to end these 'views.'"[17]

To "Treason"

At the end of July 1937, three weeks after the Marco Polo Bridge Incident, Beijing fell into Japanese hands. Five months later, a provisional government was installed by the occupying army in the city to govern the five northern provinces of Hebei, Chahar, Suiyuan, Henan, and Shandong. The inauguration of this puppet regime was followed by the organization of the New People Society (Xin Min Hui), the propaganda arm of the Japanese military. With its hundreds of county-level branches conducting educational activities in schools, movie theaters, radio stations, and teahouses, the New People Society tried to promote "a new cultural order" and legitimize Japanese rule on Chinese territory. One theme of its propaganda centered on Confucianism, with the claim that Japan came to China with an intention to "rejuvenate the people" and to help the Chinese return to their tradition.[18]

During those clamorous months of changing authority in occupied Beijing, Zhou, as he promised his friends, withdrew into his "Living-in-Bitterness Studio" and worked on a translation of Greek mythology through the first year of the occupation. From the American-owned Yenching University he also obtained a visiting professorship that entailed a few hours of lecturing each week. Occasionally he wrote essays—mostly notes from his readings that appeared "leisurely" and apolitical—for the *Chen bao Supplement*. Several universities under the administration of the puppet regime, such as Manchuria University, Beijing Normal University, Women's Normal University, and Beijing University, had offered Zhou positions throughout 1938; relying on support from private institutes, he resisted the pressure.[19]

Zhou might have been able to continue his passive withdrawal for the rest of the war, if not for a sudden turn of events in 1939. On New Year's Day morning, two assassins broke into Zhou's residence, killed a rick-shaw puller, and wounded several others; the bullet intended for Zhou bounced off a button on his cardigan, just grazing his skin. The assassins fled, leaving behind a puzzle that invited various interpretations for the next half century. Based on his common sense, as well as other indicators, Zhou concluded that the assassination attempt was a final warning from the Japanese occupiers.[20] And his judgment seemed to be confirmed by the fact that, immediately after the assassination attempt, police came to provide

Zhou "protection" and were to be stationed in his house until the end of war. Twelve days later, Zhou accepted an appointment to become the curator of Beijing University library, a position that he "had no choice but to accept," as he noted in his diary.[21] Two years later, in 1941, he accepted an appointment as minister of education for the North Chinese Political Committee, the puppet regime in north China.

Zhou's political collaboration seemed to have confirmed many people's assumptions about him when he had refused to evacuate at the beginning of the war. At war's end, he was arrested by the National Government, tried for treason, and was given a ten-year prison sentence. For nearly half a century after the war, he was described in standard textbooks of Chinese literature as a cultural traitor. Among the people who denounced his "treason" were those, mainly from the Communist side, who called him a traitor at heart even before the war, due to his pro-Japanese sentiments.[22]

He was not without supporters and sympathizers, however. The court records, now available in print, reveal the staunch support that the liberal community provided to Zhou when he stood trial. Several schools in Beijing and many intellectuals sent petitions on Zhou's behalf, attesting to his various efforts and successes in protecting school property, at rescuing more than half a dozen underground resistance workers, and at resisting orders from the occupation authorities to force students to show support for the war effort.[23] Feng Wenbing (Fei Ming), a former student of Zhou and himself a well-known writer, captured the spirit of this shared judgment in the words of a protagonist in his novel: "Master Zhitang [Zhou Zuoren] ... hates to simply talk about the world and the future but tries to do good for the nation.... Master Zhitang is indeed a number-one patriot."[24] In the 1980s, those involved in Zhou's decision to join the government under Japanese occupation finally stepped forward and wrote memoirs to testify to what they saw as the truth. According to them, Zhou was mobilized by underground agents of both the Communists and the Guomindang; they had persuaded Zhou to preside over the Ministry of Education so that Miao Bin, a contender for the position and an active leader of the New People Society, would have fewer opportunities to carry out the indoctrination of the young generation. Although Zhou initially hesitated because of his lack of bureaucratic skills, he was persuaded to accept the position when he was assured that underground friends would come to his assistance in times of need.[25]

Zhou Zuoren himself believed that he had never betrayed his nation. He believed that his acceptance of a position in the puppet regime was "neither forced nor voluntary," and he took the offer only "after consideration."[26] The testimony of the immediate participants and observers of his collaboration attested to the credibility of Zhou's argument, yet none spoke more convincingly than Zhou himself, who left a trail of essays that revealed his true thoughts during those trying years.

The first sign of Zhou's changing attitude regarding his vow of silence and withdrawal is found in an essay, "Commemorating Xuantong," written on April 28, 1939, a hundred days after his old friend's sudden death from apoplexy. A philologist by training, Qian Xuantong had been Zhou's close friend since their student years in Tokyo. He was the one who had argued with Zhou and Lu Xun in 1917 for the need to act and to initiate a cultural revolution, while the two brothers hesitated. For two decades, while teaching at Beijing University, Qian had been perhaps the most frequent visitor to the Zhou household. He "did not care about petty things," wrote Zhou about his late friend, "but whenever he gave advice he always tried to be understanding and to benefit others." Qian's death, Zhou knew, resulted partly from his distress under the occupation and, especially, the recent assassination attempt on his old friend. Zhou's late friend not only carried away an important part of their life together, but also the support he could have extended in this time of dire need. Now Zhou had to face the darkness alone, and "there will be no one to give me sincere admonitions anymore." Although writing this essay could not do enough to honor his venerable friend, Zhou remarked, it "has broken my vow of silence of the past two years, since it is not a trivial decision for me, and perhaps it is the only proper way to memorialize my late friend."[27]

As if to defy the threat of death, Zhou stepped out of his passivity and resumed his social duties as a writer. On the first day of 1940, he began writing essays for *Yong bao,* a newspaper in Tianjin, and his essays were published in two columns titled "Yaocaotang suibi" (Essays from the medicine hall) and "Yaocaotang yulu" (Quotations from the medicine hall). In appearance, most of his essays were notes from his random readings on various subjects regarding the "life of animals, sexual relationships, primitive civilizations, and the evolution of ethics" that he viewed as "good for the youth." Implicitly, the title hinted at his intention to prescribe medicine for his readers in a troubled age, but none, he admitted, had "yet expressed a central idea in my thought" as he started the columns.[28] He kept testing the waters until March, when he finally stepped on solid ground with an essay titled "The Buddhist and the Confucianist," from which several of his important essays would develop later. In an attempt to clarify the spirit of pristine Confucianism, Zhou argued that the true Confucius "was originally pragmatic *[jiang shiji]* and emphasized actual results *[zhong gongli]*." Although scholars in the Han and Song dynasties turned his ideas into dogma, Confucius' ideas "were in fact motivated by his 'concerns for the people' *[youmin]*." Zhou insisted that it was necessary to clarify the difference, or "the hope for the revival of Confucianism will be doomed."[29]

That Zhou, an anti-Confucian iconoclast during the May Fourth era, was calling for the return to pristine Confucianism at this moment was indeed significant. On the surface he seemed to echo the ideological indoctrination of Confucianism promoted by the New People movement under the occupation. What Zhou actually meant, however, followed the same strand of thought he had voiced in "Commemorating Xuantong," and it had nothing in common with the New People propaganda. His intent, in fact, was to combat that movement, though he knew his task was akin to prescribing bitter, but curing, medicine, though he had "yet to find a way to [get others to] swallow it."[30]

The Chinese Antithesis to the New Order in East Asia

If a writer's activism were measured by the immediacy of his engagement with the great issues of his time, it is beyond doubt that between 1940 and 1943, when Zhou wrote a series of critical essays on Confucianism, he had committed himself to a revived activism, comparable to his impassioned participation in the discussion of "human literature" and his advocacy of the New Village during the May Fourth era. This revival of activism was also manifested in—or, to be more accurate, necessitated—Zhou's return to the genre of the critical essay, in which he assumed the didactic tone he had abandoned for quite some time. The four major, and unusually long, essays he wrote and published—"The Tradition of Han

Literature" in March 1940, "The Thought Problem of China" in November 1942, "Two Strands of Thought in Chinese Literature" in April 1943, and "The Future of Han Literature" in July 1943— were the boldest attempts ever made by a writer living under the occupation to criticize Japan's aggression and to discredit its claim for leadership in Asia.

Zhou worked on the premises of his first essay by marking the difference between the Chinese and the invader and by reclaiming the Chinese origin of Confucianism. In his definition of Chinese literature, he pointedly used the word "Han," instead of "Chinese," to include only works "that are written in Han language" and to exclude those by "foreigners." Those often-heard "claims about Asian culture and about Chinese national character," wrote Zhou, were either wishful or distorted assertions that "are not worth listening to [bukanwen]." Authorship aside, he also noted the importance of the authenticity of the message. The true meaning of Chinese tradition as contained in Han literature was "a kind of commonsensical, pragmatic thing, which can be called 'humanism,' or the Confucianism of ancient times." Announcing that he was "optimistic" about that commonsensical spirit of Confucianism, Zhou boldly declared:

> Since Confucianism is owned by ourselves, it is like the root of a tree, growing from under the deep ground. If there is no outside interference, either by restraint or artificial cultivation [zhuzhang], it can grow up again even if the tree temporarily withers.[31]

The rejection of Japanese claims to ideological leadership and to helping the Chinese return to their tradition is unmistakable in these lines; yet in this first move Zhou was understandably cautious and used metaphor, hinting that the propaganda for a new order in Asia was an "artificial cultivation." He also included a great many quotations from literature in the Confucian tradition to explicate the content of that "commonsensical" idea of "humanism," sometimes leaving his argument buried in a language difficult for contemporary readers to understand. That scholarly manner, masked by allusion, gave way to a combative stance when Zhou wrote "The Thought Problem of China" in late 1942. It was a posture he had already adopted in 1941, when he addressed the Third Summer

Training Program of Middle School Teachers in North China, sponsored by the puppet regime and attended by officers of the occupation force. He titled that speech "The National Thought of China" and made an emphatic note at the beginning that these were his "own opinions, very ordinary and very old," but there was "no lie, said as it should be said, and not a word of what may just sound good to say." In the two-hour speech, he lectured on the "most important aspects" of Confucian thought, which he defined as "altruism" or "benevolence" *[ren]*, "being pragmatic, rather than emphasizing theory," and "pursuing the mean." These were subtle rejections of Japan's call to unify East Asia under Confucianism in order to establish a glorious New Order—points related to his argument that the Chinese had no such religious craze for the god's way as seen in Japan. The pursuit of the mean was not only required by life, because "life, including eating, walking, sleeping, is [meant to maintain] the mean," but it was also a Chinese idea endorsed by all, "from Confucius to the average people." Leading from this fact was a logical but subversive conclusion: that a Chinese "is incapable of pursuing a great cause, yet he has huge strength for endurance over a very long time."[32]

Zhou pursued the same strands of thought in the 1942 essay, but with an even sharper argument and greater force. The essay began with a pointed objection to the occupation propaganda: "I usually do not feel optimistic about almost everything, yet I feel nothing but optimism about the thought problem in China.... Although there is indeed a bit of confusion in Chinese intellectual circles recently, that is simply a superficial phenomenon; seeing from afar and into its depth, the thought of the Chinese people is basically very healthy."

To further underscore this confident tone, Zhou approached his discussion of "Chinese central thought" with a precise definition: what he meant by Confucianism was its pristine form, "the Confucian thought that was represented by Confucius and Mencius and exemplified by Yu and Ji," the two sages whose thoughts centered on the idea of *ren* and the two legendary kings whose administration demonstrated altruistic service for the people. Regardless of how *"ren"* had been made by some to sound so lofty, Zhou argued, its meaning was "extremely pragmatic, or even low and intimate," because, in the final analysis, *"ren"* derived from the instinct for survival. But human beings' need to survive, unlike other organisms' primal instinct, was achieved more often through mutual aid. That was how the ideas of loyalty *(zhong)* and empathy *(shu)* were elaborated to implement *ren,* or the human way *(ren zhi dao).* Since this "central idea of Chinese thought" followed nature and human feelings, indicated Zhou, it was understood not only by intellectuals, but also by the illiterate common people who had never read a sentence from the sage's book.

A bolder stroke came after Zhou's lengthy clarification of *"ren."* Simply because the "human way" meant the need for survival, Zhou reminded his audience, its goal indeed was "the so-called 'co-existence and co-prosperity' that has now become a cliché," if viewed from a positive angle. Yet such a philosophy of survival also had its negative side, he added, for violating its rule, or "opposing the human way," as he put it, would inevitably lead to chaos, a historical lesson proved by recurrent popular revolts in China's long past. And from such a this-worldly philosophy of survival Zhou also found a fundamental difference between the Chinese and "the religious people of another nation":

> The living demand of the Chinese is very simple, and thus becomes very urgent. He wants to live, and his morality of survival does not allow him to harm others in order to benefit himself; yet on the other hand he cannot harm himself to benefit others like a saint. The religious people of other nations might dream of the coming of the millennium and be willing to endure immense torture in order to attain immortality. The Chinese has no such belief and confidence. He will not sacrifice himself for god or for a cause [C: *shendao,* J: *shintō*]. He will, however, take great risk without turning back, if he feels that there is no hope for survival, as is usually said, "making a reckless move in desperation."[33]

While holding several distinguished positions in the collaboration regime, Zhou as minister of education was in fact making "reckless moves." His covert efforts at resisting the New People Society's indoctrination education in north China, as he later recalled, "was the most troublesome work every day." His intentional neglect of an order from the occupation army had once so enraged the Japanese military that he would have been arrested had the Japanese embassy not intervened. As a high-ranking official in the

government, he had also helped secure the release of some intellectuals.[34] Zhou must have appeared to the Japanese occupation
authorities as too unreliable after these incidents. In early 1943, he
was removed from his ministry position, but as a celebrity, he was
kept on the Political Affairs Committee of North China without administrative power.[35]

In April 1943, Zhou, now removed from the Ministry of Education, received an invitation from Wang Jingwei, the head of the
puppet regime in Nanjing, to undertake a lecture tour in the south.
In Nanjing Zhou gave a public lecture to the students at Central
University, "Two Strands of Thought in Chinese Literature." There
were two traditions in Chinese political ethics, defined by divergent
purposes, argued Zhou. One was for the people, which "emerged
early"; the other was for the emperor, which "emerged later but
became dominant." Citing classical literature from *The Book of Songs*
to poetry in the Tang dynasty as well as Confucian scholars from
Mencius to Yu Lichu (1775–1840), Zhou asserted that the tradition
for the people "has long and deep roots." Only by following that
tradition, he admonished his young audience, could writers produce "good literature."[36]

Are these discussions of the past merely empty words, irrelevant to the harsh reality of the war? As if to expel such doubt from
his readers' minds, Zhou followed the Nanjing lecture with yet another essay, "The Future of Han Literature." In this last of his four
wartime essays on Confucianism, Zhou urged his fellow Chinese to
look beyond the dark reality of the present. Although it was often
said, he reminded them, that the Chinese were like "a plate of
loose sand," there was a force of internal unity that held the nation
together: the Chinese language, which by its unique ideographical
form and phonetic characteristics served the Chinese nation as a
centripetal force *(weiji li)*. The simple fact of using Chinese characters that enabled the communication of feelings and thoughts to
transcend great geographical distances, Zhou wrote, was a small fact
of "tremendous importance."[37]

With these essays Zhou became the most outspoken person in
occupied China to combat the Japanese military's ideological campaign through the New People movement. Although there were
others who wrote in a covert fashion to remind the Japanese to live
up to their words of "co-existence,"[38] none had written so con-
sistently, as Zhou had, to underscore the diverging directions of

humanism in pristine Confucianism, on the one hand, and the "New Order" of the Japanese military, on the other. Under the circumstances of the occupation, as it would soon turn out, Zhou's essays were applauded in secrecy by many who remained in the occupied area. But only when he was picked up by Kataoka Teipei, a former leftist writer "converted" [tenkō] to the cause of the Greater East Asia New Order, did Zhou's personal resistance become a public affair.

In August 1943, the Literature Patriotic Association (Bungaku Hōkokukai), controlled by the intelligence agency of the Japanese army headquarters, sponsored the Second Conference of East Asian Literature Workers. During the discussions of the second panel, Kataoka made a speech announcing that in "the pacified area" in China there was still an "old reactionary writer" who continued to resist the Great East Asia War with his "extremely passive reactionary thoughts and activities." For the sake of China's future, Kataoka insisted, that "special literary enemy" must be "relentlessly crushed." Kataoka's attack passed unnoticed at first because Zhou did not attend the conference, and most of the Chinese writers there did not understand Japanese. But when Hu Lancheng, a Chinese writer who had remained in the occupied area, reported Kataoka's speech in the *Zhonghua ribao* (China daily), the incident began to produce widespread ramifications.[39]

Piecing sporadic evidence together, Zhou realized that Kataoka's attack originated from Shen Qiwu, one of his former students, who had become resentful because of Zhou's refusal to support him in a personal dispute regarding the editing of two journals in north China. Shen brought Zhou's essays to the attention of Hayashi Fusao, another "converted" leftist writer and colleague of Kataoka in the Literature Patriotic Association who had come to visit north China that summer. Shen's behavior was not simply a matter of personal betrayal, but an act of treason that Zhou could not tolerate, and he made several public moves to make that point. First he renounced his mentor-pupil relationship with Shen in an "Excommunication Statement" and had it published in the *Zhonghua ribao*. Then, in a formal letter to Kume Masao, the president of the Literature Patriotic Association, he demanded an official explanation of Kataoka's attack, setting mid-April (about twenty days from the date on his letter) as the deadline for a response.[40] And without waiting for a response, he had the letter published in the *Zhonghua ribao* almost immediately.

Instantly, Chinese writers in occupied areas seized the moment to make their points. One typical response came in an editorial for the newspaper *Xin zhongguo* that insisted that "the realization of friendly cooperation must be based on the spirit of mutual respect, even criticism or correction should be presented with good intention"; that if the "misunderstanding provokes the passive withdrawal" of such a prestigious writer as Zhou Zuoren, it would be "detrimental to the future of Sino-Japanese cultural exchanges." Tao Jingsun, a Japan-educated scientist and writer in the former Creation Society who remained in Shanghai, demanded in *Xin shen bao* (New Shanghai newspaper) that Kataoka withdraw his "mistaken words." Even a Japanese newspaper in Shanghai, *Tairiku shinpō* (New continental newspaper), complained that the Literature Patriotic Association should never have allowed Kataoka to speak in such a reckless way, expressing "deep regret" at the incident.[41] From Japan, Mushanokoji Saneatsu and Nagayo Yoshirō sent Zhou Zuoren letters of support. Public opinion from all corners sided with him.[42]

Finally, in a letter to Zhou, Kataoka admitted that his speech was directed toward Zhou's essay, "The Thought Problem of China." While admitting to being "very irreverent," Kataoka nevertheless warned Zhou "not to underestimate the ability of the Japanese to understand [your] writing."[43]

New Order for Japan in East Asia: "A Toy of Sorrow"

When Zhou exclaimed with utter despair, "I do not understand," in his fourth "Limited View of Japan," he also announced the closing of his "Japanese Shop." Yet like his return to the critical essay, his commentaries on Japan, too, resumed at the end of 1941. It was the 2,600th anniversary of the founding of the Japanese state, and Zhou was asked by the Japanese Association for Promoting International Cultures to write an essay commemorating the event.

"Re-understanding Japan," the title that Zhou chose for this essay, suggested his inclination to revisit, revise, and refine the points he had previously made. In appearance, the essay simply combined his second and fourth "Limited View of Japan," with some editing. Yet once merged, these two emotionally distant essays, one nostalgic about an old Japan and the other frustrated and angry with the irreversible conflict of the present, took a new direction.

Taking up the theme of his second "Limited View," Zhou began "Re-understanding Japan" with emphatic praise of the past. Although what he knew about Japan was limited to the old Tokyo of some thirty years ago, he said, he "liked" everything he had experienced in Meiji Japan, from food to clothing, dwelling, and customs because they were "clean, polite, and unpretentious." Life in Tokyo at that time, he maintained, "had more Japanese characteristics than what has become more Westernized later."

And then in a sudden change of tone Zhou stated that his purpose in saying so much about the good things of the past "is to rescind all of them in one stroke now, and to illustrate that the road taken is wrong." Because of his propensity to pay attention only to what he could "understand," he "had never taken Japan to be a special country." That approach of "looking at Japan straightforwardly" through his own experiences misled him to simply "seek commonality in differences [yizhong qiutong]" and "hence feel deeply Japan's East Asian characteristics [Dongya xing]." As a result he missed "the uniqueness that makes Japan different."

To understand Japan's "innate spirit" and find its "original face," Zhou wrote with emphasis, it was necessary to adopt a new attitude of "seeking especially what made Japan different from China."[44] Religion, he said, reiterating his view in the fourth "Limited View," might be a promising path to reach that difference. Citing once again Yanagita Kunio's description of Shintō ritual, Zhou reemphasized that the "fusion of god and man" in such rituals "is rarely seen and hardly understood in China." Although the Chinese had seen words like "the kingdom of God" (kami no kuni) and "God's way" (kaminagara no michi) so often, "we will never understand their true meanings as the Japanese understand them." The reason was simple: "Such things ... must resort to feelings, hence any rational explanation is probably pointless, or at least useless." As for himself, Zhou declared, "it is deplorable that I have no faith.... Although I have found the door, I have no way to get in."[45]

Having thus reiterated his aversion to Japan's ideological justification for war in Asia, Zhou pursued further the idea of the "Greater East Asian War" in his next essay, "Recollections of Studying Abroad." It was amazing, he wrote, how passionately the Chinese had responded to Japan's achievement around the turn of the century. Chinese students, including himself, were excited and motivated by a sense of national crisis and an aspiration to "resist the West and preserve East Asia." The Chinese admired and praised the Meiji Restoration and wished for Japanese victory in the Russo-Japanese War "with an enthusiasm much greater than that when the Greater East Asian War broke out last year." But the opportunity for a better relationship between the two had been wasted and lost because of the many "unexpected turns in the past thirty years."

Yet who was to blame for the conflict? The Chinese enthusiasm for Japan lost its momentum, stated Zhou, not because of anti-Japanese feelings growing from the discrimination the Chinese students experienced in Japan, as "Japanese so often say"; instead, the problem lay in the opposite direction, he insisted. Most Chinese students in Japan, "except a few who saw only Japan's imitation of the Western civilization," actually "attained a good feeling toward Japan after having contacted its life and culture," a good feeling that grew out of "admiration for a progressive society and an affinity with an Oriental nation *[dongyang minzhu]*." What changed their minds was Japanese behavior in China, "especially of the so-called 'China Hands' *[zhina tong]* who followed the example of some British and American missionaries and made their careers writing books only to publicize China's evil traits." It was a particularly rude awakening for the Chinese students returning from Japan because they read Japanese and understood that "it was not the way Japanese behave in their own country, nor was it the way they behave toward the West. Hence they [the Chinese students] are upset, and small things turn into big problems." With a tinge of sarcasm Zhou remarked that recollecting his student years in Japan was rather "unseasonable." But being so "fond of old ways" he could not but feel, "somehow, under the Greater East Asian War, it is the 'Western' influence that is dominating East Asia. Writing an old-fashioned recollection about East Asia at this time is nothing but 'a toy of sorrow.'"[46]

Directing his criticism against "the West" was probably the best possible way, under the occupation, to criticize Japan's pursuit of the "material culture" of warfare. The time of fighting was the time of heroes. But Zhou had long declared his disinterest in the so-called "heroes in Japan's past and present," who were simply "a kind of big hooligan." He respected only "men of wisdom" such as the producers of *ukiyo-e,* who "lived like worms."[47] These people defined what he meant by "Orientals," who shared the same sorrowful fate, being abused by the powerful. "Now China and Japan stand as enemy countries," wrote Zhou in 1936, "but if we detach ourselves from their relations at present and look at their permanent traits, then the two are born as Orientals, whose fate and fortunes are so different from that of the Westerners."[48] In 1943, six years deep into a war between China and Japan, Zhou reiterated: "We are born as Orientals whose fate and circumstances are different from those of white people." To have "the self-consciousness of an Oriental" was "necessary" because "it was like hanging a mirror by our side, so we can constantly look into it and not forget who we are."[49]

This argument about the shared fate of the Orientals aside, Zhou continued to hold to the belief that there were Japanese, though small in number, who shared a rational tradition with the Chinese, a belief sustained by his repeated citation of Kafū, Yanagita, and a few other writers. While criticizing the war through his emphasis on the differences between Chinese and Japanese religious feelings, Zhou in "Re-understanding Japan" explicitly noted that "the intellectuals [in Japan] have not attained such a god-obsessed state as seen in those palanquin carriers for god."[50] The negativity of his original sentence, however, was translated into a positive when Zhou's essay was published in Japan.[51] In correcting that "absurd and strange mistake" Zhou had to append a note when he included the essay in the *Book on the Taste of Medicine (Yao-wei ji)* in 1941. Although a small incident, it was enough to remind Zhou that his secret hope for the survival of rational thinking among Japanese intellectuals might also become "a toy of sorrow."

It was perhaps because of the fear that Japan would completely lose its conscience that news on August 22, 1943, of the death of Shimazaki Tōson, the literary giant of the Meiji era, could have given Zhou such a feeling of profound loss. His first reaction was "not surprise but, instead, an urgent sense of loneliness." While leafing once again through Tōson's *Paper Window in Snowy Days (Yuki no shōji),* he thought that "the person who can write such essays does not exist anymore." And he felt that "there is one more person lost on my side of the front, thus the loneliness becomes almost cowardice."

Zhou had been an avid reader of Tōson's works since his student years in Tokyo, and he was especially fond of Tōson's essays
because "here, his image is the most distinct." He admired Tōson's
thoughtfulness, the feel of spatial and temporal magnanimity in his
writings. Only after many years did Zhou finally meet Tōson, when
Zhou was a well-established Chinese writer and Tōson already an
old man. In 1934, the two writers had met twice when Zhou visited
Tokyo, and then again in 1941, when Zhou went to Japan in an official capacity as the head of a Chinese delegation from the puppet
regime to attend a meeting of the East Asian Cultural Association.

In none of the three meetings, as Zhou recalled, did he talk
much with Tōson, for he revered the old writer "as the great senior
in the East Asian literary circles." He took these meetings as opportunities "to pay respects." Nevertheless, the "old thinker," as
Zhou called Tōson, left him with the impression that he "is on the
same front as we and thus makes us feel close to him." From the
second meeting on August 20, 1934, Zhou carried away the fondest
memories because it was a small party, hosted by Tōson and attended by only three other writers: Watsuji Tetsurō, Arishima
Ikuma, and Xu Yaochen (Zuzheng). When they met, the host and
the guests exchanged books and wrote or painted paper fans, and a
short song by Saigyō Hōshi (1118–1190) was Tōson's gift to Zhou:

> Those summer nights were
> Like bitter bamboo
> Bamboo slender, their joints dense
> Daylight will come
> Before too long.[52]

***

Indeed, daylight came before too long. Two years after Zhou Zuoren wrote down this symbolic song to commemorate Tōson, an exhausted and devastated Japan finally surrendered. Perfectly confident about his motivations and activities during the occupation,
Zhou remained in liberated Beijing, looking forward to a return to
the scholarly life of teaching and writing. He even hoped that the
returning Chinese government would send him with the mission to
Japan to retrieve the cultural artifacts looted by the Japanese army
during the war.[53] What he received, however, was an arrest warrant
at the end of 1945. His trial, held with that of other prominent

political figures in the collaboration regime under the occupation, lasted a year and a half and concluded with a guilty verdict and a ten-year sentence for "collaborating with the enemy country." Zhou was released from prison before the end of his term, just as Nanjing was about to be taken over by the Communists in 1949. He chose, once again, to remain on the mainland and continue his translations of Japanese literature and Greek mythology. The younger generation born after the war did not know him, as he was allowed to publish under pen names only. Only in the 1980s, more than a decade after Zhou died from beatings and abuse by the Red Guards in 1967, did he once again catch the attention of the Chinese. A so-called "Zhou Zuoren Craze" (Zhou Zuoren Re) swept the country from the mid-1980s to the early 1990s, and his works have been reprinted and his essays recompiled into new collections. In addition to two major biographies published recently, scholars have written hundreds of articles on Zhou Zuoren. While his literary contribution has been fully acknowledged, his collaboration continues to remain a divisive and much-debated question.

At the time Zhou began serving his prison term in 1948, Guo Moruo's wife, Anna, who had been separated from her husband since he stepped out of their house in 1937, was planning a trip to China. Because of her marriage to Guo, she had lost her Japanese citizenship the previous year. Meanwhile, Guo had journeyed from Shanghai to Hong Kong at the end of 1947 by the arrangement of the Communist Party in order to avoid being harmed by the ongoing civil war. His articles and memoirs began to appear in Hong Kong newspapers and literary journals as soon as he arrived there. It is likely that Anna got the news of Guo's whereabouts around that time. "I have been living with the thought that China is my homeland," said Anna to newspaper reporters before she left Ichikawa in May 1948. Taking three of their children with her and leaving one to watch their home, she made a three-week stop in Taiwan, where their eldest son was teaching at Taiwan University, and then proceeded to Hong Kong.[54] How devastating a shock it must have been when she arrived at Guo's residence and saw a young woman with five small children at Guo's side! "It was the Japanese militarists who caused all this," Guo reportedly said upon the moment of their reunion.[55] Facing the five young children in Guo's new family, Anna finally realized that she had no choice but to resign herself to fate. In 1949, she took Chinese citizenship and moved to Dalian, where her eldest son got a job at a research institute. "I am a stray dog all my life," Anna told the Japanese writer Sawachi Hisae, who visited her to write Anna's life story in 1980, when she was 86, "but whatever bitterness can be said about this bitter life, that was because of my own foolishness."[56] She outlived Guo by sixteen years and died in 1994, at the age of 99.[57]

During the war years, Dai Jitao had remained absent from the public scene. Following his service for the Special Diplomatic Committee after the Manchurian Incident, he no longer held any official position relating to Japan. His health had been in a steady decline since his suicide attempt in 1922, and to quell his physical and spiritual pains he had taken up the habit of smoking opium. He also tried, without success, to resign from the various positions that he had held in the party and in the government.[58] Sadness overwhelmed him as he watched the war turn both China and Japan into ruins. At the time of Japan's surrender, he could feel no joy over China's victory but only immense anxiety about a dangerous future. He perceived that the fate of humanity would be dominated by the most disastrous weapon—the atomic bomb—which not only had destroyed cities in Japan that held his youthful memories, but also had manifested the loss of man's belief in nature. Looking back at Japan over the past twenty years, he could not help grieving over the unfortunate death of Saburi Sadao, the once energetic minister to China, his co-visionary in Pan-Asianism, and a member of the opposition to the rising militarism in Japan.[59] Looking back at Japan's dramatic path toward power in the past three hundred years, what else could he say but "how sorrowful, the three islands in the Sea!"[60] On February 12, 1949, while his beloved Japan still struggled in ruins and poverty and the National Government under the Guomindang crumbled from within and without, Dai took an overdose of sleeping pills and died in Guangzhou.

CONCLUSION

The once vibrant and multidimensional Sino-Japanese interactions came to an abrupt end when China and Japan stopped fighting in 1945. Violent clashes between these two close neighbors during the previous fifteen years not only left both devastated, but also created a host of disturbing sentiments of denial, suspicion, and resentment on both sides that remain potent even today.[1] At war's end, the swing over the preceding fifty years from a generally positive attitude among the Chinese to a negative one is unmistakable.

In this study, I have set out to probe the reasons beneath this dramatic swing in Chinese sentiments and found Chinese consciousness about Japan through these fifty years a more complex affair. The four individuals' experiences and thoughts investigated here point toward the diversity in Chinese approaches to Japan and Chinese understanding of Japan. Such diversity originated primarily from the many impulses in China's revolutionary changes, with the goals of reconstructing its political, military, intellectual, and social orders. Their different emphases on what was the primary need for China's reconstruction, in turn, directed the Chinese to seek various kinds of assistance or inspiration from Japan. The resulting intimate and intense interactions with Japan and the Japanese in the five decades between the two Sino-Japanese Wars developed parallel to China's ongoing revolutionary changes and its changing relations with Japan, and shaped and reshaped Chinese understanding of Japan.

Rediscovering Japan

How the Chinese changed their attitude toward Japan in the two decades following the first Sino-Japanese War may best be told by the emergence of a new Chinese term, *"Dong-yang,"* or the Exotic East (literally, Eastern Ocean), for Japan. It was a term used by Zhou Zuoren's father when he expressed the wish to send one son to Japan *(Dong-yang)* and another to the West *(Xi-yang)*—an expression that placed Japan parallel to the West. At the time, this change in nomenclature from *"Dongyi"* (Eastern Outsiders, Eastern Barbarians) signified the altered mind and a rising admiration and amazement at Japan's swift rise to power. The recognition of Japan's success as well as the desire to learn its secret motivated many Chinese to journey east. Going to study in Japan became "a passage to a world of new ideas" originating from the West.[2] Indeed, high-ranking officials and popular writers at the time shared the view that Japan, by its modern success, its cultural affinity, and its geographical proximity, provided a convenient bridge to the West.

Looking more comprehensively into the individual experiences before, during, and after each one's journey east, however, this study has found that Japan offered more than just a bridge to the West. In addition to making use of Japan's cultural media to reach the many ideas from the West, the Chinese also rediscovered Japan itself. With firsthand experiences, they not only identified certain distinctive aspects of Japanese society and culture, but their discoveries also took divergent directions unique to the individual. The crucial reason for such distinctiveness and divergence, as the four individuals examined here have demonstrated, originated from the experiences at home. Exposures to Japan's education and other cultural media often served to modify or reinforce the existing impulses and inclinations.

Yet such individual impulses and inclinations were more than personal. Above all, they were generated by the widely felt need to make changes in China in big ways. And the discovery of Japan by the four individuals in this study illustrates the deep impulses for political, cultural, and social changes within China.

Jiang Baili's discovery of Japan paralleled the rise of radical nationalism, which had motivated his pursuit of modern education and political activism while still at home. Arriving in Japan with only an abstract awareness of its military strength, Jiang touched the pulse of Japan's energetic drive for national power on the training grounds of the Army Officers' Academy. Although he said little about his explorations in Japan beyond his studies and political activities, his writings in the *Tides of Zhejiang* revealed a wide-ranging exposure to literature on the histories of modern nations and on Social Darwinism. But more than serving as a cultural medium for ideas from the broadly defined West, Meiji Japan impressed Jiang most with its effective modernization and military strength. Observing the ongoing imperialist expansion in Asia and elsewhere at the turn of the century, he was convinced that military readiness, as Japan's experience demonstrated, would be China's best chance for survival and rejuvenation.

Like Jiang, Zhou Zuoren brought with him to Japan an intense concern with the fate of the Chinese nation; yet unlike Jiang, he was deeply mistrustful of institutional authority. His encounter with Meiji Japan, therefore, led him to discover not Japan's material power, but its unique cultural appeal. His anti-authoritarian inclination steered him away from institutionalized education in Japan, from Japan's power and its martial spirit, and from the power-oriented political activities that absorbed Jiang and other Chinese radicals in the opening decade of the century. This more humanistic inclination oriented Zhou to the unpretentious folk life in Japan, or its "human culture" as he later called it, which in turn reinforced his anti-authoritarian propensity. Although he made use of Tokyo's trend-sensitive bookstores to access literary and scholarly publications from the West, Zhou quickly realized that there was more that Japan could offer. Zhou's experience with and attentive observation of Japan's everyday life, as well as his study of Japan's un-Westernized literature, altered his presumption that Japan was a mere transmitter of Western ideas. The almost instant change in his view of Japan once he landed on its soil was not fickle, but logical to his awareness of the social and political crises at home, as seen in China's patriarchal family and the ossified mandarinization in modern schools.

Either being absorbed by youthful adventure or being skeptical of organized protest, both Dai Jitao and Guo Moruo were not as politically active and radical as Jiang was during their student years in Japan. Yet dissatisfaction with the existing education system, in Dai's case, and clashing with the oppressive institution of arranged marriage, in Guo's case, were moving forces behind their search for alternatives beyond home. Therefore, both found life without close bureaucratic surveillance or familial constraint liberating; both echoed Zhou's fascination with Japanese culture in their discovery of the romantic charm of Japanese literature and the empathetic spirit of Japanese life. On the other hand, Japan during the Meiji and Taisho transition—with a state exerting more control in repressing radical thinkers and activists in the late Meiji period and the growing racism of the Taisho period—prevented them from being totally captivated by Japan's "human culture." At once drawn to Japan's cultural appeal and repelled by its blunt social and political repression, they were unable to define Japan intellectually as sharply as did Jiang and Zhou; rather, they perceived it in more emotional terms.

As selective, limited, and perhaps biased as each of these individuals' experiences with and impressions of Japan were, their partiality did not necessarily connote triviality. Rather, it registered in particular and specific ways the great complexity of the two societies, both of which were undergoing profound political and cultural transformation. It was in this context of revolutionary change that their discoveries of Japan illustrated new departures of Chinese consciousness of Japan from the old.

Engaging Japan

Unlike the majority of others, Jiang, Zhou, Dai, and Guo did not keep individually specific experiences and perceptions of Japan in early encounters to themselves, but instead carried them forth and translated them into future activities of national and intercultural magnitude. The separate courses they pursued in relation to Japan defy sweeping generalizations. There was, however, a common theme in their relationships with Japan during the first three decades of the century, one that was present from the turn of the century: what to borrow from Japan's modern experience and how to assimilate? They had approached this question mostly beyond the boundaries of state-to-state diplomatic relations; diverging beliefs, organizational needs, and personal imperatives had played uneven roles in shaping and directing their experiments to engage Japan in China's reconstruction.

The importance of intellectual persuasion was most evident in the experiments of Jiang and Zhou, despite the fact that the two had followed different beliefs, embraced different Japanese inspirations, and worked with different social groups to attain their goals. Although he was a radical anti-establishment student in Japan, Jiang made a surprising about-face to work within the government's military establishment when he returned home. The reason lies in the influence of the Japanese model in nation-building. Jiang was convinced by Japan's experience that strong military strength provided a shortcut to national strength and that reform from within (such as in the Meiji Restoration) would be the best approach to China's rejuvenation. From the viewpoint of a nationalist as well as a professional soldier, Jiang chose to remain aloof from the partisan struggles that so often led to compromising national interests. Pragmatic and realistic, he made use of a wide range of social connections with liberal reformers, wealthy bankers, and conservative warlords; these connections in turn added moderate or even conservative colors to his career.

Guided by the ideal of intellectual enlightenment, Zhou connected Japan's inspiration to a cultural revolution that reached full bloom in the late 1910s. His was an experiment to make use of inspirations from outside China to meet the demands from within. Through his theoretical discussion and articulation, Japan's inspiration of "human feelings" and "creative emulation" influenced the New Culture community and became vital components of the new agenda for China's cultural revolution. These new elements of Japanese origin added force to Zhou's iconoclastic attacks on traditional ethics during the New Culture Movement and inspired his new vision for China's cultural transformation.

In the realm of politics, Japan was perceived most often in terms of material aid. Motivated by special interests and necessitated by internal power struggles, Chinese political leaders both in and out of power during the early Republic could rarely forego external support.[3] The fate of the Guomindang was especially bound to Japan for decades during its struggle for national power. When facing political repression at home, its leaders anxiously sought protection and aid in Japan. Dai Jitao's growth from an adventurous youth to an anti-imperialist journalist, and finally to a Pan-Asian advocate, best illustrates the force of the political imperative in reshaping an individual's outlook on the world in general and on China's relationship with Japan in particular. Before his commitment to the Guomindang's cause, Dai vacillated between his hatred of Japanese imperialism and his admiration for Japan's wealth and empathetic culture. Involvement in the Guomindang's political struggle moderated his anti-imperialism. Dai's turn toward Pan-Asianism at the moment of the Guomindang's rise to national power derived from both the domestic power struggle with the radical Communists and the partisan need for international support. It appeared to offer Dai and his party the best solution for potentially conflicting forces to reconcile: the rhetoric of a racial war between the white and the yellow races subsumed his anti-imperialism, his affection for Japan transformed into the idea of international alliance, and the partisan needs of Japanese support were guaranteed by a partnership in a Sino-Japanese coalition.

In contrast to others' engagements with Japan, Guo Moruo's Japan connection was primarily in the domains of private life, personal literary pursuit, and personal association. In an age of radical cultural transformation, his engagement with Japan and with the Japanese aided not only his contribution to China's new literature, but also his liberation from the traditional family. Of the four men, he lived in Japan for the longest period—twenty years—and his autobiographical writings reveal the intensely emotional aspect that may be emblematic of many other private engagements between the Chinese and the Japanese. From a social point of view, his quiet rebellion foreshadowed the theoretical discussion and the radical practice of the next generation in the May Fourth era.

Thus through their varied endeavors, these Chinese internalized the influences of Japan on Chinese life. But the impact was uneven. In the political realm, the use of Japanese influence, whether in the form of a model (as Jiang did in reforming the military) or material assistance (as when Dai sought Japan's commitment to the Guomindang's cause), achieved little success because either internal resistance to change was too strong or the desired Japanese aid was not forthcoming. In the cultural realm, connections with and inspirations from Japan made a considerable impact, which can be seen in two broad areas. First, as has been detailed in several studies, Japan served as a transmitter of ideas from the West, including the radical theories of anarchism, socialism, and Marxism, as well as "the seminal terms and concepts of Western literature."[4] Second, as the findings in this study suggest, Japan also provided its own cultural inspiration, which was best explicated by Zhou, who brought it into Chinese national discourse and used it to shape the theory of a new literature. The positive impact of Japanese inspiration in reorienting China's cultural movement thus sharply contrasted with the small dimensions of Japan's influence on China's political landscape before the 1930s.

Confronting Japan

Throughout the years between the two Sino-Japanese Wars, Japan was not an idle reservoir with bountiful resources to draw upon. Japan itself was changing. Directly or indirectly, its government and its people were active participants in China's revolutionary changes. Although its imperial ambition had been present since the late nineteenth century, a generally accepted trajectory of Sino-Japanese relations marks 1915 as the turning point, when the notorious Twenty-One Demands caused a shift from largely positive interactions to negative ones. This periodization holds true concerning the rise of Chinese public opinion against Japan, but it becomes less valid if considering the Chinese central government under various warlords, which never stopped actively seeking Japanese aid. When Japan's impact on Chinese experiments in the areas of politics and culture are taken into consideration, this broad division also appears less useful.

The diverse efforts by the Chinese to engage Japan in China's cultural and political changes—as seen in Jiang's experiments in the military, in Dai's in politics, in Guo's in his quiet social rebellion, and in Zhou's in the New Culture movement—did not stop in 1915. In fact, most Chinese engagements with Japan and with Japanese inspiration either continued or even intensified in much of the 1920s. Jiang Baili stopped lauding Japanese bushidō after his failed experiments in reforming the Baoding Military Academy, mainly because of internal opposition rather than the external conflict with Japan. He was the first to reject the Japanese model after his trip to post–World War I Europe made him realize the bankruptcy of militarism after the Prussian—and Japanese—model. Yet at the same time in the early 1920s, Guo was making his debut in the May Fourth literary scene with the support of Satō Tomiko, and his autobiographical novels, as has been pointed out by several scholars,[5] were strongly influenced by the Japanese naturalist genre, the I-novel. Zhou was energetically promoting the New Village Movement and becoming a nationally recognized figure in promoting Chinese understanding of Japan, especially its cultural strength.

The more decisive turn that would affect these Chinese's engagements with Japan, especially Dai's, came in 1928, when a momentous shift in the power relationship began to take place both within China and Japan and between the two. In that year, the Chinese state attained internal unification under the Guomindang. Dai had been one of the most enthusiastic proponents of Pan-Asianism since the early 1910s, but his attempt to shore up his party's weakness at the time with racial sentiment failed to affect the cold calculations of realpolitik on the Japanese side. By the late 1920s, his dream of a Pan-Asian alliance again clashed with harsh reality, though this time it was not the weakness of his party but the perceived strength of his nation. Japan responded to the prospect of a strong nation on the continent with a power shift within the Japanese government from the more moderate Minseitō to the aggressive Seiyūkai.[6] As Dai learned firsthand on his mission to Japan, cultural affinity or racial sentiment could never bridge the enormous gap between the divergent national interests of China and Japan.

The worsening Sino-Japanese relations after 1928, on the other hand, generated the necessary conditions for Jiang's plan for national rejuvenation. Having learned from his failures in his single-minded pursuit of military strength after the Japanese model, Jiang broadened his perspective to include cultural forces and the Western democratic tradition. Japan in this context became a useful adversary that, by his dialectic logic, would help to enhance China's national strength through confrontation. Although his connection with rebellious forces led to clashes with the new regime in the late 1920s, Nanjing's commitment to defense preparation during the 1930s finally opened up common ground for cooperation with the nationalist Jiang Baili.

The approaching Sino-Japanese confrontation also narrowed the space of cultural liminality and ambivalent loyalty, which had been essential for Guo Moruo's social liberation and literary creation. Guo, who remained a quiet rebel while living an intercultural life in Japan, was thrown into the torrent of events by the Japanese

invasion of China. The war cut short his search for personal liberation and ended his twenty-year marriage to his Japanese wife. By
forcing him back into a China where the efforts for national salvation were complicated by the partisan struggle between the Guomindang and the Communist Party, the war also redefined Guo's
engagement with Japan within the perimeter of national and partisan loyalty.

While Japanese imperial expansion and the eventual invasion
had caused others to retreat from engagement (Dai) or turn toward
confrontation (Jiang and Guo), it compelled Zhou to seek an
approach that may be termed antagonistic engagement. Zhou appeared to be "a scholar who withdrew" from active participation in
national life during the 1930s.[7] But close examination of Zhou's
thoughts and actions reveals the fact that he had never retreated
from his position of individualist humanism as first inspired by
the Shirakaba school. His wartime activities, which unified private
and public morality around humanist concerns, further defied
characterization as either passivity, resistance, or collaboration[8]—
categories meaningful only within the borders of a nation-state. His
service in the "client regime" in north China may appear to be an
"accommodation" of the Japanese invasion, as seen in several cases
analyzed in a recent collection of essays edited by David P. Barrett
and Larry N. Shyu,[9] but in fact Zhou did not choose to work *with*
the enemy but *against* it. As a writer, he never put his weapon down;
"[h]is immediate contribution," as Edward Gunn aptly summarizes,
"was his dissent with the authoritarian traditions of Confucianism
being advocated by the Japanese, and his counterclaim that the
value of Confucianism lay in its espousal of humaneness, modera-
tion and skepticism."[10] In his writings before, during, and after the
war, Zhou's sympathies and hatreds transcended national boundaries. He never hesitated to criticize those who abused power,
whether Chinese or Japanese. There is a consistency in his admiration for the empathetic spirit in Japanese culture, in his efforts at
advocating "human literature" during the May Fourth era, and in
his use of the pristine Confucian idea of "benevolence" *(ren)* to
criticize Japan's military atrocities during the war. The war did not
quench the spirit of humanism that Zhou discovered in Tokyo at
the turn of the century; instead, it shone even more brightly and
defiantly through the darkness of savage brutality.

Re-understanding Japan

By 1945, it was clear that most of the objectives that these individuals hoped to achieve by applying Japanese inspirations or with Japanese assistance—a strong nation, intellectual enlightenment, or personal liberation from institutional authority—had not been met. Their greatest accomplishment lay in having begun a new chapter with multiple voices in the Chinese understanding of Japan. Through their writings and by engaging issues that concerned a growing number of Chinese, they articulated several distinct perspectives on Japan and hence departed in different measures from the premodern Chinese representation of Japan.

Unlike the premodern scholar-officials who wrote about Japan mostly within the folds of dynastic histories, modern Chinese writings about Japan, as these four individuals' work exemplifies, served a different function and developed on a new institution.[11] Print media, despite its limited reach to the literate and concerned Chinese,[12] was a new cultural phenomenon that grew by leaps and bounds in their generation's time. It offered a new arena where Chinese concerns about Japan could be presented and debated and the new knowledge of Japan formed and disseminated. Through the print media, all four individuals transcended their professional boundaries to share the function of modern publicist and join the national discourse on Japan.

Although emotionally close to the Chinese public when facing Japan's continental ambitions and territorial expansion, the four Chinese studied here often stood in opposition to the nation's mood swings. Assuming the role of opinion leaders, they intended to lead the public away from ignorance, arrogance, or fear by offering them carefully observed knowledge. In the late 1910s, for instance, Guo Moruo argued against the Chinese boycott of Japanese goods, which he believed achieved little tangible result. With the hope of eliminating stereotypical Chinese contempt for Japanese culture and habitual Chinese indifference to Japanese imperialism, Zhou Zuoren during the 1920s pursued a two-pronged strategy: to popularize Japan's creative cultural spirit while writing the harshest criticisms of Japanese colonial behavior in China. For Dai Jitao, writing about Japan, of course, had an explicit political purpose: to steer the population toward his partisan cause. And his ultimate treatise on Japan, *Riben lun,* which summarized his lifelong observation of Japanese politics and culture, was an attempt to direct the growing national sentiment for resisting Japan toward supporting the government's effort at internal unification[13] and a final appeal to the Japanese leaders to turn an emerging aggressive policy toward China into a cooperative one.[14] But even Jiang Baili, who often appeared more congenial to the public sentiment, was writing in wartime with the aim of changing popular fears of a technologically more advanced enemy.

The engagement with prevalent problems and attitudes among the Chinese revealed more than a gap between the ordinary and the extraordinary. It was by their pointed, nuanced, and diverse writings for the public that these four publicists made a significant breakthrough from stereotypes to knowledge based on firsthand experience and studied observation, with works that redefined the scope and depth of Chinese understanding of Japan in modern times. Noticeable ambivalence toward Japan and Japanese culture marked the thoughts of all four Chinese we have discussed, but their departures from premodern representations of Japan can be found in three divergent tendencies, each concerned with repositioning Japan in the modern world and re-understanding China's relationship with it.

One tendency took Japan as a model of Westernization. Such was the main orientation of Chinese attitudes toward Japan at the beginning of the century, but its intellectual genealogy can be traced to the nineteenth-century Self-strengtheners, who wanted to use Western technology to revive the Chinese nation. Training in Meiji Japan's Westernized educational institutions, as Jiang Baili and, to some extent, Guo Moruo had, provided these Chinese Westernizers with a passage of acculturation to a desirable modernity. But Japan as a culture was not taken seriously in their intellectual quest. Viewed from the perspective of modern achievement, with its archetypes located in the West, they tended to look down on Japan as a mere "imitator" of the West. The need to find the true source of modern greatness thus led Jiang to pursue enlightenment in Europe and, when looking back during the Sino-Japanese confrontation, to taunt Japan's ill-matched "desire" and "fate."

The second tendency, while recognizing the influence of the West on modern Japan, viewed the Japanese experience as an unusually successful case of cultural assimilation. This tendency rejected the view that Japan was either a cultural variant of Chinese civilization or a mere imitator of the Western type of modernization. Instead of attributing Japan's strength to influences from outside, it recognized Japan's own ability to select and to absorb such influences. "Creative emulation," a phrase that Zhou Zuoren used to describe Meiji literary innovation and development, best summarized this more cosmopolitan view of Japan's cultural strength and uniqueness.

If both these tendencies, emphasizing either Japan's parody of the West or Japan's difference from it despite its assimilation of Western influence, present an image of Japan's separateness from Chinese civilization, the third tendency, as best articulated by Dai Jitao, argued the opposite. Motivated by a partisan interest and substantiated by a longer perspective of Japan's mythical and historical past, Dai viewed Chinese cultural influence, and above all Confucianism, as "providing the foundation for Japan's civilization." The influences from the West, such as liberalism, were taken only as complementary forces in a civilization process that had been developing for three hundred years. Although Dai spoke highly of Japanese spiritual life while criticizing the Chinese, he rejected the view of Japan as a Westernization model and, instead, attempted to place it within the borders of Chinese civilization.

While Jiang Baili, Zhou Zuoren, and Dai Jitao made the most prominent and influential articulations on these three perspectives, they were aware of each other's viewpoints and would concur with these viewpoints to a degree but with qualifications. How these divergent perspectives coexisted in the modern Chinese consciousness of Japan may be seen in Guo Moruo's shifting attitude and sentiment toward Japan. Being primarily a Westernizer like Jiang, who viewed Japan as merely a bridge to the West, Guo held considerable appreciation for Japan's unique culture. This appreciation that grew out of his intimate observation of Japanese life over a long period of time was substantiated by his scholarship on language and history. He also made frequent reference to the shared past between China and Japan, as Dai did, and such reference was also often prompted by his concern for the present. The three perspectives in viewing Japan thus became not isolated viewpoints, but layers of consciousness in understanding Japan by Guo and many of his fellow Chinese.

All these perspectives, in retrospect, were scarcely conceivable before the first Sino-Japanese War, when the Sinocentric order had been taken for granted by educated Chinese. Nor were they visible during the Cold War era, when ideological rigidity locked Chinese understanding of Japan into a single mode. But here and there we now begin to hear echoes of these not-so-distant voices, as another age of the exchange of people and ideas between China and Japan is unfolding with renewed vibrancy.[15] The goals and priorities of those pioneers who traversed the unknown territory of modern Sino-Japanese relations may now be replaced by new ones in this age of faster communication, relative political stability, and greater, though uneven, affluence and economic opportunities; yet their footprints, their insights, and their bias, as well as their all too human hopes and despair, remain, challenging the latecomers to achieve greater success in forging human fellowship in an increasingly smaller world.

ABBREVIATIONS

DJTBN	*Zengding Dai Jitao xiansheng biannian zhuanji*
DJTJ	*Dai Jitao ji, 1909–1920*
DJTWC	*Dai Jitao xiansheng wencun*
DJTWJ	*Dai Jitao xinhai wenji (1909–1913)*
DJTJNTK	*Dai Jitao xiangsheng shishi shizhounian jinian tekan*
GMRNP	*Guo Moruo nianpu*
JBLNP	*Jiang Baili nianpu*
JBLJNC	*Jiang Baili xiansheng jinance*
JBLQJ	*Jiang Baili xiansheng quanji*
SZSQJ	*Sun Zhongshan quanji*
SZSNP	*Sun Zhongshan nianpu changbian*
ZTHXL	*Zhitang huixianglu*
ZZRNP	*Zhou Zuoren nianpu*
ZZRRJ-LXYJZL	*Zhou Zuoren riji*
ZZRWLB	*Zhou Zuoren wen leibian*

NOTES

Introduction

1. For studies of pioneering advocates for the Japanese model before 1895, see Noriko Kamachi, *Reform in China: Huang Tsun-hsien and the Japanese Model* (Cambridge, Mass.: Harvard University Press, 1981); and Zheng Hailin, *Huang Zunxian yu Jindai Zhongguo* [Huang Zunxian and Modern China] (Beijing: Shenghuo dushu xinzhi sanlian shudian, 1988), especially chapter 6.

2. See chapter 2 for a discussion on the rapidly growing influx of Chinese students to Japan. For a detailed analysis of the study-in-Japan movement, see Sanetō Keishū, *Chūgokujin Nihon ryūgakushi* (Tokyo: Kuroshio shuppan, 1970); Huang Fu-ch'ing, *Chinese Students in Japan in the Late Ch'ing Period,* trans. Katherine P. K. Whitaker (Tokyo: Centre for East Asian Cultural Studies, 1982); and Paula S. Harrell, *Sowing the Seeds of Change: Chinese Students, Japanese Teachers, 1895–1905* (Stanford: Stanford University Press, 1992). An earlier work by Roger F. Hackett, "Chinese Students in Japan, 1900–1910," in *Papers on China,* vol. 3 (Cambridge, Mass.: Committee on International and Regional Studies, 1949), 134–170, provides important arguments that are more fully developed in later book-length studies by others.

3. Douglas R. Reynolds, *China, 1898–1912: The Xinzheng Revolution and Japan* (Cambridge, Mass.: Harvard University Press, 1993).

4. Y. C. Wang, *Chinese Intellectuals and the West, 1872–1949* (Chapel Hill: University of North Carolina Press, 1966), 68, 119–120, 177, 178–179. Wang draws on a comparison of several editions of *Who's Who in China* and *The China Yearbook* to show that in 1923, 47.5 percent listed in *Who's Who* were educated in China, 29.5 percent held degrees from Japan, and 12.9 percent had educational backgrounds in the United States; in 1932, the numbers were 31.2 percent, 20.3 percent, and 31.3 percent, respectively. Ching-mao Cheng indicates that most Chinese writers who were active and influential during the 1920s and 1930s had studied in Japan; see Ching-mao Cheng, "The Impact of Japanese Literary Trends on Modern Chinese Writers," in Merle Goldman, ed., *Modern*

Chinese Literature in the May Fourth Era (Cambridge, Mass.: Harvard University Press, 1977), 63–88.

5. Joshua A. Fogel, *The Literature of Travel in the Japanese Rediscovery of China, 1862–1945* (Stanford: Stanford University Press, 1996).

6. For examples see Maruyama Noboru, *Aru Chūgoku tokuhain* (Tokyo: Chūo kōronsha, 1976); and Joshua A. Fogel, *Nakae Uchikichi in China: The Mourning of Spirit* (Cambridge, Mass.: Harvard University Press, 1989).

7. Peter Duus, Ramon H. Myers, and Mark R. Peattie, *The Japanese Informal Empire in China, 1895–1937* (Princeton, N.J.: Princeton University Press, 1989). For the colonization of Manchuria in the 1930s, see Louise Young, *Japan's Total Empire: Manchuria and the Culture of Wartime Imperialism* (Berkeley: University of California Press, 1998).

8. Two excellent collections of articles by leading political scientists, historians, and literary scholars of China and Japan provide the best guides to this issue of twentieth-century Sino-Japanese conflict: Alvin D. Coox and Hilary Conroy, eds., *China and Japan: A Search for Balance since World War I* (Santa Barbara, Calif.: Clio Books, 1978); James C. Hsiung and Steven I. Levine, eds., *China's Bitter Victory: The War with Japan, 1937–1945* (New York: M. E. Sharpe, 1992). The figure of Chinese war casualties is a Chinese estimate, cited by Hsi-sheng Ch'i, "The Military Dimension, 1942–1945," in Hsiung and Levine, 179.

9. Allen S. Whiting, *China Eyes Japan* (Berkeley: University of California Press, 1989), 41.

10. Marius B. Jansen, *Japan and China: From War to Peace, 1895–1972* (Chicago: Rand McNally College Publishing Co., 1975), xiv.

11. Persistence of the previously existing force in social organization and intellectual repertoire may be sampled in Emily Honig, *Sisters and Strangers: Women in the Shanghai Cotton Mills, 1919–1949* (Stanford: Stanford University Press, 1980); Brian Martin, *The Green Gang: Politics and Organized Crime, 1919–1937* (Berkeley: University of California Press, 1996); Guy Alitto, *The Last Confucian: Liang Shu-ming and the Chinese Dilemma of Modernity* (Berkeley: University of California Press, 1979); and Christina Kelley Gilmartin, *Engendering the Chinese Revolution: Radical Women, Communist Politics, and Mass Movements in the 1920s* (Berkeley: University of California Press, 1995).

12. Douglas R. Reynolds, *China, 1898–1912;* Marius B. Jansen, *The Japanese and Sun Yat-sen* (Cambridge, Mass.: Harvard University Press, 1954); Chalmers A. Johnson, *Peasant Nationalism and the Communist Power: The Emergence of Revolutionary China, 1937–1945* (Stanford: Stanford University Press, 1962).

13. See Kojima Shinji, Itō Teruo, Mitsuoka Gen, Itagaki Nozomu, Sugiyama Fumihiko, and Kō Seibu, *Chūgokujin no Nihonjinkan hyakunenshi* (Tokyo: Jiyū kokuminsha, 1974), for a comprehensive anthology of Chinese views of Japan, which consists of seventy-eight excerpts from writings by thirty-eight Chinese during the period from the 1870s to 1972. The four individuals in this

study, of course, are among the thirty-eight authors, but no businessman's writing is included. A case study of a Chinese woman and businessman certainly would enhance our understanding of Sino-Japanese interactions in modern times, but so far I have not found a case comparable in depth and length to the four that I have selected.

14. See Jerome Bruner, *Acts of Meaning* (Cambridge, Mass.: Harvard University Press, 1990), 120.

15. See, e.g., Michael Elliot Lestz, "The Meaning of Revival: The Kuomintang 'New Right' and Party Building in Republican China, 1925–1936," Ph.D. dissertation, Yale University, 1982; and John Fitzgerald, *Awakening China: Politics, Culture, and Class in the Nationalist Revolution* (Stanford: Stanford University Press, 1996), 19.

16. I have briefly discussed the debate in "Revisiting Wartime Collaboration: Chinese Debate on Zhou Zuoren, 1945–1995," a paper presented to the New England Association of Asian Studies annual meetings in 1997.

17. Zhou Zuoren, "Liuxue de huiyi" [Reminiscence of studying abroad], in *Yaotang zawen* (Beijing: Xinmin yinshuguan, 1944; reprint, Hong Kong: Beixin shuju, n.d.), 93–94.

18. Wang Xiangrong, a Chinese scholar who did extensive intertextual study on premodern records of Sino-Japanese exchange, indicates that the name "Wo," a word used in the *History of Wei* to refer to the Japanese, first appeared in the *Classic of Mountains and Seas [Shanhai jing]*, the ancient fable collection dated from the third century B.C. to the second century A.D. Wang cautions against treating *Shanhai jing* as a definitive record of the Japanese without sufficient corroborating sources. See Wang Xiangrong, "Zhongguo zhengshi zhong de Riben zhuan [The biographies of Japan in China's official dynastic histories]," in *Zhongri guanxishi wenxian lunkao* (Changsha: Yuelu shushe, 1985), 1–65, esp. 5–6. Also see Shi Xiaojun, *Zhongri liangguo huxiang renshi de bianqian* (Taibei: Taiwan shangwu yinshuguan, 1992), 24. The eleven-word reference to "Wo" in *Shanhai jing* appeared in book twelve, "The Classic of Regions within the Seas: The North" (ca. first century B.C.). For an English translation, see Anne Birrell, trans., *The Classic of Mountains and Seas* (London and New York: Penguin Books, 1999), 147.

19. For the most comprehensive and insightful study in English of Japanese discussion on the subject, see John Young, *The Location of Yamatai: A Case Study in Japanese Historiography, 720–1945* (Baltimore, Md.: Johns Hopkins Press, 1958). For the more recent development of Japanese archaeological and historical discoveries and discussion in the second half of the twentieth century, see Walter Edwards, "In Pursuit of Himiko: Postwar Archeology and the Location of Yamatai," *Monumenta Nipponica* 51.1: 53–79.

20. Wang Xiangrong indicates the following intertextual relationships: *The Treatise of Wei* serves as the original source for *The History of Late Han [Hou Han shu]*, *History of Jin [Jin shu]*, and *History of Liang [Liang shu]*; *History of Song*

[Song shu] serves as the original source for *History of Southern Qi [Nan Qi shu]* and *History of the Southern Dynasties [Nan shi]*; and *The History of Sui [Sui shu]* serves as the original source for *The History of Northern Dynasties [Bei shi]*. The worst case of plagiarizing with ridiculous alteration occurred in *The History of Southern Dynasties* and *The History of Northern Dynasties*. See Wang Xiangrong, "Zhongguo zhengshi zhong de Riben Zhuan," in *Zhongri guanxishi wenxian lunkao*, 1–65, esp. 4–14. Some of the information regarding Japan's internal division recorded in *The History of Wei* can also be found unaltered in the *Riben Kaolue*, an important work in the Ming dynasty. See Shi Xiaojun, *Zhongri liang-guo huxiang renshi de bianqian*, 57, 88.

21. Wang Xiangrong, *Zhongri guanxishi wenxian lunkao*, 239–245.

22. D. R. Howland, *Borders of Chinese Civilization: Geography and History at Empire's End* (Durham, N.C., and London: Duke University Press, 1996), passim.

23. Edwin O. Reischauer, *Ennin's Travels in Tang China* (New York: The Ronald Press, 1955), 41.

24. Instead of using "barbarian," a traditional translation of the Chinese word *"yi"* as established in the volume edited by John K. Fairbank, *The Chinese World Order* (Cambridge, Mass.: Harvard University Press, 1968), I opt for "outsiders" in order to avoid a telescopic view of Sino-Japanese relations in history. The English word "barbarian," as demonstrated by Fairbank's classic volume, connotes not only contempt but also antagonism in nineteenth-century diplomatic relations between China and the West. For an erudite discussion on the inclusiveness of Chinese civilization and the elasticity of its borders, see D. R. Howland, *Borders of Chinese Civilization*, esp. "Civilization and Proximity" in chap. 1.

25. In ancient Chinese, *"wo"* also connotes *"wei,"* meaning supple or nimble. See Xu Shen (ca. 100 A.D.), *Shuowen Jiezi zhu [Annotated Shuowen Jiezi]*, annotated by Duan Yucai (1735–1815) (Shanghai: Shanghai guji chubanshe, 1981), 368.

26. Noriko Kamachi, *Reform in China*, esp. chap. 3.

27. D. R. Howland, *Borders of Chinese Civilization*, 148, 201.

Part I: Paths to Japan

1. Marius B. Jansen, *Japan and China*, 149.

2. Mary Backus Rankin, *Early Chinese Revolutionaries: Radical Intellectuals in Shanghai and Chekiang, 1902–1911* (Cambridge, Mass.: Harvard University Press, 1971), 3–17; Robert A. Scalapino, "Prelude to Marxism: The Chinese Student Movement in Japan, 1900–1910," in Albert Feuerwerker, Rhoads Murphey, Mary C. Wright, eds., *Approaches to Modern Chinese History* (Berkeley and Los Angeles: University of California Press, 1967), 190–215.

3. Douglas Reynolds, *China, 1898–1912*, 2–5, 194; citation on page 2.

1. Riding the Crest of Chinese Nationalism

1. Yamazaki Masao, ed, *Rikugun Shikan Gakkō* (Tokyo: Shūgen Shobō, 1969), esp. 37–38; Hillis Lory, *Japan's Military Masters: The Army in Japanese Life* (New York: Viking Press, 1943), 95–99.

2. Chiyoda shiryō, no. 921; *Rikugun Shikan Gakkō Chūka Minkoku Ryūgakusei Meibo* (Bōeichō reprinted, 1965), in Bōeichō Kenshujo Senshishitsu, call no. chūō.guntai kyōiku.shikan gakkō.60; Jiang Fucong and Xue Guangqian, eds., *Jiang Baili xiansheng quanji*, vol. 6 (Taibei: Zhuanji wenxue chubanshe, 1971), 23–24 (hereafter cited as *JBLQ J*); Tao Juyin, *Jiang Baili zhuan* (Beijing: Zhonghua shuju, 1985), 9–11. For the practice of honoring the Top Five graduates in the Army Officers' Academy (Shikan Gakkō), see Alvin Coox, *The Year of the Tiger* (Tokyo: Orient/West Incorporated, 1964), 58.

3. Liang Qichao, *Zhongguo jin sanbainian xueshushi [A history of Chinese scholarship in the last three hundred years]* (1924), reprinted in Zhu Weizheng, ed., *Liang Qichao lun Qing xue shi erzhong* [Two works by Liang Qichao on the scholarship in the Qing dynasty] (Shanghai: Fudan daxue chubanshe, 1985), esp. chap. 5.

4. Xu Yiyun, *Jiang Baili nianpu, 1882–1938* (Beijing: Tuanjie chubanshe, 1992), 8 (hereafter cited as *JBLNP*).

5. Ibid., 1.

6. Ibid., 10.

7. Jiang Baili, "Shi-bu-shi shechi de zhuang-shi-pin?" [A decoration of luxury] *Gaizao* 4.1 (December 1921).

8. Zhang Hecao, "Jiang Baili suiyuan riji" [Journals from the days serving Jiang Baili], cited in *JBLNP*, 11.

9. Zhang Zongxian, "Jiang Baili Xiaozhuan" [A brief biography of Jiang Baili], *Wenshi ziliao xuanji*, vol. 10, reprinted in He Suihua, Xu Yiyun, and Chen Boliang, eds., *Jiang Baili xiansheng jiniance* (Haining: Zhongguo renmin zhengzhi xieshang huiyi zhejiang sheng haining shi wenshi ziliao weiyuanhui, 1993), 3 (hereafter cited as *JBLJNC*).

10. *JBLNP*, 16.

11. Ibid., 16.

12. Jiang went without an official fellowship. Fang Yuting, who had been providing occasional financial support to Jiang, promised to do the same in the future. But Fang died soon after Jiang sailed to Japan. In Japan, Jiang supported himself mostly through writing and translation. See Jiang Baili, "Shi-bu-shi shechi de zhuang-shi-pin?"

13. Sanetō Keishū, *Chūgokujin Nihon ryūgakushi*, 544.

14. Fang Hanqi, *Zhongguo jindai baokanshi* [A history of modern press in China] (Taiyuan: Shanxi jiaoyu chubanshe, 1981), 189.

15. Table 1 indicates an overwhelming tendency among the Chinese students in Japan during the first half of the 1900s to enroll in military schools. See Sanetō Keishū, *Chūgokujin Nihon ryūgakushi*, 138.

Table 1. Chinese Students Graduated from Japanese Schools

	1901	1902	1903	1904	1905	1906	1907	1908
Total	40	30	6	109	15	42	57	623
Army/Navy	39	25	–	93	–	–	–	254

16. *JBLNP*, 23. For the position of Seijō Gakkō in the Japanese educational system, see Sanetō Keishū, *Chūgokujin Nihon ryūgakushi*, 65; Kobayashi Tomoaki, "Rikugun Shikan Gakkō to Chūgoku ryūgakusei," *Hitori kara*, vol. 6 (Tokyo: 1985), which indicates that the Japanese naval academy only started to accept Chinese students in 1906, and the program stopped in 1909.

17. Seijō had two prominent figures serving as top administrators when Jiang enrolled. General Kodama Gentarō, the most able strategist in the army at the time, was its nominal president, and Okamoto Noribumi, one of the four leading mathematicians of the early Meiji era, was the principal and the actual administrator. Its foreign student department opened in 1895, first admitted Chinese in 1898, and offered a comprehensive curriculum at the middle-school level that included English, geography, geology, mathematics, nature, physics, chemistry, drawing, physical education, and a specially designed course in the Japanese language. See Nakamura Tadashi, "Seijō Gakkō to Chūgokujin ryūgakusei," in Shingai Kakumei Kenkyūkai, ed., *Chūgoku kingendai shi ronshū* (Tokyo: Kyūko shoyin, 1985), 251–275; and Inagaki Haruhiko et al., eds., *Seijō Gakkō Hyakunen [A Hundred Years of Seijō Gakkō]* (Tokyo: Seijō Gakkō, 1985), 52, 247, 254, 269, 314.

18. *JBLNP*, 25.

19. Ibid., 28; *Zhejiang chao* 2.

20. Fang Hanqi, *Zhongguo jindai baokan shi*, 208.

21. Articles signed with such pen-names as "Huiseng," "Wanseng," "Weizeng," "Weichen," and "Feishi" are also possibly written by Jiang Baili; see *JBLNP*, 27–28. Also see *Zhejiang chao* 1–10.

22. Yu Yi [Jiang Baili], "Minzu zhuyi lun" [On nationalism], *Zhejiang chao* no. 1, 1–2.

23. "Guohun lun" [On national soul], *Zhejiang chao* no. 1.

24. Yu Yi, "Minzu zhuyi lun," *Zhejiang chao* no. 2 (February 1903), 17.

25. Feisheng, "Guohun pian" [On national soul], *Zhejiang chao* no. 3 (March 1903), 21.

26. Feisheng, "Guohun Pian," *Zhejiang chao* no. 7, 39.

27. Ibid., 34, 38.

28. Ibid., 32.

29. "Guohun Pian," *Zhejiang chao* no. 3, 6–7.

30. Feisheng, "Zhen Junren" [The true soldier], *Zhejiang chao* no. 3, 65–72.

31. Feisheng, "Guohun Pian," *Zhejiang chao* no. 3, 11.

32. See Fukuzawa Yukichi, *An Outline of a Theory of Civilization,* trans. David A. Dilworth and G. Cameron Hurst (Tokyo: Sophia University, 1970), esp. chap. 2; and John D. Pierson, *Tokutomi Sohō, 1863–1957: A Journalist for Modern Japan* (Princeton, N.J.: Princeton University Press, 1980), 54–56.

33. Philip C. Huang, *Liang Ch'i-ch'ao and Modern Chinese Liberalism* (Seattle: University of Washington Press, 1972), esp. 56–61.

34. Paula Harrell, *Sowing the Seeds of Change,* chap. 6, esp. 132–133, 193–194.

35. *JBLNP,* 26–27; Mary Backus Rankin, *Early Chinese Revolutionaries,* 22–24.

36. See Paula Harrell, *Sowing the Seeds of Change,* 131–139.

37. Feisheng, trans., "E-ren zhi xingzhi" [The nature of the Russians], *Zhejiang chao* nos. 1 and 2.

38. Feisheng, "E-luo-si zhi dongya xin zhengce [Russia's new East Asia policy]," *Zhejiang chao* nos. 1 and 2.

39. The publication as printed in the monthly is dated the tenth lunar month, which should fall within the year 1903. Yet the article discussed here is obviously written *after* Japan's successful attack on the Russian Pacific Fleet at Port Arthur in early February 1904 and Japan's declaration of war.

40. Mingxin, "Ri-E kaizhan yu Zhongguo zhi diwei" [The outbreak of the Russo-Japanese War and China's position in it], *Zhejiang chao* no. 10.

41. Zhang Hecao, "Jiang Baili suiyuan riji" [Journal from the days following Jiang Baili], cited in *JBLNP,* 11–12.

42. Feisheng, "Jinshi erda xueshuo zhi pinglun" [Critique on the two current major theories], *Zhejiang chao* no. 8, 25, 28.

43. Feisheng, "Jinshi erda xueshuo zhi pinglun," *Zhejiang chao* no. 9, 16, 17.

44. Ibid., 19–20.

45. Liang in 1903 began to consider it necessary to use strong government as a means for effective change after a trip to America, where he visited Chinese communities. The social problems there caused him to reconsider his view on cultivating new citizenry. See Philip C. Huang, *Liang Ch'i-ch'ao and Modern Chinese Liberalism,* chap. 4, esp. 80–81.

46. Jiang probably became acquainted with the famous reformer through the introduction of Cai E, his close friend at Seijō Gakkō and later at the Army Officers' Academy, who was Liang's student in Hunan before their abortive reform attempts. See *JBLNP,* 25–26.

47. Liang Qichao, "Da Feisheng" [A response to Feisheng], in Lin Zhijun, ed., *Yinbingshi heji,* vol. 3 (Shanghai: Zhonghua shuju, 1932), 40–45.

48. Liang also gave critical help that enabled Jiang to enter the Army Officers' Academy. Although sent to Japan by the provincial government of Zhejiang, Jiang received no governmental aid, as Fang Yuting, who promised a yearly one-hundred-yuan stipend, died soon after Jiang left for Japan. Either earning income by translation or being helped by friends, Jiang supported himself through preliminary schools. Being a self-subsidized student, he lacked the social connections to obtain an official recommendation, as stipulated by the Japanese authorities at the request of the Qing government, for all Chinese who wished to enter military schools. Through Liang's connection, Jiang finally obtained a recommendation from Zhao Erxun, then the governor-general of Shengjing, after waiting for one and a half years. See Xu Yiyun, *Jiang Baili nianpu*, 32; Seijō Gakkō Gakuseibu, *Seijō Gakkō ryūgakuseibu shusshinsha meibo* [Register of foreign students in Seijō Gakkō] (Tokyo: Seijō Gakkō Gakuseibu, 1937), 3; and "Meiji sanjūroku nen jūnigatsu nyūkō shinkoku rikugon gakusei kōka retsujō hyo" [Examination ranking chart of Chinese military students enrolled in December 1903], Chiyoda shiryō no. 921.

49. Yamazaki Masao, ed., *Rikugun Shikan Gakkō*, 211.

50. Tao Juyin, *Jiang Baili zhuan*, 10; *JBLNP*, 33.

51. Tao Juyin, *Jiang Baili zhuan*, 10–11.

52. Ibid., 11. Qian's son, the famous missile expert Qian Xuesen, later married Jiang's third daughter, Jiang Ying.

2. Beyond Chinese Nationalism

1. Sanetō Keishū, *Chūgokujin Nihon ryūgakushi*, 58–59; Li Xisuo, "Qingmuo liuri xuesheng renshu xiaokao" [An estimate on the number of Chinese students in Japan], *Wenshizhe* no. 3 (1982), 28–30. All evidence considered, Sanetō's estimate of eight thousand is probably closer to the actual number of Chinese students who *went to* Japan in 1906.

2. Sanetō Keishū, *Chūgokujin Nihon ryūgakushi*, 138–139.

3. Lu Xun, "Preface to the First Collection of Short Stories, *Call to Arms*," in *Selected Works of Lu Hsun*, vol. 1 (Beijing: Foreign Languages Press, 1956), 3.

4. As it turned out, Zhou Zuoren was never able to follow through with his translation plan, being afraid of ruining the nuance and the beauty of the masterpiece. Nevertheless, he kept the eight-volume collection for nearly three decades, until the 1930s. Zhou Zuoren, *Zhitang huixianglu* (Hong Kong: Sanyu tushu wenju gongsi, 1974), 166 (hereafter cited as *ZTHXL*).

5. Ibid., 173.

6. Ibid., 176–177.

7. Zhang Juxiang and Zhang Tierong, eds., *Zhou Zuoren nianpu* (Tianjin: Nankai daxue chubanshe, 1985), 1 (hereafter cited as *ZZRNP*); also see Zhou Xiashou [Zhou Zuoren], *Lu Xun de gujia* (Hong Kong: Datong shuju, 1962), 111–112.

8. Lu Xun, "Cong baicaoyuan dao sanwei shuwu [From hundred-plant garden to three-flavor study]," *Lu Xun Qianji*, vol. 2, 384.

9. *ZTHXL*, 15; *Lu Xun de gujia*, 59, 62.

10. *Lu Xun de gujia*, 38–41, 45.

11. Ibid., 156–157.

12. Ibid., 148, 158.

13. Lu Xun, "Suoji" [Random notes], in *Zhaohua xishi* [Dawn blossoms plucked at dusk], reprinted in *Lu Xun quanji* (Shanghai: Lu Xun quanji chubanshe, 1938), 399–401.

14. *ZTHXL*, 11.

15. Zhou Xiashou, *Lu Xun de gujia*, 46.

16. *ZTHXL*, 11–12.

17. Zhou Xiashou, *Lu Xun de gujia*, 50.

18. Ibid., 29–30.

19. *ZTHXL*, 12–13.

20. Zhou Xiashou, *Lu Xun de gujia*, 48, 90; Zhou Zuoren, "Wo xue guowen de jingyan" [My experience of learning written Chinese]," in *Tanhu Ji* (Shanghai: Beixin shuju, 1929; reprint, Hong Kong: Shiyong shuju, 1967).

21. *Zhou Zuoren riji, 1898–1899*, printed in *Lu Xun yanjiu ziliao*, vol. 8 (1981), 67–69, 84–85; vol. 9, 108 (hereafter cited as *ZZRRJ-LXYJZL*).

22. *ZZRRJ-LXYJZL*, vol. 8, 89. The fourth brother whom Zhou Zuoren mentioned was Zhou Fengyi's fourth son, who was born in 1893 and died in 1899. Zhou Zuoren, as the oldest male heir remaining at home, assumed the responsibility of seeking medical treatment for the younger brother and took care of the sad business of his burial.

23. *ZTHXL*, 69.

24. *ZZRRJ-LXYJZL*, vol. 8, 96.

25. Ibid., 91; *ZTHXL*, 67, 69.

26. Lu Xun, "Zi xu" [One's own preface], *Nahan* [Call to arms], *Lu Xun quanji*, vol. 1, 270.

27. Fudan Daxue, Shanghai Shida, and Shanghai Shiyuan, eds., *Lu Xun nianpu* (Hefei: Anhui renmin chubanshe, 1979), 27–32.

28. Zhou Xiashou, *Lu Xun de gujia*, 80–81; *ZZRRJ-LXYJZL*, vol. 10, 105.

29. *ZTHXL*, 93, 100, 101.

30. *ZZRRJ-LXYJZL*, 1901, 1902, vol. 10–11, passim.

31. Ibid., vol. 10, 122.

32. *Lu Xun quanji*, vol. 2, 405–406.

33. *ZZRRJ-LXYJZL*, vol. 10, 120; Lin Shu was China's first major translator of Western literature and left some 180 translated works. See Leo Ou-fan Lee, *The Romantic Generation of Modern Chinese Writers* (Cambridge, Mass.: Harvard University Press, 1973), 45–46.

34. Benjamin Schwartz, *In Search of Wealth and Power: Yen Fu and the West* (Cambridge, Mass.: Harvard University Press, 1964), 98–112; also see James

Pusey, *Charles Darwin and China* (Cambridge, Mass.: Harvard University Press, 1983).

35. *ZZRRJ*, 1901–1905, in *LXYJZL*, vols. 10–13, passim.

36. *ZZRRJ-LXYJZL*, vol. 11, 72.

37. Ibid., vol. 12, 115.

38. "Zhou Zuoren riji," July 20, 1903, in *ZZRRJ-LXYJZL*, vol. 12, 135.

39. Ibid., August 10, 1903, vol. 12, 137.

40. Zhou Zuoren, "Wo xue guowen de jingyan" [My experience of learning Chinese], *Tanhu ji*, vol. 2 (Shanghai: Beixin Shuju, 1929), 404.

41. *ZTHXL*, 107; *ZZRNP*, 44–45; Ernst Wolff, *Chou Tso-jen* (New York: Twayne Publishers, 1971), 18.

42. *ZTHXL*, 105–106.

43. "Zhou Zuoren riji," 1904, in *ZZRRJ-LXYJZL*, vol. 12, 141; "Zhou Zuoren riji," 1905, in *ZZRRJ-LXYJZL*, vol. 13, 29–30 and passim.

44. *ZTHXL*, 167–170.

45. "Zhou Zuoren riji," January 11, 1903, in *LXYJZL*, vol. 11, 96; *ZTHXL*, 110.

46. "Zhou Zuoren riji," March 18, 1903 and April 20, 1903, in *LXYJZL*, vol. 12, 114, 125.

47. *ZTHXL*, 151–166.

48. *ZTHXL*, 192–194; Y. C. Wang, *Chinese Intellectuals and the West*, 69, 478; Ching-mao Cheng, "The Impact of Japanese Literary Trends on Modern Chinese Writers," in Merle Goldman, ed., *Modern Chinese Literature in the May Fourth Era* (Cambridge, Mass.: Harvard University Press, 1977), 63–88. For the popular reputation of students returning from Japan, see especially two works of fiction by Li Jieren, *Dabo* (Beijing: Zuojia chubanshe, 1958–1963); and Bu-xiaosheng, *Liudong waishi*, 2 vols. (Shanghai: Minquan chubanshe, 1992). One example of pay scale, in the prestigious Commercial Press during the early Republic period, is revealing of the general treatment of returned students. A graduate of a Japanese college was paid $100–$200 and was allowed a desk three by two feet; graduates from Western colleges were paid a $200 monthly salary; graduates from Harvard, Yale, Oxford, and Cambridge received a $250 monthly salary and were allowed to have custom-made desks. See Tao Xisheng, "A Story of the Desk," in *Zi-you Tan* [Discourse on freedom], vol. 9, no. 9; cited in Y. C. Wang, *Chinese Intellectuals and the West*, 90.

49. *ZTHXL*, 196–197.

50. Ibid., 208.

51. Ibid., 211.

52. Ibid., 207, 231–233.

53. Ibid., 232.

54. Ibid., 212–213, 219–220.

55. Ibid., 223–224.

56. Ibid., 201; also see Zhou Xiashou, *Lu Xun de gujia*, 180, 185.

57. Leo Ou-fan Lee, *Voices from the Iron House: A Study of Lu Xun* (Bloomington and Indianapolis: Indiana University Press, 1987), 24.

58. *ZTHXL*, 206, 263; Zhou Xiashou, *Lu Xun de gujia*, 205.

59. Zhou Zuoren, "Riben de yi-shi-zhu" [The clothing, food, and dwellings in Japan]," in *Kuzhu zaji* (Shanghai: Liangyou tushu yinshua gongsi, 1936), 225–226.

60. Ibid., 228–229.

61. Ibid., 233.

62. Zhou Zuoren, "Riben zhi zairenshi" [Re-understanding Japan], in *Zhitang Yiyou wenbian* (Hong Kong: Sanyu tushu wenju gongsi, 1962), 148; also see *ZTHXL*, 178.

63. Zhou Zuoren, "Riben de yi-shi-zhu," 234–235.

64. Kiyama Hideo, *Pekin kujōan ki: Nitchū sensō jidai no Shū Sakujin* (Tokyo: Chikuma shobō, 1978), 5. About the Zhou brothers in Nishikata-chō in 1908–1909, see Zhou Xiashou, *Lu Xun de gujia*, 181.

65. Xu Shoushang, *Wangyuo Lu Xun yinxiang ji* (Shanghai: Sanlian shudian, 1949), 36.

66. For the cultural divide in Tokyo during the Meiji period, see Edward Seidensticker, *Low City, High City: Tokyo from Edo to the Earthquake, 1867–1923* (New York: Alfred A. Knopf, 1983; reprint New York: Viking Penguin, 1985), esp. 240, 246, on Azabu.

67. *ZTHXL*, 247–248.

68. Ibid., 233–236.

69. Ibid., 250.

70. Ibid., 245.

71. Tokutomi Roka's words are cited in Mikiso Hane, *Modern Japan: A Historical Survey* (Boulder, Colo.: Westview Press, 1986), 182; Edward Seidensticker, *Kafū the Scribbler: The Life and Writings of Nagai Kafū, 1879–1959* (Stanford: Stanford University Press, 1965; reprint Ann Arbor: Center for Japanese Studies, University of Michigan, 1990), 46.

72. *ZTHXL*, 245–246.

Part II: "Can China and Japan Be Friends?"

1. See Paul A. Cohen, *Between Tradition and Modernity: Wang T'ao and Reform in Late Ch'ing China* (Cambridge, Mass.: Harvard University Press, 1974), 103, for a brief discussion on the Kō-A Kai and Chinese response to it.

2. Marius B. Jansen, "Konoe Atsumaro," in Akira Iriye, ed., *The Chinese and the Japanese: Essays in Political and Cultural Interactions* (Princeton, N.J.: Princeton University Press, 1980), 107–123; Douglas R. Reynolds, "Training Young China Hands: Tōa Dōbun Shoin and Its Precursors, 1886–1945," in Peter Duus, Ramon H. Myers, and Mark R. Peattie, eds., *The Japanese Informal*

Empire in China, 1895–1937 (Princeton, N.J.: Princeton University Press, 1989), 210–271, esp. 254–256 on official subsidies.

3. A Case of Ambivalence

1. Marius B. Jansen, *The Japanese and Sun Yat-sen,* chaps. 1–3, 9.
2. Zhongguo Shehui Kexueyuan Jindaishi Yanjiusuo Zhonghua Minguoshi Yanjiushi, ed., *Sun Zhongshan quanji,* vol. 3 (Beijing: Zhonghua shuju, 1984), 14, emphasis added (hereafter cited as *SZSQ J*).
3. Chen Xiqi et al., eds., *Sun Zhongshan nianpu changbian,* vol. 1 (Beijing: Zhonghua shuju, 1991), 793 (hereafter cited as *SZSNP*).
4. Tianchou, "Qiangquan yinmou zhi heimu" [A sinister story of power politics], *Minquan bao,* April 3, 1913, reprinted in Sang Bing, Huang Yi, and Tang Wenquan, eds., *Dai Jitao xinhai wenji (1909–1913)* (Hong Kong: Zhongwen daxue chubanshe, 1991), 1401–1403 (hereafter cited as *DJTWJ*).
5. The Dais migrated from Xiuning in Anhui Province to Wuxing in Zhejiang Province and eventually settled down in Sichuan at the end of the Qianlong reign (1735–1795). See Chen Tianxi, *Zengding Dai Jitao xiansheng biannan zhuanji* (Taibei: Zhonghua Minguo Zhongshan xueshu wenhua jijin dongshihui, 1967), 1 (hereafter cited as *DJTBN*). The genealogical history made Dai feel attached to the land in which his ancestors once resided, and he claimed, often, that he was a native of Wuxing.
6. Dai Jitao to Zhong Fuchang, March 6, 1937, in Chen Tianxi, ed., *Dai Jitao xiansheng wencun,* vol. 4 (Taibei: Zhongguo Guomindang zhongyang weiyuanhui, 1959), 1572 (hereafter cited as *DJTWC*).
7. Dai Jitao, "Yanju yu pingmin" [Performance and the common people] (March 1913), in *DJTWC,* vol. 4, 1752–1759.
8. *DJTWC,* vol. 2, 544–545.
9. *DJTBN,* 8–9.
10. Wang Xiangrong, *Riben jiaoshi* (Beijing: Sanlian shudian, 1988), 95–97.
11. Hattori Misao's father, Hattori Shō (Shisai, 1847–1910), had also been in Sichuan for seven years as a teacher and, upon his return to Japan, became a teacher at the Seijō Gakkō. See Nakamura Tadayoshi, "Hattori Shisai jiryaku" [A brief biography of Hattori Shisai, in Hattori Misao, ed., *Aigen yibun* (Tokyo: Seishindō, 1911), n.p.
12. Dai Jitao, "Yanju yu pingmin" [Drama performance and the common people], *DJTWC,* vol. 4, 1756; "Yu zhi dushu ji" [My learning experiences], *DJTWC,* vol. 2, 547.
13. Dai Jitao, "Yu zhi dushu ji," *DJTWC,* vol. 2, 541–549.
14. Xie Jian, "Dai Jitao xiansheng shishi erzhounian jinian xianci" [Remembering Mr. Dai Jitao on the second anniversary of his death], in *DJTWC,* 3rd suppl. vol., 289–297.

15. *DJTBN*, 12.

16. Xie Jian, "Preface," *DJTWC*.

17. Ibid.

18. Ibid.

19. Dai Jitao, "Yu zhi dushu ji," *DJTWC*, 549; also see Xie Jian, "Preface," *DJTWC*.

20. Xie Jian, "Preface," *DJTWC*.

21. *DJTBN*, 15.

22. Xie Jian, "Preface," *DJTWC*.

23. Dai Jitao, "Tianchou conghua" [Comments from Tianchou], *Minquan bao*, April 1–April 28, 1912, in *DJTWJ*, 730.

24. *DJTBN*, 15.

25. The three characters of Dai Tian-chou come from a six-word idiom "bu-gong *dai tian* zhi *chou*" [foes that cannot share the same sky].

26. *DJTBN*, 18; Sang Bin, Huang Yi, and Tang Wenquan, "Dai Jitao xiaozhuan" [A brief biography of Dai Jitao], in *DJTWJ*, xiv.

27. Sanhong [Dai Jitao], "Rihan hebang yu zhongguo zhi guanxi [The merge of Korea into Japan and its implication to China]," *Zhongwai ribao*, August 5, 1910, reprinted in *DJTWJ*, 30–32.

28. Tianchou [Dai Jitao], "Shehui zhi dabuxing" [The great misfortune of our society], *Tianduo bao*, November 12, 1910, reprinted in *DJTWJ*, 271.

29. Tianchou [Dai Jitao], "Wudao guo [Cruel country]," *Tianduo bao*, February 2, 1911, reprinted in *DJTWJ*, 516; "Bupingming" [Cries against inequality], February 4, 1911, *Tianduo bao*, reprinted in *DJTWJ*, 524.

30. Tianchou, "Er wen yan jian" [What I have heard and seen], *Tianduo bao*, October 28, 1910, reprinted in *DJTWJ*, 235; "Zhuji shali" [Pearls and sands], *Tianduo bao*, November 1, 1910, reprinted in *DJTWJ*, 237.

31. Tianchou, "Ribenren zhi qizhi" [The Japanese character], *Tianduo bao*, October 17–20, 1910, reprinted in *DJTWJ*, 177–178.

32. Tianchou, "Pianpian de Riben wenxue guan" [Bits and pieces of a view on Japanese literature], *Tianduo bao*, November 7–8, 1910, reprinted in *DJTWJ*, 261–262.

33. Tianchou, "Eren zhi zhongguo zhengzhi guan" [The Russian's view on Chinese politics], *Tianduo bao*, January 22, 1911, reprinted in *DJTWJ*, 508.

34. The phrase is Marie-Claire Bergère's and describes the accidental outbreak of the 1911 Revolution. See Marie-Claire Bergère, *Sun Yat-sen*, trans. Janet Lloyd (Stanford: Stanford University Press, 1998), 140.

35. Dai Jitao, "Shibai zhi geming" [The failed revolution], March 1913; "Da zai siren xinyong" [How great is that personal credibility], *Minquan bao*, April 9, 1912; "Danda wangwei zhi Yuan Shikai" [The Reckless Yuan Shikai], *Minquan bao*, April 18–22, 1912; "Yuan Shikai zhi zuizhuang" [The crimes that

Yuan Shikai committed], *Minquan bao,* April 19–20, 1912; "Qilun" [Strange talk], *Minquan bao,* April 24, 1912; "Tao Yuan Shikai" [Against Yuan Shikai], *Minquan bao,* April 26, 1912; "Gao beifang baojie" [A statement to the journalists in the north], *Minquan bao,* April 28, 1912; "Zhuo zai *Minsheng bao*" [How clumsy, *Minsheng bao*], *Minquan bao,* May 10, 1912; all reprinted in *DJTWJ,* 725, 756, 779, 781–783, 812, 815–816, 817–818, 852–853.

36. *DJTBN,* 24.

37. *SZSNP,* 767–791.

38. Dai Jitao, *Riben lun* (Shanghai: Minzhi shuju, 1928), 95–96.

39. Ibid., 97.

40. Tianchou, "Qiangquan yinmou zhi heimu" [A sinister story of power politics], *Minquan bao,* April 3, 1913, reprinted in *DJTWJ,* 1401–1403.

41. Dai Jitao, *Riben lun,* 98.

42. Foreign Minister Makino to Consulate General Ariyoshi in Shanghai, July 30, 1913; Foreign Minister Makino to Governor-General Sakuma in Taiwan, August 5, 1913, in Gaimushō, ed., *Nihon gaikō bunsho, 1913–1915,* vol. 2 (Tokyo: Gaimushō, 1964–1966), 379, 392; Marius B. Jansen, *The Japanese and Sun Yat-sen,* 166.

43. Sun Wen to Ōkuma Shigenobu, May 11, 1914, reprinted in Wang Yunsheng, *Liushinian lai Zhongguo yu Riben,* vol. 6 (Tianjin: Dagongbao she, 1933), 35–38; Sun's letter to Koike Chōzō, head of the political affairs section of the Foreign Ministry, is cited in Marius B. Jansen, *The Japanese and Sun Yat-sen,* 192–193; the contract between Sun and the former Mantetsu administrators was signed on February 5, 1915; see Fujii Shōzō, "Er-shi-i-tiao jiaoshe shiqi de Sun Zhongshan he zhongri mengyue" [Sun Yat-sen and the 'Sino-Japanese Contract' during the negotiation of the Twenty-One Demands, *Guowai xinhai geminshi yanjiu dongtai* [Recent Works by Foreign Researchers on the 1911 Revolution], vol. 5.

44. Japanese secret police daily report, January 10, 1914 [no. 31]; February 3, 1914 [no. 289]; February 4, 1914 [no. 310]; in Yu Xinchun and Wang Zhensuo, trans. and eds., *Sun Zhongshan zai ri huodong milu 1913.8–1916.4: Riben waiwusheng dangan* (Tianjin: Nankai daxue chubanshe, 1990), 82–83, 96, 666–672.

45. *SZSNP,* 832–970, passim.

46. Ibid., 938; also see Japanese secret police report, March 1, 1915 [no. 435], in *Nihon gaikō bunsho, 1915,* vol. 2 (Tokyo: Gaimushō, 1966), 265–266.

47. Dai Jitao to Xin Shuzhi, July 12, 1933, in *DJTWC,* vol. 2, 673–674.

48. Dai Jitao, "Ou-luo-ba Datongmeng lun" [On Greater European Alliance], *Minguo* no. 3, July 10, 1914, reprinted in Tang Wenquan and Sang Bing, eds., *Dai Jitao ji, 1909–1920* (Wuhan: Huazhong shifan daxue chubanshe, 1990), 730–753 (hereafter cited as *DJTJ*).

49. Yunchao Daoshi [Dai Jitao], "Zuijin riben zhi zhengju jiqi duihua zhengche" [The recent political situation in Japan and its China policy], *Minguo ribao,* December 14, 1917, to January 24, 1918.

50. *Minguo ribao,* December 13, 1917; January 5–6, 1918; January 10–12, 1918.

51. Marius B. Jansen characterizes Japan's disastrous policy toward China after 1911 as "following a vacillating policy of drift," except for the brief period of the Twenty-One Demands fiasco. He also evaluates Terauchi's policy as "short-sighted" and "reckless." See *The Japanese and Sun Yat-sen,* chaps. 6–8, esp. 131, 197.

52. *Minguo ribao,* December 15–17, 1917; December 20–21, 1917; January 15, 1920; January 20, 1918.

53. Ibid., December 23, 1917; January 16, 1918.

54. Ibid., January 23, 1918.

55. Dai Jitao, *Riben lun,* chap. 19.

56. Dai Jitao, "Dao Huzhou hou de Ganxiang" [Thoughts after arriving at Huzhou], *Jianshe* 2.6 (July 1, 1920).

57. Shen Yanbin, "Huiyi Shanghai gongchan zhuyi xiaozu" [Recollection about the Communist group in Shanghai], in Zhongguo shehui kexueyuan xiandaishi yanjiushi, ed., *Yida qianhou* (Beijing: Renmin chubanshe, 1980), 44; also see Arif Dirlik, *The Origins of Chinese Communism* (New York: Oxford University Press, 1989), passim.

58. Yang Zhihua, a student of the Third Women's Normal Academy in Hangzhou, first received radical influence from Shen Dingyi [Shen Xuanlu], her father-in-law. Yang later divorced Shen's son and married a Communist, Qu Qiubai. See Yang Zhihua, "Yang Zhihua de huiyi" [Reminiscences by Yang Zhihua], in *Yida Qianhou,* 25–26.

59. Xu Zhizhen, "Guanyu Yuyangli liouhao de huodong qingkuang" [The activities at no. 6 Yuyang Lane], in *Yida qianhou,* 58–60; Shao Lizi, "Dang chengli qianhou de yixie qingkuang" [Memories about events around the time of the establishment of the party], in *Yida Qianhou,* 61–70.

60. Dai Jitao, "Minguo jiunian de gongzuo" [The work for 1920], *Minguo ribao,* January 1, 1920; reprinted in *DJTJ,* 1089–1091.

61. Qimin, "Rendao zhuyi lun" [On Humanism], *Minli bao,* October 12, 1910; reprinted in *DJTWJ,* 152–155.

62. Qimin, "Shehui zhuyi zhi dahuodong" [Great Actions of Socialism], *Minli bao,* November 12–18, 1910, reprinted in *DJTWJ,* 266–269.

63. Tianchou, "Dangdai diyi weiren du-tui-si zhuanlie" [A biography of the number one great man of our time: Tolstoy], *Zhongwai ribao,* August 23, 1910; Qimin, "Tuo-er-si-tai xiansheng zhuan" [A biography of Mr. Tolstoy], *Minli bao,* November 22–December 13, 1910; Tianchou, "Du-tui-si xiansheng xuean" [A comment on Mr. Tolstoy], *Tianduo bao,* October 9–18, 1910; Tian-

chou, "Dushi zuie lun" [On the evils of the city], *Minquan bao,* June 11–12, 1911; all reprinted in *DJTWJ,* 111–112, 291–303, 143–144, 936–940; also see *DJTWJ,* 304, 306, 513, for short comments on Tolstoy.

64. Dai Jitao, "Baixun" [A hundred lessons], *Minguo zazhi,* 1.6 (December 1914), reprinted in *DJTWC,* suppl. vol., 273–283, esp. 279; *DJTWJ,* 427, 442, 603, 653.

65. Tianchou, "Wuzhengfu zhuyi zhi shensui" [The spirit of anarchism], *Tianduo bao,* February 2–3, 1911; reprinted in *DJTWJ,* 518–521.

66. *DJTWC,* suppl. vol., 280.

67. "Yu Dai Jitao de tanhua" [A conversation with Dai Jitao], June 22, 1919, *SZSQ J,* vol. 5, 68–71.

68. Dai Jitao, "Wo de riben guan" [My view of Japan], *Jianshe* 1.1 (August 1919): 103–133.

4. A Case of Frustration

1. *Heichao* was sponsored by the Pacific Society (Taipingyang Xueshe) in Shanghai and edited by Lu Youbai. The choice of title indicates its sponsor's familiarity with the history of Sino-Japanese exchange. The Black Tides, or the Japan Current, is a warm current that flows through Tsushima Strait between southern Japan and Korea, and in ancient times, when navigation tools were limited, its counterclockwise turn aided travel between the continent and the Japanese island. It was a short-lived magazine, lasting for three issues only. For a comprehensive discussion on *Black Tides,* see Zhonggong Zhongyang Makesi Engesi Liening Sidalin Zhuzuo Bianyiju Yanjiushi, ed., *Wusi shiqi qikan jieshao,* vol. 3 (Beijing: Sanlian shudian, 1959), 368–369.

2. Editor, "Heichao yuekan bianji dagang" [Editorial proposal for the monthly *Black Tides*], *Heichao* no. 1, cited in *Wusi shiqi qikan jieshao,* 365.

3. Guo Kaizhen, "Tongwen Tongzhong Bian [On the same culture and same race]," *Heichao* 1.2, reprinted in Wang Jinhou, Xiao Binru, and Wu Jialun, eds., *Guo Moruo yiwenji, 1906–1949,* vol. 1 (Chengdu: Sichuan daxue chubanshe, 1988), 5–16.

4. Xia She, "Dizhi rihuo zhi jiujing" [The inner story of the anti-Japanese boycott], in *Guo Moruo yiwenji,* 17–23.

5. Although the name Moruo was adopted after 1920, hereafter I will use Guo Moruo for readers' convenience.

6. Guo Moruo, "Wo de tongnian" [My childhood], in Guo Moruo, *Shaonian shidai* (Shanghai: Haiyan shudian, 1947), esp. 3–19; Li Baojun, *Guo Moruo qingnian shidai pingzhuan* (Chongqing: Chongqing chubanshe, 1984). Li's book contains materials from his investigation of Guo's family background.

7. Guo Moruo, *Shaonian shidai,* 42. The following discussion of Guo's childhood in Sichuan, if not otherwise noted, is based on this autobiography of his childhood.

8. Ibid., 45.

9. Ibid., 46.

10. Guo described his marriage arrangement with Zhang Qionghua in detail in "Heimao" [Black cat], a short autobiography that focused on his experience in 1912. The title is said to come from a Sichuan idiom: "Buying a white cat covered by a cloth bag and finding a black cat when opening the bag at home," implying a dishonest deal. See *Shaonian shidai,* 305–351.

11. Guo Moruo, "Heimao," 329.

12. Guo Moruo, "Chuchu kuimen [First time out of the gate of Sichuan]," in *Shaonian shidai,* 369.

13. Guo Kaizhen to parents, February 1914, March 1914, June 1914, July 1914, August 1914, in Tang Mingzhong and Huang Gaobin, eds., *Yinghua shujian: Guo Moruo 1913 zhi 1923 nian jiaxin xuan* (Chengdu: Sichuan renmin chubanshe, 1981), 11–31.

14. Qian Chao, "Huiyi Moruo zaonian zai Riben de xuexi shenghuo" [Moruo's early years in Japan as I remembered], in Wang Xunzhao et al., eds., *Guo Moruo yanjiu ziliao* (Beijing: Zhongguo shehui kexue chubanshe, 1981), 532–533.

15. Guo Moruo, "Wang Yangming," written on June 17, 1921, reprinted in Guo Moruo, *Lishi renwu* (Shanghai: Haiyan shudian, 1947), 75–90, esp. 76.

16. Guo Moruo, "Wo de zuoshi de jingguo" [How I began to write poetry], *Zhiwen* 2.2 (November 10, 1936), reprinted in *Moruo wenji,* vol. 11 (Beijing: Renmin wenxue chubanshe, 1959), 137–148.

17. Tao Jingsun, Guo's fellow writer in the Creation Society as well as his brother-in-law by marriage to Satō Tomiko's younger sister, transformed the Guo-Satō episode into a story, "Sen toraru sapurai no dorobō: Aru kangofu no hanashi" [The thief who stole things from the supply room: A nurse's story], *Nihon e no isho* (Tokyo: Sōgensha, 1953), 94–101.

18. Guo Moruo to Tian Shouchang, February 15, 1920, in Tian Shouchang, Zong Baihua, and Guo Moruo, *Sanye ji,* 5th ed. (Shanghai: Yadong tushuguan, 1927), 33–43.

19. Sawachi Hisae, *Zoku Showashi no onna* (Tokyo: Bunkei shunju, 1986), 127–130.

20. Ibid., 132–136; Guo Moruo to Tian Shouchang, February 15, 1920, in *Sanye ji,* 33–43.

21. Tang Mingzhong and Huang Gaobing, eds., *Yinghua shujian,* 140–143.

22. Guo Moruo, *Chuangzao shinian* (Shanghai: Xiandai shuju, 1932), 32–33.

23. Guo Moruo, "Wo de zuoshi de jingguo," 72.

24. Ibid.

25. Guo Moruo, *Chuangzao shinian,* 72; Nakajima Midori, "Xia-she ziliao" [Source materials on Xia-she], in *Guo Moruo yanjiu* no. 3 (Beijing), 371–374.

26. Wang Jinhou, Wu Jialun, and Zhong Dehui, "Guo Moruo diyici kanjian de baihua shi [The modern colloquial poem that Guo Moruo had seen for the first time], in *Xinwenxue shiliao* no. 13 (1981), 233; Guo Moruo, *Chuangzao shinian*, 73.

27. Zong Baihua (1897–1986), was then a member of the Young China Society (Shaonian Zhongguo Xuehui). He went to Germany to study aesthetics in 1920 and returned to teach at Dongnan University and Beijing University until his death. He was considered one of the leading theorists on aesthetics in China.

28. Tian Shouchang (1898–1968), who later used the name Tian Han, was one of the initiators of the Creation Society. He was interested in European literature and became a prolific dramatist during the later 1920s and 1930s. In 1932, Tian Han joined the Chinese Communist Party. He composed the lyrics to *March of the Voluntary Army (Yiyongjun jinxingqu)*, which was inspired by and in turn inspired the anti-Japanese fighters during the war and was chosen as the Chinese national anthem after 1949.

29. Zong Baihua, "Qiuri tanwan" [Talking about the past in autumnal days], *Beijing ribao*, October 19, 1980, reprinted in Wang Xunzhao et al., eds., *Guo Moruo yanjiu ziliao*, vol. 1 (Beijing: Zhongguo shehui kexue chubanshe, 1981), 545–547.

30. Bing Xin, "Dao Guo lao" [Mourning for the venerable Guo]; Cao Yu, "Chentong de zhuidao" [A deep mourning]; and Zhang Ruifang, "Guo-lao women de yidai zongshi!" [Venerable Guo, the teacher for our generation], all in Yu Liqun, Mao Dun et al., *Huhuan chuntian de shiren* (Chengdu: Sichuan renmin chubanshe, 1978), 39–42; 43–47; 131–136.

31. The enduring impact of Guo's translation was well captured in a scene of Mao Dun's *Midnight (Ziye)*, when Captain Lei, a cadet of the Huangpu Academy, meets his lover from his student years and presents her with "an old, well-worn copy of *Die Leiden des jungen Werther* with a pressed white rose in it," saying, "This book and this white rose are dearer to me than all else.... I made my way over thousands, indeed tens of thousands of corpses. Innumerable times I escaped death by a hair's breadth, I lost everything. Only from this rose and book I never parted." Cited in Jaroslav Průšek, *The Lyrical and the Epic: Studies of Modern Chinese Literature* (Bloomington: Indiana University Press, 1980), 4.

32. Guo Moruo, *Chuangzao shinian*, 86, 89–90, 101.

33. Guo Moruo, *Chuangzao shinian*, 87.

34. Ibid., 105–107.

35. Ibid., 161.

36. Yu Yun, "Yu Dafu yu Chuangzaoshe" [Yu Dafu and the Creation Society], in Rao Hongjing et al., eds., *Chuangzaoshe ziliao* [The materials of the Creation Society] (Fuzhou: Fujian renmin chubanshe, 1985), 1007.

37. Qian Chao, "Huiyi Moruo zaonian zai Riben de xuexi shenghuo" [The student years in Japan during Moruo's youth], in Wang Xunzhao et al., eds., *Guo Moruo yanjiu ziliao,* vol. 1, 532–540.

38. Gong Jimin and Fang Rennian, *Guo Moruo nianpu* (Tianjin: Tianjin renmin chubanshe, 1982), 109–129 (hereafter cited as *GMRNP*).

39. Guo Moruo, *Chuangzao shinian,* 239.

40. Ibid., 248.

41. Xu Zhimo diary, October 11, 1923, in Lu Xiaoman, ed., *Zhimo riji,* reprinted in Jiang Fucong and Liang Shiqiu, eds., *Xu Zhimo quanji,* vol. 4 (Taibei: Zhuanji wenxue chubanshe, 1969), 499.

42. Ibid.

43. Guo Moruo, *Chuangzao shinian,* 247.

44. Jaroslav Průšek, "Subjectivism and Individualism," in *Lyrical and the Epic: Studies of Modern Chinese Literature* (Bloomington: Indiana University Press, 1980), 5.

45. Guo Moruo, *Chuangzao shinian,* 88, 109–111.

46. Ibid., 111–112.

47. Ibid., 114–115.

48. Guo Moruo, "Yueshi" [Lunar eclipse], written on August 28, 1923, reprinted in *Moruo Wenji,* vol. 5, 29–42.

49. Guo Moruo, "Qilu" [The crossing], in *Moruo Wenji,* vol. 5, 120.

50. Guo Moruo, *Chuangzao shinian xubian* (Shanghai: Beixin shuju, 1946), 24, 37; Guo to Cheng Fangwu, August 9, 1924, in Huang Chunhao, ed., *Guo Moruo shuxin ji* (Beijing: Zhongguo shehui kexue chubanshe, 1992), 227–228.

51. Guo Moruo to Cheng Fangwu, August 9, 1924, in *Guo Moruo shuxin ji,* 230.

52. David Tod Roy, *Kuo Mo-jo: The Early Years* (Cambridge, Mass.: Harvard University Press, 1971), chap. 7, esp. 160–161.

53. Guo Moruo to Cheng Fangwu, August 9, 1924, in *Guo Moruo shuxin ji,* 230.

54. Guo Moruo, "Lupang de qiangwei" [Roses by the roadside], "Ximu" [Dusk], and "Baifa" [Gray hair], all in *Shanzhong zaji* (Shanghai: Guanghua shuju, 1931).

55. Guo Moruo to Cheng Fangwu, August 9, 1924, in *Guo Moruo shuxin ji.*

56. Guo Moruo, *Ganlan* [Olive] (Shanghai: Xiandai shuju, 1929), 95–102. Sima Zhao was a general who served the king of Wei during the era of the Three Kingdoms. His scheming to usurp the throne had become such an open secret that the king once commented that "the heart of Sima Zhao is known by all common folks" *[Sima Zhao zhi xin, luren suo zhi ye].* In 263, Sima Zhao gave himself the title Duke of Jin. His son Sima Yan ended the rule of Wei and be-

came the emperor of Jin. *"Sima Zhao zhi xin, luen jie zhi,"* or simply *"Sima Zhao zhi xin,"* has since become a commonly used Chinese expression for ignoble plotting and scheming. The story of Sima Zhao's scheming was first recorded by Chen Shou in "Weishu. Gaogui Xianggong zhuan" in his *Sanguo zhi* [History of Three Kingdoms], which has many editions with annotations by later scholars, since the book was first compiled in the third century. The modern reader may find good references in Lu Bi, *Sanguo zhi jizhu* [History of Three Kingdoms, with annotation] (Beijing: Zhonghua shuju, 1982), 150–164.

57. Guo Moruo to Cheng Fangwu, August 9, 1924, in *Guo Moruo shuxin ji.*

58. Martin Wilbur, *Sun Yat-sen: Frustrated Patriot* (New York: Columbia University Press, 1976), 134–135.

59. Sun Yat-sen, "Speech at Kobe Women's High School," November 28, 1924, reprinted in *SZSNP,* 2080–2081.

Part III: Culture and Politics

1. Akira Iriye, *China and Japan in the Global Setting* (Cambridge, Mass.: Harvard University Press, 1992), 45.

5. Pro-Japanese or Anti-Japanese?

1. Kaiming, "Waiguoren yu minxin [Foreigners and popular sentiment], *Jingbao fukan* no. 5 (December 9, 1924).

2. *ZZRNP,* 60, 68, 70.

3. Zhitang, "Riben de xiangtu yanjiu" [The folklore studies in Japan], *Gujin* no. 52 (August 1944); Zhou Zuoren's diary, 1912–1917, printed in *LXYJZL,* vols. 13, 14, 18, passim.

4. Zhou Xiashou, *Lu Xun de gujia,* 216.

5. Lu Xun, "Preface to the First Collection of Short Stories, *Call to Arms,*" in *Selected Stories of Lu Hsun,* trans. Yang Hsien-yi and Gladys Yang (Beijing: Foreign Languages Press, 1960), 3–4.

6. *ZTHXL,* 293–294.

7. Ibid., 313.

8. Zhou Xiashou, *Lu Xun de gujia,* 213–215.

9. *ZTHXL,* 323–328.

10. Ibid., 319.

11. Lu Xun, "Preface to the First Collection of Short Stories," 5.

12. Zhou Zuoren, "Du Wuzhexiaolu jun suo zuo Yige Qingnian de Meng" [Reading Mr. Mushanokoji's 'A Youth's Dream'], *Xin qingnian* 4.5 (May 1918).

13. Lu Xun, "Yizhe xu" [Translator's introduction], *Xin qingnian* 7.2 (August 1919).

14. Lin Yü-sheng and Leo Ou-fan Lee have argued persuasively of the importance of humanist moral ethos in Lu Xun's literary activities. See Lin Yü-sheng, "The Morality and Immorality of Politics: Reflections on Lu Xun, the Intellectual," in Leo Ou-fan Lee, ed., *Lu Xun and His Legacy* (Berkeley: University of California Press, 1985); Leo Ou-fan Lee, *Voices from the Iron House*, 196. The spirit obviously was drawn on several sources, traditional and foreign, and shared by the two brothers during this period of their close collaboration.

15. Zhou Zuoren, "Du Wuzhexiaolu jun suo zuo Yige Qingnian de Meng," *Xin qingnian* 4.5 (May 1918).

16. Zhou Zuoren, "Ren de wenxue" [Human literature], in *Yishu yu shenghuo* (Shanghai: Qunyishushe, 1931; reprint, Kowloon: Shucheng chubanshe, n.d.), 11–30.

17. See Mushanokoji Saneatsu, "'Jiko no Tame' oyobi sonota ni tsuite [Concerning Matters Related to 'For the Self']," *Shirakaba*, vol. 3, no. 2 (February 1912), 95–102; esp. 98–99.

18. *"Renjian"* in Chinese is closer in meaning to "society" rather than "human" *(ningen)* in Japanese, though the characters are exactly the same. For the Shirakaba school, Mushanokoji, and their influence on Chinese intellectuals, see Kuno Osamu and Tsurumi Shunsuke, *Gendai Nihon no shisō*, 17th printing (Tokyo: Iwanami shoten, 1968), 6; Hosoya Sōko, "Go ten yon shinbunka no rinen to Shirakabaha no jindō shugi," *Yasō* no. 6 (1972); Honda Shūgo, *Shirakabaha no bungaku* (Tokyo: Dainihon yūbengai kōdensha, 1955), 39–43.

19. Hu Shi, "Daoyan" [Preface], in Hu Shi, ed., *Zhongguo xinwenxue daxi: Jianshe lilun ji* (Shanghai: Liangyou tushu gongsi, 1935), 29, 30.

20. See, for example, Zhou Zuoren, "Pingmin wenxue" [Literature about common people] (1919), "Ertong de wenxue" [Children's literature] (1920), "Ouzhou gudai wenxueshang de funuguan" [Views on women as expressed in ancient European literature] (1921), "Guoyu gaizao de yijian" [My views on Chinese language reform] (1922), all in *Yishu yu shenghuo;* Zhong Mi [Zhou Zuoren], "Lun Heimu" [On 'inside stories'], "Zai lun heimu" [Recomment on 'inside stories'], in *Xin qingnian* 6.2 (February 1919).

21. I refer to the New Culture community in a broader sense than that defined by Timothy B. Weston, whose study focuses on the early phase of the New Culture Movement and demonstrates the importance of the journal *Tiger* as a gathering place during the early phase of the movement for one group of New Culture leaders, particularly Chen Duxiu and Li Dazhao. See Timothy B. Weston, "The Formation and Positioning of the New Culture Community, 1913–1917," *Modern China*, 24.3 (July 1998):255–284.

22. *ZZRNP*, 1919–1924, passim.

23. Zhou Zuoren, "Xinwenxue de yaoqiu" [The Requirements of new literature], *Yishu yu shenghuo*, 41.

24. Zhou Zuoren, "Riben de Xinchun" [Japan's New Village], *Yishu yu shenghuo*, 401.

25. Zhou Zuoren, "Fang Riben Xinchun Ji" [My visit to New Village in Japan], *Yishu yu shenghuo*, 441–468.

26. Zhou Zuoren, "Xinchun de lixiang yu shiji" [The ideal and reality of the New Village], *Yishu yu shenghuo*, 437.

27. Zhou Zuoren, "Fang Riben Xinchun ji," 462.

28. Zhou Zuoren, "Fang Riben Xinchun ji," *Xinchao* [New Tide] 2.1 (October 1919), reprinted in *ZZRWLB*, vol. 7, 113–126; "Xinchun yundong de jieshuo" [An explanation on the New Village movement], *Chen bao,* January 20, 1920; "Gongxue zhuyi yu Xinchun de taolun" [The debate on the "Work-study program" and the New Village], *Gongxue* 1.5, March 28, 1920, reprinted in *ZZRWLB*, vol. 7, 139–143; "Du Wuzhexiaolu guanyu Xinchun de zhuzuo" [Reading works on the New Village by Mushanokoji], *Piping* no. 4, December 5, 1920; "Xinchun de taolun" [The discussion on the New Village], *Piping* no. 5, December 26, 1920, reprinted in *ZZRWLB*, vol. 7, 152–155; "Xinchun de jingsheng" [The spirit of the New Village], speech given at the Tianjin xueshu jiangyanghui [Scholarship talks at Tianjin], November 8, 1919, printed in *Juewu,* November 23–24, 1919; "Xinchun de lixiang yu shiji" [The ideal and reality of the New Village], speech at the Shehui Shijinhui [Society of Social Progress] on June 19, 1920, printed in *Chen bao fukan,* June 23–24, 1920.

29. *ZZRNP*, 98.

30. Qian Liqun, *Zhou Zuoren zhuan* (Beijing: Beijing shiyue wenyi chu-banshe, 1990), 231–232.

31. Zhonggong Zhongyang Makesi Engesi Liening Sidalin Zhuzuo Bian-yiju Yanjiushi, ed., *Wusi shiqi qikan jieshao*, 299–301, 411–412.

32. Arif Dirlik, *Anarchism in the Chinese Revolution* (Berkeley and Los Angeles: University of California Press, 1991), chap. 5, esp. 194–195. Dirlik considers the New Village movement as one strand of the anarchist movement during the May Fourth era and indicates its difference from the mainstream in its "agrarian impulse." I would further stress that the New Village's philosophical emphasis on peaceful coexistence departed sharply from some of the participants of the anarchist movement (however amorphous it was), who became more inclined to violence as a means of change.

33. See Charles W. Hayford, *To the People: James Yen and Village China* (New York: Columbia University Press, 1990), for the Rural Reconstruction experiments in Ding County in the 1920s to 1940s.

34. See Guy S. Alitto, *The Last Confucian: Liang Shu-ming and the Chinese Dilemma of Modernity* (Berkeley: University of California Press, 1979), esp. 193–215.

35. Cai Yuanpei, "Fuji" [A postscript], *Xin qingnian* 7.3 (February 1920):415–417.

36. Lu Xun, "Toufa de gushi" [A story about hair], *Lu Xun qianji*, vol. 1 (Beijing: Remin wenxue chubanshe, 1973), 331.

37. Hu Shi, "Fei geren zhuyi de xinshenghuo" [Non-individualistic new life], *Shishi xinbao,* January 15, 1920, reprinted in Gen Yunzhi, ed., *Hu Shi lunzheng ji* [A collection of critical articles by Hu Shi], vol. 1 (Beijing: Zhongguo shehui kexueyuan chubanshe, 1998), 423–428.

38. Chen Duxiu, "Fuji" [A postscript], *Xin qingnian* 7.3 (February 1920), 419–420.

39. Zhou Zuoren, "Qinri pai" [Japanophiles], *Tanhu ji*, 3d ed. (Shanghai: Beixin shuju, 1929), 19.

40. Zhou Zuoren, "Pairi de ehua" [Worsening of Japanophobia], *Tanhu ji,* 17–18.

41. Zhou Zuoren, "Riben jin sanshinian xiaoshuo zhi fada" [The development of Japanese fiction in recent thirty years], *Yishu yu shenghuo,* 294; "Riben yu Zhongguo" [Japan and China], *Tanhu ji,* 498.

42. Ibid., 265.

43. Zhou Zuoren, "Sen Ouwai boshi" [Dr. Mori Ōgai], *Tanlong ji* (Shanghai: Kaiming shudian, 1927), 37–39.

44. Zhou Zuoren, "Riben yu Zhongguo," 496–498.

45. Qiming, "Riben zhi paiju" [Japan's haiku], and "Riben zhi penyong" [Japan's bon-odori], both in *Ruoshe congkan* 3 (June 1916); "Riben de fushihui" [Japan's ukiyo-e], *Ruoshe congkan* 4 (March 1917); all reprinted in Zhong Shuhe, ed., *Zhou Zuoren wen leibian,* vol. 7 (Changsha: Hunan wenyi chubanshe, 1998), 231–232 (hereafter cited as *ZZRWLB*).

46. Zhou Zuoren, "Riben de shige" [Japanese poetry], *Yishu yu shenghuo,* 215–243, esp. 217–218. Lafcadio Hearn, or Yakumo Koizumi, the Japanese name Hearn chose for himself, remains the most fascinating interpreter of Japan from his time at the turn of the century to the present. For the quotation, see Lafcadio Hearn, *In Ghostly Japan* (Boston: Little, Brown, & Co., 1899; reprint, Rutland, Vt., and Tokyo: Charles E. Tuttle, 1971), 149; for a recent and comprehensive biography of Hearn, see Jonathan Cott, *Wandering Ghost: The Odyssey of Lafcadio Hearn* (New York: Knopf, 1991). Also see Carl Dawson, *Lafcadio Hearn and the Vision of Japan* (Baltimore, Md., and London: Johns Hopkins University Press, 1992).

47. Zhou Zuoren, "Riben de shige," 215–244.

48. Zhou Zuoren's diary, January to September 1921, in *LXYJZL,* vol. 18 (1987), 65–73.

49. Zhongmi, "The Sorrow of a Dreamer," "At Crossroads," both in *Xin Qinnian* 9.5 (September 1, 1921).

50. Zhou Zuoren, "Shanzhong zaxin: Zhi Sun Fuyuan" [Letters from the hills: To Sun Fuyuan], *Yutian de shu* (Shanghai: Beixin shuju, 1933), 198.

51. Zhou Zuoren, "Ziji de yuandi" [One's own garden], "Wenyi shang de kuanrong" [Tolerance in literature and arts], both in *Ziji de yuandi*, 10th ed. (Shanghai: Beixin shuju, 1927), 1–4, 5–8.

52. Zhou Zuoren, "Riben de fengcishi" [Japan's satirical poetry], *Tanlong ji*, 201–202, 207.

53. Zhou Zuoren, "Youdao Wulang" [Arishima Takeo], *Tanlong ji*, 45–46.

54. Zhou Zuoren, "Xinzhong" [Love suicide], *Zexie ji* (Shanghai: Beixin shuju, 1927), 124–135.

55. Zhou Zuoren, "Riben de renqing mei" [The beauty of human feelings in Japan], *Yutian de shu*, 177–178.

56. Hu Shi's diary, May 7, 1921, in Zhongguo shehui kexueyuan jindaishi yanjiusuo zhonghua minguoshi yanjiushi, ed, *Hu Shi de riji* (Hong Kong: Zhonghua shuju, 1985), 39–40.

57. Zhou Zuoren, "Riben de renqing mei," 180.

58. Sophia Lee, "The Foreign Ministry's Cultural Agenda for China: The Boxer Indemnity," in Peter Duus, Ramon H. Myers, and Mark R. Peattie, eds., *The Japanese Informal Empire in China, 1895–1937* (Princeton, N.J.: Princeton University Press, 1989), 272–306, esp. 275–279.

59. In response to Chinese opposition to the use of the term "Shina," which had a derogatory connotation at the time, the China Cultural Affairs Bureau (Tai-Shi Bunka Jimukyoku) was redesignated the Cultural Affairs Division (Bunka Jigyōbu). See Lee, "The Foreign Ministry's Cultural Agenda for China," 280. The bureau was the first of several such official bureaus on cultural relations with China created from the 1920s to the 1940s within the Japanese government, which, in See Heng Teow's words, established "a framework of operations" for Japan's cultural diplomacy till the end of the war. See See Heng Teow, *Japan's Cultural Policy toward China, 1918–1931* (Cambridge, Mass.: Harvard University Press, 1999), 1–2, 199.

60. *ZZRNP*, 159–160; *ZTHXL*, 427–431.

61. Zhou Zuoren, "Pairi de ehua" [The degeneration of anti-Japanese boycott], *Tanhu ji*, 17; Jingsheng [Zhou Zuoren], "Hai buru junguozhuyi" [Better to pursue jingoism], *Chen bao fukan*, July 19, 1923, reprinted in *ZZRWLB*, vol. 7, 628.

62. Zuoren, "'Shenhu tongxin' fuji" [A postscript to 'Kobe Correspondence'], *Yusi* 59 (December 1925), reprinted in *ZZRWLB*, vol. 7, 656; Qiming, "Pai-Ri—Riben shi Zhongguo de choudi" [Anti-Japan—Japan is China's enemy], *Jing bao fukan*, March 16, 1926, reprinted in *ZZRWLB*, vol. 7, 674–675.

63. For a succinct account of the Ōsugi Sakae incident in English, see Mikiso Hane, *Modern Japan: A Historical Survey* (Boulder, Colo.: Westview Press, 1986), 232.

64. Jingsheng [Zhou Zuoren], "Dashan rong zhi si" [Ōsugi's death], *Chen bao fukan*, September 25, 1925.

65. Jingsheng [Zhou Zuoren], "Dashan rong shijian de ganxiang" [Reflections on the Ōsugi incident], *Chen bao fukan,* October 17, 1923.

66. Comprehensive accounts on the event can be found in Shen Yiyun, *Yiyun huiyi* (Taibei: Zhuanji wenxue chubanshe, 1968), chaps. 14–15; Jian Youwen, *Feng Yuxiang zhuan* (Taibei: Zhuanji wenxue chubanshe, 1982), chap. 10.

67. Zhou Zuoren, "Zhi Puyi-jun shu" [A letter to Mr. Puyi], November 30, 1924, *Yusi* no. 4 (December 1924).

68. A detailed account of Puyi's eviction and his decision to seek refuge in the Japanese embassy is given in his autobiography. See Aixinjueluo Puyi, *Wo de qianbansheng* (Beijing: Zhonghua shuju, 1977), 162–197.

69. For a brief description of background of *Shuntian shibao,* see Iikura Shohei, "*Peikin Shuhō* to *Junten Jihō*" *[Beijing Weekly* and *Shuntian shibao],* in Takeuchi Yoshimi and Hashikawa Bunsō, eds., *Kindai Nihon to Chūgoku,* vol. 1 (Tokyo: Asahi shinbun, 1974), 342.

70. See, for example, "San-bai-nian Qing-yun zuori gaozong: guominjun shiyan bigong ju" [The three-hundred-year fortune of the Qing ended yesterday: The National Army staged the real drama of coercing the court], *Shuntian shibao,* November 6, 1923; "Nairen xunwei shi bigong shijian" [The incident of coercing the court called for reflection], *Shuntian shibao,* November 7, 1923; "Muo taifei liuxue xun Qingchao [One empress dowager spilled her blood to die for the Qing dynasty], *Shuntian shibao,* November 8, 1923; "Sun Zhongshan yu gongchanzhuyi" [Sun Yat-sen and communism], *Shuntian shibao,* December 18, 1923; also see Aixinjueluo Puyi, *Wo de qianbansheng,* 176, 181, for his citations and impressions.

71. Cited in Zhou Zuoren, "Jieshao Ribenren de guailun" [Presenting a strange commentary by the Japanese], *Jing bao fukan,* January 6, 1925.

72. Kaiming [Zhou Zuoren], "'Ribenren de Guailun' shuhou" [After writing 'Presenting a Strange Commentary by the Japanese'], *Jing bao fukan,* January 13, 1925.

73. Kaiming, "Qing-chao de yuxi" [Qing dynasty's imperial seal], *Yusi* no. 1 (November 1924).

74. Zhou Zuoren, "Sixiangjie de qingxiang" [The tendencies in intellectual circles], *Tanhu ji,* 137–139.

75. Zhou Zuoren, "Yuandan shibi" [Testing the brush on New Year's Day], *Yutian de shu,* 191.

76. Zhou Zuoren, "Zai shi *Shuntian shibao*" [Again on *Shuntian shibao*], *Tanhu ji,* 515.

77. Zhou Zuoren, "Riben yu Zhongguo" [Japan and China], *Tanhu ji,* 499–502.

78. *ZTHXL,* 432, 439.

79. Ibid., 459–460.

80. Teow, *Japan's Cultural Policy toward China,* 214.

81. *ZZRNP,* 209; Zhao Jinghua, *Xunzhao jingsheng jiayuan: Zhou Zuoren wenhua sixiang yu shenmei zhuiqiu* (Beijing: Zhongguo renmin daxue chubanshe, 1989), 148, n. 1; Kiyama Hideo, "Wo zhi Zhou Zuoren yanjiu" in *Lu Xun yanjiu dongtai* 1 (1987): 22.

82. Zhou Zuoren, "Riben langren yu *Shutian shibao*" [Japanese *rōnin* and *Shuntian shibao*], *Tanhu ji,* 506–507.

6. The End of a Pan-Asian Vision

1. Sun Yat-sen, "Sun Zhongshan zhi Su-E yishu" [Sun Yat-sen's parting letter to Soviet Russia], reprinted in *SZSNP,* 2131–2132.

2. For the labor movement in the early 1920s, see Jean Chesneaux, *The Chinese Labor Movement, 1919–1927,* trans. H. M. Wright (Stanford: Stanford University, 1968), esp. chaps. 8, 10, 11. The numbers of labor strikes in 1918 and 1922 are from Harold R. Isaacs, *The Tragedy of the Chinese Revolution,* rev. ed. (Stanford: Stanford University Press, 1951), 65.

3. Yang Zhihua, "Yang Zhihua de huiyi" [The reminiscence by Yang Zhihua], in Zhongguo shehui kexueyuan xiandaishi yanjiushi, ed., *Yida qianhou,* 26. Also see Shao Lizi, "Dang chengli qianhou de yixie qingkuang" [The circumstances before and after the founding of the party], and Yuan Zhenying, "Yuan Zhenying de huiyi" [Reminiscence by Yuan Zhenying], both in *Yida qianhou,* 61–70, 467–479; Chen Gongbo, "Wo yu Zhongguo gongchandang" [The Chinese Communist Party and I], *Hanfeng ji* (Shanghai: Shanghai difang xingzhengshe, 1945), 214.

4. Dai Jitao, "Xie 'Ba-jue' de jingguo ji mudi jiangci" [The process and the goal of writing the 'Eight Enlightenments'], *DJTWC,* suppl. vol. 2, 738–748.

5. Ibid.

6. Chen Tianxi, "Xiaoyuan xiansheng fuyou renqingwei zhi wuojian" [My opinion on Mr. Xiaoyuan's rich human feelings], *DJTWC,* suppl. vol. 3, 360.

7. Ding Wenyuan, "Wo suo renshi de Dai Jitao xiansheng" [What I know about Mr. Dai Jitao], *DJTWC,* suppl. vol. 3, 284.

8. Jiang Weiguo's true identity became a news topic in 1986, when newspapers and magazines in Hong Kong and Taiwan reported that he intended to reveal that he was Dai Jitao's son in his planned autobiography (which was never published); the synthesis of these reports about Jiang Weiguo's familial relationship is seen in Li Da, *Jiang Weiguo mishi* (Hong Kong: Wide Angle Press, 1986), and *Jiang Weiguo zhuan* (Hong Kong: Wide Angle Press, 1988). A brief account in English first appeared in 1993, when Ch'en Chieh-ju, Jiang Jieshi's second wife, published her memoirs; see Lloyd E. Eastman, ed., *Chiang Kai-shek's Secret Past: The Memoir of His Second Wife, Ch'en Chieh-ju* (Boulder, Colo.: Westview Press, 1993), 72–75. In 1996, Jiang Weiguo authorized Wang Shi-chun, a journalist from *Lianhe Bao* in Taiwan, to write his

biography, *Qianshan duxing: Jiang Weiguo de rensheng zhilü* (Taibei: Commonwealth Publishing Co., 1996), for which Jiang Weiguo wrote a preface and still holds co-copyright with Wang. The book identifies Shigematsu Kaneko, a nurse, as the mother of Jiang Weiguo. See *Qianshan Duxing,* 20. Most recently, Zhang Yuping, a graduate student at Tokyo University and a member of the Research Society on the Documents Concerning Umeya Shōkichi (Umeya Shōkichi Kankei Shiryō Kenkyūkai), cites two letters from Dai to Umeya Shōkichi, a loyal supporter and friend to the Chinese revolutionaries. The letters, one dated September 29, 1916, before the boy was born, and the other dated November 21, 1916, two weeks after the boy's birth, asked Umeya to take care of "O-Kin," the boy's mother, in Tokyo, and then informed him that Jiang Jieshi had promised to adopt the boy as his own child. See Zhang Yuping, "Tō-En undōki ni okeru Tai Kitō no Nihon ninshiki (1913–1916)" *Chikaki ni arite* (Tokyo) no. 36 (December 1999): 59–73, esp. 62–63.

9. Zhao Wentian, the nephew of Niu Youheng and the younger brother of Zhao Wenshu, provided collaborative evidence in his reminiscences. Zhao Wentian was on the ship to Sichuan with Dai in 1922. After his rescue, Dai confessed to Zhao in private his affair with Zhao's sister, who was to be married to a Mr. Wang that year. The marriage pact was dissolved through negotiation and monetary compensation. See Zhao Wentian, "Dai Jitao zisha de zhenxiang" [The true story of Dai Jitao's suicide], *Jiangsu wenshi ziliao,* vol. 2 (1981), 119–121. Dai's official biographer noted that Zhao Wenshu "came to serve Mr. Dai" in 1922. In 1944, she formally became Dai's wife, two years after Niu Youheng died in 1942. See *DJTBN,* 53, 277, 322.

10. Dai Jitao, "Xie Bajue Jingguo ji Mudi Jiangci," in Chen Tianxi, ed., *Dai Jitao xiansheng wenchu,* suppl. vol. 2 (1968), 738–748.

11. Dai to Jiang Jieshi, December 13, 1925, *DJTWC,* 979–986, esp. 980–981.

12. *DJTBN,* 59–61.

13. *SZSNP,* 1929.

14. Zou Lu, *Hui gu lu,* vol. 1 (Taibei: Wenhai chubanshe, n.d.), 159–161.

15. Dai Jitao, preface to the 1927 edition of *Zhongguo gemin yu Zhongguo Guomindang* [Chinese revolution and the Chinese Nationalist Party] (n.p.: Zhongguo Guomindang zhongyang zhixing weiyuanhui xuanchuanbu, n.d.).

16. Xia Yanyue, "Zhongguo Qingnian Junren Lianhehui yu Sun Wen Zhuyi Xuehui," in Zhongguo gemin bowuguan dangshi yanjiushi, ed., *Dangshi yanjiu ziliao,* vol. 2 (Chengdu: Sichuan renmin chubanshe, 1981), 279–291.

17. Dai Jitao, "Sun-wen-zhu-yi zhexue de jichu," reprinted in *Sun-wen-zhu-yi lunji* (Taibei: Wenxin shudian, 1965), 1–38, esp. 5, 9.

18. Ibid., 11–12, 17, 23, 25.

19. Dai Jitao, *Guomin gemin yu Zhongguo Guomindang* [National revolution and the Chinese Nationalist Party], reprinted in *DJTWC,* suppl. vol. 2, 424–452, esp. 437, 441, 444, 449.

20. Huang Jilu, "Dai Jitao xiansheng yu zaoqi fangong yundong" [Mr. Dai Jitao and the early anti-Communism movement], in *DJTWC*, suppl. vol. 3, 319–326.

21. Chen Duxiu, "Gei Dai Jitao de yi feng xin," *Xiangdao* no. 129, September 18, 1925; no. 130, September 25, 1925.

22. From a cartoon by the leftist United Association of Young Chinese Soldiers during the period of late 1925 and early 1926. See Xia Yanyue, "Zhongguo Qingnian Junren Lianhehui yu Sun Wen Zhuyi Xuehui," 286.

23. Dai Jitao, "Sanmin zhuyi de yiban yiyi yu shidai beijing jiangci" [A lecture on the general ideas of 'Three Principles of the People' and its historical background], lecture given at the Army Officers' Academy in Guangzhou between April and May 1925, in *DJTWC*, suppl. vol. 3, 658–668, esp. 660.

24. Dai Jitao, "Sun-wen-zhu-yi zhi zhexue de jichu," 20, 22.

25. Akira Iriye, *After Imperialism: The Search for a New Order in the Far East, 1921–1931* (Cambridge, Mass.: Harvard University Press, 1965), 110–121.

26. Li Enhan, *Beifa Qianhou de "Gemin Waijiao," 1925–1931* (Taibei: Institute of Modern History in Academia Sinica, 1993), 263–264.

27. Shen Yiyun, *Yiyun huiyi* (Taibei: Zhuanji wenxue chubanshe, 1968), 168–169, 254.

28. Ibid., 168–169, 228, 231, 247.

29. Ibid., 247, 255–257.

30. Trying to conceal his real intentions from the rival leftist Nationalists in Wuhan, Dai made vague statements regarding the purpose of his visit to Japan, painstakingly avoiding contact with news reporters. Yet Wuhan soon was informed of Dai's mission to Japan. Xia Yan, a leftist Guomindang member in Kobe and later an underground Communist playwright in Shanghai, was ordered to receive and to monitor Dai for the Wuhan Nationalists. See Xia Yan, *Lanxun jiumeng lu* (Beijing: Sanlian shudian, 1985), 103–113.

31. Given the semiofficial nature of the visit, no complete record of these speeches and talks is available except three sets of published transcriptions: the first is Chen Yiyi, ed., *Dongya zhi dong: Dai Jitao xiansheng fu-Ri jiang-yanlu*, published in February 1928 in Shanghai; the second, a few reminiscent essays written by Dai in 1945 and 1947 when the war was over; and the third, a brief record of the two luncheons between Dai and a handful of leading businessmen, published in *Shibusawa Eiichi denki shiryō* in 1964 in Tokyo.

32. Chen Yiyi, ed., *Dongya zhi dong*, 48.

33. *Shibusawa Eiichi denki shiryō*, vol. 39, 457–458.

34. Chen Yiyi, ed., *Dongya zhi dong*, 24–26, 37.

35. Dai Jitao, "Ji minguo shiliunian shi-ri shi shilue" [Reminiscence of the experience of the mission to Japan in 1927], written in the winter of 1945, in *DJTWC*, 1438–1439.

36. Chen Yiyi, ed., *Dongya zhi dong*, 41–44.

37. Dai Jitao, "Ji minguo shiliunian shi-ri shi shilue," *DJTWC,* 1438–1439.

38. Iriye, *After Imperialism,* 146; Ronson Ping-nan Yueh, *Riben chubing Shandong yu Zhongguo pairi yundong: Minguo shiliunian-shibanian* (Taibei: Academia Historica, 1988), 73–74.

39. Xiangjun, "Dai Jitao shi zairi yanlun zhi pianduan" [A few paragraphs of the speeches by Mr. Dai Jitao in Japan], *Shishi xinbao,* May 30, 1927–June 3, 1927; reprinted in *Dongya zhi dong,* 37–47.

40. Dai Jitao, *Riben lun* (Shanghai: Minzhi shuju, 1928), 12.

41. Ibid., 10, 15–16.

42. Ibid., 8, 32.

43. Ibid., 75, 78, 86, 87.

44. Ibid., 88–89.

45. Ibid., chap. 18.

46. Ibid., chap. 19.

47. Ibid., 131–133.

48. Ibid., chap. 23.

49. Ibid., chap. 24.

50. This is a view also voiced by Japanese scholars in the late 1960s. When the monthly *Chūgoku* in Tokyo serialized the sixth version of *Riben lun* from July 1968 to February 1969, it provoked impassioned discussion among Japanese scholars of modern China. They considered *Riben lun* first and foremost "an admonition against a destructive Japanese diplomacy." See Komatsu Shigeo et al., "Nihon gaikō no kiro: Tai Kitō *Nihon Ron* o meggute," *Chūgoku* no. 62 (January 1969); Nakajima Itaru, "Kōchi de no Tai Kitō," *Chūgoku* no. 63 (February 1969); Matsuda Michio et al., "Tai Kitō *Nihon Ron* o yonde," *Chūgoku* no. 64 (March 1969); Murakami Ichirō, "Kanashii kana kaijō sanzan," *Chūgoku* no. 65 (April 1969).

51. Dai Jitao, *Riben lun,* 140.

52. *Riben lun* was first translated into Japanese in 1928–1929, according to Wu Anlong and Xiong Dayun. By 1970, six Japanese versions of *Riben lun,* by different translators, had been published in Japan. See Wu Anlong and Xiong Dayun, *Chūgokujin no Nihon kenkyushi* (Tokyo: Rikko shuppan, 1989), 195–196.

53. Zhou Zuoren, "Nanbei" [South-north], *Tanhu ji,* 217.

54. Zhou Zuoren, "Luoti youxing kao" [On naked parade], *Tanhu ji,* 525–532.

55. Zhou Zuoren, "Huisang yu maishui" [Funeral's aftermath and water purchase], *Ziji de yuandi,* 226.

56. Shanshu [Zhou Zuoren], "Mingyun" [Fate], *Yusi* no. 126 (April 1927); Qiming [Zhou Zuoren], "Yujian" [My stupid opinion], *Yusi* no. 132 (May 1927); Qiming, "Renliche yu zhanjue" [Rickshaw and beheading], *Yusi* no. 140 (July 1927); Qiming, "Ougan size" [Four pieces of occasional thoughts], *Yusi* no. 140 (July 1927); Qiming, "Kao qiutu" [Torturing cap-

tives], *Yusi* no. 151 (October 1927); Zirong [Zhou Zuoren], "Gongcheng" [Heroes], *Yusi* no. 153 (October 15, 1927); Qiming [Zhou Zuoren], "Correspondence," *Yusi* 4.28 (July 9, 1928).

57. Shanshu, "Kepa ye" [How appalling], *Yusi* no. 143 (August 6, 1927).

58. Shanshu, "Huoshan zhi shang" [On the volcano], *Yusi* no. 148 (September 10, 1927).

59. Zhou Zuoren, "Bihu dushu lun" [On reading behind a closed door], *Yongri ji* (Shanghai: Beixin shuju, 1929), 256–262.

60. Ibid., 260, 261.

61. *DJTBN*, 121; Yan Huiqing, *Yan Huiqing zizhuan* [Autobiography of Yan Huiqing] (Zhuanji wenxue congkan, no. 29), 164–165.

7. For Survival

1. Guo Moruo, "Kua zhe Donghai" [Crossing the Eastern Sea], in *Moruo wenji*, vol. 8, 313.

2. Mao Dun, *Wo zouguo de daolu* [The roads that I have taken], vol. 1 (Beijing: Remin wenxue chubanshe, 1981), 237–238, 255–258.

3. Guo Moruo, *Chuangzao shinian xubian*, 122–123.

4. *GMRNP*, 144–145.

5. Guo Moruo, *Chuangzao shinian xubian*, 140–165, 201–202; "Kua zhe Donghai."

6. Guo Moruo, "Tuoli Jiang Jieshi yihou" [After leaving Jiang Jieshi], in *Moruo wenji*, vol. 8, 147; *GMRNP*, 160–161.

7. *GMRNP*, 160.

8. Guo Moruo, "Qing kan jingri zhi Jiang Jieshi" [Please look at the Jiang Jieshi of today], *Moruo wenji*, vol. 8; also see Guo Muoro, "Tuoli Jiang Jieshi yihou."

9. Guo Moruo, "Lihu zhiqian" [Before leaving Shanghai], *Moruo wenji*, vol. 8, 276.

10. Guo Moruo, "Kua zhe Donghai," 286–313.

11. Ibid., 308.

12. Gregory J. Kasza, *The State and the Mass Media in Japan, 1918–1945* (Berkeley: University of California Press, 1988), 38–43; Mikiso Hane, *Modern Japan, A Historical Survey* (Boulder, Colo.: Westview Press, 1986), 236.

13. The derogatory term in Japanese for the Chinese, equivalent to "Chink."

14. Guo Moruo, "Wo shi Zhongguoren" [I Am a Chinese], *Moruo wenji*, vol. 8, 116–117.

15. Guo Moruo, *Moruo wenji*, vol. 8, 347; vol. 14, 12.

16. Guo Moruo, "Wo shi Zongguoren," 121–122; Maruyama Noboru, *Aru Chūgoku Tokuhain* (Tokyo: Chūō kōrun sha, 1976), 19–40, 92–93.

17. Gu Jiegang, *Dangdai Zhongguo shixue* [Contemporary Chinese historiography] (Hong Kong, 1964 [1947]), 100, cited in Arif Dirlik, *Revolution and History: The Origins of Marxist Historiography in China, 1919–1937* (Berkeley: University of California Press, 1978), 138. Dirlik's book provides a detailed analysis in English of the social history debate; for the discussion on Guo's contribution, see chap. 5.

18. Guo Moruo, *Moruo wenji*, vol. 8, 353.

19. Guo Moruo, "Wo shi Zhongguoren," 348.

20. Du Xuan, "Xiaye xingkong" [Starry sky in summer nights], *Jiefang ribao* [Liberation daily] (Shanghai), June 23, 1978.

21. Guo Moruo to Rong Geng, September 27, 1931, in Zeng Xiantong, ed., *Guo Moruo shujian* (Guangzhou: Guangdong renmin chubanshe, 1981), 115–116.

22. Qiming [Zhou Zuoren], "Xinnian Tongxin" [Correspondence of the New Year], *Yusi* 4.8 (February 4, 1928).

23. Meidi, "Guo Moruo yinxiangji" [Impression of Guo Moruo], in Huang Renyin, ed., *Wentan yinxiangji* [Impression of literary circles] (Shanghai: Lehua tushu gongsi, 1931), reprinted in Wang Xunzhao et al., eds., *Guo Moruo yanjiu ziliao*, 463–465.

24. *GMRNP*, 271; Gong Jimin and Fang Rennian, *Guo Moruo zhuan* (Beijing: Shiyue wenyi chubanshe, 1988), 174.

25. About the founding of Zuolian, see Xia Yan, *Lanxun jiumeng lu* (Beijing: Sanlian shudian, 1985), esp. chap. four, "Zuoyi Shinian" [Ten years of the left wing].

26. Ling Huanping, "Guo Xiansheng yu liudong tongxue de wenyi huodong" [Mr. Guo and the literary activities of the Chinese students in Japan], *Dagong bao*, Hong Kong, November 16, 1941, reprinted in Wang Xunzhao et al., eds., *Guo Moruo yanjiu ziliao*, 470–474; "Zhongguo Zuoyi Zuojia Lianmeng Dongjing Zhimeng de qingkuang" [About the Tokyo branch of the Chinese Leftist Writers' Association], *Xinwenxue shiliao* no. 49 (1990).

27. Lin Lin, "Zheshi dang laba de jingshen" [This is the spirit of the party's trumpet], *Xinwenxue shiliao* no. 2 (1979).

28. Yu Gong, "Zai Riben de Guo Moruo huijianji" [Meeting Guo Moruo in Japan], *Xinren zhoukan* 2.24 (February 15, 1936), reprinted in Wang Xunzhao et al., eds., *Guo Moruo yanjiu ziliao*, 466–468. The essay is a memoir about a meeting with Guo around 1933.

29. *GMRNP*, 108.

30. See note 22 above.

31. Guo Moruo, "Langhua shiri" [Ten days in Namihana], *Haitao* (Shanghai: Xinwenyi chubanshe, 1951), 164.

32. Kong Haizhu, "Guo Moruo shuxin shierfeng" [Twelve letters by Guo Moruo], *Baihuazhou* no. 1 (1981), cited in *GMRNP*, vol. 1, 235.

33. Guo Moruo, "Langhua shiri," 164.

34. Zhou Zuoren's diary, July 30, 1934, cited in Qian Liqun, *Zhou Zuoren zhuan*, 383–384.

35. Tao Kangde, "Zhitang yu Dingtang" [Zhitang and Dingtang], *Gujing* (Shanghai) nos. 20 and 21 (April 1943), 14–15.

36. Guo Moruo, "Guanglin san" [Parting at Guanglin], *Haitao*, 170–173.

37. Guo Moruo, "Guanglin san," *Haitao*, 176.

38. Takeuchi Yoshimi, "Kaku Matsujiaku shi no koto" [Things about Guo Moruo], *Takeuchi Yoshimi zenshū*, vol. 13 (Tokyo: Chikuma shobō, 1981), 56–58.

39. Guo Moruo, "Zai tan Yu Dafu" [Once again about Yu Dafu], *Tiandi Xuanhuang* (Shanghai: Dafu chuban gongsi, 1947), 575–586; Wang Yingxia, Yu Dafu's estranged wife, provided in her memoirs corroborating information on the official nature of Yu's contact with Guo in Japan. See Wang Yingxia, *Wuo yu Yu Dafa* (Nanning: Guangxi jiaoyu chubanshe, 1992), 58–61.

40. See Alvin D. Coox, "Recourse to Arms: The Sino-Japanese Conflict, 1937–1945," in Coox and Conroy, eds., *China and Japan*, 295–321, esp. 299–301, for the initial reaction of high-level decision makers on both sides; for popular reaction in China, see Mao Dun, *Wuo zuo guo de daolu*, vol. 2 (Beijing: Renmin wenxue chubanshe, 1981), chap. 1.

41. Guo Moruo, *Moruo wenji*, vol. 8, 417.

42. See Yin Chen [Jin Zutong], *Guo Moruo guiguo miji* (n.p.: Yanxing chubanshe, 1947?), passim.

43. Guo Moruo, *Moruo wenji*, vol. 8, 417–418. In the short story of his escape from Japan, "You Riben huilai le," Guo dramatized the experience and wrote that Anna was already awake and reading a book in bed and, not knowing he was leaving for good, did not respond or say a word when he kissed her good-bye. In an interview in the 1980s, Anna indicated that she "came to sense" Guo's preparations for leaving but "did not know" that he would leave that particular day; she found out about his departure only when she awoke and saw two letters on the table. See Tang Mingzhong, "Fang Anna Furen" [An interview with Mme. Anna], in Sichuan shehui kexueyuan wenxue yanjiusuo kangzhan wenyi yanjiushi, ed., *Guo Moruo mimi guiguo ziliao xuan* [Select source materials on Guo Moruo's secret return to China] (n.p., 1984), 12–21. Citation on 15.

44. Yin Chen, *Guo Moruo guiguo miji*, 121–124.

45. Guo Moruo, "You Riben huilai le" [Back from Japan at last], *Moruo wenji*, vol. 8, 418–419.

46. Ibid., 419.

47. Ibid., 427.

48. Yin Chen, *Guo Moruo guiguo miji*, 166–167; Guo Moruo, "Zai tan Yu Dafu," 575–586.

49. *GMRNP*, 286–287.

50. Xia Yan, *Lanxun jiumeng lu*, 76, 376–377.

51. *GMRNP,* 289, 302.

52. Sawachi Hisae, *Zoku Showashi no onna,* 188–202; Tang Mingzhong, "Fang Anna Furen"; author's interviews with Tao Fangzi, the nephew of Anna, on February 20, 1994, in Tokyo, and with Tao Titu, Tao Fangzi's brother, on March 6, 1994, in Kyoto.

53. *GMRNP,* 302.

54. Xia Yan, *Lanxun jiumeng lu,* 409–410; Guo Moruo, *Hongbo qu* [Song of great waves] (Tianjin: Baihua wenyi chubanshe, 1959), 12–13.

55. Xia Yan, *Lanxun jiumeng lu,* 410.

56. *GMRNP,* 344.

57. Guo Kaixin and Wang Hao, "Furen Yu Liqun" [Madame Yu Liqun], in Lai Zhenghe, ed., *Guo Moruo de hunlian yu jiaoyou* (Chengdu: Chengdu chubanshe, 1992), 97–99. Guo Kaixin is Guo Moruo's cousin.

58. Guo Moruo, "Qianxian guilai" [Coming back from the battle front], "Zai hongzha zhong laiqu" [Going back and forth amid the bombing], both in *Moruo wenji,* vol. 8, 439–454, 458–488.

59. Xia Yan, *Lanxun jiumeng lu,* 375–381.

60. Gong Jimin and Fang Rennian, *Guo Moruo zhuan,* 199.

61. Guo Moruo, "Lixing yu shouxing zhi zhan" [A war between reason and animal instinct], *Wenhua zhanxian* no. 1, September 1, 1937, reprinted in *Quanmian kangzhan de renshi* (Guangzhou: Beixin shuju, 1938), 17–20.

62. Guo Moruo, "Wuomen weisheme kangzhan" [Why we wage a war of resistance], *Kangzhan sanrikan* no. 2, August 23, 1937, reprinted in *Quanmian kangzhan de renshi,* 1–5.

63. Guo Moruo, "Gao guoji youren shu" [A letter to our international friends], *Jiuwang ribao,* August 24–25, 1937, reprinted in *Quanmian kangzhan de renshi,* 6–16.

64. Guo Moruo, "Zhonggao Riben de zhengzhijia" [Admonition to Japanese politicians], *Jiuwang ribao,* September 7, 1937, reprinted in Guo Moruo, *Yushu ji* (Shanghai: Qunyi chubanshe, 1947), 178–182.

65. Guo Moruo, "Wenhua yu zhanzheng" [Culture and war], *Da gong bao,* March 19, 1939, reprinted in *Moruo wenji,* vol. 12, 6–13.

66. Guo Moruo, "Riben de guoqu, xianzai, weilai" [The past, the present, and the future of Japan], *Yushu ji,* 173–177.

67. Guo Moruo, "Wuomen weisheme kangzhan," 4–5.

68. Guo Moruo, "Riben minzu fazhan gaiguan" [An overview of the development of the Japanese nation], written February 27, 1942, first published in *Xinhua ribao,* March 3, 1942, reprinted in *Moruo wenji,* vol. 12, 148–158.

69. Gong Jimin and Fang Rennian, *Guo Moruo zhuan,* 225–265.

70. Guo Moruo, "Riben minzu fazhan gaiguan."

71. *GMRNP,* 402–403.

72. Lin Lin, "Zuo dang de laba," in Yu Liqun and Mao Dun et al., *Huhuan chuntian de shiren,* 48.

73. Zhou Enlai, "Wo yao shuo de hua" [The few words I have to say], *Xinhua ribao,* November 16, 1941, cited in *GMRNP,* 387.

8. For Rejuvenation

1. Alvin D. Coox, "Recourse to Arms," 302.

2. Fangzhen is Jiang Baili's given name, though Jiang had been using his style, Baili, throughout his life. See *JBLNP,* 1.

3. Huang Pingsun, "Yu Jiang Baili xiangsheng yixitan" [A conversation with Mr. Jiang Baili], *JBLQ J,* vol. 6, 308–309.

4. Jiang Baili, "Ribenren: Yige waiguoren de yanjiu" [The Japanese: A foreigner's analysis], in *JBLQ J,* vol. 3, 206.

5. Cao Juren, *Caifang waiji* (Hong Kong: Chuangken chubanshe, 1955), 242–243; Sun Zhen, "Huai Jiang Baili shi" [Remembering Master Jiang Baili], in *JBLQ J,* vol. 6, 280; author's interview with Lo Fu, a journalist with *Da gong bao* in 1938, at Hong Kong on December 11, 1993; Zhang Hecao, "Jiang Baili suiyuan riji" [Journals from the days serving Jiang Baili], cited in *JBLNP,* 161.

6. Shi Sheling, "Baoding Junguan Xuexiao Cangsangshi" [Vicissitudes of the Baoding Army Officers' Academy], *Yiwen zhi* no. 34 (July 1, 1957), 16–21.

7. Shen Yunlong, *Wan Yaohuang xiansheng fangwen jilu* (Taibei: Academia Sinica, 1993), 67–69; Shi Sheling, "Baoding Junguan Xuexiao cangsangji," 16–17.

8. Shi Sheling, "Baoding Junguan Xuexiao cangsangji," 18.

9. Tao Juyin, *Jiang Baili zhuan* 25; Shi Sheling, "Baoding Junguan Xuexiao cangsangji," 18.

10. Shen Yunlong, *Wan Yaohuang xiansheng fangwen jilu,* 70; Tao Juyin, *Jiang Baili zhuan,* 25; Gong Hao, "Shicheng ji" [Memories of my education], in *JBLQ J,* vol. 6, 271.

11. Shen Yunlong, *Wan Yaohuang xiansheng fangwen jilu,* 71.

12. Zhang Zongxiang, "Jiang Baili xiaozhuan" [A brief biography of Jiang Baili], in He Suihua, Xu Yiyun, and Chen Boliang, eds., *Jiang Baili xiansheng jiniance* (Haining: Zhongguo renmin Zhengzhi xieshang huiyi Zhejiangsheng Hainingshi wenshi ziliao weiyuanhui, 1993), 6 (hereafter cited as *JBLJNC*).

13. Without access to Japanese sources, the biographies of Jiang Baili in Chinese draw information mostly from Tao Juyin's work, which was based on his personal interviews with Jiang; all of these biographies indicate that it was a Dr. Hirato who took care of Jiang's wound, and all claim that Satō Yato was from Hokkaidō. Although a small detail, the connection with Japanese personnel was important because it led to a significant change in Jiang's personal life. The documents in the Japanese Foreign Ministry have shown that Satō was a native of Niigata. In my search for information on Japanese medical person-

nel, I have received generous help from Dr. Izumi Hyōnosuke of the Fujui Prefectural University, who, as a medical doctor, researches and writes on the history of Japanese medical activities in China in his spare time. Dr. Izumi has been able to locate *A Forty-Year History of Dōjingai [Dōjingai yonjūnen shi]*, a history of the *only* Japanese general hospital in Beijing, but he found no Dr. Hirato listed. He did find a Dr. Hiraga Seijirō, who was a medical attaché to the Japanese legation in the early 1910s with a title equivalent to colonel. Based on the sources he discovered and sent to me, I decided to use the name Hiraga instead of Hirato.

14. Izumi Hyōnosuke's letter to the author, December 12, 1994.

15. See *JBLNP*, 41; Zhang Zongxiang, "Jiang Baili xiaozhuan," *JBLJNC*, 4; Registration of Satō household, Niigata-ken Minamikanbara-gun Katōge-mura Iida 1398 banchi, eleventh year of Taishō (1922). Dr. Izumi (see note 14), who made several research trips to Tokyo and Niigata in order to ascertain Satō Yato's identity, acquired information of a nurse registration from the Association of Nurses in Niigata, which listed Satō Yato as a registered midwife there on December 27, 1913. Letter, December 7, 1994, from the Association of Nurses in Niigata to Dr. Izumi Hyōnosuke (copy in author's possession).

16. Despite their happy union and their lifelong companionship, Satō Yato was accepted by the Jiang clan as Baili's concubine *[qie]*. Because Satō failed to bear a son, Jiang's mother arranged yet another marriage for Jiang in 1918, to Wang Ruomei. Wang remained in their hometown of Xiashi and did not bear any children. See Zhang Zongxiang, "Xiashi Jiang-shi zhipu" [Branch genealogy of the Jiang clan in Xiashi]; a copy of the manuscript, given by Mr. Jiang Zukang, grandnephew of Jiang Baili, is in author's possession; also see *JBLNP*, 68.

17. Shen Yunlong, *Wan Yaohuang xiansheng fangwen jilu*, 70–71.

18. Shi Sheling, "Baoding Junguan Xuexiao cangsangji," 19; *JBLNP*, 52.

19. Jiang Baili, "Zhongguo guofanglun zhi shizu" [The founder of the Chinese theory of national defense]," excerpt from *Sunzi xinlun* (1913), *JBLQ J*, vol. 2, 289.

20. See *JBLQ J*, vol. 2, 289–321.

21. Jiang Baili, *Sunzi qianshuo* [A preliminary explanation of Sunzi], in *JBLQ J*, vol. 2.

22. Jiang Baili, "Ershinian qian zhi guofanglun" [The theory of national defense of twenty years ago], in *JBLQ J*, vol. 2, 219–250.

23. Liang Shuming, "Jiang Baili yishi shuze" [A few anecdotes about Jiang Baili], *JBLJNC*, 116.

24. Jiang Baili, *Junshi changshi [Common knowledge in military science]*, reprinted in *JBLQ J*, vol. 2, 219.

25. Jiang Baili, "Shijie junshi dashi yu Zhongguo guoqing" [The general military trend in the world and China's situation], *Gaizao* 3.9 (August 1921). Also see Jiang Baili, "Caibing jihuashu" [On arms reduction] (1921), *JBLQ J*,

vol. 3, 160; Jiang Baili, "Kanzhan yinian zhi qianyin yu houguo" [The causes and consequences of the one-year-old resistance war] (1938), *JBLQJ*, vol. 1, 369.

26. Tao Juyin, *Jiang Baili zhuan*, 44.

27. Charlotte Furth, *Ting Wen-chiang: Science and China's New Culture* (Cambridge, Mass.: Harvard University Press, 1970), 67.

28. Ding Wenjiang, *Liang Rengong xiansheng nianpu changbian chugao* [A preliminary edition of the annotated chronological biography of Mr. Liang Rengong] (Taipei: Shijie shuju, 1958), 6, 541, 551.

29. See Liang Qichao, *Ouyou xinying lu* (Hong Kong: Sanda chuban gongsi, n.d.).

30. Zhonggong Zhongyang Makesi Engesi Liening Sidalin Zhuzuo Bian-yiju Yanjiushi, ed., *Wusi Shiqi Qikan Jieshao*, 352, 369. Also see Ding Wenjiang and Zhao Fengtian, eds., *Liang Qichao nianpu changbian* (Shanghai: Shanghai renmin chubanshe, 1983), 874–927.

31. Liang Qichao, "Xu" [Preface], *Ouzhou wenyi fuxingshi* [A history of the European Renaissance], in *JBLQJ*, vol. 3, 5.

32. *JBLQJ*, vol. 3, 13–15.

33. Jiang Baili, "Junguo zhuyi zhi miewang yu Zhongguo" [The demise of jingoism and China], *Gaizao* 3.1 (September 1920).

34. Jiang Baili, "Shijie junshi dashi yu Zhongguo guoqing" [The grand trend of the military situation in the world and the national conditions of China], *Gaizao* 3.9 (August 1921).

35. Ibid.

36. Jiang Baili, "Lun junshi yu liansheng zizhi" [On military matters and federalism], *JBLQJ*, vol. 4, 163–171.

37. Jiang Baili, "Shijie junshi dashi yu zhongguo guoqing."

38. Jiang Baili, "Junguo zhuyi zhi shuaiwang yu Zhongguo."

39. Jiang Baili, "Zizhi wenti yanjiu" [On the question of autonomy], *Gaizao* 3.4 (March 1921).

40. Tao Juyin, *Jiang Baili zhuan*, 55.

41. Ibid., 51–66; *JBLNP*, 98–110.

42. Tao Juyin, *Jiang Baili zhuan*, 62–66; Furth, *Ting Wen-chiang*, chap. 7, esp. 173, 182–187.

43. Jiang's visit to Japan in June 1926 was followed closely by the Japanese police, who reported to higher authorities at every stop of his itinerary; see Gaimushō, 3.9.4.110-3, *Gaikokujin dōsei zatsusan: Shinajin bu* [Miscellaneous collections of foreigners' activities: Part on Chinese]; also see *JBLNP*, 106. The Satō household still keeps the scroll of calligraphy that Jiang wrote for Satō Yato's brother, Satō Saijirō, which expressed his frustration over the situation in China. A photocopy of the scroll is in the author's possession.

44. Liang Qichao speculated in late September 1926: "If Sun [Chuan-fang] were defeated (Baili will be ruined too), the area south of the Yellow

River will all become the sphere of influence of Red Russia. If Sun defeated Jiang [Jieshi], then the future will depend on Baili's maneuver. Baili's plan is to separate Jiang [Jieshi] and Tang [Shengzhi], then make an alliance between Sun and Tang after Jiang [Jieshi] is defeated. If this can be achieved, there will be a totally different situation, and great things can be achieved for our country in the future; but whether success or failure will much depend on luck." Liang Qichao to children, September 27, 1926, in Ding Wenjiang, *Liang rengong xiansheng nianpu changbian chugao,* 709. Liang expressed his concerns over Russian pressure on Jiang Jieshi in several other letters during these tumultuous months in 1926; see letter to Liang Lingxian, January 18, 1927; letter to children, January 27, 1927; letter to children, March 30, 1927; all in *Liang rengong xiansheng nianpu changbian chugao,* 719–720, 722, 727.

45. *JBLNP,* 111.

46. Jiang Jieshi in early January ordered Zhang Qun, the mayor of Shanghai, to advise Jiang Baili to "go to Hangzhou for 'recuperation,'" which Jiang refused to do. The decision to jail Jiang Baili was made in late January, though he had already been taken to Hangzhou and put under house arrest in mid-January. See Zhang Zongxiang, "Jiang Fangzhen xiaozhuan," 9–10; *JBLNP,* 117; Jiang Jieshi to He Yingqin, January 8, 1930, "Choubi" [Jiang Jieshi's own handwriting] no. 2574; Jiang Jieshi to Zhang Qun, "Choubi" no. 2581; Jiang Jieshi to Zhang Renjie [Jingjiang], January 21, 1931, "Choubi" no. 2654; Jiang Jieshi to Liu Wendao, January 27, 1930, "Choubi" no. 2672, all in *Daqi Dangan* [Daqi documents], Academia Historica, Xindian, Taiwan.

47. Jiang Jie, "Baili xiansheng yanxing fengdu de zhuihuai" [Reminiscence of Mr. Baili's words and deeds], cited in *JBLNP,* 120–121.

48. In 1931, Chen Mingshu was a rising star in the military and political circles because he had helped in the negotiations and the reconciliation of the Guangdong faction in the Guomindang with Jiang Jieshi. He was also an acting president of the Administration Yuan and was elected to the Standing Committee of the Guomindang's Central Committee. See Tao Juyin, *Jiang Baili zhuan,* 85.

49. *JBLNP,* 123–124; Tao Juyin, *Jiang Baili zhuan,* 89–90.

50. Tao Juyin, *Jiang Baili zhuan,* 89.

51. Ibid., 94–95.

52. Ibid., 95–98. Tao indicated that Jiang was able to make these trips because his financial situation improved when he was elected to the board of directors of the Bank of Agriculture and Commerce in 1934.

53. Jiang Baili to Jiang Jieshi, spring 1935, 1936, *JBLQ J,* vol. 1, 2–7.

54. See John Hunter Boyle, *China and Japan at War, 1937–1945: The Politics of Collaboration* (Stanford: Stanford University Press, 1972), 68–70.

55. For the two missions, see William C. Kirby, *Germany and Republican China* (Stanford: Stanford University Press, 1984), chap. 8, esp. 234–239; also see *JBLQ J,* vol. 6, 50–51.

56. Xue Guangqian, *Jiang Baili de wannian yu junshi sixiang* (Taibei: Zhuanji wenxue chubanshe, 1969), 39–45.

57. Jiang Baili, Berlin (?), to Generalissimo Jiang Jieshi, confidential telegraph, November 8, 1937, in "Kong Xiangxi and Jiang Fangzhen cheng waijiao baogao" [Diplomatic reports from Kong Xiangxi and Jiang Fangzhen [Baili]], *Guomin Zhengfu Dangan Waijiaobu*, 0600.04/1238.01-01, Academia Historica, Taibei.

58. Zhang Hecao, "Jiang Baili suiyuan riji," cited in *JBLNP*, 161.

59. Tao Juyin, *Jiang Baili zhuan*, 155.

60. Jiang Baili, "Xinsichao zhi laiyuan yu beijing" [The sources and background of new intellectual tides], *Gaizao* 3.1 (September 1920).

61. Jiang Baili, "Ribenren: Yige waiguoren de yanjiu" [Japanese: A foreigner's analysis], reprinted in *JBLQ J*, vol. 3, 173.

62. Ibid., 175–176.

63. Ibid., 179–181.

64. Ibid., 183–184.

65. Ibid., 187–190.

66. By the time of his assassination, Takahashi in fact was eighty-two.

67. Jiang Baili, "Ribenren: Yige waiguoren de yanjiu," 192.

68. Ibid., 186, 196–198.

69. Ibid., 199.

70. Ibid., 201–202.

71. In accordance with the central government's rule of practice at the time, Jiang Jieshi held concurrently the presidencies of all military academies in China. See *JBLNP*, 172.

72. Xue Guangqian, *Jiang Baili de wannian yu junshi sixiang*, 56.

73. Jiang Baili, "Kaocha yiguo kongjun jianshe zhi shunxu yu yijian" [Report on the procedure of building an air force in Italy], August 8, 1936, reprinted in *JBLQ J*, vol. 1, 9–19.

74. Jiang Baili, "Xiandai wenhua zhi youlai yu xin renshengguan zhi chengli" [The sources of modern culture and the foundation of new perspective on life], *Guofang lun* [On national defense], reprinted in *JBLQ J*, vol. 2, 324.

75. Jiang Baili, "Kangzhan de jiben guannian" [The Premises of Resistance War], *JBLQ J*, vol. 1, 343–348.

76. Jiang Baili, "Kangzhan yinian zhi qianyin yu houguo" [The causes and consequences of the one-year-old war], *JBLQ J*, vol. 1, 349–374.

77. Tao Juyin, *Jizhe shenghuo sanshinian* [Thirty years in journalism], cited in *JBLNP*, 173; Cao Juren, *Jiang Baili pingzhuan* [A critical biography of Jiang Baili] (Taibei: Yiqiao chubanshe, 1998), 12; Cao Juren, *Wo yu wo de shijie* (Beijing: Renmin chubanshe, 1983), 571.

78. Tao Juyin, *Jiang Baili zhuan*, 140.

9. With Sorrow

1. Su Xuelin, "Zhou Zuoren xiansheng yanjiu [A Study of Mr. Zhou Zuoren]," *Qingnianjie* 6.5 (December 1934), reprinted in Zhang Juxiang and Zhang Tierong, eds., *Zhou Zuoren yanjiu ziliao*, vol. 1 (Tianjin: Tianjin renmin chubanshe, 1986), 358–377; Guo Moruo, "Guonan shengzhong huai Zhitang" [Thinking about Zhitang amid national crisis], *Yijing, Yuzhoufeng, Xifeng: Feichang Shiqi Lianhe Xunkan* no. 1 (August 30, 1937).

2. Mao Dun et al., "Zhi Zhou Zuoren de yifeng gongkaixin" [An open letter to Zhou Zuoren], *Kangzhan wenyi* no. 4 (May 14, 1938), reprinted in *Zhou Zuoren yanjiu ziliao*, 382–383.

3. Hu Shi to Zhou Zuoren, received on September 20, 1938; Zhou Zuoren to Hu Shi, September 21, 1938, cited in *ZZRNP*, 406–407.

4. Letters, Zhou Zuoren to Tao Kangde, August 6, 1937; August 20, 1937; September 26, 1937; October 9, 1937, all reprinted in Kangde, "Zhitang zai Beiping" [Zhitang in Beiping], *Yuzhoufeng* no. 50 (November 1, 1937).

5. Zhou Zuoren, "Guanyu zhengbing" [About conscription], a speech to the Anti-Japanese National Salvation Association, organized by the students of Beijing University, October 27, 1931, in *Kan yun ji* (Shanghai: Kaiming shudian, 1932), 265–272, citations on 268, 271.

6. Xu Jie, "Zhou Zuoren lun" [On Zhou Zuoren], in Tao Mingzhi, ed., *Zhou Zuoren lun* (Shanghai: Beixin shuju, 1934), 32–65.

7. Zhou Zuoren, "Yuxieye xiansheng jinian" [Commemorating Mr. Yosano], in *Kucha suibi* (Shanghai: Beixin shuju, 1935), 173–177.

8. Zhou Zuoren, *"Yin chashi"* [Silver teaspoon], in *Bingzhu tan [Chats by candlelight]* (Shanghai: Beixin shuju, 1936), 117–127. Zhou, however, was deeply disappointed by Naka's support, in his poetry, of Japan's invasion of China after 1937, and he wrote in early 1945 that "I still remain respectful to Mr. Naka who wrote 'Silver Teaspoon,' but I cannot but feel so regretful [for him], as I remember seeing a number of his poems after the China Incident.... The poet Naka is not the one I know." Citation from "*Yin Chashi* yingyan" [Introduction to *Silver Teaspoon*], in *Yiwen zazhi,* January 1945, reprinted in *ZZRWLB*, vol. 7, 418–419.

9. Zhou Zuoren, "Fanren congbai" [Worshipping the ordinary men], in *Bingzhu tan*, 137–149.

10. Nagai Kafū, "Edo geijutsuron" [On Edo arts], quoted in Zhou Zuoren, *"Dongjing Sanceji [Tokyo Sansakuki]";* English translation from Edward Seidensticker, *Kafū the Scribbler,* 71, with modification in reference to Zhou's translation and to the original, reprinted in *Kafū zenshū* [Complete collection of the works by Kafū], vol. 14 (Tokyo: Iwanami shoten, 1963), 5–6.

11. For a discussion on the event in English, see Frank O. Miller, *Minobe Tatsukichi: Interpreter of Constitutionalism in Japan* (Berkeley: University of California Press, 1965), chap. 7; and Gregory J. Kasza, *The State and the Mass Media in Japan, 1918–1945* (Berkeley: University of California Press, 1988), 126–137.

12. Zhou Zuoren, "Riben guankui" [A limited view of Japan], in *Kucha suibi*, 231–247.

13. Zhou Zuoren, "Riben de yi-shi-zhu" [The clothing, food, and dwellings in Japan], in *Kuzhu zaji*, 225–239.

14. Zhou Zuoren, "Riben guankui zhi san" [A third limited view of Japan], in *Fengyu tan* (Shanghai: Beixin shuju, 1936), 241–256.

15. Zhou Zuoren, "Tan Riben wenhua shu" [A letter on Japanese culture], in *Guadou ji* (Shanghai: Yuzhoufeng she, 1937), 72–79, citation on 77–78.

16. Zhou Zuoren, "Riben guankui zhi san," citation on 256.

17. Zhou Zuoren, "Riben guankui zhi si" [A fourth limited view of Japan], in *Zhitang yiyou wenbian* (Hong Kong: Sanyu tushu wenju gongsi, 1962), 131–142.

18. Akira Iriye, "Toward a New Cultural Order: The Hsin-min Hui," in Akira Iriye, ed., *The Chinese and the Japanese*, 254–274.

19. *ZZRNP*, 395–409; Zhou Zuoren, *ZTHXL*, 493, 498–499.

20. *ZTHXL*, 573–575. The mystery was finally solved in the early 1990s, when one of the assassins wrote his reminiscences in 1990. The assassination attempt was carried out by several students who joined a Guomindang secret agent–directed underground group, Kangri Shajian Tuan (Killing Traitors to Resist Japan Corps). See Yu Haocheng, "Zhou Zuoren yuci shijian zhenxiang" [The truth about the assassination attempt on Zhou Zuoren], *Lu Xun yanjiu yuekan* no. 9 (1991), 54–55; Huang Kaifa, "Zhou Zuoren yuci shimo" [The Incident of the assassination attempt on Zhou Zuoren], *Lu Xun yanjiu yuekan* no. 8 (1992), 34–39.

21. *ZZRNP*, 412–413.

22. See, for examples, He Qifang, "Liangzhong butong de daolu" [Two different paths], October 17, 1942, reprinted in Zhang Juxiang and Zhang Tierong, eds., *Zhou Zuoren yanjiu ziliao*, 393–394; Zheng Zhenduo, "Xi Zhou Zuoren" [Regret for Zhou Zuoren], *Zhou bao* no. 19 (January 12, 1946); Mao Dun, "Zhou Zuoren de 'zhi cankui'" [Zhou Zuoren's knowing 'shame'], *Mengya* 1.3 (September 15, 1946); Zhang Juxiang and Zhang Tierong, "Zhou Zuoren churen weizhi de qianqian houhou" [What happened before and after Zhou Zuoren's taking positions in the puppet regime], *Nankai xuebao* no. 2 (1982), reprinted in Zhang Juxinag and Zhang Tierong, eds., *Zhou Zuoren yanjiu ziliao*, 126–149, 383–399; Ni Moyan, *Zhongguo de pantu yu yinshi: Zhou Zuoren* (Shanghai: Shanghai wenyi chubanshe, 1990), chap. 7; Qian Liqun, *Zhou Zuoren zhuan*, chap. 8.

23. See Nanjingshi Danganguan, ed., *Shenxun Wangwei hanjian bilu* (Nanjing: Jiangsu guji chubanshe, 1992), chap. 22, "Zhou Zuoren," esp. docs. 4–7, 11–13, 15, 17, 21, 22.

24. Fei Ming, "Moxuyou xiansheng zuo feiji yihou" [What happened after Mr. Fabricated riding the airplane], *Wenxue zazhi* no. 4 (1948).

25. Xu Baokui, "Zhou Zuoren churen huabei jiaoyu duban weizhi de jingguo" [Zhou Zuoren's experience in taking up the position of minister of education in the north China puppet regime], *Xinwenxue shiliao* no. 35 (1987).

26. Zhou's appeal to the high court, on July 15, 1946, listed the facts of his appointment by Beijing University, his contact with underground agents, and his various efforts at protecting school property and resisting the "enslavement education" by the occupation authorities. After his release from prison, Zhou also wrote to Zhou Enlai, on July 4, 1949, seeking fair judgment. See "Zhou Zuoren de yifengxin," in *Xinwenxue shiliao* no. 35 (1987), 213–216, 221; the quotation is from a letter by Zhou to Bao Yaoming (Bau Yiu-ming), July 18, 1964, in Bao Yaoming (Bau Yiu-ming), ed., *Zhou Zuoren wannian shuxin* [Zhou Zuoren's correspondence in his late Years] (Hong Kong: Zhenwenhua chubanshe, 1997), 409.

27. Zhou Zuoren, "Xuantong jinian" [Commemorating Xuantong], *Yaowei ji* (Beijing: Xinmin yinshuguan, 1942), 47–57.

28. Zhou Zuoren, "Preface," *Shufang yijiao* (Beijing: Xinmin yinshuju, 1944; reprint, Hong Kong: Shiyong shuju, 1974), 4–5.

29. Zhou Zuoren, "Shizi yu Rusheng" [The Buddhist and the Confucianist], *Yaotang zawen* (Beijing: Xinmin yinshuguan, 1944; reprint, Hong Kong: Beixin shuju, n.d.), 81–83.

30. Zhou Zuoren, "Daode mantan" [Random talk on morality], *Yaotang zawen*, 53.

31. Zhou Zuoren, "Han Wenxue de Chuantong" [The tradition of Han literature], *Yaotang zawen*, 2.

32. Zhou Zuoren, "Zhongguo de guomin sixiang" [The national thought of China], speech on July 17, 1941, to the Third Summer Training Program of Middle School Teachers in North China, first printed in *Jiaoyu shibao* no. 2 (September 1941), reprinted in Zhong Shuhe, ed., *ZZRWLB*, vol. 1, 796–809.

33. Zhou Zuoren, "Zhongguo de sixiang wenti" [The thought problem of China], *Yaotang zawen*, 13.

34. Zhou Zuoren to Zhou Enlai, July 4, 1949, *Xinwenxue shiliao* no. 35 (1987); Yu Haocheng, "Guanyu Zhou Zuoren de ersanshi" [A few things about Zhou Zuoren]," *Lu Xun yanjiu dongtai* no. 3 (1987); Yu Li (Dong Luan), *Rengui zaju de Beijing shi [Beijing as a World for human and devils]* (Yanan: *Jiefang ribao*, 1942; reprint, Beijing: Qunzhong chubanshe, 1984), 16.

35. *ZZRNP*, 435, 483–484.

36. Zhou Zuoren, "Zhongguo wenxue shang de liangzhong sixiang" [Two strands of thought in Chinese literature], *Yaotang zawen*, 17–23.

37. Zhou Zuoren, "Han wenxue de qiantu" [The future of Han literature], *Yaotang zawen*, 25–32.

38. Akira Iriye, "Toward a New Cultural Order: The Hsin-min Hui," in Akira Iriye, ed., *The Chinese and the Japanese*.

39. Hu Lancheng, "Zhou Zuoren he Luyishi" [Zhou Zuoren and Lewis], in Yang Yiming, ed., *Wentan shiliao* (Dalian: Dalian shudian, 1944), 112–115; *ZTHXL*, 589–590.

40. Letter, Zhou Zuoren to Kume Masao, March 20, 1944, reprinted in Kiyama Hideo, *Pekin Kujōan Ki*, 242–243.

41. Cited in Qian Liqun, *Zhou Zuoren zhuan*, 475.

42. Mushanokoji Saneatsu to Zhou Zuoren, no date; and Nagayo Yoshirō to Zhou Zuoren, July 24, 1944, both reprinted in Kiyama Hideo, *Pekin Kujōan Ki*, 262–265, 265–267.

43. Cited by Zhou Zuoren in *Zhitang huixianglu* (Hong Kong: Sanyu tushu wenju gongsi, 1974), 591–592. For a discussion on the Kataoka incident in English, see Edward Gunn, *Unwelcome Muse: Chinese Literature in Shanghai and Peking, 1937–1945* (New York: Columbia University Press, 1980), 165–171.

44. Zhou Zuoren, "Riben de zairenshi" [Re-understanding Japan], *Yaowei ji*, 246.

45. Ibid., 230–254.

46. Zhou Zuoren, "Liuxue de huiyi," 93–98.

47. Zhou Zuoren, "Tan Riben wenhua shu (qi er)" [A Second Letter on Japanese Culture], *Guadou ji*, 80–85, citations on 83, 85.

48. Zhou Zuoren, "Huai Dongjing" [Remembering Tokyo], August 8, 1936, *Guadou ji*, 70.

49. Zhou Zuoren, "Guanyu Riben huajia" [About Japanese Painters], *Yaotang zawen*, 102.

50. Zhou Zuoren, "Riben de zairenshi," 250.

51. Ibid., 254.

52. Zhou Zuoren, "Daoyi Tengcun Xiansheng" [Mr. Shimazaki Tōson], *Yaotang zawen*, 111–113.

53. Chang Feng, "Guanyu Zhou Zuoren" [About Zhou Zuoren], in Chen Zishan, ed., *Xianhua Zhou Zuoren* (Hangzhou: Zhejiang wenyi chubanshe, 1996), 93–102, citation on 102.

54. In 1946, Anna's sister, Satō Misao, who married Tao Jingsun, met Guo in Shanghai. Guo brought along Yu Liqun and introduced her as "my wife." But it appears that Misao kept the devastating news from Anna for the next two years. See Sawachi Hisae, *Zoku Shōwashi no onna*, 205, 207, 208. Anna's arrival in Taiwan is reported by the Zhongyangshe, the official news bureau of the National Government, in "Guo Moruo qian riji furen xiedai ernu wanli xunfu [With children, Guo Moruo's ex-Japanese wife looking for her husband on a ten-thousand-mile trip], *Zhongyang ribao*, May 13, 1947.

55. Liu Zhiqing, "Yidai wenhao de hunlianshi" [A literary giant's love and marriages], *Wenxue daguan* no. 1 (1990), reprinted in Lai Zhenghe, ed., *Guo Moruo de hunlian yu jiaoyou* (Chengdu: Chengdu chubanshe, 1992), 63–77, quotation on 75. Liu interviewed Anna in Dalian in 1988 when Anna was 93. Also see Sawachi Hisae, *Zoku Shōwashi no onna*, 208.

56. Sawachi Hisae, *Zoku Shōwashi no onna*, 126.

57. "Guo Anna zai Shanghai shishi" [Guo Anna died in Shanghai], *Guo Moruo xuekan* no. 3 (1994), 80.

58. Dong Zhujun, a famous woman entrepreneur whose estranged husband was a fellow Sichuanese and a friend of Dai Jitao, met Dai soon after his first suicide attempt in Sichuan and noticed his habit of opium smoking. It is the earliest record by a contemporary of Dai's addiction I have seen so far. See Dong Zhujun, *Wo de yige shiji* (Beijing: Shenghuo dushu xinzhi sanlian shudian, 1997), 120–121. Also see Zhao Wentian, "Dai Jitao zisha de zhenxiang," in which Zhao indicated that Dai began to use the medical substitute for opium (*yanwan*) after he became president of the Examination Yuan. For Dai's perennial nervous pain and illness, see also Zhu Jiahua, "Dai Jitao xiansheng yu Zhongshan Daxue" [Mr. Dai Jitao and Zhongshan University], in *DJTJNTK*, 1; and Dai's letter to Ding Dingchen, May 3, 1937, in *DJTWC*, 704–705. Dai had attempted to resign from his various official positions during the 1930s and 1940s; see *DJTWC*, 1088, 1093, 1126–1127, 1423, 1480, 1506, 1627, 1636, 1638, 1644, 1669, 1706, 1712; Dai Jitao to the Central Executive Committee of the Guomindang, letter of resignation from the presidency of the Examination Yuan, November 27, 1935, in Guomindang Zhongyang Dangshi Shiliao Bianzhuan Weiyuanhui (Taibei), doc. 241/1177.2; Dai Chuanxian [Jitao] to the Central Executive Committee of the Guomindang, resignation letter, March 1946, in Zhongguo Dier Lishi Danganguan (Nanjing), doc. 3024/28.

59. Dai Jitao, "Ji Minguo shiliunian shiri shi shilue," 1438–1440; "Ji Riben Zuofenli shi" [Remembering things about Saburi of Japan], April 1947, Shanghai, *DJTWC*, vol. 4, 1458.

60. Dai Jitao, "Ai Riben" [Grieving for Japan], *DJTWC*, vol. 4, 1449.

Conclusion

1. See Chalmers Johnson, "How China and Japan See Each Other," in Coox and Conroy, eds., *China and Japan*, 5–16; Whiting, *China Eyes Japan*, esp. chap. 4, "The Anti-Japanese Student Demonstration." The emblematic case of Sino-Japanese enmity with broad implications in domestic and international politics is probably the Nanjing Massacre; see Joshua A. Fogel, ed., *The Nanjing Massacre in History and Historiography* (Berkeley: University of California Press, 2000).

2. Harrell, *Sowing the Seeds of Change*, chap. 9, especially 183–195.

3. In his study of "the response of a range of Chinese political leaders to the possibility of Japanese assistance in the first few years of the Chinese Republic," Earnest P. Young concludes that none of them "automatically rejected Japanese aid under any circumstances." See Young, "Chinese Leaders and Japanese Aid in the Early Republic," in Akira Iriye, ed., *The Chinese and the Japanese*, 124–139.

4. See, for examples, Harrell, *Sowing the Seeds of Change,* 184–189, for the influence of various Western ideas on Chinese students in Japan at the beginning of the century; for the transmission of anarchism through the Japanese medium, see Peter Zarrow, *Anarchism and Chinese Political Culture* (New York: Columbia University Press, 1990), esp. chap. 2, "The Route to Anarchism through Tokyo." The influence of Marxism through Japanese translation on the early Chinese Communist Li Dazhao during his years in Japan is briefly discussed in Maurice Meisner, *Li Ta-chao and the Origins of Chinese Marxism* (Cambridge, Mass.: Harvard University Press, 1967), 55–56; the transmission of Western literary terms and concepts through Japan is mentioned in Leo Ou-fan Lee, *Shanghai Modern: The Flowering of a New Urban Culture in China, 1930–1945* (Cambridge, Mass.: Harvard University Press, 1999), 315.

5. See Jaroslav Průšek, *Three Sketches of Chinese Literature* (Prague: Oriental Institute in Academia, 1969); Ching-mao Cheng, "The Impact of Japanese Literary Trends on Modern Chinese Writers," in Merle Goldman, ed., *Modern Chinese Literature in the May Fourth Era,* esp. 80.

6. See Akira Iriye, *After Imperialism,* 142–145.

7. See David E. Pollard, "Chou Tso-jen: A Scholar Who Withdrew," in Charlotte Furth, ed., *The Limits of Change: Essays on Conservative Alternatives in Republican China* (Cambridge, Mass.: Harvard University Press, 1976), 332–358.

8. See Poshek Fu, *Passivity, Resistance, and Collaboration: Intellectual Choices in Occupied Shanghai, 1937–1945* (Stanford: Stanford University Press, 1993).

9. David P. Barrett and Larry N. Shyu, *Chinese Collaboration with Japan, 1932–1945: The Limits of Accommodation* (Stanford: Stanford University Press, 2001), esp. 4, 8–10.

10. Edward Gunn, *Unwelcome Muse,* 267.

11. The official function of writing about Japan surely continued to exist in modern times, but it was largely limited to the works of a small number of people who were often referred to as "Japan Hands," who worked in institutions affiliated with the government (Qian Shoutien in chap. 7 is an example) and whose writings were often specifically oriented to and limited by policy-making. For the general public, the reach of the Japan Hands' writings was indirect, more through the function of government policy rather than through direct participation in public discourse.

12. Leo Ou-fan Lee and Andrew J. Nathan estimate that the readership of newspapers and popular journals was around 1 percent of the total population; see Lee and Nathan, "The Beginning of Mass Culture: Journalism and Fiction in the Late Ch'ing and Beyond," in David Johnson, Andrew J. Nathan, and Evelyn S. Rawski, eds., *Popular Culture in Late Imperial China* (Berkeley and Los Angeles: University of California Press, 1985), 360–395, citation on 373. Parks M. Coble estimates that the readership reached 5 to 10 percent in the 1930s; see Coble, *Facing Japan: Chinese Politics and Japanese Imperialism, 1931–1937* (Cambridge, Mass.: Harvard University Press, 1991), 76.

13. For the growing sentiment in favor of resistance to Japanese aggression, see Parks M. Coble, *Facing Japan,* chaps. 2 and 8.

14. A view taken by several Japanese scholars in 1969. See note 49 in chap. 6.

15. As China began to pursue an open policy starting in the 1970s, Japan has once again become one of the most popular destinations for Chinese students seeking higher education abroad. By 1989, the number of Chinese students in Japan reached 15,850. See Abe Hiroshi, *Chūgoku no kindai kyōiku to Meiji Nihon* (Tokyo: Fukumura shuppan, 1990), 1. By the late 1990s, the number was estimated at 100,000, according to the Ministry of Education (Monbushō); cited in Liu Qingyun, "Manman dongying lu, qiusuo xin tiandi" [A long path to eastern oceans, a search for the new world], in Huang Shuai et al., *Dongying rensheng lu* (Shanghai: Shijie tushu chuban gongsi, 1999), 1–16. Liu also cited the statistics of the Ministry of Justice (Hōmushō), which put Chinese from the People's Republic of China at 252,164 by the end of 1997; he estimates that the total number of Chinese, including all who are naturalized and those who entered illegally, at 350,000 to 400,000. Citation on 3.

CHARACTER LIST

Akiyama Masayuki 秋山貞之
Amakasu Masahiko 甘粕正彦
Araki Sadao 荒木貞夫
Arishima Ikuma 有島生馬
Arishima Takeo 有島武郎
Aru Seinen no Yume ある青年の夢
Asahi Shinbun 朝日新聞

Ba Jin 巴金
Bai Lang 白朗
Baicao Yuan 百草園
bansei ikkei 万世一系
"*Bao He er yu bodowan*" "抱和兒浴
　　博多灣"
Bao Yaoming (Bau Yiu-ming) 鮑耀明
Biexia Zhai 別下齋
(Xie) Bing Xin（謝）冰心
bukanwen 不堪聞
Bungaku Hōkokukai 文学報国会
Bunkyūdō 文求堂
buren 不忍
bushidō 武士道
Bushūkō Hiwa 武州公秘話

Cai E 蔡鄂
Cai Hesen 蔡和森
Cai Yuanpei 蔡元培
Cao Juren 曹聚仁

Cao Yu 曹禺
Cen Chunxuan 岑春煊
Chen bao 晨報
Chen Cheng 陳誠
Chen Duxiu 陳獨秀
Chen Gongbo 陳公博
Chen Mingshu 陳銘樞
Chen Shou 陳壽
Chen Wangdao 陳望道
Chen Yi 陳儀
Chen Zhongshu 陳仲恕
Chen Ziying 陳子英
Cheng Fangwu 成仿吾
"*Chiisaki sha e*" "小さき者へ"
Chuangzao 創造
chuangzao de moni 創造的模擬
Chuangzao Zhoukan 創造週刊
Chūgoku Bungaku Kenkyukai
　　中國文學研究会

Dai Jitao (Chuanxian, Tianchou)
　　戴季陶（傳賢, 天仇）
Dangkou zhi 蕩寇誌
dapingyuan de wenhua 大平原的文化
datsu-A nyū-Ou 脱亜入欧
Deng Yanda 鄧演達
Deng Zeru 鄧澤如
Ding Wenjiang 丁文江

Doihara Kenji 土肥原賢二
Dongliu She 東流社
dongtu ximo 東塗西抹
Dongya xing 東亞性
Dongyang 東洋
Dongyang minzu 東洋民族
Dongyang Ren 東洋人
Dongyi 東夷
Dongyou Yubei Xuetang 東遊預備
　　學堂
Duan Qirui 段祺瑞
"duanji huazhou" 斷薺劃粥

Eiko 栄子

fan wenhua 反文化
Fan Zhongyan 范仲淹
Fang Yuting 方雨亭
feichangshi / hijōji 非常時
feiren de wenxue 非人的文學
Feisheng 飛生
Feng Wenbing (Fei Ming)
　　馮文炳 (廢名)
Feng Yuxiang 馮玉祥
Fengshen Bang 封神榜
fugu sixiang 復古思想
Fujimori Seikichi 藤森成吉
Fujiwara Seika 藤川惺窩
Fukuzawa Yukichi 福沢諭吉

Gaizao 改造
Gao Erdeng 高爾登
geren zhuyi de renjian benwei zhuyi
　　個人主義的人間本位主義
Gong Hao 龔浩
Gong Weisheng 龔未生
Gongche shangshu ji 公車上書記
Gongdu Huzhutuan 工讀互助團
gonggong zhi guannian 公共之觀念
Gongxue 工學
Gongxue She 共學社
Guan Zhixiang 管芷湘
guanfeng juan 觀風卷

Guangfu Hui 光復會
Guanghan 廣漢
Guanghua bao 光華報
Guer ji 孤兒記
Guo Kaizhen (Moruo, Dingtang)
　　郭開貞 (沫若, 鼎堂)
guocui 國粹
guomin jingshen bing 國民精神病
Guoxue jikan 國學季刊
guqi zhuyi 鼓氣主義

Habuto Nobuko 羽太信子
Haga Yaichi 芳賀矢一
Haiyan 海鹽
hamon 破門
hanjian wenren 漢奸文人
Hara Kei 原敬
Hatano Akiko 波多野秋子
Hattori Misao 服部操
Hattori Shō (Shisai) 服部章 (子裁)
Hayashi Fusao 林房雄
He Lian 何廉
He Wei 何畏
Heichao 黑潮
Heigakkō 兵學校
hinin 非人
Hongxing yishi 紅星佚史
Honjō Shigeru 本庄繁
Hōsei Daigaku 法政大學
houbei / kohai 後輩
Hu Hanmin 胡漢民
Hu Lancheng 胡蘭成
Hu Linyi 胡林翼
Hu Shi 胡適
Huan Huangdi 煥皇帝
Huan Qiangdao 煥強盜
Huang Fu 黃郛
Huang qiangwei 黃薔薇
Huang Xing 黃興
Huang Zongxi 黃宗羲
Huang Zunxian 黃遵憲

Iino Yoshisaburō 飯野吉三郎

Ikigakari 行き掛り

Inoue Junnosuke 井上準之助

Inukai Tsuyoshi 犬養毅

Itagaki Seishirō 板垣征四郎

Itagaki Taisuke 板垣退助

Itō Hirobumi 伊藤博文

Itō Noe 伊藤野枝

Ji 稷

Jiang Baili (Fangzhen) 蔣百里 (方震)

Jiang Jieshi 蔣介石

Jiang Shengmu 蔣生沐

jiang shiji 講實際

Jiang Weiguo 蔣緯國

Jiang Xuelang 蔣學琅

Jiang Zungui 蔣尊簋

Jiangnan Lushi Xuetang 江南陸師
     學堂

Jiangnan Shuishi Xuetang 江南
     水師學堂

Jianshe zazhi 建設雜誌

Jiefang yü gaizao 解放與改造

Jieguang 潔光

jiejie 姐姐

Jin Shengtan 金聖嘆

Jin Zutong 金祖同

Jing bao 京報

Jingguo meitan 經國美談

Jingji Xuetang 經濟學堂

Jiuliancheng 九連城

Jiuwang ribao 救亡日報

Ju-E Yiyong Dui 拒俄義勇隊

junguo zhuyi 軍國主義

Kaizō 改造

Kakei Katsuhiko 筧克彦

kami no kuni 神の国

kaminagara no michi 神ながらの道

Kan'innomiya Kotonohito 閑院宮
     載仁

Kang Youwei 康有為

katakiuchi 敵討ち

Kataoka Teipei 片岡鉄兵

Katō Hiroyuki 加藤弘之

Katō Kōmei 加藤高明

Katsura Tarō 桂太郎

Kawai Senrō 河井荃廬 (仙郎)

Kawakami Hajime 河上肇

Kawashima Naniwa 川島浪速

Kenteki 涓滴

Kido Takayoshi 木戸孝允

Kita Ikki 北一輝

Kō-A Kai 興亜会

Kobayashi Issa 小林一茶

Kōbun Gakuin 弘文学院

kōdō-ha 皇道派

kokunan / guonan 國難

Konishi Sanshichi 小西三七

Konoe Atsumaro 近衛篤麿

Kōtō Shihan Gakkō 高等師範学校

Kōtoku Shūsui 幸德秋水

Kuangwu Tielu Xuetang 礦物鐵路
     學堂

"Kuanren Riji" "狂人日記"

Kume Masao 久米正雄

Kuriyagawa Hakuson 廚川白村

Kuyu Zhai 苦雨齋

Kuzhu Zhai 苦住齋

Kyōdo kenkyū 鄉土研究

Kyōgen nijū ban 狂言二十番

kyōson kyōei 共存共榮

kyotō 巨頭

Li Bai 李白

Li Da 李達

Li Dazhao 李大釗

Li Hanjun 李漢俊

Li Shiceng 李石曾

Li Yimang 李一氓

Li Yuanhong 黎元洪

Liang Qichao (Rengong) 梁啓超
     (任公)

Liao Zhongkai 廖仲愷

Lin Boqu 林伯渠

Lin Lin 林林

Lin Shu (Qinnan) 林紓 (琴南)

Liu Chongjie 劉崇傑
liu-Ri 留日
Luo Zhenyu 羅振玉
Lushan Junguan Xunliantuan
　　盧山軍官訓練團
"Lusi" 鷺鷥

makanai 賄い
Makura no sōshi 枕の草子
mamu buren 麻木不仁
Manzhouguo 滿洲國
Mao Dun 茅盾
Mao Zedong 毛澤東
Matsuoka Yōsuke 松澤洋右
Mazaki Jinzaburō 真崎甚三郎
Meiji Senmon Gakkō 明治專門學校
Meizhou pinglun 每週評論
Miao Bin 繆斌
Min She 民社
Minguo ribao 民國日報
Mingxin 明心
Minobei Tatsukichi 美濃部達吉
Minquan bao 民權報
Minquan She 民權社
minzu qijie 民族氣節
minzu zhuyi de shidai 民族主義的時代
Miyazaki Tōten 宮崎滔天
Miyazaki Sanmai 宮崎三昧
Mori Ōgai 森鷗外
Mu Mutian 穆木天
Muramatsu Shōfū 村松梢風
Mushanokoji Saneatsu 武者小路
　　実篤

Nagai Kafū 永井荷風
Nagata Tetsuzan 永田鉄山
Nagayo Yoshirō 長与善郎
Naka Kansuke 中勘助
Nakae Tōju 中江藤樹
Niijima Jō 新島襄
Niu Youheng 鈕有恆
Nomizu Shinji 野水新司
Nüzi shijie 女子世界

Ohara Eijirō 小原栄次郎
Okamura Yasuji 岡村寧次
Ōsugi Sakae 大杉栄
Ouyang Xiu 歐陽修
Ouzhou wenyi fuxingshi 歐洲文藝
　　復興史

Pan Hannian 潘漢年
Putian zhongfen lu 普天忠憤錄
Puyi 溥儀

Qian Chao 錢潮
Qian Junfu 錢均甫
Qian Shoutie 錢瘦鐵
Qian Xuantong 錢玄同
Qilu 岐路
Qimeng huabao 啓蒙畫報
Qimin yaoshu 齊民要術
Qingyi bao 清議報
Qiushi Shuyuan 求是書院
Qü Qiubai 瞿秋白
Qu Yuan 屈原
"Quan yu Hua Ren bu zhun ru"
　　"犬與華人不准入"

Rakugo Sen 落語選
ren 仁
ren-ai 仁愛
ren de wenhua 人的文化
Ren xue 仁學
ren zhi dao 人之道
renqing wuli 人情物理
renru zhuyi 忍辱主義
Riben guozhi 日本國誌
Rikkyō Daigaku 立教大學
Rikugun Shikan Gakkō 陸軍士官
　　學校
Rong Geng 容庚
Ruicheng 瑞澂

Saburi Sadao 佐分利貞男
Saigō Takamori 西鄉隆盛
Saigyō Hōshi 西行法師

Saionji Kinmochi 西園寺公望
Saitō Makoto 斎藤実
Sanguo yanyi 三國演義
Sanhong Sheng 散紅生
Sanye ji 三葉集
Satō Tomiko 佐藤富子
Satō Yato 佐藤やと
Sei Shōnagon 清少納言
Seijō Gakkō 成城學校
Seika Gakkō 清華學校
senpai 先輩
Shakai soshiki to Shakai kakumei
　　社會組織と社會革命
Shanhai 上海
Shao Lizi 邵力子
Shaonian weite zhi fannao 少年維特
　　之煩惱
Shaonian Zhongguo Xuehui
　　少年中國學會
Shawan 沙灣
she-shuo 社説
shehui zhuyi de shidai 社會主義的時代
Shen Dingyi (Xuanlu) 沈定一 (玄盧)
Shen Qiwu 沈啓無
Shen Yinmo 沈尹默
shendao / shintō 神道
Shi Cuntong 施存統
Shibue Tomotsu 渋江保
Shibusawa Eiichi 渋沢栄一
Shidehara Kijūrō 幣原喜重郎
Shimazaki Tōson 島崎藤村
Shin shina 新支那
Shinbu Gakkō 振武學校
shinjū 心中
Shirakaba 白樺
shishi / zhishi 志士
Shishi xinbao 時事新報
"Shiwu Xiaohaojie" "十五小豪傑"
Shiwu Xuetang 時務學堂
Shixue 實學
Shōsetsu shinzui 小説神髄
shu 恕
Shuangshan Shuyuan 雙山書院

Shuihu zhuan 水滸傳
Shuntian shibao 順天時報
Sima Zhao 司馬昭
sixiang de zhanzheng 思想的戰爭
sixiang geming 思想革命
Song Jiaoren 宋教仁
Song Zheyuan 宋哲元
Su Xuelin 蘇雪林
suketachi 助太刀
Sun Chuanfang 孫傳芳
Sun Wen Zhuyi Xuehui 孫文主義
　　學會

Tai-Shi Bunka Jimukyoku 対支文化
　　事務局
Tairiku shinpō 大陸新報
Takahashi Korekiyo 高橋是清
Takeuchi Yoshimi 竹内好
Tamura Kōkon 田村黄昏
Tan Sitong 譚嗣同
Tanaka Giiji 田中義一
Tang Jiyao 唐繼堯
Tang Shengzhi 唐生智
Tao Chengzhang (Huanqing)
　　陶成章 (煥卿)
Tao Jingsun 陶晶孫
Tao Juyin 陶菊隱
Tao Kangde 陶亢德
Tao Wangchao 陶望潮
tenkō 転向
Tensoku hyaku wa 天竸百話
Terauchi Masatake 寺内正毅
Tian Han (Shouchang) 田漢 (壽昌)
Tianduo bao 天鐸報
Tianyan lun 天演論
tianze 天擇
Tianzu Yundong 天足運動
Tō-A Dōbunkai 東亜同文会
Togawa Shūkotsu 戸川秋骨
Tokutomi Roka 徳富蘆花
Tokutomi Sohō 徳富蘇峰
Tokyo Joshi Isha Senmon Gakkō
　　東京女子醫者專門學校

tongbao guannian 同胞觀念
tonghua de gongshi 同化的攻勢
Tongmenghui 同盟會
Tōno monogatari 遠野物語
Tōyama Mitsuru 頭山滿
Tōyō Bunko 東洋文庫
Toyotomi Hideyoshi 豊臣秀吉
Tsubouchi Shōyō 坪内逍遙
Tsurezuregusa 徒然草

Wang Jingwei 汪精衛
Wang Yangming 王陽明
Watsuji Tetsurō 和辻哲郎
Wei lue 魏略
Wei zhi 魏志
weiji li 維繫力
weiyou 畏友
"Woren Zhuan" "倭人傳"
wu de wenhua 物的文化
Wu Cheng 吳誠
Wu Peifu 吳佩孚
Wu Yizhai 吳一齋
Wu Zhihui 吳稚輝
wudao guo 無道國
wujing 物競
wuli de shoushi 武力的守勢

Xia Mianzun 夏丏尊
Xia Nünu 俠女奴
Xia She 夏社
Xia Yan 夏衍
Xiandai 現代
Xiangdao zhoubao 嚮導週報
xiangshang de jingshen 向上的精神
Xiaoshuo yuebao 小說月報
xiaozhu 小注
Xiashi 硤石
Xie Chi 謝持
Xie Jian 謝健
Xin Min Hui 新民會
Xin shen bao 新申報
Xin Zhongguo 新中國
Xinhua ribao 新華日報

Xinmin congbao 新民叢報
Xingqi pinglun 星期評論
Xinren 新人
Xinsheng 新生
Xinshige She 新詩歌社
Xinxiaoshuo 新小說
xinxue 新學
Xiongnu qishilu 匈奴奇士彔
Xiyang 西洋
Xiyou ji 西遊記
Xu Guangzhi 許光治
Xu Shoushang 許壽裳
Xu Xilin 徐錫麟
Xu Xinliu 徐新六
Xu Zhimo 徐志摩
Xu Zixiu 徐子休
Xu Zuzheng (Yaochen) 徐祖正
　　(耀辰)
"Xuedeng" "學燈"
xundao 殉道
xunzhi 殉職

Yamagami Masayoshi 山上正義
Yamakawa Hitoshi 山川均
Yamamoto Gonnohyōe 山本権兵衛
Yamamoto Jōtarō 山本條太郎
Yan Fu (Jidao) 嚴復 (幾道)
Yanagita Kunio 柳田国男
Yang Zhenhe 楊振和
Yang Zhihua 楊之華
Yang Zihong 楊子鴻
"Yaocaotang Suibi" 藥草堂隨筆
"Yaocaotang Yulu" 藥草堂語錄
Yashan 牙山
yi renyi wei ben 以仁義為本
yin 因
yinxi 因襲
yizhong qiutong 異中求同
Yokoda Heizaemon 橫田兵左衛門
Yong bao 庸報
"yong su er li su" "用俗而離俗"
Yosano Akiko 与謝野晶子
Yosano Hiroshi 与謝野寛

Yoshida Kenkō 吉田兼好
youmin 懶民
Yu 禹
Yu Dafu 郁達夫
Yu Lichen 于立忱
Yu Lichu 俞理初
Yu Liqun 于立群
Yu Manzi 余蠻子
Yu Yue 俞樾
yuan 緣
Yuan Shikai 袁世凱
Yuan Wensou 袁文藪
Yue Fei 岳飛
"Yueshi" "月蝕"
Yuki no shōji 雪の障子
Yun Daiying 惲代英
Yusi 語絲
Yuwai xiaoshuo ji 域外小説集
Yuyi 余一
Yuzhou feng 宇宙風

Zeng Guofan 曾國藩
Zha Pinzhen 查品珍
"Zhaixiang duanbing xiangjie chu, sharen rucao buwen sheng"
    窄巷短兵相接處,
    殺人如草不聞聲
Zhang Ji 張繼
Zhang Jingjiang 張靜江
Zhang Junmai (Carsun Chang)
    張君勱
Zhang Qionghua 張瓊華
Zhang Taiyan 章太炎
Zhang Xun 張勛
Zhang Ziping 張資平
Zhang Zuolin 張作霖
zhanjianhou 斬監候
Zhao Erxun 趙爾巽
Zhao Wenshu 趙文淑
Zhehui 浙會

Zhejiang chao 浙江潮
Zhejiang Tongxiang Hui 浙江同鄉會
Zheng Boqi 鄭伯奇
Zhexue Hui 浙學會
zhina tong 支那通
zhishan zhi mudi 至善之目的
Zhiwen She 質文社
zhong, cheng, zhi, yong 忠, 誠, 智, 勇
zhong gongli 重功利
zhongjun 忠君
Zhongguo Qingnian Junren
    Lianhehui 中國青年軍人
    聯合會
Zhongguo Zuoyi Zuojia Lianmeng
    中國左翼作家聯盟
Zhonghua Gemingdang 中華革命黨
Zhonghua ribao 中華日報
Zhonghua xinbao 中華新報
Zhong-Ri Jiaoyuhui 中日教育會
Zhong-Ri Xueshu Xiehui 中日學術
    協會
Zhong-Ri Xueyuan 中日學院
Zhongwai ribao 中外日報
Zhou Enlai 周恩來
Zhou Fengyi 周鳳儀
Zhou Fuqing 周福清
Zhou Jianren 周建人
Zhou Shuren (Zhangshou)
    周樹人 (樟壽)
Zhou Zuoren (Kuishou, Qiming,
    Zhitang) 周作人 (櫆壽, 启明,
    知堂)
Zhou Zuoren Re 周作人熱
Zhu Xingbo 朱杏伯
Zhu Xizu 朱希祖
zhuzhang 助長
Zong Baihua 宗白華
zuier daoguo 蕞爾島國
Zuolian 左聯
zuoren zhidao 做人之道

SELECT BIBLIOGRAPHY

Unpublished Sources

ARCHIVAL SOURCES

Academia Historica 國史館, Xindian, Taiwan.
Bōeichō Kenshūjo Senshishitsu 防衛廳研修所戰史室 [Archive of the History of War, the Research Institute of the Defense Ministry], Tokyo.
Gaikō Shiryōkan 外交史料館 [Archive of Historical Materials of Foreign Affairs], Gaimushō 外務省 [Foreign Ministry], Tokyo.
Seijō Gakkō Gakuseibu 成城学校学生部 [Student Department of Seijō School], Seijō Gakkō 成城學校, Tokyo.
Zhongguo Dier Lishi Danganguan 中國第二檔案館 [Second History Archive of China], Nanjing.
Zhongyang Dangshi Shiliao Bianzhuan Weiyuanhui 中央黨史史料編撰委員會 [Editorial Committee of the Historical Materials of the Guomindang], Taibei.

GENEALOGICAL DOCUMENTS

Household Registration, Satō 佐藤, Niigata-ken Minamikambara-gun Katōge-mura Iida 1398 banchi 新潟県南蒲原郡鹿峠村飯田 1398 番地, Taishō jūichinen 大正十一年 [1922].
Zhang Zongxiang 張宗祥. "Xiashi Jiang-shi zhipu 硤石蔣氏支譜 [Branch genealogy of the Jiang Clan in Xiashi]," circa 1960.

INTERVIEWS

Bau Yiuming 鮑耀明, December 12, 1993, Hong Kong.
        April 27, 1995, Hong Kong.
        June 30, 1995, Toronto.
Iguchi Hirokazu 井口洋一, March 10, 1994, Tokyo.

Jiang Ying 蔣英, October 27, 1993, Beijing.
Jiang Zukang 蔣祖康, November 11, 1993, Haining, Zhejiang.
Lo Fu 羅孚, December 11, 1993, Hong Kong.
Qian Yonggang 錢永剛 and Zhou Jin 周瑾, May 13, 1994.
Satō Kihachirō 佐藤喜八郎 and family, March 12, 1994, Minamikanbara, Niigata.
Tao Fangzi 陶坊資, February 20, 1994, Tokyo.
Tao Naihuang 陶乃煌, November 24, 1993, Nanjing.
Tao Titu 陶堤土, March 6, 1994, Kyoto.
Tao Yiwang 陶易王, March 24, 1994, Tokyo.
Zhang Jue 張玨, May 13, 1995, Shanghai.

Published Sources

Abe Hiroshi 阿部洋. *Chūgoku no kindai kyōiku to Meiji Nihon* 中國の近代教育と明治日本 [Chinese modern education and Meiji Japan]. Tokyo: Fukumura shuppan, 1990.

Aixinjueluo Puyi 愛新覺羅・溥儀. *Wo de qian bansheng* 我的前半生 [The first half of my life]. Beijing: Zhonghua shuju, 1977.

Alitto, Guy S. *The Last Confucian: Liang Shu-ming and the Chinese Dilemma of Modernity.* Berkeley: University of California Press, 1979.

Arima, Tatsuo. *The Failure of Freedom: A Portrait of Modern Japanese Intellectuals.* Cambridge, Mass.: Harvard University Press, 1969.

Barrett, David P., and Larry N. Shyu, eds. *Chinese Collaboration with Japan, 1932–1945: The Limits of Accommodation.* Stanford: Stanford University Press, 2001.

Bergère, Marie-Claire. *Sun Yat-sen.* Trans. Janet Lloyd. Stanford: Stanford University Press, 1998.

Biduan 筆端 [Tip of a pen]. Hong Kong, 1968.

Boorman, Howard, ed. *Biographical Dictionary of Republican China*, 6 vols. New York: Columbia University Press, 1967.

Boyle, John H. *China and Japan at War, 1937–1945: The Politics of Collaboration.* Stanford: Stanford University Press, 1972.

Buxiaosheng 不肖生. *Liudong waishi* 留東外史 [An unofficial history of study in Japan], 2 vols. Shanghai: Minquan chubanshe, 1922.

Cao Juren 曹聚仁. *Caifang waiji* 採訪外記 [Additional notes from interviews]. Hong Kong: Chuangken chubanshe, 1955.

———. *Wentan wushinian* 文壇五十年 [Fifty years in literary circles], 2 vols. Hong Kong: Xinwenhua chubanshe, 1955.

———. *Lu Xun pingchuan* 魯迅評傳 [A critical biography of Lu Xun], 2 vols. Hong Kong: Xinwenhua chubanshe, 1956.

———. *Wo yu wo de shijie* 我與我的世界 [I and my world]. Beijing: Renmin chubanshe, 1983.

Chapman, Nancy Elizabeth. "Zhou Zuoren and Japan." Ph.D. dissertation, Princeton University, 1990.

Chen Bao 晨報 [Morning newspaper]. Beijing.

Chen bao fukan 晨報副刊 [*Chen bao* supplement]. Beijing, 1921–1928.

Chen Duxiu 陳獨秀. "Gei Dai Jitao de yi feng xin 給戴季陶的一封信" [A letter to Dai Jitao], *Xiangdao* 向導 no. 129 (September 18, 1925); no. 130 (September 25, 1925).

Chen Gongbo 陳公博. *Hanfeng ji* 寒風集 [A collection in chilling winds]. Shanghai: Shanghai difang xingzhengshe, 1945.

Chen Tianxi 陳天錫, ed. *Dai Jitao xiansheng wencun* 戴季陶先生文存 [A collection of works by Mr. Dai Jitao], 4 vols. and 3 suppl. vols. Taibei: Zhongguo guomindang zhongyang weiyuanhui, 1959–1971.

———. *Zengding Dai Jitao xiansheng biannian zhuanji* 增訂戴季陶先生編年傳記 [A revised and enlarged chronological biography of Mr. Dai Jitao]. Taibei: Zhonghua Minguo Zhongshan xueshu wenhua jijin dongshihui, 1967.

Chen Xiqi 陳錫祺 et al., eds. *Sun Zhongshan nianpu changbian* 孫中山年譜長編 [A chronological biography of Sun Zhongshan with source materials]. Beijing: Zhonghua shuju, 1991.

Chen Yiyi 陳以一, ed. *Dongya zhi Dong: Dai Jitao xiansheng fu-Ri jiangyan lu* 東亞之東: 戴季陶先生赴日講演錄 [East of East Asia: The records of Mr. Dai Jitao's speeches in Japan], 2nd print. Nanjing: Zhonghua shuju, 1928.

Chen Yutang 陳玉堂. *Zhongguo jinxiandai renwu minghao dacidian* 中國近現代人物名號大詞典 [A grand dictionary of names and pseudonyms of historical figures in modern and contemporary China]. Hangzhou: Zhejiang guji chubanshe, 1993.

Chen Zishan 陳子善, ed. *Xianhua Zhou Zuoren* 閑話周作人 [Reminiscences about Zhou Zuoren]. Hangzhou: Zhejiang wenyi chubanshe, 1996.

Cheng Ching-mao. "The Impact of Japanese Literary Trends on Modern Chinese Writers." In Merle Goldman, ed., *Modern Chinese Literature in the May Fourth Era.* Cambridge, Mass.: Harvard University Press, 1977, 63–88.

Chesneaux, Jean. *The Chinese Labor Movement, 1919–1927.* Trans. H. M. Wright. Stanford: Stanford University Press, 1968.

Chow, Tse-tsung. *The May Fourth Movement: Intellectual Revolution in Modern China.* Cambridge, Mass.: Harvard University Press, 1960.

Chow, William Cheong-loong. "Chou Tso-jen: A Serene Radical in the New Culture Movement." Ph.D. dissertation, University of Wisconsin–Madison, 1990.

Chūgoku 中國 [China]. Tokyo, 1963–1972.

Cohen, Paul A. *Between Tradition and Modernity: Wang T'ao and Reform in Late Ch'ing China.* Cambridge, Mass.: Harvard University Press, 1974.

Coox, Alvin D., and Hilary Conroy, eds. *China and Japan: A Search for Balance since World War I.* Santa Barbara, Calif.: ABC-Clio, 1978.

Coble, Parks M. *Facing Japan: Chinese Politics and Japanese Imperialism, 1931–1937.* Cambridge, Mass.: Harvard University Press, 1991.

Cott, Jonathan. *Wandering Ghost: The Odyssey of Lafcadio Hearn.* New York: Knopf, 1991.

Dai Jitao 戴季陶. *Riben lun* 日本論 [On Japan]. Shanghai: Minzhi shuju, 1928.

———. "Sun-wen-zhu-yi zhexue de jichu 孫文主義哲學的基礎" [The philosophical foundation of Sun Yat-senism]. Reprinted in *Sun-wen-zhu-yi lunji* [Treatises on Sun Yat-senism]. Taibei: Wenxin shudian, 1965.

———. *Guomin geming yu Zhongguo Guomindang* 國民革命與中國國民黨 [National Revolution and the Chinese Nationalist Party]. Zhongguo Guomindang Zhongyang Zhixing Weiyuanhui Xuanchuanbu, n.p., n.d.

Dawson, Carl. *Lafcadio Hearn and the Vision of Japan*. Baltimore and London: Johns Hopkins University Press, 1992.

Ding Wenjiang 丁文江 and Zhao Fengtian 趙豐田. *Liang Qichao nianpu changbian* 梁啓超年譜長編 [A chronological biography of Liang Qichao with source materials]. Shanghai: Shanghai renmin chubanshe, 1983.

Dirlik, Arif. *Revolution and History: The Origins of Marxist Historiography in China, 1919–1937*. Berkeley: University of California Press, 1978.

———. *The Origins of Chinese Communism*. New York: Oxford University Press, 1989.

———. *Anarchism in the Chinese Revolution*. Berkeley and Los Angeles: University of California Press, 1991.

Dong Shouyi 董守義. *Qingdai liuxue yundongshi* 清代留學運動史 [A history of study abroad during the Qing period]. Shenyang: Liaoning remin chubanshe, 1985.

Dong Zhujun 董竹君. *Wo de yige shiji* 我的一個世紀 [My life through a century]. Beijing: Shenghuo dushu xinshi sanlian shudian, 1997.

Duus, Peter, Ramon H. Myers, and Mark R. Peattie. *The Japanese Informal Empire in China, 1895–1937*. Princeton, N.J.: Princeton University Press, 1989.

Eastman, Lloyd E. *The Abortive Revolution: China under Nationalist Rule, 1927–1937*. Cambridge, Mass.: Harvard University Press, 1974.

———, ed. *Chiang Kai-shek's Secret Past: The Memoir of His Second Wife, Ch'en Chieh-ju*. Boulder, Colo.: Westview Press, 1993.

Edwards, Walter. "In Pursuit of Himiko: Postwar Archeology and the Location of Yamatai." *Monumenta Nipponica* 51.1 (Spring 1996), 53–79.

Fei Ming 廢名 [Feng Wenbing 馮文炳]. "Moxuyou xiansheng zuo feiji yihou 莫須有先生坐飛機以後" [What happened after Mr. Fabricated riding the airplane], *Wenyxue zazhi* no. 4 (1948).

Fitzgerald, John. *Awakening China: Politics, Culture, and Class in the Nationalist Revolution*. Stanford: Stanford University Press, 1996.

Fogel, Joshua A. *Nakae Ushikichi in China: The Mourning of Spirit*. Cambridge, Mass.: Harvard University Press, 1989.

———. *The Literature of Travel in the Japanese Rediscovery of China, 1862–1945*. Stanford: Stanford University Press, 1996.

———, ed. *The Nanjing Massacre in History and Historiography*. Berkeley: University of California Press, 2000.

Fu, Poshek. *Passivity, Resistance, and Collaboration: Intellectual Choices in Occupied Shanghai*. Stanford: Stanford University Press, 1993.

Furth, Charlotte. *Ting Wen-chiang: Science and China's New Culture*. Cambridge, Mass.: Harvard University Press, 1970.

——, ed. *The Limits of Change: Essays on Conservative Alternatives in Republican China*. Cambridge, Mass.: Harvard University Press, 1976.

Fudan Daxue 復旦大學, Shanghai Shida 上海師大, and Shanghai Shiyuan 上海師院, eds. *Lu Xun nianpu* 魯迅年譜 [A chronological biography of Lu Xun]. Hefei: Anhui renmin chubanshe, 1979.

Gaiji Keisatsu Hō 外事警察報 [Newsletter of the Police of Foreign Affairs]. Tokyo, 1924–1926.

Gaizao 改造 [Reconstruction]. Beijing, 1920–1922.

Gaimushō 外務省, ed. *Nihon gaikō bunsho* 日本外交文書 [Documents on Japanese Foreign Policy, 1913–1915]. Tokyo: Gaimushō, 1964–1966.

Gaimushō Gaikō Shiryōkan 外務省外交史料館. *Nihon gaikōshi jiten* 外交史辭典 [A dictionary of diplomatic history of Japan]. Tokyo: Ōkurashō insatsukyoku, 1980.

Goldman, Merle, ed. *Modern Chinese Literature in the May Fourth Era*. Cambridge, Mass.: Harvard University Press, 1971.

Gong Jimin 龔濟民 and Fang Rennian 方仁念, eds. *Guo Moruo nianpu* 郭沫若年譜 [A chronological biography of Guo Moruo], 2 vols. Tianjin: Tianjin remin chubanshe, 1982.

Gong Jimin and Fang Rennian. *Guo Moruo zhuan* 郭沫若傳 [A biography of Guo Moruo]. Beijing: Shiyue wenyi chubanshe, 1988.

Gujin 古今 [Past and present]. Shanghai, 1942–1944.

Gunn, Edward M. *Unwelcome Muse: Chinese Literature in Shanghai and Peking, 1937–1945*. New York: Columbia University Press, 1980.

Guo Moruo 郭沫若. *Piaoliu sanbuqu* 漂流三部曲 [A trilogy of wandering]. Shanghai: Guanghua shuju, 1930.

——. *Shanzhong zaji* 山中雜記 [Miscellaneous notes from living in the hills]. Shanghai: Guanghua shuju, 1931.

——. *Chuangzao shinian* 創造十年 [Ten years of Creation Society]. Shanghai: Xiandai shuju, 1932.

——. *Quanmian kangzhan de renshi* 全民抗戰的認識 [Recognizing the need of a war of total resistance]. Guangzhou: Beixin shuju, 1938.

——. *Chuanzao shinian xubian* 創造十年續編 [Sequel to ten years of Creation Society]. Shanghai: Beixin shuju, 1946.

——. *Lishi renwu* 歷史人物 [Historical figures]. Shanghai: Haiyan shudian, 1947.

——. *Shaonian shidai* 少年時代 [My early youth]. Shanghai: Haiyan shudian, 1947.

——. *Tiandi xuanhuang* 天地玄黃 [Heaven, earth and stars]. Shanghai: Dafu chuban gongsi, 1947.

——. *Yushu ji* 羽書集 [Book of feather]. Shanghai: Qunyi chubanshe, 1947.

——. *Haitao* 海濤 [Sea waves]. Shanghai: Xinwenyi chubanshe, 1951.

——. *Moruo wenji* 沫若文集 [A collection of works by Moruo], 17 vols. Beijing: Renmin wenxue chubanshe; Hong Kong: Sanlian shudian, 1957–1963.

———. *Hongbo Qu* 洪波曲 [Song of great waves]. Tianjin: Baihua wenyi chubanshe, 1959.

Guo Moruo yanjiu 郭沫若研究 [Studies on Guo Moruo]. Beijing, 1985–present.

Guo Tingyi 郭廷以, Xie Wensun 謝文孫, and Liu Fenghan 劉鳳翰. *Deng Jiayan xiansheng fangwen jilu* 鄧家彥先生訪問記錄 [The reminiscences of Mr. Deng Jiayan]. Taibei: Academia Sinica, 1990.

Hackett, Roger F. "Chinese Students in Japan, 1900–1910." In *Papers on China*, vol. 3. Cambridge, Mass.: Committee on International and Regional Studies, 1949, 134–169.

Hane, Mikiso. *Emperor Hirohito and His Chief Aide-De-Camp: The Honjō Diary, 1933–1936*. Tokyo: University of Tokyo Press, 1982.

———. *Modern Japan: A Historical Survey*. Boulder, Colo.: Westview Press, 1986.

Harrell, Paula. *Sowing the Seeds of Change: Chinese Students, Japanese Teachers, 1895–1905*. Stanford: Stanford University Press, 1992.

Hattori Misao 服部操. *Aigen yibun* 愛軒遺文 [Articles of Aigen collected posthumously]. Tokyo: Seishindō, 1911.

Hay, Stephen N. *Asian Ideas of East and West: Tagore and His Critics in Japan, China, and India*. Cambridge, Mass.: Harvard University Press, 1970.

Hayford, Charles W. *To the People: James Yen and Village China*. New York: Columbia University Press, 1990.

He Suihua 何葳華, Xu Yiyun 許逸雲, and Chen Boliang 陳伯良, eds. *Jiang Baili xiangsheng jiniance* 蔣百里先生紀念冊 [Essay collection in memory of Mr. Jiang Baili]. Haining: Zhongguo renmin zhengzhi xieshang huiyi Zhejiangsheng Hainingshi wenshi ziliao weiyuanhui, 1993.

Hearn, Lafcadio. *In Ghostly Japan*. Boston: Little, Brown & Co., 1899; reprint, Rutland, Vt., and Tokyo: Charles E. Tuttle, 1971.

Hō Kisei [Fang Jisheng] 方紀生. *Shū Sakujin sensei no koto* 周作人先生のこと [Things about Mr. Zhou Zuoren]. Tokyo: Kōfūkan, 1944.

Honda Shūgo 本多秋五. *Shirakabaha no bungaku* 白樺派の文学 [Literature of the White Birch School]. Tokyo: Dainihon yūbengai Kōdensha, 1955.

Hosoya Sōko 細谷草子. "Gō ten Yon shinbunka no rinen to Shirakabaha no jindō shugi 五・四新文化の理念と白樺派の人道主義" [The concept of new literature of May Fourth and Shirakaba School's humanism]. *Yasō* 野草 no. 6 (1972).

Howland, D. R. *Borders of Chinese Civilization: Geography and History at Empire's End*. Durham, N.C., and London: Duke University Press, 1996.

Hsia, C. T. *A History of Modern Chinese Fiction*. New Haven, Conn.: Yale University Press, 1961.

Hu Shi 胡適, ed. *Zhongguo xinwenxue daxi: Jianshe lilun ji* 中國新文學大系: 建設理論集 [Grand collection of new literature in China: The volume on constructive theories]. Shanghai: Liangyou tushu gongsi, 1935.

Huang Chunhao 黃淳浩, ed. *Guo Moruo shuxin ji* 郭沫若書信集 [A collection of

Guo Moruo's correspondence], 2 vols. Beijing: Zhongguo shehui kexue chubanshe, 1992.

Huang Fu-Ch'ing. *Chinese Students in Japan in the Late Ch'ing Period.* Trans. Katherine P. K. Whitaker. Tokyo: Center for East Asian Cultural Studies, 1982.

Huang Meizhen 黄美真 and Hao Shengchao 郝盛潮, eds. *Zhonghua minguoshi shijian renwu lu* 中華民國史事件人物錄 [An anthology of events and historical figures in the history of republican China]. Shanghai: Shanghai renmin chubanshe, 1987.

Huang, Philip C. *Liang Ch'i-ch'ao and Modern Chinese Liberalism.* Seattle and London: University of Washington Press, 1972.

Huang Shuai 黄帥 and Deng Xing 鄧星, et al. *Dongying rensheng lu* 東瀛人生路 [Passages of life in eastern oceans]. Shanghai: Shijie tushu chuban gongsi, 1999.

Hung Chang-tai. *War and Popular Culture: Resistance in Modern China, 1937–1945.* Berkeley and Los Angeles: University of California Press, 1994.

Inagaki Haruhiko 稻垣晴彦 et al. *Seijō Gakkō hyakunen* 成城学校百年 [A hundred years of Seijō School]. Tokyo: Seijō Gakkō, 1985.

Iriye, Akira. *After Imperialism: The Search for a New Order in the Far East, 1921–1931.* Cambridge, Mass.: Harvard University Press, 1965.

———. *The Chinese and the Japanese: Essays in Political and Cultural Interactions.* Princeton, N.J.: Princeton University Press, 1980.

———. *China and Japan in the Global Setting.* Cambridge, Mass.: Harvard University Press, 1992.

Isaacs, Harold R. *The Tragedy of the Chinese Revolution.* Rev. ed. Stanford: Stanford University Press, 1951.

Jansen, Marius B. *The Japanese and Sun Yat-sen.* Cambridge, Mass.: Harvard University Press, 1954.

———. *Japan and China: From War to Peace, 1894–1972.* Chicago: Rand McNally College Publishing Co., 1975.

Jian Youwen 簡又文. *Feng Yuxiang zhuan* 馮玉祥傳 [A biography of Feng Yuxiang]. Taibei: Zhuanji wenxue chubanshe, 1982.

Jiang Fucong 蔣復璁 and Xue Guangqian 薛光前, eds. *Jiang Baili xiansheng quanji* 蔣百里先生全集 [Complete collection of Mr. Jiang Baili], 6 vols. Taibei: Zhuanji wenxue chubanshe, 1971.

Jianshe 建設 [Construction]. Shanghai, 1919–1920.

Jingbao fukan 京報副刊 [*Jing bao* supplement]. Beijing.

Johnson, Chalmers A. *Peasant Nationalism and Communist Power: The Emergence of Revolutionary China, 1937–1945.* Stanford: Stanford University Press, 1962.

Kamachi, Noriko. *Reform in China: Huang Tsun-hsien and the Japanese Model.* Cambridge, Mass.: Harvard University Press, 1981.

Kasza, Gregory J. *The State and the Mass Media in Japan, 1918–1945.* Berkeley: University of California Press, 1988.

Kirby, William C. *Germany and Republican China*. Stanford: Stanford University Press, 1984.

Kiyama Hideo 木山英雄. *Pekin Kujōan Ki: Nitchū Sensō Jidai no Shū Sakujin* 北京苦住庵記: 日中戰爭時代の周作人 [About the Living-in-Bitterness studio in Beijing: Zhou Zuoren during the Sino-Japanese War]. Tokyo: Chikuma Shobō, 1978.

———. "Wo zhi Zhou Zuoren yanjiu 我之周作人研究" [My studies on Zhou Zuoren]. *Lu Xun yanjiu dongtai* 魯迅研究動態 [Current Studies on Lu Xun] no. 1 (1987).

Kobayashi Tomoaki 小林共明. "Rikugun Shikan Gakkō to Chūgoku ryūgakusei 陸軍士官學校と中國留学生" [The Army Officers' Academy and the Chinese students in Japan]. *Hitori kara* ひとりから vol. 6. Tokyo: 1985, 62–75.

Kojima Shinji 小島晉治 et al. *Chūgokujin no Nihonjinkan hyakunenshi* 中國人の日本人観百年史 [One-hundred-year history of Chinese views of the Japanese]. Tokyo: Jiyū kokuminsha, 1974.

Komatsu Shigeo 小松茂夫 et al. "Nihon gaikō no kiro: Tai Kitō Nihon Ron o meggute 日本外交の岐路: 戴季陶『日本論』をめぐて" [The crossroads of Japanese diplomacy: Concerning Dai Jitao's *Riben lun*]. *Chūgoku* 中國 no. 62 (January 1969).

Kōsaka Masaaki. *Japanese Thought in the Meiji Era*. Trans. and adapt. David Abosch. Tokyo: Pan-Pacific Press, 1958.

Kuno Osamu 久野収 and Tsurumi Shunsuke 鶴見俊輔. *Gendai Nihon no shisō* 現代日本の思想 [Modern Japanese thought]. Tokyo: Iwanami shoten, 1968.

Lai Zhenghe 賴正和, ed. *Guo Moruo de hunlian yu jiaoyou* 郭沫若的婚戀與交游 [Guo Moruo's marriages and friends]. Chengdu: Chengdu chubanshe, 1992.

Lee, Leo Ou-fan. *The Romantic Generation of Modern Chinese Writers*. Cambridge, Mass.: Harvard University Press, 1973.

———. *Voices from the Iron House: A Study of Lu Xun*. Bloomington and Indianapolis: Indiana University Press, 1987.

———. *Shanghai Modern: The Flowering of a New Urban Culture in China, 1930–1945*. Cambridge, Mass.: Harvard University Press, 1999.

Lee, Leo Ou-fan, and Andrew J. Nathan. "The Beginnings of Mass Culture: Journalism and Fiction in the Late Ch'ing and Beyond." In David Johnson, Andrew J. Nathan, and Evelyn S. Rawski, eds., *Popular Culture in Late Imperial China*. Berkeley: University of California Press, 1985, 360–395.

Lee, Sophia. "The Foreign Ministry's Cultural Agenda for China: The Boxer Indemnity." In Peter Duus, Ramon H. Myers, and Mark R. Peattie, eds., *The Japanese Informal Empire in China, 1895–1937*. Princeton, N.J.: Princeton University Press, 1989, 272–306.

Lestz, Michael Elliot. "The Meaning of Revival: The Kuomintang 'New Right' and Party Building in Republican China, 1925–1936." Ph.D. dissertation, Yale University, 1982.

Li Baojun 李保均. *Guo Moruo qingnian shidai pingzhuan* 郭沫若青年時代評傳 [A critical biography of the young Guo Moruo]. Chongqing: Chongqing chubanshe, 1984.

Li Da 李達. *Jiang Weiguo mishi* 蔣緯國秘史 [A secret history of Jiang Weiguo]. Hong Kong: Wide Angle Press, 1986.

———. *Jiang Weiguo zhuan* 蔣緯國傳 [A biography of Jiang Weiguo]. Hong Kong: Wide Angle Press, 1988.

Li Enhan 李恩涵. *Beifa qianhou de "Gemin waijiao," 1925–1931* 北伐前後的"國民外交" 1925–1931 [The nationalist China's "Revolutionary diplomacy," 1925–1931]. Taibei: Institute of Modern History in Academia Sinica, 1993.

Li Jieren 李劼人. *Dabo* 大波 [Great waves], 4 vols. Beijing: Zuojia chubanshe, 1958–1963.

Li Xisuo 李喜所. *Jindai Zhongguo de liuxuesheng* 近代中國的留學生 [Chinese students abroad in modern times]. Beijing: Remin chubanshe, 1987.

Liang Qichao 梁啓超. "Da Feisheng 答飛生" [A response to Feisheng]. In Lin Zhijun, ed., *Yinbingshi heji* [Collection of works from Yinbingshi], vol. 3. Shanghai: Zhonghua shuju, 1932.

———. *Ouyou xinying lu* 歐遊心影錄 [Reflections on the trip to Europe]. Hong Kong: Sanda chuban gongsi, n.d.

Lin Lin 林林. "Zuo dangde laba 作黨的喇叭" [Be a trumpet of the party]. In Yu Liqun 于立群 and Mao Dun 茅盾 et al., *Huhan chuntian de shiren* 呼喚春天的詩人 [A poet who calls for spring]. Chengdu: Sichuan renmin chubanshe, 1978, 48–51.

Lin Yü-Sheng. *The Crisis of Chinese Consciousness: Radical Antitraditionalism in the May Fourth Era*. Madison: University of Wisconsin Press, 1979.

Lory, Hillis. *Japan's Military Masters: The Army in Japanese Life*. New York: Viking Press, 1943.

Lu Xiaoman 陸小曼, ed. *Zhimo riji* 志摩日記 [The diary of Zhimo], reprinted in Jiang Fucong 蔣復璁 and Liang Shiqui 梁實秋, eds., *Xu Zhimo quanji* 徐志摩全集 [Complete collection of works by Xu Zhimo]. Vol. 4. Taibei: Zhuanji wenxue chubanshe, 1969.

Lu Xun Xiansheng Jinan Weiyuanhui 魯迅先生紀念委員會, ed. *Lu Xun quanji* 魯迅全集 [Complete collection of works by Lu Xun]. Vols. 1–2. Shanghai: Lu Xun quanji chubanshe, 1938.

Lu Xun yanjiu dongtai 魯迅研究動態 [Current studies on Lu Xun]. Beijing, 1980–present.

Ma Qibin 馬齊彬, Zhang Tongxin 張同新, and Li Jiaquan 李家泉, eds. *Zhongguo Guomindang lishi shijian, renwu, ziliao jilu* 中國國民黨歷史事件, 人物, 資料輯錄 [An anthology on the events, historical figures, and source materials in the history of the Chinese Nationalist Party]. Beijing: Jiefangjun chubanshe, 1988.

Mao Dun 茅盾. *Wo zuoguo de daolu* 我走過的道路 [The roads that I have taken], 3 vols. Beijing: Remin wenxue chubanshe, 1981.

Maruyama Noboru 丸山昇. *Aru Chūgoku tokuhain* ある中國特派員 [A special correspondent of China]. Tokyo: Chūō kōrun sha, 1976.

Mast, Herman Wm. III. "An Intellectual Biography of Tai Chi-tao, 1891–1928."
    Ph.D. dissertation, University of Illinois, 1970.

Matsuda Michio 松田道雄 et al. "Tai Kitō *Nihon Ron* o yonde 戴季陶『日本論』を読
    んで" [Reading Dai Jitao's *Riben lun*]. *Chūgoku* 中國 no. 64 (March 1969).

Meisner, Maurice. *Li Ta-chao and the Origins of Chinese Marxism*. Cambridge, Mass.:
    Harvard University Press, 1967.

Minguo ribao 民國日報 [Republican daily]. Shanghai, 1918.

Miller, Frank O. *Minobe Tatsukichi: Interpreter of Constitutionalism in Japan*. Berkeley:
    University of California Press, 1965.

Murakami Ichirō 村上一郎. *Kanashii kana kaijō no sanzan* 哀しいかな海上の三山
    [The sorrowful three mountains on the sea]. *Chūgoku* no. 65 (April 1969).

Mushanokoji Saneatsu 武者小路実篤. "'Jiko no Tame' oyobi sonota ni tsuite 自己
    の為及び其他について" [Concerning matters related to 'For the Self'].
    Shirakaba 白樺 3.2 (February 1912).

Nakajima Itaru 中島及. "Kōchi de no Tai Kitō 高知での戴季陶" [Dai Jitao at Kōchi].
    Chūgoku 中國 no. 63 (February 1969).

Nakamura Tadashi 中村義. "Seijō Gakkō to Chūgokujin ryūgakusei 成城學校と中
    國人留学生" [The Seijō School and Chinese students]. In Shingai Kakumei
    Kenkyūkai 辛亥革命研究會, ed., *Chūgoku kingendaishi ronshū* 中國近現代史
    論集 [An essay collection on modern and contemporary China]. Tokyo:
    Kyūko shoin, 1985, 251–275.

Nanjingshi Danganguan 南京市檔案館, ed. *Shenxun Wangwei hanjian bilu* 審訊汪
    偽漢奸筆錄 [Court records of the trials of the traitors in the collaborationist
    Wang regime]. Nanjing: Jiangsu guji chubanshe, 1992.

Ni Moyan 倪墨炎. *Zhongguo de pantu yu yinshi: Zhou Zuoren* 中國的叛徒與隱士: 周
    作人 [A rebel and hermit of China: Zhou Zuoren]. Shanghai: Shanghai
    wenyi chubanshe, 1990.

Pierson, John D. *Tokutomi Sohō, 1863–1957: A Journalist for Modern Japan*. Princeton,
    N.J.: Princeton University Press, 1980.

Pollard, David E. *A Chinese Look at Literature: The Literary Values of Chou Tso-jen in
    Relation to the Tradition*. Berkeley: University of California Press, 1973.

———. "Chou Tsuo-jen: A Scholar who Withdrew." In Charlotte Furth, ed., *The
    Limits of Change: Essays on Conservative Alternatives in Republican China*.
    Cambridge, Mass.: Harvard University Press, 1987, 332–356.

Průšek, Jaroslav. *Three Sketches of Chinese Literature*. Prague: Oriental Institute in
    Academia, 1969.

———. *The Lyrical and the Epic: Studies of Modern Chinese Literature*. Bloomington:
    Indiana University Press, 1980.

Pusey, James. *China and Charles Darwin*. Cambridge, Mass.: Harvard University
    Press, 1983.

Qian Liqun 錢理群. *Zhou Zuoren zhuan* 周作人傳 [A biography of Zhou Zuoren].
    Beijing: Beijing shiyue wenyi chubanshe, 1990.

———. *Zhou Zuoren lun* 周作人論 [Essays on Zhou Zuoren]. Shanghai: Shanghai
    renmin chubanshe, 1991.

Rankin, Mary Backus. *Early Chinese Revolutionaries: Radical Intellectuals in Shanghai and Chekiang, 1902–1911.* Cambridge, Mass.: Harvard University Press, 1971.

Reischauer, Edwin. *Ennin's Travels in Tang China.* New York: The Ronald Press, 1955.

Reynolds, Douglas R. "Training Young China Hands: Tōa Dōbun Shoin and Its Precursors, 1886–1945." In Peter Duus, Ramon H. Myers, and Mark R. Peattie, eds., *The Japanese Informal Empire in China, 1895–1937.* Princeton, N.J.: Princeton University Press, 1989.

———. *China, 1898–1912: The Xinzheng Revolution and Japan.* Cambridge, Mass.: Harvard University Press, 1993.

Roy, David Tod. *Kuo Mo-jo: The Early Years.* Cambridge, Mass.: Harvard University Press, 1971.

Sanetō Keishū 實藤惠秀. *Chūgokujin Nihon ryūgaku shi* 中國人日本留學史 [A history of Chinese students in Japan]. Tokyo: Kuroshio shuppan, 1970.

Sang Bing 桑兵, Huang Yi 黃毅, and Tang Wenquan 唐文權, eds. *Dai Jitao xinhai wenji, 1909–1913* 戴季陶辛亥文集 [A collection of works by Dai Jitao during the 1911 Revolution, 1909–1913]. Hong Kong: Zhongwen daxue chubanshe, 1991.

Sawachi Hisae 沢地久枝. *Zoku Shōwashi no onna* 続昭和史のおんな [Women in Showa history, a sequel]. Tokyo: Bunkei shunju, 1986.

Scalapino, Robert A. "Prelude to Marxism: The Chinese Student Movement in Japan, 1900–1910." In Albert Feuerwerker et al., eds., *Approaches to Modern Chinese History.* Berkeley: University of California Press, 1967, 190–215.

Schwartz, Benjamin. *In Search of Wealth and Power: Yen Fu and the West.* Cambridge, Mass.: Harvard University Press, 1964.

Seidensticker, Edward. *Kafū the Scribbler: The Life and Writings of Nagai Kafū, 1879–1959.* Stanford: Stanford University Press, 1965; reprint, Ann Arbor: Center for Japanese Studies at the University of Michigan, 1990.

———. *Low City, High City: Tokyo from Edo to the Earthquake, 1867–1923.* New York: Alfred A. Knopf, 1983; reprint, New York: Viking Penguin, 1985.

Shanghai Tushuguan 上海圖書館 and Huadong Shifan Daxue 上海師範大學, eds. *Guo Moruo zhuanji* 郭沫若專集 [A collection on Guo Moruo]. In *Zhongguo dangdai wenxue yanjiu ziliao* [Research materials collection on contemporary Chinese literature]. Chengdu: Sichuan, 1984.

Shan Yanyi 單演義, ed. *Lu Xun yu Qu Qiubai* 魯迅與瞿秋白 [Lu Xun and Qu Qiubai]. Tianjin: Tianjin remin chubanshe, 1986.

Shen Yiyun 沈亦雲. *Yiyun huiyi* 亦雲回憶 [Recollections by Yiyun]. Taibei: Zhuanji wenxue chubanshe, 1968.

Shen Yunlong 沈雲龍. *Wan Yaohuang xiansheng fanwen jilu* 萬耀煌先生訪問記錄 [The reminiscences of Mr. Wan Yaohuang]. Taibei: Academia Sinica, 1993.

Shi Jian 史劍. *Guo Moruo pipan* 郭沫若批判 [A critique of Guo Moruo]. Hong Kong: Yazhou chubanshe, 1954.

Shi Sheling 史射陵. "Baoding junguan xuexiao cangsangji 保定軍官學校滄桑記" [The vicissitudes of the Baoding Military Academy]. *Yiwen zhi* 藝文誌 no. 34

(Taibei, July 1957), 16–21; no. 35 (August 1957), 9–14; no. 36 (September 1957), 19–21; no. 37 (October 1957), 35–38.

Shi Xiaojun 石曉軍. *Zhong-Ri liangguo huxiang renshi de bianqian* 中日兩國互相認識 的變遷 [The changes in the mutual understanding between China and Japan]. Taibei: Taiwan shangwu yinshuguan, 1992.

Shibusawa Eiichi Denki Shiryō Kankōkai 渋沢栄一伝記史刊行會. *Shibusawa Eiichi denki shiryō* 渋沢栄一伝記資料 [Biographical sources of Shibusawa Eiichi]. Vols. 38, 39, 55. Tokyo: Shibusawa Eiichi denki shiryō kankōkai, 1961–1964.

Shinano Yūjin 信濃憂人. *Shinajin no mita Nihonjin* 支那人の見た日本人 [The Japanese in Chinese eyes]. Tokyo: Seinen shobō, 1941.

Shu Wu 舒蕪. *Zhou Zuoren de shifei gongguo* 周作人的是非功過 [Zhou Zuoren's achievements and failures]. Beijing: Renmin wenxue chubanshe, 1993.

Shuntian shibao 順天時報 [Shuntian daily]. Beijing, 1923–1924.

Sun Fuyuan 孫伏園. *Lu Xun xiansheng ersanshi* 魯迅先生二三事 [A few things about Mr. Lu Xun]. Shanghai: Zuojia shuwu, 1945.

Sun Tzu. *Art of War*. Trans. Ralph D. Sawyer. Boulder, Colo.: Westview Press, 1994.

Takeuchi Yoshimi 竹内好. "Kaku Matsujaku shi no koto 郭沫若氏のこと" [Things about Guo Moruo]. In *Takeuchi Yoshimi zenshū* 竹内好全集 [A complete collection of works by Takeuchi Yoshimi]. Vol. 13. Tokyo: Chikuma shobō, 1981.

Takeuchi Yoshimi 竹内好 and Hashikawa Bunzō 橋川文三, eds. *Kindai Nihon to Chūgoku* 近代日本と中國 [Modern Japan and China]. Tokyo: Asahi shinbun, 1974.

Tang Mingzhong 唐明中 and Huang Gaobin 黄高斌, eds. *Yinghua shujian: Guo Moruo 1913 zhi 1923 nian jiaxin xuan* 櫻花書簡: 郭沫若 1913 至 1923 年家信 選 [Sakura letters: Guo Moruo's letters to home between 1913 and 1923]. Chengdu: Sichuan remin chubanshe, 1981.

Tang Wenquan 唐文權 and Sang Bing 桑兵, eds. *Dai Jitao Ji, 1909–1920* 戴季陶集 1909–1920 [A collection of works by Dai Jitao, 1909–1920]. Wuhan: Huazhong shifan daxue chubanshe, 1990.

Tao Jingsun [Tō Shōson] 陶晶孫. *Nihon e no isho* 日本への遺書 [A farewell note to Japan]. Tokyo: Sōgensha, 1953.

Tao Juyin 陶菊隱. *Jiang Baili zhuan* 蔣百里傳 [A biography of Jiang Baili]. Beijing: Zhonghua shuju, 1985.

Tao Mingzhi 陶明志, ed. *Zhou Zuoren lun* 周作人論 [On Zhou Zuoren]. Shanghai: Beixin shuju, 1934.

Teow, See Heng. *Japan's Cultural Policy toward China, 1918–1931*. Cambridge, Mass.: Harvard University Press, 1999.

Tian Shouchang tian 田壽昌, Zong Baihua 宗白華, and Guo Moruo 郭沫若. *Sanye ji* 三葉集 [Kleeblatt]. Shanghai: Yadong tushuguan, 1927.

Tsurumi, Shunsuke. *An Intellectual History of Wartime Japan, 1931–1945*. London: KPI, 1986.

Wang Jinhou 王錦厚, Xiao Binru 肖斌如, and Wu Jialun 伍加倫, eds. *Guo Moruo yiwenji, 1906–1949* 郭沫若佚文集 1906–1949 [Uncollected essays by Guo Moruo, 1906–1949]. Chengdu: Sichuan daxue chubanshe, 1988.

Wang Shichun 汪士淳. *Qianshan duxing: Jiang Weiguo de rensheng zhi lü* 千山獨行: 蔣緯國的人生之旅 [Through mountains alone: The life's journey of Jiang Weiguo]. Taibei: Commonwealth Publishing Co., 1996.

Wang Xiangrong 汪向榮. *Zhongri guanxishi wenxian lunkao* 中日關係史文獻論考 [A critical evaluation of the source materials of the history of Sino-Japanese relations]. Changsha: Yuelu shushe, 1985.

———. *Riben jiaoshi* 日本教師 [Japanese teachers]. Beijing: Sanlian shudian, 1988.

———. *Gudai de Zhongguo yu Riben* 古代的中國與日本 [China and Japan in ancient times]. Beijing: Shenghuo dushu xinzhi sanlian shudian, 1989.

Wang Xiangron 汪向榮 and Xia Yingyuan 夏應元, eds. *Zhongri guanxishi ziliao huibian* 中日關係史資料彙編 [A collection of source materials of the history of Sino-Japanese relations]. Beijing: Zhonghua shuju, 1984.

Wang Xunzhao 王訓詔 et al., eds. *Guo Moruo yanjiu ziliao* 郭沫若研究資料 [Research materials on Guo Moruo]. 3 vols. Beijing: Zhongguo shehui kexue chubanshe, 1981.

Wang, Y. C. *Chinese Intellectuals and the West, 1879–1949.* Chapel Hill: University of North Carolina Press, 1966.

Wang Yingxia 王映霞. *Wo yu Yu Dafu* 我與郁達夫 [Yu Dafu and I]. Nanning: Guangxi jiaoyu chubanshe, 1992.

Wang Yunsheng 王芸生. *Liushinian lai Zhongguo yu Riben* 六十年來中國與日本 [Sixty-year relations between China and Japan]. 6 vols. Tianjin: Dagongbao she, 1933.

Wenxue zazhi 文學雜誌 [Literary magazine]. Shanghai, 1947–1948.

Weston, Timothy B. "The Formation and Positioning of the New Culture Community, 1913–1917." *Modern China* 24.3 (July 1998): 255–284.

Whiting, Allen S. *China Eyes Japan.* Berkeley: University of California Press, 1989.

Wolff, Ernst. *Chou Tso-jen.* New York: Twayne Publishers, 1971.

Wu Anlong 武安隆 and Xiong Dayun 熊達雲. *Chūgokujin no Nihon kenkyushi* 中國人の日本研究史 [A history of Chinese studies on Japan]. Tokyo: Rokko shuppan, 1989.

Xia Yan 夏衍. *Lanxun jiumeng lu* 懶尋舊夢錄 [Searching old dreams with reluctance]. Beijing: Sanlian shudian, 1985.

Xia Yanyue 夏燕月. "Zhongguo Qingnian Junren Lianhehui yu Sun Wen Zhuyi Xuehui 中國青年軍人聯合會與孫文主義學會" [On the United Association of Young Chinese Soldiers and the Association of Sun Yat-senism]. *Dangshi yanjiu ziliao* [Research materials of the party history], vol. 2 (Chengdu: Sichuan renmin chubanshe, 1981).

Xin qingnian 新青年 [New youth]. Beijing, 1918–1920.

Xinwenxue shiliao 新文學史料 [Source materials on the new literature]. Beijing, 1978–present.

Xu Shoushang 許壽裳. *Wangyou Lu Xun yinxiangji* 亡友魯迅印象記 [Reminiscences of the late friend Lu Xun]. Shanghai: Sanlian shudian, 1949.

Xu Yiyun 許逸雲. *Jiang Baili nianpu, 1882–1938* 蔣百里年譜 [A chronological biography of Jiang Baili, 1882–1938]. Beijing: Tuanjie chubanshe, 1992.

Xue Guangqian 薛光前. *Jiang Baili de wannian yu junshi sixiang* 蔣百里的晚年與軍事思想 [Jiang Baili's later years and his military thoughts]. Taibei: Zhuanji wenxue chubanshe, 1969.

Yamada Keizo 山田敬三 and Lü Yuanming 呂元明 [Ro Genmei]. *Jugonen sensō to bungaku: Nitchū kindai bungaku no hikaku kenkyū* 十五年戰爭と文學: 日中近代文學の比較研究 [Fifteen-year war and literature: Comparative studies of Japanese-Chinese literature]. Tokyo: Tōhō shuppo, 1991.

Yamazaki Masao 山崎正男, ed. *Rikugun Shikan Gakkō* 陸軍士官学校 [The Army Officers' Academy]. Tokyo: Shūgen shobō, 1969.

Yang Yiming 楊一鳴, ed. *Wentan shiliao* 文壇史料 [Historical materials in literary circles]. Dalian: Dalian shudian, 1944.

Yin Chen 殷塵 [Jin Zutong 金祖同]. *Guo Moruo guiguo miji* 郭沫若歸國秘記 [An account of Guo Moruo's secret return to China]. N.p.: Yanxing chubanshe, 1947?

Young, John. *The Location of Yamatai: A Case Study in Japanese Historiography, 720–1945*. Baltimore, Md.: Johns Hopkins University Press, 1958.

Yu Liqun 于立群, Mao Dun 茅盾 et al. *Huhuan chuntian de shiren* 呼喚春天的詩人 [A poet who calls for spring]. Chengdu: Sichuan renmin chubanshe, 1978.

Yu Xinchun 俞辛焞 and Wang Zhensuo 王振鎖, eds. *Sun Zhongshan zairi huodong milu, 1913.8–1916.4: Riben Waiwusheng Dangan* 孫中山在日活動密錄: 日本外務省檔案 [Secret documents on Sun Yat-sen's activities in Japan from August 1913 to April 1916: From the archive of the Japanese Foreign Ministry]. Tainjin: Nankai daxue chubanshe, 1990.

Yueh, Ronson Ping-nan 樂炳南. *Riben chubing Shandong yu Zhongguo pairi yundong: Minguo shiliunian-shibanian* 日本出兵山東與中國排日運動: 民國十六年–十八年 [The Japanese military expeditions to Shandong and the Chinese anti-Japanese movement, 1927–1929]. Taibei: Academia Historica, 1988.

Yusi 語絲 [Threads of talk]. Beijing-Shanghai, 1924–1930.

Yuzhou feng 宇宙風 [Cosmic wind]. Shanghai, 1935–1947.

Zarrow, Peter. *Anarchism and Chinese Political Culture*. New York: Columbia University Press, 1990.

Zeng Xiantong 曾憲通, ed. *Guo Moruo shujian* 郭沫若書簡 [Letters of Guo Moruo]. Guangzhou: Guangdong renmin chubanshe, 1981.

Zhang Juxiang 張菊香 and Zhang Tierong 張鐵榮, eds. *Zhou Zuoren nianpu* 周作人年譜 [A chronological biography of Zhou Zuoren]. Tianjin: Nankai daxue chubanshe, 1985.

———. *Zhou Zuoren yanjiu ziliao* 周作人研究資料 [Research materials on Zhou Zuoren]. 2 vols. Tianjin: Tianjin renmin chubanshe, 1986.

Zhang Yuping 張玉萍. "Tō-En undōki ni okeru Tai Ki-tō no Nihon ninshiki (1913–

1916) 討袁運動期における戴季陶の日本認識" [Dai Jitao's understanding of Japan during the anti-Yuan movement]. *Chikaki ni Arite* 近きに在りて (Tokyo) no. 36 (December 1999), 59–73.

Zhang Zongxiang 張宗祥. *Riben youxue zhinan* 日本遊學指南 [A guide for study in Japan]. N.p., 1901.

Zhao Jinghua 趙京華. *Xunzhao jingsheng jiayuan: Zhou Zuoren wenhua sixiang yu shenmei zhuiqiu* 尋找精神家園: 周作人文化思想與審美追求 [Seeking spiritual home: The cultural ideas and aesthetic pursuit of Zhou Zuoren]. Beijing: Zhongguo renmin daxue chubanshe, 1989.

Zhao Jun 趙軍. *Xinhai Geming yu dalu langren* 辛亥革命與大陸浪人 [The 1911 Revolution and continental *rōnin*]. Beijing: Zhongguo dabaike quanshu chubanshe, 1991.

Zhao Wentian 趙文田. "Dai Jitao zisha de zhenxiang 戴季陶自殺的真相" [The true story of Dai Jitao's suicide]. *Jiangsu wenshi ziliao* 江蘇文史資料 vol. 2 (1963; reprint 1981), 119–121.

Zhejiang chao 浙江潮 [Tides of Zhejiang]. Tokyo, 1903.

Zheng Boqi 鄭伯奇. *Yi Chuangzaoshe ji qita* 憶創造社及其他 [Recollections about the Creation Society and other matters]. Hong Kong: Sanlian shudian, 1982.

Zhong Shuhe 鐘叔河, ed. *Zhou Zuoren wen leibian* 周作人文類編 [A collection of the works by Zhou Zuoren according to categories]. 10 vols. Changsha: Hunan wenyi chubanshe, 1998.

Zhongguo Gemin Bowuguan Dangshi Yanjiushi 中國革命博物館黨史研究室, ed. *Dangshi yanjiu ziliao* 黨史研究資料 [Research materials of the party history]. Vol. 2. Chengdu: Sichuan renmin chubanshe, 1981.

Zhongguo Guomindang Zhongyang Dangshi Shiliao Bianzhuan Weiyuanhui 中國國民黨中央黨史史料編撰會, ed. *Geming xianlie xianjing shiwen xuanji* 革命先烈先進詩文選集 [Poems and essays by revolutionary pioneers and martyrs]. 6 vols. Taibei: Zhonghua Minguo Gejie Jinian Sun Wen Bainian Dancheng Choubei Weiyuanhui Xueshu Lunzhu Bianzhuan Weiyuanhui, 1965.

Zhongguo Shehui Kexueyuan Jindaishi Yanjiusuo Zhonghua Minguoshi Yanjiushi 中國社會科學院近代史研究所中華民國史研究室, ed. *Sun Zhongshan quanji* 孫中山全集 [A complete collection of the works by Sun Zhongshan]. Vol. 3. Beijing: Zhonghua shuju, 1984.

Zhongguo Shehui Kexueyuan Xiandaishi Yanjiushi 中國社會科學院現代史研究室, ed. *Yida qianhou* 一大前後 [Around the time of the first conference of the CCP]. Beijing: Renmin chubanshe, 1980.

Zhonggong Zhongyang Makesi Engesi Liening Sidalin Zhuzuo Bianyiju Yanjiushi 中共中央馬克思恩格斯列寧斯大林著作編譯局研究室, ed. *Wusi shiqi qikan jieshao* 五四期刊介紹 [Introduction to the periodicals during the May Fourth era]. 6 vols. Beijing: Sanlian shudian, 1959.

Zhongguo Shehui Kexueyuan Jindaishi Yanjiusuo Zhonghua Minguoshi Yanjiushi 中國社會科學院近代史研究所中華民國史研究室, ed. *Hu Shi de riji* 胡適的日記 [Hu Shi's diary]. Hong Kong: Zhonghua shuju, 1985.

Zhonghua minguo waijiao wenti yanjiuhui 中華民國外交問題研究會, ed. *Guomin zhengfu beifa hou zhongri waijiao guanxi* 國民政府北伐後中日外交關係 [The Sino-Japanese relations after the Nationalist Government's Northern Expedition]. Taibei: Zhonghua minguo waijiao wenti yanjiuhui, 1964.

Zhou Jinyu 趙金鈺. *Riben langren yu Xinhai geming* 日本浪人與辛亥革命 [Japanese *Ronin* and the 1911 Revolution]. Chengdu: Sichuan renmin chubanshe, 1988.

Zhou Xiashou 周遐壽 [Zhou Zuoren 周作人]. *Lu Xun de gujia* 魯迅的故家 [Lu Xun's old home]. Hong Kong: Datong shuju, 1962.

Zhou Zuoren 周作人. *Tanlong ji* 談龍集 [Book on dragon]. Shanghai: Kaiming shudian, 1927.

———. *Zexie ji* 澤瀉集 [Book on Zexie]. Shanghai: Beixin shuju, 1927.

———. *Ziji de yuandi* 自己的園地 [One's own garden]. 10th ed. Shanghai: Beixin shuju, 1927.

———. *Tanhu ji* 談虎集 [Book on tigers]. Shanghai: Beixin shuju, 1929; reprint, Hong Kong: Shiyong shuju, 1967.

———. *Yongri ji* 永日集 [Eternal days]. Shanghai: Beixin shuju, 1929.

———. *Yishu yu shenghuo* 藝術與生活 [Arts and life]. Shanghai: Qunyi shushe, 1931; reprint, Kowloon: Shucheng chubanshe, n.d.

———. *Kan yun ji* 看雲集 [Book on watching clouds]. Shanghai: Kaiming shudian, 1932; reprint, Hong Kong: shiyong shuju, 1972.

———. *Yutian de shu* 雨天的書 [Letters from rainy days]. Shanghai: Beixin shuju, 1933 [1925]; reprint, Kowloon: Shiyong shuju, 1967.

———. *Kucha suibi* 苦茶隨筆 [Notes on bitter tea]. Shanghai: Beixin shuju, 1935.

———. *Fengyu tan* 風雨談 [Chats amid wind and rain]. Shanghai: Beixin shuju, 1936.

———. *Kuzhu zaji* 苦竹雜記 [Notes on bitter bamboo]. Shanghai: Liangyou tushu yinshua gongsi, 1936.

———. *Guadou ji* 瓜豆集 [Book on melons and beans]. Shanghai: Yuzhoufeng she, 1937; reprint, Changsha: Yuelu shushe, 1989.

———. *Bing zhu tang* 秉燭談 [Chats by candlelight]. Shanghai: Beixin shuju, 1940; reprint, Changsha: Yuelu shushe, 1989.

———. *Yaowei ji* 藥味集 [Book on the taste of medicine]. Beijing: Xinmin yinshuguan, 1942.

———. *Kukou gankou* 苦口甘口 [Bitter taste, sweet taste]. Shanghai: Taiping shuju, 1944; reprint, Hong Kong: Shiyong shuju, 1973.

———. *Shufang yijiao* 書房一角 [A corner of the study]. Beijing: Xinmin yinshuju, 1944; reprint, Hong Kong: Shiyong shuju, 1974.

———. *Yaotang zawen* 藥堂雜文 [Essays from the medicine hall]. Beijing: Xinmin yinshuguan, 1944; reprint, Hong Kong: Beixin shuju, n.d.

———. *Zhitang Yiyou wenbian* 知堂乙酉文編 [Essays compiled in the year of Yiyou]. Hong Kong: Sanyu tushu wenju gongsi, 1962.

————. *Zhitang huixianglu* 知堂回想錄 [Reminiscences of Zhitang]. Hong Kong: Sanyu tushu wenju gongsi, 1974.

————. *Zhou Zuoren riji* 周作人日記 [Zhou Zuoren diary]. Printed in *Lu Xun yanjiu ziliao* 魯迅研究資料 [Research materials on Lu Xun], vol. 8 (1981), vol. 9 (1982), vol. 10 (1982), vol. 11 (1982), vol. 12 (1983), vol. 13 (1984), vol. 14 (1984), vol. 18 (1987), vol. 19 (1988); and in *Xinwenxue shiliao* 新文學史料 no. 22 (1984:1), no. 23 (1984:2), no. 24 (1984:3), no. 25 (1984:4).

Zou Lu 鄒魯. *Hui gu lu* 回顧錄 [Reminiscences]. 2 vols. Taibei: Wenhai chubanshe, n.d.

INDEX